D1765762

Liberation Diaries

Leeds Beckett University

17 0602890 6

Liberation Diaries

Edited by Busani Ngcaweni

LEEDS BECKETT
UNIVERSITY
LIBRARY
1706028906
FRF-CR
CC-147984/2014
14·1·15
968.06 LIB

First published by Jacana Media (Pty) Ltd in 2014

10 Orange Street
Sunnyside
Auckland Park 2092
South Africa
+2711 628 3200
www.jacana.co.za

© Individual contributors, 2014

All rights reserved.

ISBN 978-1-4314-1004-0

Cover design by publicide
Set in Sabon 11/14pt
Printed by Mills Litho, Cape Town
Job no. 002184

See a complete list of Jacana titles at www.jacana.co.za

Contents

Contents

Contents

Contents

Foreword

Twenty years into democracy, South Africa has a good story to tell

SOUTH AFRICA HAS REACHED A VERY important milestone of 20 years of democracy. This book is an important reflection on those 20 years of hard work to change a country that was once the skunk of the world to a model modern democracy, which enshrines freedom, equality, justice and socio-economic rights for all.

In 1975, in his address at the ninth extraordinary session of the Council of Ministers of the Organisation of African Unity (OAU), President Oliver Tambo asserted that it is only when political power has been won by the masses in South Africa, that we will be able to begin the immense task of completely dismantling the structures and institutions of apartheid.

Twenty years into our democracy, this ideal has come true. Volumes of evidence attest to the fact that South Africa has changed tremendously from the mire of poverty and deprivation that it was to the land of freedom and equal opportunities, where everyone can realise their potential.

Not only have the institutions of apartheid been dismantled and new democratic institutions been established but there has also been a substantial transformation across a broad spectrum in the country, where race and gender disparities within workplaces and in various other settings have been levelled considerably.

Our democratic Constitution gave birth to a new legal dispensation based on access, equity and human rights, including the right to dignity. The justice system has been changed substantially, with black judges now constituting 61% of the judiciary, something that was inconceivable pre-1994. The irrationalities of separate amenities have been buried with all their disgrace. Many human development indices strongly attest to the fact that the lives of the people of South Africa have improved dramatically in the past 20 years, which is essentially the lived experience shared in this book by various authors.

In education, for example, the 99% primary school enrolment rate indicates that we have made tremendous strides in achieving the goal of universal access to primary education before 2015 – the target period for achieving the second Millennium Development Goal.

We have improved drastically in the provision of basic services such as water, electricity, sanitation and housing. Since 1994, over 3 million houses have been built to ease the burden of homelessness, and the right of abode in urban areas has been restored to black people. Almost 95% of households now have access to water, a remarkable increase from 60.7% in 1996.

It is also important to highlight that during the apartheid era, only 34% of households had access to electricity, but that in the 20th year of our democracy, more than 86% of households now have access to electricity, which is, without doubt, a very great milestone. There are impressive strides in health as well – in primary healthcare, reduced HIV and AIDS infection rates and improved TB detection technologies. We have also received international acclaim for our achievements in combating malaria. Through our robust policies, we have propelled this country on an upward trajectory in terms of life expectancy. Social grants for about 16 million people have provided a safety net for orphans and vulnerable children, older persons and people with disabilities.

This country has not only expanded the base for higher education, but has also increased funding as well. All these are cause for celebration. South Africa is a far better place than it was in 1994 and no objective mind can deny this.

This book is, therefore, very important in the sense that it provides the human dimension to the hard statistics and data that are often presented. It provides first-hand experiences of people from both the rural and urban perspectives, most of whom lived under apartheid. Its significance lies in the fact that it opens the celebration of democracy by giving room for academic and non-academic voices.

It is significant that this book gives agency to emerging and non-academic scholars as well; democracy should be embraced and celebrated by this mix of voices that fought collectively for it. As much as the story of the struggle and its challenges should continue to be told, it is right that the outcome of that very struggle, the achievements and challenges, be documented with the same fervour.

This achievement not only validates the principles we espoused during the struggle but also continues to inspire us and other nations to appreciate the importance of freedom and democracy to human progress. It also inspires us to strive hard to overcome some of the still outstanding challenges regarding our transformation, knowing that change is possible.

As we move ahead to deal with the challenges of poverty, unemployment and inequality that still persist, we are happy that scholars will analyse this journey and provide a mirror for us to look at ourselves critically, to consolidate where we have done well and to improve further where we need to do more.

Jacob G Zuma
President of the Republic of South Africa

Introduction

Busani Ngcaweni

Backdrop

AT THE TIME OF COMPILING THIS BOOK, democratic South Africa lost its founding father, President Nelson Mandela. And so the temptation to change the narrative from answering the question *What democracy means to me* to *What Mandela did for South Africa* was palpable. Fortunately, many of the contributors understood that telling the story of transformation, of life and experiences in post-apartheid South Africa is itself a fitting tribute to this international icon. We make so bold an assertion believing that, working with many celebrated and unsung heroes and heroines of our liberation struggle, Nelson Mandela made it possible for South Africans to tell their stories without fear of harassment or imprisonment.

Under apartheid, some of the stories covered in this collection would either be banned or shunned, its authors imprisoned, killed or exiled. Besides, even the opportunity to publish such material was limited, especially for black people, since many publishing houses either feared publishing black writers or attached no value to the material they produced.

Thanks to selfless and visionary leaders like Nelson Mandela, today we give to the world these *Liberation Diaries*, a collection of essays by fifty diverse South Africans, young and old, from all walks of life, who reflect on South Africa's journey of democratisation and transformation. In so doing, these writers honour former president Nelson Mandela and countless other icons of our nation who did not live long enough to witness South Africa celebrate two decades of democracy, let alone torchbearers like Oliver Tambo who did not even witness the inauguration of free South Africa.

The book's hypothesis

This book was conceived in 2013 at the height of the debate about the centenary of the 1913 Natives Land Act. Commentators and ordinary members of the public debated the extent to which this atrocious piece of legislation balkanised South Africa, eventually turning the black majority into *subjects* with no land rights and the white minority into *citizens* who owned the majority of the land and the wealth beneath it.

It is recorded by historians and economists that the inequality and poverty we witness in South Africa today owes its legacy to the 1913 Natives Land Act, its predecessors and subsequent laws which 'legalised' the idea of segregation and uneven development along racial lines. Many scholars have documented that the racialised poverty and inequality in South Africa predates the outcomes of the work of the democratic dispensation. The seeds were laid by colonial dispossession, the introduction of the migrant labour system after the discovery of gold, late 19th-century colour-bar acts, the Land Act and later by apartheid.

Among the most authoritative accounts of the effects of the Natives Land Act is a tome by Sol Tshekisho Plaatje, *Native Life in South Africa*. It described how overnight the majority of the population was disposed, criminalised and dehumanised. But, as Govan Mbeki would later demonstrate in *The Peasant's Revolt*, black people did not accept dispossession and exclusion. They revolted against an unjust system and, as the founding fathers of the leading force in the struggle against apartheid colonialism would envision, only national unity and democracy would save South Africa and incubate the seeds of progress. Education, as Dr JL Dube explained in *Izikhali Zanamuhla* (Weapons of Today), featured prominently in the thinking of these torchbearers.

We are now accustomed to the reality that, in many instances, very few voices and partial analysis dominate the public discourse and therefore shape our imagination of how the demise of apartheid has transformed our body politic and improved the quality of life of the majority of citizens. This was clearly evident in the centenary of the Land Act discourse, as it is in this year's reflections on twenty years of democracy. To the extent that colonial history and its long-lasting legacies are removed as the basic unit of analysis, we believe that gauging the democratic dividend would be inconclusive.

We therefore put together the concept of this book hoping to achieve two objectives: firstly, to unearth new voices that, through this collection, offer new and dynamic insights into the making of two decades of democracy in South Africa; secondly, we hope to initiate a new analytical architecture for assessing what this democracy means to South Africans, especially the majority that was oppressed under colonialism and apartheid. Let us briefly elaborate on the latter.

We have stated already that the 1913 Natives Land Act features among the most decisive and devastating pieces of legislation that officialised and consolidated segregation as conceived in colour-bar laws of the late 19th century and the 1910 Union of South Africa Act. It disposed Africans and denied them any real chance to earn sustainable livelihood outside the poor-paying jobs in the mines, agriculture and supporting industries. Most importantly, it criminalised the majority of South Africans and set the tone for subsequent laws that demanded identity documents and permits whenever Africans moved outside the native reserves that were consolidated after 1948 as ethnically defined Bantustans.

Women suffered the most as their livelihoods now depended on remittances and wages from men working as migrant labourers. Their movement was even more restricted. In years to come, the franchise was taken away from all black people who lost all rights to participate in the political life of their country.

Consequently, South Africa became a racialised, sexist and authoritarian country. Growth and development were stunted as a result of the exclusion of the majority of the populations from the education and training system and, most importantly, from meaningful participation in the economy. The victory of the National Party in 1948 consolidated and deepened the idea of racial segregation through the formal policy of apartheid, which gave privileges to the minority and condemned the majority to servitude.

Alongside the consolidation of apartheid colonialism, flourished a call from the liberation movement, led by the African National Congress, for the dismantling of segregation. The leaders of our struggle posited a counter vision of society and sought to build a non-racial, non-sexist, united, democratic and prosperous South Africa. In the new society, inclusivity and citizen participation would be the antithesis of polarisation anchored in the 1910 Union of South Africa, the introduction of apartheid in 1948, as well as the 1961 Declaration of the Republic.

As I was contemplating this introduction, a strange coincidence happened. Its due date, Monday 3 March, coincided with my attendance of *A Service to Celebrate the Life and Work of Nelson Mandela* at Westminster Abbey, London. A twist of fate because here I am conceiving an introduction to a book that celebrates twenty years of democracy on the same day as the inseparable companion of the citadel of the British Empire celebrates the life of the man who founded free South Africa. Need we restate that it was the same British Empire that formalised the exclusion of the majority from mainstream politics in the Union of South Africa and for the better part of the second half of the 20th century turned a blind eye on the suffering of the majority under apartheid, a system dubbed by the United Nations as a crime against humanity. Yet today, under conditions of freedom and universal suffrage, historic institutions like Westminster Abbey can convene a special service to honour Madiba and the people of South Africa for the role they have played in redefining modernity, characterised by values of inclusivity, reconciliation and national unity.

Consequently, the storehouse of world civilisation proudly contains the word South Africa alongside Nelson Mandela for proving it possible that a nation so deeply divided over centuries can embark on a path of national reconciliation and development without retribution, to the extent that today South Africans can congregate, through platforms like the *Liberation Diaries*, and ponder *what it means to live in a free society.*

Living in the new South Africa

The new analytical architecture therefore proposes that, in order to conscientiously and honestly measure what it means to live in the new South Africa, the founding vision should be the principal variable. In other words, the key question should be: how far has South Africa progressed in its journey to create a non-racial, non-sexist, united, democratic and prosperous society.

Apart from what the essays in this edition conclude in their gauging of progress, we can assert here that, indeed, South Africa has made significant progress towards the attainment of a non-racial, non-sexist, democratic and prosperous society. Although numbers tell much of this story (as did the 2011 Census), we can summarise the good story of South Africa as follows.

On non-racialism and national unity

In spite of South Africans' occasional outbursts, perceived and lived racial fissures, many ordinary people would agree that twenty years on, as state policy, racism has been dismantled and replaced with progressive laws and programmes that encourage unity in diversity. All South Africans enjoy full citizenship rights under the Constitution which has the Bill of Rights that extends and complements political rights with socio-economic entitlements.

The constitution and many subsequent sets of laws set out the path towards correcting racial distortions in society and, especially, in the labour market. Chapter 9 institutions have been created to promote the values of inclusivity enshrined in the constitution and to promote non-racialism and national unity.

With the exception of very few prisoners of history, those who yearn for what shall not return, South Africans identify with important national symbols like the national anthem, the national flag and the coat of arms. There is growing support for national teams across racial lines. Pride and dignity in being South African have been restored.

At community level, lived experiences suggest that many South Africans are exorcising themselves of the demons of racism and prejudice. Many studies by independent institutions confirm that South Africans are more united now than they were before 1994. Some of the chapters in this book elaborate on this issue.

On non-sexism

There are two important variables we can call upon to measure progress in this regard: firstly, the extent to which our legal and institutional arrangements protect women and promote equity; secondly, gauging society's attitudes towards women. On both counts, South Africa has made tremendous strides. While women (together with children) still occupy the epicentre of violence and victimisation, the country has strong laws that protect women against discrimination and sexism. There are mandatory sentences for rapists, and there are state-run and civil society initiatives that protect women and children. Most importantly, there are functioning labour laws that not only protect women but also promote their meaningful participation in the formal economy. For its part, the ruling party set a global benchmark by adopting a policy of 50/50 gender representation in all structures of political governance where it is represented, i.e. in local government as well as provincial and national legislatures.

On democracy

Within two decades, South Africa has established vibrant democracy based on one-man-one-vote and majority rule. Four free and fair national and provincial elections (1994, 1999, 2004 and 2009) have been held. There is a strong sense of political tolerance – in spite of occasional flare-ups in very limited localities.

South Africans now freely participate in the political life of the country without fearing jail or reprisal. There is an electoral system prioritising inclusivity and representation that has ensured that even smaller political parties participate in the making of laws, although some now believe that this system should be replaced by a constituency system in the hope that accountability of public representatives will increase. All we can say at this stage is that, at minimum, the current system has reversed the legacy of exclusion and given a voice to the minorities.

Depending on your locus of enunciation, the so-called service delivery protests can be seen as a living expression of South Africa's democracy, as anarchy or as a sign of weakness on the part of government. For our part we choose the former. That is, only in a true and vibrant democracy can the citizens take to the streets to demand services. In autocratic regimes, citizens are reluctant to protest against the state, fearing for their lives. Although our police forces have sometimes overreacted and applied excessive force in dealing with protestors, communities continue to exercise their democratic right to demonstrate, a right enshrined in the Constitution. The same goes for the right of workers to associate, organise and go on strike. All these rights were reserved for the white minority before 1994.

Towards a better life for all

Again, we will not use the numbers here to punctuate the conclusion that there has been a material change in the lives of many South Africans since 1994. The 2011 Census and independent reports by institutions like Goldman Sachs and the South African Institute of Race Relations all present numbers that illustrate changes in the quality of life of the previously oppressed majority.

Suffice to say that more South Africans are now engaged in formal employment across the sectors of the economy. The share of formal employment for Africans in particular has sharply increased, although lack of skills still confines the majority into certain vulnerable occupations. For the first time in the history of South Africa, women feature in the top echelons of management in government and in the private sector. The much-sought-after growth should concomitantly sustain efforts to deracialise our economy.

Challenges notwithstanding, the majority of South Africans now enjoy access to basic services like water and sanitation. More African children are accessing formal education and receiving state support to enrol in further and higher education institutions. Over a million houses have been built – giving both shelter and assets to poor households. Land continues to be redistributed and black smallholder farmers are emerging. Early childhood development and youth development tops the transformation agenda.

In short, as many essays in this contribution discuss, living in democratic South Africa cannot reasonably be compared to living in apartheid and colonial South Africa. Even for those citizens who still lack access to basic services, housing and employment, they take to the streets assured that the Constitution protects their right to demand socio-economic entitlements and, significantly, hold the belief that tomorrow will be better than yesterday.

Conclusion

How is such a big book organised, you may ask. To avoid any appearance of priority or preference given to any of the authors, essays have been ordered alphabetically by surname. Therefore, no preference has been given to any subject of inquiry either, irrespective of the profile of the contributor or my own philosophical disposition.

Another question that preoccupied the editing process was whether or not to create themes and subdivide the essays accordingly. At face value, such an organisation appears an appealing and logical proposition. However, as the readers would find out, that exercise proved difficult in a sense that there would have been a disproportionate representation of essays under certain themes, while others would have featured no more than three essays. This challenge owes its roots to the original brief carried in the call for contributions. Writers were neither commissioned nor asked to write according to themes. Many of them free-styled within the broader rubric of reflecting on twenty years of democracy, without limiting scope to commenting on gender, youth, economic, political or social transformation. Some essays differ in their usage of different referencing systems although the brief was to use endnotes, not Harvard-like formal academic referencing styles. However, it is not easy to control style in such a big volume.

Equally, let us hasten to accentuate that all articles presented in this edition differ in tenor and style. Some of the writers tell their own personal stories as a proxy for general trends in society, whereas others write in generalities, constructing a narrative of transformation through broad overviews. Some openly write for the communities they represent without claiming any authority or monopoly over the tales they tell; as the reader will experience, others are more specific and direct.

Finally, let us remind the reading public that the idea of South Africa is a contested phenomenon. Therefore, no single story or book can paint the whole and full picture of our history and accurately speculate about the future. Mao Zedong might have had South Africa in mind when he talked of letting a hundred flowers blossom and a hundred schools of thought contend. Adam Smith in *The Wealth of Nations* and Karl Marx in *The Communist Manifesto* also observed the centrality of polity in the southern tip of the African continent to the world's civilisation and expansion of capitalism. Scientific findings suggesting that Maropeng as a Cradle of Humankind also proves South Africa's special position in the annals of world civilisation which, as stated above, will be contested in future as much as it was in the decades leading up to its founding.

Dissent on the depth and impact of transformation notwithstanding, there is general consensus that, as repeated in many chapters of this book, South Africa is a better place today than it was in 1994.

Significantly, all citizens are equal before the law, enjoy universal suffrage, have a constitution that guarantees socio-economic rights and, most importantly, have the opportunity to improve their living conditions and quality of life. Even the so-called service delivery protests are, by and large, an expression and yearning of that possibility and hope that tomorrow will be better than yesterday. Thus they require recommitment from the leadership as in the words of Madiba: 'We pledge ourselves to liberate all our people from the continuing bondage of poverty, deprivation, suffering, gender and other discriminations.'

As if talking about South Africa twenty years after the introduction of universal suffrage and majority rule, Madiba instructed in his inauguration: 'We have triumphed in the effort to implant hope in the breasts of the millions of our people. We enter a covenant that we shall build the society in which all South Africans, both black and white, will be able to walk tall, without any fear in their hearts, assured of their inalienable right to human dignity – a rainbow nation at peace with itself and the world.'

The ascent of hope, my country, my freedom

Nazeema Ahmed
Researcher and Muslim scholar

IN THE LATTER PART OF THE 20TH CENTURY, South Africa penned its entry into the international journal of liberation that has been scripted since the beginning of time. That liberation journal chronicles the struggles of people who, through the ages, hoped and strived for freedom, justice, mutual consultation, the restriction of power, the rule of law and constitutionalism.

Not unlike other struggles for freedom, the South African liberation narrative pays homage to the maxim that what gives life to nations is hope, while what kills them is despair. Notwithstanding different times, different circumstances, different narrators, different oppressors, there is but one essential liberation narrative – the narrative of hope.

In reflecting on 20 years of democracy, there was the dawning realisation that, unlike the concept of time, life experiences do not conform to the clean and neat categorisation of pre- and post-liberation. The adults, parents, employees and citizens that we are today have been materially or inadvertently shaped by our experiences of living under apartheid. Thus, of necessity, that is where our story begins.

Amid the crushing difficulties of life under apartheid, communities, whether they were in Cape Town or Kliptown (in Gauteng), were not infrequently characterised by laughter, music, satire and wonderful storytelling. It would be disingenuous to not acknowledge that the apartheid system perversely presented opportunities for diverse people to co-exist, to collaborate, to assist one another, to nurture mutual respect and to sustain a common ideal – the hope of freedom. Throughout that tumultuous time, people never lost that hope, since the ideal of freedom held the tacit promise of a different life for the people in this country.

1

During apartheid, the forced coexistence of people of different faiths and cultures thus forged unanticipated bonds of solidarity and mutual assistance. Borrowing a cup of sugar to make the syrup for the koeksisters (coconut-filled doughnuts) on a Sunday morning in District Six, Cape Town, was commonplace and certainly no cause for shame. Is it at all possible that it is the erosion and demise of these kinds of uncomplicated acts of kindness that have prompted us to try to recapture and reconstruct that elusive construct termed social cohesion?

With freedom came a rather arbitrary sense of independence or self-reliance that precludes this kind of mutual assistance, borne out of need and facilitated by proximity. Interestingly, sameness and a sense of shared destiny rather than difference seemed to be the common experience.

One of my more exciting and invigorating adventures as a little Muslim girl was to sneak off to a neighbour's house in Bree Street in the city to sing what was then my favourite hymn, *Fishing for Jesus*. Belting out the tune at the top of my voice with the other children from the neighbourhood was such an exhilarating experience. There was no theory about respecting another's culture or being accepting of other people's faith, since the joyful act of singing *Fishing for Jesus*, while mimicking the act of fishing, at the Sunday school, with pure abandonment, rendered anything else unimportant.

I am certain that the lack of prohibition and censure by my parents and other adults is what laid the foundations for my respect of difference and experiential coexistence that did not require the intervention of any diversity training.

Similarly, my experience of difference was facilitated by my father and grandmother who, coincidentally, both had Jewish employers. I remember with immense fondness, travelling with my grandmother by bus during the school holidays to the 'white' suburb of Fresnaye in Cape Town, where my grandmother worked as an ironing woman at the home of a Jewish family.

To this day, I can never walk past the canned biryani at the supermarket without smiling at the memory of those forays into Fresnaye. Respecting my grandmother's practice of eating only halal food, her employer used to purchase halal canned biryani for our lunch, while she ate salad.

Notwithstanding the fact that the salad was both kosher and

halal, I remember thinking that she went to the trouble of purchasing the canned biryani from the supermarket while she could simply have offered us the salad too. Although my mother used to cook the most delicious homemade biryani, the thrill of eating food from a can, bought by my grandmother's employer from a supermarket, made me feel that her acknowledgement of this Muslim practice was truly admirable.

I also witnessed the respect and deference with which my grandmother was treated by her employer, and, as a young child, I concluded that being an ironing woman was truly a noble profession, worthy of respect and aspiration.

My grandmother imparted to me that being scrupulously honest and working hard in whatever profession you are employed, is what assures you self-respect, self-worth and dignity, rather than trying to derive these values artificially from the status of the profession itself. Furthermore, treating people with respect and compassion not only earns respect but is a sure sign that you have had a good moral upbringing, something on which she placed high value, since this was what ultimately ensured success in life's undertakings.

On a similar note, my father's employer was a magnanimous Jewish woman with big hair and an even bigger heart who, through her generosity and kind-heartedness, systematically deconstructed the prevailing caricature of the Jewish woman as a 'selfish and self-absorbed kugel'. She welcomed my family into her life and her home, and was always curious to learn about Islam and Muslim cultural practices.

She introduced me to Jewish delicacies like bagels, pickled herring, latkes (potato pancakes) and teiglach (sweet boiled pastries) and piqued my curiosity with anecdotes about the differences between orthodox and reform Jews and their respective practices. I took great delight in regaling my cousins and friends with stories about Jewish culture, since I was one of the few young Muslim people my own age who could speak with such 'authority' on what I considered to be popular Jewish custom and cuisine.

One day, my father had to drop something at his employer's apartment, and we walked in on her daughter's birthday party. There were a number of young girls at the party and they asked me which school I attended. I felt both ashamed and rather embarrassed to mention the name of my school because I attended an Afrikaans-medium school in a poor neighbourhood, so I was loathe to divulge this fact to the bevy of English-speaking girls. I mumbled the name of the school somewhat inaudibly, and was greatly relieved when my father announced our imminent departure and thus the girls could not pursue this line of questioning.

On the drive back home my father gave me quite an impassioned lecture about my earlier social discomfort. He stressed that having the opportunity to receive an education was worth far more than the location or prestige of the school one attended. He had to leave school very early to contribute to his family's livelihood, so he regarded education as a privilege to be pursued with vigour and relentless determination. Attending school in and of itself should be a source of pride and certainly not the cause for embarrassment. His passion and conviction that education allows one the freedom to pursue life's opportunities has left an indelible mark on my own consciousness in this regard.

His lecture came back to haunt me later, post apartheid, when I had to confront the pressure of enrolling my daughters at the 'right school' since this was one of the privileges attendant on living a middle-class lifestyle. I often wonder how much of our decision as parents to afford our children the opportunity of a 'quality education' was truly taken with their best interests at heart, and how much of it was merely the guise to signal our accomplishment as middle-class parents who have made good.

Later in his life, my father was also subjected to criticism and ridicule by the men folk for sending his daughters to college and university, as they considered it a waste of both time and money to educate girls. Women were supposed to be good wives and mothers, so what was the point in investing money in our education since we were destined to be housewives anyway?

Paradoxically, I was also subjected to ridicule by some family members and friends for taking the decision to send my daughters to a former Model C school (former 'white' school), and not to the Muslim school, as befits young Muslim children. They asked, how I could take the 'morally reprehensible' decision of enrolling them in a Model C school and thus take the risk of our daughters adopting 'white' culture and behaviour, characterised by 'loose morals' and a conflagration of endless partying, alcohol and drug abuse. Furthermore, how could I intentionally expose them to the

4

'real threat' of becoming Christian or, worse still, atheists?

The inference here was two-fold. I was clearly an irresponsible parent for not protecting my daughters from the corrupt influences of people who do not share 'our' culture, religion and race. Furthermore, my decision proclaimed me to be a 'bad' Muslim who did not consider that being in a school environment populated by other Muslim children was the best medium of socialisation for my daughters.

This view is premised on the assumption that Muslims are the sole custodians of values and ethics, and therefore it follows that people who do not share this faith are necessarily antithetical to the evolution of a values-based life orientation.

Thus, my ability and good standing as a parent were seriously called into question by these detractors, many of whom, incidentally, were my age contemporaries. There is really very little to top moral blackmail and the threat of eternal perdition to test one's fearlessness and resolve to forge ahead in the face of such blatant accusations, which were meant to ensure compliance and adherence to the bigotry of prevailing normative practice.

My view has always been that 'a Muslim school does not a Muslim make'. Being confronted with such views therefore strengthened my resolve and consolidated my conviction that sending the girls to a school that largely reflected the reality of a diverse society was the correct decision. The ideal of young people becoming conscious and active citizens in this country is best served in the midst of the melting pot of cultures, faiths, perspectives and divergence, rather than in an enclave of consensus, conformity and acquiescence.

I feel certain that it is primarily within the home environment that the foundational values of people are established and that through a process of development and maturation, other mediums of socialisation build onto these foundational values.

Furthermore, the formation and development of a personal identity thrives best through a process of differentiation, rather than through assimilation. We become certain about who we are and confirm that which we value, through our interactions with others and through negotiating situations in which we are called upon to take decisions guided by our values.

Then, of course, there were the 'conscientious objectors', who considered those of us who opted to send our children to former

Model C schools as 'sell-outs' because we were perceived to be desecrating the apartheid struggle and breaking rank with the working class to join the ranks of those who lived a charmed, middle-class existence. Ironically, had the school fees at these schools not been so prohibitively expensive, it is likely that many of these objectors would have been lining up to invent fictitious addresses in the suburbs in order to enrol their children at them.

On the one hand, navigating and negotiating the landscape of freedom and liberation required an arsenal of tools derived from the cumulative experience of growing up in a family and community where values and principles, hope and optimism informed action. On the other hand, it also brought with it a situation in which some of these tools were starkly absent, since there was no cumulative experience or precedent for many of the decisions that I had to make as a parent.

In the days of apartheid, my siblings and I attended the nearest school because it had to be within walking distance from home. Being driven to and from school was a luxury most parents could ill afford. In our case, the closest school was an Afrikaans-medium school in an economically deprived neighbourhood.

Although my parents were aware that Afrikaans was the language of the white oppressors, it was our closest school. Thus, pragmatism rather than ideology prevailed. To this day, I can hold my own in an Afrikaans conversation, much to the delight of Afrikaans-speaking people, and much to the chagrin of those who profess, quite proudly, 'I cannot speak Afrikaans, and nor do I ever want to'. Stripped of its pejorative connotations, Afrikaans is simply another means of communication among culturally diverse people in this country.

Then there was a plethora of unanticipated issues requiring decisions by the uninitiated, who could not look to their own parents for guidance because these contemporary dilemmas were previously largely non-existent. Dilemmas such as: requests to attend mixed-sex teenage parties; having meals at the homes of non-Muslim families; being invited to sleep over at friends' homes; being at school camp and thus away from home for three consecutive days; attending grade 10 and 12 dances; requests to have friends sleep over at our home; and whether or not it was suitable to follow our Islamic practice of eating with our hands when school friends came for meals, because they may consider eating with one's hand to be 'barbaric and gross'.

In an era of individual rights and freedoms, and assertive and articulate youth who express their opinions fearlessly, for many parents there was no precedent and neither was there collective wisdom on which to draw. We were on our own and had to be guided by whatever moral or social compass each of us favoured, or one that seemed least likely to evoke the wrath of a discontented adolescent. Many parents were caught in the vexatious grip of desperately trying to uphold moral rectitude, while simultaneously striving for the accolade of being considered 'cool and hip' parents.

Perhaps one of the supreme ironies of parenting today is the way in which parents are at pains to try and educate their children about not succumbing to peer pressure. However, these same parents often succumb to filial pressure, when their children demand the most expensive branded clothes, which are then bought for them with alacrity. Are we not sending contradictory and conflicting messages to our children in this way?

Furthermore, upon attaining political freedom, have we not of our own volition, through indulging our children's every material desire, enslaved them to rabid consumerism, with its emphasis on excess and acquisition at any and all cost? A sobering thought perhaps?

It must be acknowledged, however, that it is not easy for families to weather the storm of emotional upheavals and the torrential tears of their children. Parents and families are trying to make sense of a changed world, suddenly populated by myriad complex issues requiring decisions and interventions that resonate with the spirit of transformation – a task for which they are frequently quite ill prepared.

Going forward, I suppose the best we can hope for is that young people will be conscious of their own experiences that resulted from the choices we made as parents in negotiating multiple transitions. Inner certainty, hope and conviction derived from personal experience are probably their best safeguards in the midst of change and uncertainty since, at best, novel situations require adaptability rather than replication.

Thus, the only real precedent that has been established is recognising the need to be decisive and optimistic when decisions need to be made. Decisions must be guided by values, rather than by parental whims or filial expectations.

Furthermore, the courage to be consistent in both applying and following through with decisions is also critical, regardless of the unpopularity of the said decisions. As we well know, young people are rather adept at preying on our own parental uncertainty and insecurities to get what they want.

Beyond parenting and at a more general level, as people traverse the liberation landscape, they also consciously have to grapple with contradictions that are not easily understood or resolved. For many people, such dilemmas result in unsatisfactory outcomes and seemingly unpardonable trade-offs. One such contradiction became apparent when Parliament was processing the Termination of Pregnancy Bill.

I recall, quite vividly, the bewilderment expressed by my mother and some of her contemporaries at the outpouring of moral outrage by women who considered abortion to be one of the 'evils' of the new democratic dispensation, since abortion was 'unheard of' in the past. Her bewilderment was occasioned by her recollection of the 'mysterious women' in District Six, whose services could be procured for a hefty fee and who would come under the veil of darkness after midnight to terminate an unwanted pregnancy.

Although terminating a pregnancy was widely acknowledged to be illegal, the practice, while ostensibly quite prevalent, was shrouded in secrecy and the identities of the mysterious women were never discussed or revealed. It seems likely that fear, shame and guilt conspired to insulate this practice from public scrutiny. Our experience of life will always be peppered by contradictions and uncomfortable truths, and it seems best to deal with these honestly and with unfailing optimism.

Fast-forward to the present... There is absolutely no doubt that all freedom-loving people in South Africa and elsewhere are concertedly striving to push back the frontiers of poverty, ignorance, inequality, violence and the other social ills that bedevil a post-liberation transition. As we are all well aware, voices of gloom abound as they sometimes self-righteously and gleefully recount the varied instances of crime, violence, corruption and maladministration.

Without detracting from this reality, it remains instructive to note that our hope, fortitude, resilience, collaboration, cooperation and conviction propelled us in our struggle for freedom from despotism and tyranny. Political freedom does not automatically ensure freedom from other forms of tyranny, such as greed, selfishness, excess, brutality, crime and corruption. So we must continue to identify and fight other forms of oppression and never succumb to the debilitation of despair.

Thus, the new and pernicious frontier that we have to actively tackle, post liberation, is the struggle for freedom from pessimism and despair. As a nation we have overcome some unimaginable obstacles and we will do so again. So we look to the future with the ascendancy of hope, certain in the knowledge that we shall also overcome the challenges that currently confound us.

A long road to constitutional democracy: A retrospective reflection

Nazir Alli and Vusi Mona

CEO and deputy CEO of a state-owned enterprise

Introduction

THE DAWN OF DEMOCRACY IN SOUTH Africa in 1994 set us on a journey of constitutional democracy that has been exhilarating, enlightening and, at times, perplexing: exhilarating because we have been pioneers in some of the things we have done; enlightening because prior to 1994 we did not know, at least from practical experience, how democracy works; and perplexing because some of the pre-1994 conduct and attitudes still exist.

At 20 years of age, we are a relatively young democracy. It has bestowed upon us South Africans a sacred right to mould our country into one which future generations can be pleased with. We correctly dumped the practice of parliamentary sovereignty and substituted it with the doctrine of constitutional supremacy. Thus, we reflect on the maturity of our democracy and the institutions created in order to support it.

Paramount among these is our Constitution, widely regarded as one of the most progressive in the world, and, of course, our Constitutional Court. What sets our Constitution apart is its emphasis on human rights, including socio-economic rights, which were inscribed in a Bill of Rights. Our Constitutional Court is the highest court in the land on matters relating to the interpretation of the Constitution, while the Supreme Court of Appeal is the final appellate court on non-constitutional matters.

The independence of our courts is guaranteed by the same Constitution. The courts are tasked with protecting the fundamental rights of all citizens. Therefore the emerging trend of 'politicising' the judiciary by those who do not accept an outcome of democratic Parliament is unfortunate. We are perturbed by the stance taken by our detractors: when court decisions go against them they place the integrity of the courts in doubt – opening the doors to anarchy. Judges are not beyond reproach but it is unsettling when we see statements in the public domain that question the integrity of our courts. It is this unfortunate conduct that prompted this essay and a general reflection on the institutions we have created to support our democracy.

Litigation over e-tolling and the rule of law
On the eve of our 20 years of freedom and democracy, our organisation, the South African National Roads Agency (SANRAL), was involved in litigation over the Gauteng Freeway Improvement Project, otherwise known as e-tolling. Those who opposed the project went to court to seek an interdict preventing SANRAL from implementing it, pending a full review on the matter. They succeeded, albeit temporarily. In April 2012, the North Gauteng High Court in Pretoria granted the Opposition to Urban Tolling Alliance (OUTA) the interdict, approving a full judicial review before electronic tolling could be implemented.

Understanding the rule of law and the social contract we signed among ourselves as South Africans in 1994, that we shall settle our disputes through the courts, we accepted the judgement but chose to exercise our right to appeal it at the Constitutional Court. In October 2012, the Constitutional Court set aside the interim interdict that had prevented SANRAL from levying tolls on certain Gauteng freeways. In a landmark judgement for our democracy, particularly the principle of the separation of powers, Deputy Chief Justice Dikgang Moseneke said: 'Courts must refrain from entering the exclusive terrain of the executive and legislative branches of government, unless the intrusion is mandated by the Constitution.' Technically, this meant SANRAL could go ahead with electronic tolling while waiting for the full judicial review.

We were cut to the quick, following the Constitutional Court ruling, when we saw headlines, inspired by a political leader who had commented on the judgement, reading 'When judges falter'. There is a thin line between commenting on a judgement and making remarks that undermine the judiciary. In this case, we submit, it was more of the latter. This was disturbing, especially coming from one of the leaders of a political party such as the Democratic Alliance, which has always projected itself as libertarian, respecting the rule of

11

law and committed to the independence of the judiciary.

At any rate, the full judicial review came in December 2012 and was heard by Judge Louis Vorster. He dismissed OUTA's application with costs. Again, the comments thereafter, especially from the chairman of OUTA, are tantamount to urging citizens to make our democracy ungovernable. But OUTA was in a fighting mood and didn't care about the damage to the judiciary caused by the pronouncements of some of its leaders and allies.

In October 2013, the Supreme Court of Appeal heard OUTA's appeal and dismissed it but gave the organisation a reprieve by setting aside the earlier costs order. Though seriously bruised, this time around OUTA was more guarded in its reaction, stating that it was going to study the judgement and would comment on its implications at a press conference later. It is now history that OUTA exited the legal battlefield but continues to whip up emotions and galvanise citizens to revolt against the courts' judgements. There is no doubt that these comments and those of OUTA's allies caused harm to the judiciary.

Also disturbing during the build-up to the appeal being heard were comments in some newspapers suggesting that the Supreme Court of Appeal would rule in favour of SANRAL and government because the bench at that court, it was alleged, would want to curry favour and be considered for appointments to the Constitutional Court in the future. One newspaper editor even wrote a column accusing the judiciary of 'ganging up' with the state against citizens on the e-tolling matter. It is very unfortunate when professionals and former captains of industry, whose training and station in life ought to have instilled in them some sense of responsibility, indulge in attitudes and pronouncements that are inimical to our constitutional democracy. We have witnessed court abuses during the apartheid regime and it will be a sad day if we subject the courts now to behaviours that are similar to that time.

These kinds of attacks against the judiciary were a very low moment in our democracy. But they were by no means the first. Certain leaders of the ruling party once described some of our judges as counter-revolutionary and portrayed some as apartheid apologists, prompting the late former Chief Justice Pius Langa to call for an end to unjustified attacks against judges. The Pan Africanist Congress once said about the Constitution and the judiciary that 'they are not

God-ordained entities that function outside the realm and exigencies of an evolving society'.

While comments about court rulings should be welcomed in the spirit of debate and enriching our democratic institutions and while the judiciary is not filled with infallible human beings who are not amenable to common frailties, a toxic relationship between society, on the one hand, and the judiciary, on the other, should be avoided. We diminish our constitutional democracy when we make pronouncements that veer towards undermining or delegitimising judges. And we shall do our democracy great service if we make all efforts not to blur the line between fair criticism of the judiciary and irresponsible demagoguery.

State institutions supporting democracy

In order to strengthen our constitutional democracy, promote accountability and give life to the human and socio-economic rights contained in the Bill of Rights, South Africa established in the Constitution itself a range of institutions. These are commonly known as Chapter 9 institutions, owing to their place in the Constitution. They include the Auditor-General, the Public Protector, the South African Human Rights Commission and the Independent Electoral Commission, among others. Section 181(2) of the Constitution states that these 'institutions are independent, and subject only to the Constitution, and they must be impartial and must exercise their powers and perform their functions without fear, favour or prejudice'.

It is not our intention to assess the effectiveness and efficiencies of these institutions for the period they have existed under our democratic dispensation but a reflection on some of the work they have carried out would help, hopefully, to demonstrate their value to our democracy. Described by some as 'watchdogs', these institutions keep government in check (a role often overemphasised) and ensure that society is transformed (a role often underplayed). Let us look at four of them.

The Auditor-General

The Office of the Auditor-General in South Africa was established prior to 1994. In fact, in 2011 the Auditor-General celebrated its centenary, having been established in 1911. It is only a year older than the oldest liberation movement in Africa, the African National Congress.

But the Auditor-General prior to 1994 was totally different from today's. Then the Auditor-General was geared towards serving minority interests and, one would argue, did not probe as deeply and lay bare as it does today. As President Jacob Zuma stated in an address to the gala dinner celebrating the centenary of the Auditor-General, 'the world in which the levels of transparency we cherish today [was] unheard of' prior to 1994. Blacks were confined to low-level positions within the institution. Although the transformation of the office of the Auditor-General is a subject on its own, it is worth mentioning that post-1994 the institution has seen some of the most talented black professionals rise to top positions.

As the supreme audit institution of our country, empowered by the Constitution to audit and report on how government across all three spheres – national, provincial and local, including its agencies – is spending the South African taxpayers' money, the Auditor-General plays a critical role in ensuring that government activities are carried out and accounted for.

Without the Auditor-General, Parliament – which is supreme in our system of government and to which the executive arms of government accounts – would find it difficult to scrutinise government performance and activities. Through the audit information the Auditor-General has provided to Parliament over the past 20 years, it has contributed a great deal to the framework of accountability of government and its agencies.

Also noteworthy about the Auditor-General is the sense of independence with which it has carried out its work. Although there are perceptions that this independence was once compromised when the Auditor-General was roped in to be part of a joint investigative team (which included the Public Protector and the National Director of Public Prosecutions) that looked at the arms deal in 2000 and found that no wrong had been committed, there is consensus that the Auditor-General is free from direction by the executive and free from political bias. That freedom is evident in the manner the Auditor-General has uncovered and pronounced on wasteful and fruitless expenditure, underspending, overspending and other instances of mishandling public finances.

In spite of the shortcomings that sometimes exist in the handling of public finances, these have not been hidden. The Auditor-

General has shone its spotlight on them, without fear or favour, and contributed immensely to the accountability of the South African public sector. This legacy, firmly established in the past 20 years of our freedom and democracy, must be carried forward.

The Independent Electoral Commission

One of the key ingredients of a successful constitutional democracy is the integrity of its electoral process and the credibility of its elections.

In our democracy, the body charged with ensuring such integrity and credibility is the Independent Electoral Commission (IEC). Section 190 of the Constitution mandates the Electoral Commission to:

- manage elections of national, provincial and municipal legislative bodies in accordance with national legislation;
- ensure that those elections are free and fair; and
- declare the results of those elections within a period that must be prescribed by national legislation and that is as short as reasonably possible.

With regard to all the functions mentioned above, the IEC has generally come out with flying colours. South Africa has an Electoral Act that is strictly adhered to. Although there will always be areas where improvements can be made, never have we had a situation in the past 20 years where an election, at whatever level, could not be held. The management of our elections from voter registration to the establishment of a network of voting stations across the country has ensured accessibility to and participation in our democracy.

Although the issue of voting stations and that of the voters' roll were raised as concerns in some elections, these have since been addressed by the IEC and, critically, have never affected the credibility of our elections. According to the IEC, the number of voting stations has increased from 20 859 in 2011 to an estimated 22 225 in 2013 and at last count the commission had 25 308 331 voters registered on the voters' roll. The voters' roll is regularly updated and copies handed out to parties and candidates contesting the elections.

It is a measure of the maturity of our democracy and the integrity of our electoral processes that the IEC has never had to declare any of our elections not free and fair. Free political participation in South Africa is first made possible by our Constitution, the Electoral Act and the Electoral Code of Conduct that are enforced by our Electoral Court. Running for office is encouraged and the number of registered political parties in our country, reportedly over 200, although only about 19 have participated in an election, attests to free political participation.

Unlike in other countries where courts have had to be roped in before an election outcome was announced, the IEC has always announced the election results within a reasonable period, as contemplated by law. Bar the ructions that we have seen within the IEC on the eve of our most important election which will mark 20 years of our democracy, which have nothing to do with the integrity of our electoral processes per se, the Commission has served the country with distinction.

Indeed, the fact that the IEC has on several occasions been asked to do work in other countries is an indication of the high regard in which it is held. In the relatively short period of our 20 years of democracy, the IEC has succeeded in driving the message that the government in South Africa is chosen through the ballot.

The South African Human Rights Commission
Given South Africa's history of gross human rights violations and the majority of its citizens being deprived of the most basic human rights – including civil, political, social and economic rights – the establishment of the South African Human Rights Commission (SAHRC) was one of the most groundbreaking steps in the new order to entrench constitutional democracy.

Human rights are the most basic of all rights, simply because they are human. In our country, human rights are inscribed in the Bill of Rights that forms Chapter 2 of our Constitution. Thus, human rights are a constitutional matter, enshrined in and protected by the Constitution. Section 184 of the Constitution states that the SAHRC has the responsibility to:

- Promote respect for human rights and a culture of human rights;
- Promote the protection, development and attainment of human rights; and
- Monitor and assess the observance of human rights in the Republic.

Some of the direct tasks of the SAHRC include:

- Developing an awareness of human rights among the people of South Africa;
- Making recommendations to the state to improve the carrying out of human rights;
- Conducting studies and reporting to Parliament on matters relating to human rights; and
- Investigating complaints of violations of human rights and seeking appropriate relief.

While investigating complaints about human rights violations is what tends to receive prominence in the Commission's work, the studies it has carried out are particularly instructive if we are to transform our society and promote a culture of human rights. Violations are a symptom and the underlying causes must be understood if the problem is to be dealt with effectively.

To this end, the SAHRC must be commended for some of the groundbreaking inquiries it has conducted in the past 20 years. These include its inquiry into racism in the media, its investigation into racism in the justice system and the inquiry into access to healthcare services, among others.

The racism in the media inquiry, conducted in 2000, generated a lot of controversy but was very enriching for our democracy. It is not usual for the fourth estate to have its cherished ideals interrogated and its assumptions challenged in the manner they were when that inquiry was conducted. The fault lines and contradictions it exposed within the media and between the media and society were an eye-opener. Editors and journalists were at loggerheads with each other in the glare of the public as a result of their ideological and racial differences. Concepts like freedom of expression and press freedom were interrogated and it was shown how these are differently understood by different role players in society.

It is reports like these that have helped us to understand our society better. We wish the SAHRC inquiries and reports could be given much more media coverage and be subjected to broader societal debate and analysis. Be that as it may, the commission has contributed towards transforming our society, securing the rights and restoring the dignity of South Africans in the last 20 years. One of its highlights, for us, was when, in 2013, it hauled before it all the provincial ministers of education and their heads of departments to come and answer questions about the availability of learning material at schools. Although this happened behind closed doors, which some may argue was inimical to the principles of transparency and accountability, the SAHRC proved that it will assert the right of South African children to receive an education.

The Public Protector

The last institution we want to examine is that of the Public Protector. The office of the Public Protector derives its existence and mandate from Section 182 of the Constitution. The role of the Public Protector is to investigate any conduct in state affairs, public administration or sphere of government that is alleged or suspected to be improper. Any citizen may lay a complaint when he or she feels that the state or a state official has committed wrongdoing or something that amounts to maladministration.

In general, the state is a huge bureaucracy and can be intimidating to an ordinary citizen. Individual citizens sometimes feel powerless in the face of a government that neither sees nor hears them. Against this background, the Public Protector, although independent of government, gives the state a face that people can relate to and an ear that can listen to them.

The Public Protector has, in the last few years, caught public imagination because of the perceived greater independence the incumbent is prepared to assert. The narrative is that she is prepared to investigate political principals and find against them without any fear or favour. Whether this perception about 'greater independence' is true or not is a moot point. There have been Public Protectors in the past that have investigated and found against ministers and very senior state officials.

The predecessor to the current incumbent once investigated and made a finding against a former minister of justice and the director of national public prosecutions. For his part, he was insulted and ridiculed in public by those officials. As is the case with the judiciary, uncontrolled activism against the Public Protector does not deepen our democracy. Rather, it weakens it.

The Public Protector, who is appointed by the president, is one of the institutions that are supposed to support our constitutional democracy. Therefore, when we hear rambling attacks against that office, we must pause and reflect on the damage that we may be causing. While any incumbent in this office must resist the temptation of being a partisan advocate for or against any person or entity in society, we as citizens and commentators have a responsibility to be temperate and self-controlled in how and what we say about that office. And let us be clear on this – lack of criticism of the Public Protector or of any of our democracy supporting institutions is not a virtue. Dissention and differences will always be there but we can disagree without being disagreeable.

Conclusion

As stated earlier, this essay focused on only four Chapter 9 institutions. They are undoubtedly the most prominent because of, among other factors, the media interest they generate. As we celebrate 20 years of our freedom and democracy, it is important to pause and reflect on the institutions of democracy and the role of citizens when exercising their rights. On the whole, South Africa can be proud of its track record in protecting the rights of its citizens. The Chapter 9 institutions have placed our democracy on a sound footing. Critically, they have provided the republic with sufficient cushion from the possibility of it becoming a failed state.

My experience of democracy

Kim Catherine
Student

Forward we will march
Forward we will march
Forward we will march to a people's government
There shall be houses, security and comfort
Forward we will march to a people's government.

A CRITICISM MOST OFTEN LEVELLED against the field of Sociology is that it is the study of the obvious – the observation and description of 'common sense facts'. The counter-argument is that Sociology is a social science that challenges accepted assumptions about society by making use of scientific methods; it is an empirical investigation of society that is deductive, verifiable and replicable.

In this essay, I deliberately attempted to avoid using the lexicon of my field (terms such as anomie, class, elite, false-consciousness, gender, heterogeneous, homogeneous, institutions, labelling, norms and values, peer pressure, positive sanction, race, self-fulfilling prophecy, segregation, significant other, social engineering, social mobility, stereotype, symbolism and role-model), because I did not want to state the obvious. But I could not avoid mentioning that my earliest memories revolve around my family, religion, education and the state. And there was always music playing in the background.

I grew up in the community of Eldorado Park. In our community, the majority of families, grandparents, parents and children all lived in the same household or in close proximity. The days started very early. Parents left for work in the mornings, returning in the evenings. Few people could afford to buy a car, much less afford to drive to work every day. That was a luxury often reserved for Fridays. Some used public transport, others using lift-clubs. Children of school-going age went to school. Maternal grandparents looked after the younger children.

As a child, being sent to the shops with my cousins was more of a daily adventure than a chore. The walk from Mapelaberg Road up to Witteberg Avenue or down to Milnerton Street was about finding shortcuts through the flats, greeting friends along the away and avoiding the 'bad elements'. On the way to buy bread and milk we would compete to see who the fastest runner was or who could count in twos and threes.

On Sundays we walked to church on Heerengracht Road to hear the Good News. The good news was that Jesus Christ was a just man and he condemned injustice and oppression against the poor.

We encountered graffiti on every street. It was only years later that the graffiti started to make sense. The slogans of protest against the State of Emergency and the tricameral Parliament: 'Don't Vote!' 'Remember June 16!' 'Stay Away!' 'UDF Unites – Apartheid Divides.'

Apartheid was not normal. The apartheid state was abnormal. In order for individual citizens, communities and South Africa as a whole to become normal, every aspect of apartheid had to be dismantled and something new created, noting that there is continuity in change.

The years 1990 to 1994 were characterised by rapid and extensive change. In the months following the unbanning of political parties and the release of political prisoners, members of the United Democratic Front (UDF) and its affiliates in the Mass Democratic Movement (MDM) had to redefine their roles and form alliances with like-minded organisations and progressive political parties. The scrapping of apartheid legislation, for example, the Group Areas Act, the Influx Control Act and the Job Reservations Act, meant that there were greater numbers of people migrating from rural areas to urban areas in search of work. This precipitated the establishment and growth of new informal settlements, including Freedom Park, close to Devland on the Golden Highway.

There were mixed reactions to the strained political processes. The heightened tension was diffused with comic relief. While the political parties were negotiating the future of the power-sharing agreement, the Convention for a Democratic South Africa (CODESA) at Kempton Park, we were lining up and dancing the Codesa (line dancing) at gatherings. Various artists composed songs to narrate unfolding events and instil optimism after heinous acts of violence were perpetuated against defenceless communities; songs like *Boipatong* by Sello 'Chicco' Twala and *Peace in Our Land* by Mzwakhe Mbuli. Ordinary people also got involved. As soon as a song was released, they would make their own remix. Lyrics were added to a popular track, 'Everybody Everybody', by house group, Black Box. The section that had only instrumentals was supplemented with, 'Mandela *slaan vir* Buthelezi down!' Other communities had their own versions, with their own lyrics, but ours was hilarious.

In April 1994, election fever did not pass us by in Eldorado Park. There were posters and pamphlets everywhere. The Department of Home Affairs and the Independent Electoral Commission set up an interim office at the shopping centre in Extension 5. The office was inundated with people trying to obtain documents that would allow them to be part of history – temporary voter's cards and applications for the green, bar-coded identity document.

Somewhere in my memory box, I have recollections of uTata Walter Sisulu visiting Eldorado Park to campaign for the African National Congress (ANC). I can't remember if it was prior to election day or on 27 April, but I know – for sure – he came to my neighbourhood. The motorcade stopped close to the civic centre and the news spread that Tata Sisulu was in our area. He was old, but still walking strong. A huge crowd gathered to wave and pay tribute to him in song.

The Constitution
I followed developments around the Constitution-drafting process, the Multi-Party Negotiation Process (MPNP) and the Constitutional Assembly. To me, the draft proposals were basically a duplication of UDF and ANC documents. Even if the MPNP was a compromise, I could swear I had seen these words and ideas expressed elsewhere before. In 1992, the ANC declared that it was *Ready to Govern*. In 1994, the ANC produced an election manifesto in the form of the Reconstruction and Development Programme (RDP). The ANC obtained 62.65% of the votes in the national election. The ANC would have a majority in the executive and the legislature. Therefore, we were in good hands.

Chapter 1 – Founding Provisions
  1. Republic of South Africa
  The Republic of South Africa is one, sovereign, democratic state founded on the following values:

a. Human dignity, the achievement of equality and the advancement of human rights and freedoms.
b. Non-racialism and non-sexism.
c. Supremacy of the Constitution and the rule of law.
d. Universal adult suffrage, a national common voters' roll, regular elections and a multi-party system of democratic government, to ensure accountability, responsiveness and openness.

2. *Supremacy of Constitution*
This Constitution is the supreme law of the Republic; law or conduct inconsistent with it is invalid, and the obligations imposed by it must be fulfilled.

Chapter 2 – Bill of Rights
7. Rights
1. This Bill of Rights is a cornerstone of democracy in South Africa. It enshrines the rights of all people in our country and affirms the democratic values of human dignity, equality and freedom.

Chapter 9 – State institutions supporting constitutional democracy
181. Establishment and governing principles
1. The following state institutions strengthen constitutional democracy in the Republic:
a. The Public Protector.
b. The South African Human Rights Commission.
c. The Commission for the Promotion and Protection of the Rights of Cultural, Religious and Linguistic Communities.
d. The Commission for Gender Equality.
e. The Auditor-General.
f. The Electoral Commission.

On 10 December 1996, the Constitution of the Republic of South Africa (Act 108 of 1996) was signed into law. In plain language, it was reiterated that we were a republic; that we were a democratic state; non-racial, non-sexist in outlook and orientation; that the Constitution was supreme; that we now had a Bill of Rights; and independent structures were established to strengthen constitutional democracy. I left my neighbourhood (temporarily) and entered university.

Higher learning

At the time I was a student, the Ministry of Education was in the midst of consultations on the Higher Education Bill, and other policies aimed at the restructuring and transforming of higher education. The scope included governance, student financing, the introduction of a national qualifications framework, and the regulation of public and private higher education institutions, among others.

The 'Size and Shape Debate' on the future of South Africa's higher education landscape, the proposed merger of some tertiary institutions – and not others – was a contentious issue between the Ministry of Education and the ANC-aligned South African Students Congress (SASCO). SASCO called on all South Africans to interrogate the proposed policies of the government, and asked difficult questions of the ANC leadership: 'Is that what the RDP envisioned?' The wholesale retention of the apartheid higher education architecture, where historically white institutions (HWIs) retain their autonomy, and historically black institutions (HBIs) had to relinquish their identities?

These issues were debated. Vociferously! The merits and demerits; the motivation and demotivation. Seconded. Objected to. What about the culture and traditions of the respective institutions? What would happen in the case where an HBI was merged with an HWI (or vice versa)? The admission criteria and registration fees at HWIs were notoriously onerous; what would happen to poor students (the majority of whom are black and previously disadvantaged), whose scores were too low, or who could not afford the fees at merged institutions? Would the government's funding model adequately address the imbalances of the past? It was anticipated that HWIs would experience increased student subscriptions, and numbers at HBIs would decrease or remain the same, perpetuating the stigma of inferior teaching, learning and research at HBIs.

In the end, the Ministry of Education followed the Australian and Canadian merger-models – two countries disparate from South Africa. The National Plan for Higher Education was implemented, and from 2001 to 2007, higher education institutions were reduced from 36 to 23. In mid-1998, following a number of incidents of racially motivated violence and inaction from the management, the Branch Executive Committee (BEC) of the African National Congress Youth League (ANCYL) University of Pretoria Branch invoked the authority of the South African Human Rights Commission (SAHRC). The SAHRC visited the campus in August 1998 to investigate allegations of human rights violations. The complaints from black students related to the discriminatory practices by administrative and academic staff, the allocation of bursaries and financial assistance, and racial conflict at the university residences. The findings and recommendations of the SAHRC were published in September 1999.[*]

In response to specific allegations of racism, a member of staff in the Faculty of Law not only denied the allegations made by the students, but 'demanded a withdrawal of the allegations and an apology'. At the time, it was rumoured, the member of staff threatened to pursue legal action against the SAHRC for defamation. The then-branch chairperson, Patson Khumalo, was interviewed in the weeks following the publication of the SAHRC report.[†] Khumalo called on the Minister of Education to intervene and ensure that the university implemented the recommendations, especially the revision of policy and admission criteria in the residences, which were based on racial quotas.

Ten years later the University of the Free State (UFS) embarked on a process to racially and linguistically integrate its residences – for the second time. The first attempt in the late 1990s was declared a failure after it resulted in violence. The vice chancellor explained that:

> The rationale for this step was educational: that is, to prepare students for a non-racial workplace, to provide them with the necessary diversity skills, to help them appreciate the enriching effect of working and socialising with people from different backgrounds, and so forth.[‡]

---

[*] South African Human Rights Commission (SAHRC). 1999. Special Report: Findings. University of Pretoria. Re: Allegations of racism and racial discrimination. Available at www.sahrc.org.za/home/21/files/Final%20report%20Tukkies%20Racism%20in%20 education%201999.pdf.

[†] Khumalo, P. (1999). 'Tuks Racism Report is "Tip of Iceberg"'. *iol*. Available at: www.iol.co.za/news/south-africa/tuks-racism-report-is-tip-of-iceberg-1.13621?ot=inmsa. ArticlePrintPageLayout.ot.

[‡] Fourie, F. 2008. *Reflections on the Reitz Incident: Implications.* Available at www.universityworldnews.com/article.php?story=20080320160825789.

Resistance to the initiative was registered in a 10-minute video made by four white Afrikaner male students of the Reitz Residence, which came into the public domain in February 2008. The video, presented as an 'initiation-type ceremony', showed the students putting a group of five black workers (four women and one man), through a series of obstacles, including forcing them to eat food from a bowl into which one of the students had allegedly urinated. The university instituted disciplinary proceedings against the students.

Following widespread national (and international) condemnation of the video, in March 2008 the Minister of Education announced the establishment of a Ministerial Committee on Transformation and Social Cohesion and the Elimination of Discrimination in Public Higher Education Institutions. The ministerial report, also known as The Soudien Report was completed in November 2008. On the matter of residences, The Soudien Report found that:

> There are two key issues that underpin and give rise to discriminatory practices in university residences, namely the policies on the integration of the residences and the role of residence culture and tradition.*

In October 2009, at his inauguration as rector and vice chancellor of UFS, Professor Jonathan Jansen announced that the university had decided to pardon the students (in the spirit of reconciliation). He explained that everybody involved had been consulted. The four were charged in the Equality Court, in terms of the Promotion of Equality and Prevention of Unfair Discrimination Act 4 of 2000. In July 2010, in a three-day trial presided over by a magistrate, they were found guilty of *crimen injuria* and fined R20 000. They were also sentenced to jail for six months, suspended for five years on condition that they did not commit another act of *crimen injuria* within that time period.† In 2011, a deed of settlement was agreed with the five workers, wherein the university committed to help

---

* Soudien, C, Michaels, W, Mthembi-Mahanyele, S, Nkomo, M, Nyanda, G, Nyoka, N, Seepe, S, Shisana, O, Villa-Vicencio, C. 2008. *Report of the Ministerial Committee on Transformation and Social Cohesion and the Elimination of Discrimination in Public Higher Education Institutions*. Pretoria: Department of Education, p. 84.

† Soudien C. 2010. 'Who Takes Responsibility for the "Reitz Four"? Puzzling our way through Higher Education Transformation in South Africa', South African Journal of Science,106(9/10), Art. #429, 4 pages. DOI: 10.4102/sajs.v106i9/10.429.

them establish a cleaning company with funds, training and a five-year contract at the institution. The university also pledged to establish a centre for human rights as part of remedial measures to eradicate the culture of racism. Two years later, the settlement had not been honoured.*

In April 2013, it was widely reported that the Convocation of Stellenbosch University voted in favour of a motion supporting a proposed new residence placement policy. The issue was subsequently referred to the university council.

The more I read about lack of transformation in higher education, and society in general, the more I prefer the conceptualisation of the Azanian People's Organisation (AZAPO), which continues to advocate for an 'anti-racist' society. Non-racialism seems to have been defeated by legalistic and linguistic karate. I support alternative dispute resolution, but I find it hard to come to terms with restorative justice that benefits the perpetrators more than the victims. In recent months I have been following the work of the Higher Education Transformation Network (HETN), a lobby and advocacy organisation, comprising graduates and alumni who are committed to the process of transformation of education and training. Like them, I still have confidence in the instruments of the Constitution.

Personal aspirations and reflections
While I was studying, I wished I could get a job in my field of study. I had aspirations of joining the civil service. There was a concerted effort to transform the bureaucracy and I wanted to be a part of it. The slogan was Batho Pele: People First. The eight service delivery principles are as relevant now as they were during the Mandela administration:
• Regularly consult with customers
• Set service standards
• Increase access to services
• Ensure higher levels of courtesy
• Provide more and better information about services
• Increase openness and transparency about services

---

* Koko, E. 2013. '"Reitz Four" Victims Left in the Cold'. *Iol.* Available at www.iol.co.za/news/south-africa/free-state/reitz-four-victims-left-in-the-cold-1.1518214.

- Remedy failures and mistakes
- Give the best possible value for money

In my final year I would scan the Sunday newspapers for advertised posts. I needed to find a job! I focused on the vacancies where the minimum requirements were: undergraduate degree or equivalent; good writing and verbal skills; and an ability to work independently or in a team. Affirmative action and the Employment Equity Act 55 of 1998 were not just buzz words, they were my passport into the workplace. The only thing I didn't have was a driver's licence. What was all the fuss about a driver's licence? How does having a driver's licence affect my ability to reason and do the job? It was so frustrating. What was even more frustrating was the choice between a Code 8 (light motor vehicle) and a Code 10 (heavy-duty vehicle). Initially there was a walk-in booking system at every testing-station, which was later replaced by a call-centre. Later it became mandatory to provide proof of residence in a particular catchment area. It felt like I was enrolling a child for school.

Looking for a job was difficult. There was the process of typing up my CV and printing hard copies. Then there was a document called a Z83 Form that had to be completed, even if you submitted a comprehensive CV. Finally there was packaging and posting. All these cost money, something that students had very little of.

In the early years, departments used to respond with a 'confirmation of receipt' and a few weeks later, a polite 'we regret to inform you'. As the years went by, adverts indicated an apparent scale-down on stationery, and so correspondence was limited to successful applicants only. Currently, we are told, 'if you have not heard from us within three months of the closing date, please accept that your application was unsuccessful'.

Returning to my old neighbourhood
A lot has changed in the past 20 years. I no longer live in Eldorado Park. I return to my old neighbourhood to celebrate family occasions: baptisms, birthdays, funerals, weddings, Easter, Mother's Day, Father's Day and Christmas Day. We have welcomed many new additions to the family. We have lost grandparents, parents and children.

There are new developments, including a small community radio station, and the Eldos Arts and Jazz Festival, which is part of the annual City of Joburg Arts Alive International Festival in September. There are areas of neglect in the neighbourhood. Clean water from burst pipes is wasted in the streets. Grass outside schools is overgrown. Public buildings are in disrepair. Drugs have infiltrated every family. Members of the community, who are affected by their condition and their environment on a daily basis, feel demoralised and marginalised.

It is not big events or grand-scale corruption that causes ordinary people to lose confidence in government. It is small, repeated instances of failure, where people begin to feel that the government no longer cares, that lead to the gradual erosion of trust.

In order to restore trust between the parties, namely, members of the community and officials in (local) government structures, there needs to be a frank admission that neither party is blameless, and that, over time, inaction by both parties concerned was what allowed the situation to deteriorate.

Officials in the local government are plagued by the problems cited in the Auditor-General's Consolidated General Report on the Local Government Audit Outcomes for 2011/2012:[*] 'Chief among the root causes of poor audit results, the Auditor General cited lack of capacity in local government, which affected its ability to account for the public resources it has to administer on behalf of society...' The Auditor-General also called for decisive action against political leaders and municipal officials that deliberately or negligently ignore their duties and disobey legislation.

It is obvious who has more power, so it equally needs to be acknowledged that the parties have 'differentiated responsibilities and respective capabilities', to paraphrase and borrow from the *United Nations Framework Convention on Climate Change.*[†]

---

[*] Auditor-General. 2013. *Consolidated General Report on the Local Government Audit Outcomes for 2011/2012* www.gov.za/documents/detail.php?cid=383036.
[†] United Nations (UN). 2013. *United Nations Framework on Climate Change* from unfccc.int/essential_background/convention/background/items/1355.php.
Article 3: Principles.
In their actions to achieve the objective of the Convention and to implement its provisions, the Parties shall be guided, INTER ALIA, by the following:
1. The Parties should protect the climate system for the benefit of present and future generations of humankind, on the basis of equity and in accordance with their common but differentiated responsibilities and respective capabilities. Accordingly, the developed country Parties should take the lead in combating climate change and the adverse effects thereof.

Community leaders, religious leaders, social workers, principals, teachers and parents have highlighted the drug problem using information communication technology innovations that differ from the methods of campaigning 20 years ago. Open letters from the community to President Jacob Gedleyihlekisa Zuma were posted on social media. The details contained in letters from Cordelia Bailey and Daraleen James, mothers of drug addicts desperate for (any kind of) assistance and intervention, prompted President Zuma to visit the community in May 2013. He was accompanied by various Cabinet ministers and provincial officials. President Zuma issued a public warning to the drug dealers and corrupt police, threatening them with the full might of law enforcement agencies.

The reaction from the highest office of government, although regarded by some as a public relations exercise, is a reassuring sign of a ruling party that still values the basic unit of organisation. The warning issued by the president has even become part of local vernacular. When faced with the threat of violence, the response is, '*Ek sal vir jou Zuma!*'

Collective action and the resilience of ordinary people in the first 20 years instil a sense of optimism for building the first half-century of democracy. As Karl Marx reminds us in *The German Ideology*, 'the philosophers have only interpreted the world, in various ways: the point, however, is to change it'.[*]

---

* Marx, K & Engels, F. 1932 (1846). *The German Ideology. Moscow*: Marx-Engels Institute.

Reconciling myths and realities: The return of second-generation exiles to post-apartheid South Africa

Zosa de Sas Kropiwnicki-Gruber
Academic

Introduction

THIS ESSAY IS BASED ON AN exploratory study of people who were born in exile and/or spent their formative years in exile during apartheid. It is based on 21 in-depth interviews with men and women who spent their childhoods in an average of three different countries as second-generation exiles during apartheid. I discuss how the experience and memory of exile affected their perceptions of development in South Africa and their role as potential 'agents of change'.

It will be argued that in exile, collective myths were established about the 'new' South Africa to which they would return. These myths fuelled four broad expectations: first, they would return to welcoming, empathetic and appreciative communities. Second, they would return to a free and equal post-apartheid South Africa. Third, they would return to a saf(er) society from which their parents had fled. And fourth, they would return to a progressive country, politically united around key liberation principles. Unfortunately, many of these expectations were dashed upon their return, as they faced discrimination, violence and social exclusion. They described a loss of faith in the struggle leaders and an overarching sense of disillusionment in politics. These frustrations have not led to passivity, as the majority of respondents are still fighting for equality and freedom in the name of the liberation vision.

The second-generation exiles

This study is based on anonymous, in-depth, life histories with 21 respondents who met the following criteria: they were born and/or spent their formative years (birth–18) in exile during apartheid and they were residing in South Africa at the time of the fieldwork. These respondents were identified by means of snowballing, a chain-referral sampling technique. The sample is as follows: seven (33%) were male and 14 (67%) were female; 17 (80%) were black; two (10%) were white and two (10%) were Indian. At the time of the interviews, three (14%) were younger than 30, eight (38%) were between the ages of 31 and 35, seven (33%) were aged 36 to 40 and three (14%) were older than 41 years.

The age at which the respondents went into exile is as follows: nine (43%) were born in exile, nine (43%) were aged one to five years and three (14%) were older than six years. Three (14%) returned to South Africa from exile aged zero to ten years, 11 (52%) were 11 to 18 years and seven (33%) were 19 years or older. When in exile, the respondents lived in a number of different countries: six (29%) stayed in one country, four (19%) lived in two countries, nine (43%) lived in three countries and two (10%) lived in four countries. With this in mind, the respondents listed 47 countries in six regions, in which they had lived: 16 (34%) lived in southern Africa, nine (19%) lived in East Africa, one (2%) lived in West Africa, ten (21%) lived in Europe, six (13%) lived in the United Kingdom and five (11%) lived in North America.* The majority of the respondents' parents either had refugee status or study permits in exile. They engaged in a range of political activities, including training, strategic planning, military operations, advocacy, activism and fundraising.

The myth of post-apartheid South Africa
Home for many exiles was not related to geographical space, material belongings or even interpersonal relationships, but was associated with a forward-looking vision about the 'new' South Africa: 'There was a whole language about when we go back; when we are free and when Mandela is free. So it was definitely part of my psyche growing up, that it [exile] was a temporary situation.'† 'Home' in exile was carefully constructed as a temporary sojourn on a longer journey leading back to South Africa: 'My parents

---

* The countries in which the respondents lived are as follows: United States of America (USA), Canada, United Kingdom, Northern Ireland, Spain, Denmark, Bulgaria, Tanzania, Swaziland, Namibia, Nigeria, Zimbabwe, Kenya, Zambia, Mozambique, Lesotho and Botswana.
† Interview, female respondent (Gauteng, 3 June 2013).

refused to ever buy property and take root; it was always about coming home.'*

Some spoke emotionally of returning for brief visits with their parents in the late 1980s, reinforcing the idea that South Africa was a central part of their parents' legacies and, in turn, their own:

> He [father] wanted us with him. This is his country. He hadn't been here for 30 years and he wanted us to see it and who knows what would happen, but he wanted us to be a part of it.[†]

Despite the possible risks associated with return, many respondents desperately wanted to (re)claim their South African heritage, even if they were not born on South African soil:

> We didn't know what it was like to go back home as exiles, my parents were not sure what would happen and if my dad would get arrested. I didn't want to wait, I wanted to go back home. It is ironic that I am calling it home and I had never been there.[‡]

This eagerness to return was, in part, related to heightened expectations of what 'homecoming' would be like. Second-generation exiles grew up in an environment in which their parents and social networks were actively involved in the liberation struggle. They were socialised into politics both directly and indirectly. For some it involved overhearing or participating in political discussions, observing their parents engaged in heated debates, reading political texts or giving up their beds to other exiles seeking refuge.

Many children participated in anti-apartheid events, rallies, demonstrations and even engaged in 'political play' at the Young Pioneers club for children of the struggle. For others, it involved the fear of ongoing political threats, suspicion of strangers and the loss of parents and siblings to prison or politically motivated violence. As a result, second-generation exiles were brought up with a particular vision of post-apartheid South Africa: 'I guess growing up outside of South Africa for most of their [parents'] lives, they saw the new

---

* Interview, female respondent (Gauteng, 9 June 2013).
† Interview, female respondent (Gauteng, 30 May 2013).
‡ Interview, female respondent (Gauteng, 3 June 2013).

South Africa through rose-coloured glasses and that is how we were always brought up.'[*]

The reality of return

Unfortunately, the reality did not always live up to expectations and many described the disappointment they experienced at their homecoming:

> It was such a long flight and when we were arriving the sun was just rising and it sort of burst red and it felt like a new beginning, but a heavy new beginning. They [relatives] didn't even come and meet us at the airport and that let us know that we were coming into a battle; we weren't coming home to a sea of kisses and hugs and love.[†]

For some, this disappointment centred on struggles at the level of the interpersonal. For others, it was more about the nature of politics, tensions within the ANC and the violent society to which they returned:

> I thought to myself that we were going to come back to black, green and gold flags flying but it wasn't what happened. We thought the ANC comrades would be like the ones we had grown up with, so it would be a nice safe place but I came back to a completely racist, angry space where everyone is nuts. This country is nuts.[‡]

Returning to a welcoming, empathetic and appreciative society

On the one hand, respondents recalled emotional encounters with relatives, underscoring their sense of loss and waste over the years that had past, disconnection with loved ones and the hope of meaningful reunification. For instance: 'He [grandfather] said, "You were the same age as your father when he was last here". My dad left at 19 and came back when he was 53.'[§]

---

[*] Interview, female respondent (Gauteng, 22 May 2013).
[†] Interview, female respondent (Gauteng, 22 May 2013).
[‡] Interview, female respondent (Gauteng, 6 June 2013).
[§] Interview, female respondent (Gauteng, 30 May 2013).

Initially, many were treated like 'celebrities in the family'* or curiosities, but this wore off quickly. Some respondents spoke about the resentment that was directed at them for having absconded from what many South Africans perceived to be their duties in the struggle for liberation: 'Certain uncles and aunts ignored me and there you are arriving back, expecting open arms because you have been fighting the struggle your entire life in exile.'† Their families were often resented for leading what many believed to be an elitist lifestyle, far away from the starvation, discrimination, violence and oppression facing the majority of South Africans:

> We missed the hard times that our families had to go through and we were not able to support them. This made my parents feel guilty for a long time. My family didn't blame them or make them feel guilty, but others said that we had a better life, we were lazy and at fault for not being here.‡

Another respondent stated:

> I was taken aback when one of my family members said that 'we were not here during the struggle'. We didn't live like the bloody Mbekis lived. They came from a privileged background and lived the life of diplomats. It's not the life we lived at all. My parents lived from hand to mouth.§

Some respondents complained that that the perception that exiles lived a lifestyle of 'champagne and money'¶ was a myth that did not reflect their everyday struggles:

> I suffered, maybe not in the context of being shot at by rubber bullets, but there were times when there was no food. There were times you worried about your safety. There were times when you got bullied. There were times when I felt unloved

---

* Interview, male respondent (Gauteng, 24 May 2013).
† Interview, male respondent (Gauteng, 28 May 2013).
‡ Interview, female respondent (Gauteng, 23 May 2013).
§ Interview, female respondent (Gauteng, 9 June 2013).
¶ Interview, male respondent (Gauteng, 28 May 2013).

and rejected, not by my family but by the world, like no one gave a damn.[*]

The respondents complained that South Africans did not empathise with their pain, loss and hardship. For instance, in a heated debate, one respondent was criticised by a peer who said, 'Who are you to tell us? You weren't even here.' This illustrates the lack of compassion and understanding of what it meant to be a child in exile: 'That was what I had to deal with: instead of being "Wow, your father died for us", it was more like "Who do you think you are?"'[†] Many believed that their contributions or sacrifices in exile would be appreciated upon return but this rarely coincided with reality:

> There are some kids out there who are really bitter about it. We were taught that we would be heroes, and all the stuff we were giving up was for this greater good, and it would be appreciated one day and it never was.[‡]

Language was often used as a proxy for discrimination. Their failure to speak South African languages had an adverse effect on their social inclusion. For instance, one respondent spoke about being called a 'traitor'[§] as he was sent to predominately English-speaking, white schools in town. Another spoke of comments such as, 'You weren't here, so you don't know. You can't come here and try to speak Zulu and try to be black.'[¶]

These language difficulties fuelled teasing and bullying. This made it difficult for former exiles to communicate with their relatives and peers, and many argued that language affected their sense of belonging: 'I never felt like I belonged in America, but when I came back I didn't belong here either.'[**] A respondent who spent most of her childhood in boarding school stated that insensitive comments directed at her mother for not teaching her South African languages revealed how little people understood of the exile experience: 'You

---

[*] Ibid.
[†] Interview, female respondent (Gauteng, 6 June 2013).
[‡] Ibid.
[§] Interview, male respondent (Gauteng, 17 May 2013).
[¶] Interview, male respondent (Gauteng, 17 May 2013).
[**] Interview, female respondent (Gauteng, 23 May 2013).

have no right to judge us. Our parents sacrificed everything for this country, including me.'*

Some respondents struggled to identify with cultural practices. For instance, some felt uncomfortable wearing traditional dress at family gatherings. A few males said that they were pressurised into being circumcised and participating in initiation ceremonies, even though this was not part of the cultures that they had grown up with.† Another said she was pressurised to undergo training as a traditional healer: 'It is something I can't think about because I grew up so Western.'‡

Some respondents could not relate to youth their own age in South Africa. Many spoke of being made to 'feel bad' because they are 'different'.§ As a result, many respondents formed friendships with other second-generation exiles whom they met at school or through their parents' networks. It was held that they found their own exile community within South Africa in which they were accepted. Referring to Sacred Heart School, one respondent stated:

> I would gravitate to other exile kids. It felt like a different world. We had no sense that we were different. It was like an island. We only felt different when we left the school, like when I used to visit my cousins in the township. They called me names...¶

The fact that some former exiles attended private schools upon their return fuelled comments about elitism on the backs of South Africans who had stayed behind and struggled. Many admitted that the exile experience gave them educational and career opportunities; however, this was not always the case. Reference was made to socio-inequalities within exile communities abroad and upon return. While some were attending private schools, others were sent to more affordable public schools. Some former exile families were able to afford domestic workers, while others were forced to move into domestic workers' quarters upon return. Some parents

---

* Interview, female respondent (Gauteng, 30 May 2013).
† Interview, male respondent (Gauteng, 28 May 2013).
‡ Interview, female respondent (Gauteng, 23 May 2013).
§ Interview, male respondent (Gauteng, 22 May 2013).
¶ Interview, female respondent (Gauteng, 23 May 2013).

assumed powerful political positions upon return, while others were left unemployed. Respondents noted that South Africans failed to recognise these differences and resented them for their 'elite' status.

Returning to a safe, free and equal post-apartheid South Africa
A few respondents applauded the liberation struggle and the ANC, in particular, for granting them freedom that was denied to the majority population under apartheid: 'There is a strong need to remind our society what the stalwarts of the struggle stood for, this is why we are living and enjoying our freedom.'* However, the majority of respondents argued that this 'freedom' is meaningless if it still remains the freedom of the few. Numerous respondents lamented the failure of the ANC to ensure that the utopian vision of a 'free and equal' society became reality:

> We have achieved a lot but not nearly enough and you know that so many people have died for this. You know them and you know their children who gave up their childhoods, so that their fathers could fight for the struggle. We are not free. Women in this country are not free. The freedom has been denied to us and that makes me so angry. We fought and we are not free. We are not free from racism either. So the struggle is not even halfway over, but everyone is telling us all about making money and the corruption of ANC leaders.†

Many respondents attended interracial schools in exile, embraced cosmopolitanism and questioned racial binaries. As a result, they often found it difficult to understand racial dynamics in South Africa. Many respondents referred to the playground as a political space in which white and black children were often pitted against each other in racial battles. A white respondent spoke about siding with a black child in one such fight. Another respondent spoke being called a 'good black', by his peers at private school, but then being criticised by family for associating with white people at school.‡ As a result, he felt that he is always 'betraying one side'.§ A white respondent said

---

* Interview, male respondent (Gauteng, 4 September 2013).
† Interview, female respondent (Gauteng, 6 June 2013).
‡ Interview, male respondent (Gauteng, 17 May 2013).
§ Ibid.

that at school her black friends refused to hug her 'because people are going to think that I am sucking up to white people'.* Suddenly having to learn Afrikaans – 'the language of the oppressor'† – to obtain university entrance was also a source of discontent. However, not all stories were negative. For instance, a black respondent said he was not prepared when a white girl left him a Valentine's Day card at school, and a white, Afrikaans-speaking neighbour showed him an act of kindness.

In the long term, all of the respondents spoke about the perpetuation of racial hierarchies in post-apartheid South Africa, which the liberation struggle had sought to dismantle: 'I don't understand why there has been a systematic effort to build up racial barriers, but there hasn't been a systematic effort to break down those barriers.'‡ This was evident in a number of examples. In the face of racially motivated violence on university campuses in Durban, a respondent told herself: "No, all our lives we have been fighting for justice, I am not going to let this go. I have every right to be here, to be treated like I am born-free and benefit equally from the struggle."§ She added: 'The most shocking thing was that people who experienced the horror of apartheid and discrimination have been completely uncritical in the way in which they are perpetuating it.'¶ Another respondent complained that South Africans still try to categorise her as white, adding to her discomfort:

> People are forcing this whiteness on me. It has taken ages to reconcile that. Yes I am white and that means stuff in this country. It means that when I walk into a shop, I don't get followed around in case I am going to steal, like all my black friends do. I counted myself as part of everyone else in exile, but all they care about here is that I am white.**

Reference was also made to the overlapping nature of race and socio-economic status in South Africa, such that the poorest are still the

---

* Interview, female respondent (Gauteng, 6 June 2013).
† Ibid.
‡ Interview, male respondent (Gauteng, 24 May 2013).
§ Interview, female respondent (Gauteng, 9 June 2013).
¶ Ibid.
** Interview, female respondent (Gauteng, 6 June 2013).

'previously disadvantaged'.* The black children with whom a white respondent grew up with in exile are now living in poverty-stricken townships: 'It was like, oh, this is what apartheid is. Just because the ANC was unbanned, doesn't mean apartheid was dismantled.'† A respondent referred to the example of the controversial painting, *The Spear*, to argue that value systems are distorted in South Africa: everyone seems to be more concerned about a painting than deeply entrenched socio-economic inequalities:

> Everything is politicised. So what if the president is offended? We are all offended. Poverty in a wealthy country like this is offensive. Children begging on the streets is offensive. So how can you get offended over a painting?‡

Gender discrimination was also highlighted by respondents. Female respondents spoke of being pressurised to get married upon their return. Others stated that roles and responsibilities were reversed upon return, such that women and girls were suddenly tasked with domestic responsibilities, when they were brought up with the same responsibilities as their brothers.§ A respondent recounted the inhumane treatment of women during a recent attempt to register for UIF:

> The way we were treated, I was so angry by the time I left there. All the women were over eight months pregnant and there is this picture of Zuma, the man I grew up with, who gave me my first political lesson when I was small. There is this picture of him smiling over us, with these people treating us like animals. I remember phoning my mother and saying, 'Is this what my father died for?' The whole reason we did what we did was that people could be treated like human beings no matter what colour their skin was.¶

Reference was made to sexual and gender-based violence. Many

---

* Interview, male respondent (Gauteng, 28 May 2013).
† Interview, female respondent (Gauteng, 6 June 2013).
‡ Interview, female respondent (Gauteng, 30 May 2013).
§ Interview, female respondent (Gauteng, 4 June 2013).
¶ Interview, female respondent (Gauteng, 6 June 2013).

respondents spoke about the needs of the liberation movement being placed before the needs of women and girls. They argued that sexual abuse was rife in certain exile communities and that nothing was done to bring the perpetrators to justice. For instance, a respondent spoke of being raped repeatedly by the teenage son of one of her parents' political friends when in exile. Although she told her parents about the incident, there was still an obligation on her parents to take the boy shopping for new clothes upon return to South Africa:

> That messed me up a little. A lot of this sexual abuse stuff was rife. You were sexually molested by a comrade's child or a comrade themselves. There again, in South Africa that has become part of our heritage, it has been normalised by society.*

This was reiterated by another respondent:

> Where are those rapes coming from? Others hear of comrades molesting girls in exile and think if he can get away with it so can I. Men hear it and will not fear to rape.†

Respondents bemoaned the poor institutional response to child sexual abuse in South Africa and questioned whether this is the utopia that they fought for in exile:

> You know the other day we were protesting outside a school where a teacher had been accused of raping a child and the teacher wasn't suspended. So off we go with the parents to protest and then the police came because we didn't ask for permission.‡

Another respondent reiterated this point:

> They failed in their vision of SOMAFCO [the Solomon Mahlangu Freedom College]. You know there is this saying that you can't have a hungry child go to school, that education does nothing for them because they are hungry. You can't have

---

* Interview, female respondent (Eastern Cape, 4 June 2013).
† Interview, female respondent (Gauteng, 23 June 2013).
‡ Interview, female respondent (Eastern Cape, 4 June 2013).

a molested child going to school and telling them that education is good; what are they going to do with that education? They can have the knowledge, but if there is that disconnect then they can't use it.*

Many respondents were shocked at the levels of interpersonal violence in South Africa:

I just think this is a crazy place. The family violence was not endemic in the places we grew up and it feels jarring for me and the crazy level of interpersonal stranger crime. It is pretty shocking.†

This respondent's baby and child minder were recently held up at gunpoint. Another argued that this violence is symptomatic of a 'damaged society needing help': 'Right now we are all pretending that only the kids who went into the army are damaged – rubbish.'‡ Reference was made to an institutionalised 'culture of violence' under apartheid and the perpetuation of it in post-apartheid South Africa. Respondents also raised concerns about xenophobia, particularly since many were officially treated as refugees in their host countries:

The xenophobic attacks were just a sad day for me. We are not an understanding people. We are a violent nation. We resolve things with violence and ironically the countries that I have lived in [in exile], don't.§

Returning to a progressive and politically united country

Despite the successes of the ANC leadership during the liberation struggle, it was argued that there is a need to 'bring back the values and virtues of the ANC'.¶ Disillusionment was a common theme, with reference to party political divisions within the liberation movement, corruption and government inefficiency.

Many respondents referred to the ANC's failure to live up to its

LEEDS BECKETT UNIVERSITY LIBRARY

---

* Interview, female respondent (Gauteng, 23 June 2013).
† Interview, female respondent (Gauteng, 3 June 2013).
‡ Interview, male respondent (Gauteng, 28 May 2013).
§ Interview, female respondent (Eastern Cape, 4 June 2013).
¶ Interview, male respondent (Gauteng, 4 September 2013).

obligation to returning exiles, while others argued vehemently that exile children should not receive more than children of parents who fought in South Africa. The lack of consistency and transparency in the ANC's policy towards second-generation exiles was bemoaned and a respondent associated this with the maladministration of funds: 'There was a situation where children of top ANC ranked members were going to good schools and those lower down were not able to access those funds at all.'* Some of the respondents were directly affected by corruption. One respondent's scholarship from an Umkhonto weSizwe trust fund ceased suddenly, leaving him to find alternative sources of funding for his schooling. At the time he was informed that the trust was having financial problems, but in hindsight he became aware that the 'fund was looted'† in a large corruption scandal. Another respondent, who benefitted from the fund, stated that the ANC should have systematically searched beyond the elite to returning second-generation exiles who were poor and orphaned.

Many second-generation exiles are still approaching SOMAFCO for financial assistance: 'It pains us, what we read about the history of SOMAFCO. It is supposed to be shared among us, the people of South Africa so we cannot be an exclusive group, but they [second-generation exiles] need assistance.'‡ He argued that the ANC government has failed to develop a proper social welfare scheme to assist those harmed by apartheid, both within South Africa and abroad.

One respondent spoke about the failure of the ANC to compensate her father for his activism in exile and upon return:

> My parents made millions for the ANC, because my dad would go and public speak in all kinds of spaces and that money he would give to the ANC. When we got back we had nothing. Their pension was used up because of corruption and other scandals. At one point my father couldn't get work and started selling books on the beachfront. This was deeply humiliating for me to experience for my parents.§

---

* Interview, male respondent (Gauteng, 24 May 2013).
† Interview, male respondent (Gauteng, 18 May 2013).
‡ Interview, male respondent (Gauteng, 24 May 2013).
§ Interview, female respondent (Gauteng, 9 June 2013).

These disappointments have shaped the role played by former second-generation exiles as agents of change in South Africa. For instance, one respondent was initially very active in student politics, but lost faith in the leadership that she had been brought up to believe in:

> I feel that generation let us down. They were supposed to be leaders. You can imagine there is a scandal involving Mac Maharaj; this is the person who taught me the Freedom Charter. You don't know who to believe. People who you looked up to as heroes are being exposed as 'tenderpreneurs' and you don't know who is lying. Some of them, you will meet them now and you don't know what to say to them ... I look at the ANC now and I don't know what can save it.[*]

Another described how her passionate belief in justice and change through the Truth and Reconciliation process became jaded in the face of divisions within the ANC:

> I had lots of hopes and dreams and every hope was met in the first two or three years of our young democracy. But the shine began to wear off and politics starts to look a bit shaky. Mbeki starts to do crazy things and it rubs against my family background. So do I remain loyal to the ANC and not participate in the vibrant democracy?[†]

Some argued that although they no longer believed in the ANC as a vehicle for meaningful liberation, they believed that they have an obligation to South Africa:

> I only have an obligation to South Africa, not the ANC. I think the euphoria of the ANC has worn off because the reality is the ANC is not the same as it once was. It doesn't have the principles it once did. I am an ANC member but where are our principles when a minister steals from the state?[‡]

For many respondents and their families this was a source of pain.

---

[*] Interview, female respondent (Gauteng, 6 June 2013).
[†] Interview, female respondent (Gauteng, 3 June 2013).
[‡] Interview, male respondent (Gauteng, 28 May 2013).

They spent many years believing in something – in a party and in a vision – that was distorted by power and corruption:

> We were so disillusioned. We were brought up with struggle music, but now it is too painful to listen to it. My mom made my father promise from now on, this chapter would be dedicated to us as a family and no longer to politics.[*]

Another respondent stated that she regularly argues with her father, who is a politician, about the way in which ANC leaders have used politics to enrich themselves:

> So every now and again I will emotionally blackmail my father because I am so angry: 'People died in my life, people that you put in my life, you cannot expect me to tolerate what is going on, because I have an obligation to them'.[†]

Agents of change
The following quote captures this tension between expectations and reality but it also points to the spirit of positive social change embodied in the liberation struggle, which should be recaptured and harnessed:

> I am grateful. If I hadn't gone into exile, I think I would not be me, I would not have been happy in myself. I identify my 'South Africaness' with being a political project, being a South African is about having a duty to fulfil: I have obligations to ensuring that what people fought for, is realised. I don't think other South Africans know it, there was a feeling in the house, in the pioneers that we had, there was a feeling everywhere, there was a mood. But when we came to South Africa the mood was not there.[‡]

Respondents spoke about being socialised into believing that they had to contribute to South Africa upon their return. For some, this meant pressure to get involved in politics. For others, it was

---

[*] Interview, female respondent (Gauteng, 9 June 2013).
[†] Interview, female respondent (Eastern Cape, 4 June 2013).
[‡] Interview, female respondent (Gauteng, 22 May 2013).

'a sense of responsibility or duty to take the legacy forward'* or, as another respondent stated, 'there are no debts to the ANC but a responsibility to the vision',† namely a free and equal society. Others spoke of the interpersonal debt that they owe to those who fought in the liberation struggle:

> I don't feel obligated to the government, but I owe my parents. I owe the South Africans who were denied. I feel a strong sense of obligation to service this country, but not to the state.‡

Others spoke of their obligations to their parents. For instance, one respondent was recently assisted by a stranger after a car accident in Johannesburg. This stranger recognised his surname and referred to the assistance his mother had rendered him while in exile: 'I was humbled; I started to cry, because I realised that's the legacy that my parents left me.'§

Conclusion
Disillusionment has not fuelled passivity and apathy. Instead, these former exiles have adopted new roles in relation to what they argue is an ongoing liberation struggle:

> We grew up with a vision for utopia for South Africa and we were allowed to experience some of that utopia in our childhood, but we didn't know it at the time. But now our job in the society is to create that vision for utopia from within, not from outside, but inside.¶

In order to create this vision, many have adopted the role of social commentators, as journalists, academics, writers, poets and artists, to hold South Africa's leaders accountable to the vision that they created, promised and propagated. Others are social activists, advocates or development practitioners. One respondent spoke of the inner shift that he had to make from politics to social development:

---

* Interview, male respondent (Gauteng, 24 May 2013).
† Interview, female respondent (Gauteng, 22 May 2013).
‡ Interview, female respondent (Gauteng, 3 June 2013).
§ Interview, male respondent (Gauteng, 28 May 2013).
¶ Interview, female respondent (Gauteng, 22 May 2013).

Yes, I grew up in a political home, but my parents have always stressed it's not about who sits in government, it's about what you are doing to change people's lives and the problem is we are consistently putting people in who we know are not right, because of this word 'comrade'.*

Despite their varied interpersonal and political struggles, many former second-generation exiles have chosen to remain in South Africa. This stems from a sense of obligation to their parents and the legacy left by their heroes in the liberation struggle. It is informed by an unwavering belief in the vision and the principles that were promoted in the struggle. The exile experience shaped many former exiles into 'agents of change' – change that they still believe is desperately needed. They truly believe that the utopian vision of South Africa as an equal and free society can still become reality.

---

* Interview, male respondent (Johannesburg, 28 May 2013).

I write for the invisible ones

Amanda Dlamini
Young writer

ANY LEGITIMATE REFLECTION ONE CAN have on the first 20 years of a democratic South Africa must first be contextualised by the window from which one views the world. Secondly, it must be measured against those historical factors that still impact us as a nation 20 years into democracy. The term 'Freedom Wasn't Free' has been widely used to highlight the plight of the political activists of our struggle, yet often we underestimate the plight of the ordinary person, who never spent decades in prison, will never have streets named after them and will never even get acknowledged for the price they had to pay for this new South Africa.

My parents' love story is the kind that fairy tales are made of. My father is an artistic, gentle soul who loves nature and animals. My mother is deeply spiritual, from a strict family and is all about structure and detail. They were high school sweethearts who got married ten years after they met. My mum gets a nostalgic smile each time she speaks of my dad back then in the early 1970s. Each morning they would take the same bus and he always made sure he saved her a seat. She says she loved how well-groomed and neat he was. From his perspective, he was captivated by this beautiful, head-strong young woman from a good family, who was still pure. In the mid-1970s, township girls were not big on that sort of thing.

Looking at pictures of their wedding day, I see a beautiful couple, madly in love, with every intention of building a wonderful forever together. They had this massive cake shaped like a cathedral. They saved the bell from the cake for a year, in anticipation of their first-born child as a married couple. It is a pity I came three years later.

It is very unfortunate that this beautiful romance didn't actually end with 'happily ever after' – instead it ended in divorce. Eleven years after they got married, this beautiful romance, which had lasted two decades, ended with them going their separate ways in 1993, when

I was eight years old. As mentioned earlier, any legitimate reflection I can have on the first 20 years of a democratic South Africa must first be contextualised by the window from which I view the world. I adore both my parents – they are the greatest gift the universe ever bestowed on me. Growing up, I always wondered why the relationship between these two amazing people ended so badly. They are both well accomplished and well loved by those around them, so what went wrong?

There may be a multitude of factors but a recent discovery made while reading Paulo Freire's *Pedagogy of the Oppressed* (1970) summed it up in a way that made some sense. In an oppressive society, the oppressed then become sub-oppressors. Six years into my parents' relationship, my father joined the correctional services as a prison warden. In those days there were very few options open to black people in terms of careers. So, here was an artist, a gentle and deeply emotional human being, who found himself thrust into a position where he had to be hardened in order to put food on the table. Daily he was confronted with the realities of enforcing discipline, carrying out orders from his superiors, and going against his nature to become what his job required. Being the strong man that he is, he excelled in his role, yet it came at a price. When it comes to being hardened, you either are or you are not. You can't just do it from 9:00 am to 5:00 pm and then go back to being yourself. So, as is to be expected from any oppressive cycle, he turned into a sub-oppressor.

The earliest years of my life were characterised by violence. Hearing screams in the middle of the night and waking up to find my mother with a swollen eye and busted lip was normal for me in those early years. But it was also normal for my father and me to spend hours in the garden as he tended his plants. We would go for walks to buy my dog Snoopy real meat because he didn't think dogs should eat only bones.

So the dichotomy of his personality fascinated me from an early age. I never doubted that he was a good person, but I also knew that what was taking place around me was wrong. It's only now that I view the situation with the eyes of an adult and with the context of what is likely to occur in oppressive societies, that I can make sense of this contradiction. The price that young couple paid was high, but it is not likely to be hailed as an achievement when the history books are written.

No one will ask why he drank and beat up his wife; they will just summarise him as a bad man who did awful things. No one will ask what he would have chosen to do with his life had he been given all the options. No one will erect monuments to the man who remains my hero, a father who loved us and who gave up on his true nature to give us what we needed – a chance at a better life.

There's something miraculous about South Africa's transition in the early 1990s. A country that had been wrestling with apartheid for more than 40 years suddenly found a common ground and the result was a peaceful democratic transition. Nelson Mandela, the flagship figure of the struggle, came out of prison after 27 years and preached a message of reconciliation. We all remember where we were on the day of his inauguration, hearing the speech: 'Never, never and never again shall it be that this beautiful land will again experience the oppression of one by another.' Seeing the helicopters flying the new Rainbow Nation colours, seeing our bright future up ahead, the nine-year-old kid in me felt it. Whatever had been wrong with our beautiful country was over. We were free!

What I love most about the Madiba miracle is that it drove a fundamentally divided nation towards a common goal. The oppressed black South Africans couldn't take it any longer and the oppressive white South Africans couldn't continue the cycle. We all wanted the same thing: freedom.

According to Paulo Freire, you cannot understand the notion of the oppressor and the oppressed without first having an understanding of what humanity is. At their core, the oppressor's mission is to dehumanise the oppressed, yet they themselves have a deep-seated need for humanisation because, at their core, they know very well that the act of dehumanisation is inhumane.

To contextualise the first 20 years of post-apartheid South Africa, one must first gain a fundamental appreciation for this subject of humanity and humanisation. In layperson's terms, the bully helps the bullied victim to become stronger the more they press them down. Humanity is a global principle. Therefore, when one is in the business of bullying, one must also be keenly aware of one's simultaneous role as a liberator. By bullying, you empower the bullied to want to be free, therefore driving them to their liberation. This may seem quite illogical at face value, like the notion of a parent who punishes their child in the name of strengthening the child's character. The act seems to be aimed at subduing but inevitably leads to freeing. When the apartheid government tried to subdue the black population, what they achieved was the strengthening of the core of black people. I am a human being – I will not be treated like a machine whose only role is to produce results. I will not allow you to dehumanise me. I deserve better.

Some would say that South Africans were not liberated in 1994. Not in a way that saw the oppressor reject their role, or the oppressed gain true liberation. A superficial anaesthetic was injected into our malnourished vein and a Rainbow Nation-coloured bandage was placed on a deeply-wounded people. Terms like 'truth and reconciliation' and 'Simunye, We are One' were parodied, in order to tell us how to feel. Films such as *Zulu on my Stoep* and TV series like *Suburban Bliss* reduced our suffering to a comedy; this was seen as the appropriate remedy for half a century of dehumanisation. The ultimate conclusion: 'Come on, it wasn't that bad! Where's your sense of humour? It is time for us to move on!'

Yet for those of us who saw the repercussions of apartheid break up our own families, it is difficult to 'just move on'. The truth of the matter is, apartheid wasn't an accident; it was a well-designed system of oppression that was in place for nearly half a century. There is no denying that it impacted, and continues to impact, the psyche of South Africans. Whenever you hear the 'black accent' you automatically start making assumptions about a person's intelligence. When you hear of a crime that has been committed by a black person, the immediate reaction is: 'Typical. That's all they ever do!'

Once again citing Freire, the oppressor needs to break free from the oppressive cycle just as much as the oppressed. Yet the greatest paradox of the oppressive cycle is that the oppressed ought to recognise the strength they have gained from their oppression so that they can liberate not only themselves but their oppressor as well. This results in a symbiotic situation of mutual benefit for all. The teacher in this case is the oppressed and the student is the oppressor. This is where the Mandela miracle comes into play. The greatest fear for those who benefitted from apartheid was that when black people gained freedom, they would seek revenge. Yet the wisdom of Mandela was to seek forgiveness and healing. This was a case of the oppressed liberating not only themselves but those who oppressed them.

Earlier we touched on the subject of oppressive societies. The cornerstone of oppression is dehumanisation. The process of dehumanisation holds within itself multiple layers, one of the first being injustice. There sits within the process of dehumanisation, a fundamental universal law of something that, in a logical state, would be deemed unjust or unfair. No religion would ever condone the act of deliberate dehumanisation, which is what apartheid did. Yet it was perpetuated with the full knowledge of it being unfair. No rational human being, outside of an oppressive state, could condone the atrocious acts conducted under apartheid. Yet, the fascinating thing is that, for nearly half a century, many did, and still do today.

The next level of dehumanisation is exploitation. For some, this is the most logical state in which the oppressive past of South Africa ever made sense. Poor, black South Africans, who were desperate and uneducated, afforded the state cheap labour. Cheap labour equates to lower means of production and higher returns on investment. Apartheid made business sense. The sceptics among us believe that it was not, in fact, a change of heart that made the apartheid government enter discussions with the ANC but the fear that the mounting pressure from trade unions, the international community putting sanctions on South Africa and those within the country who had vowed to make it ungovernable, were simply bad for business. The business model of exploitation became unsustainable, so the apartheid government had to cut their losses and concede defeat.

Then 1994 happened, Mandela became the first democratically elected post-apartheid president of South Africa and we all lived happily ever after.

But did we? Freire states that liberation is not an act of chance or serendipity, it takes struggle. No one can negate the fact that South Africans went through a struggle before we came to Mandela's release in 1990 and our first democratic elections in 1994. The assumption here is that the struggle ended when we got to the ballot box and could choose who governed our country. Yet the reality is that the struggle did not end in 1994; it just became more complex in nature.

The CODESA compromises ensured that there was no unsettling of the economy, plus some promises made by both sides to work towards forming what was popularly referred to as the New South Africa. The previously oppressed would not take their oppressors to task for the last 46 years of oppression, and the oppressors would surrender political power to the oppressed. But the sunset clauses ensured that where it counted for the oppressor, they still remained in power (land ownership, mineral resources, and control of the private sector and means of production).

So, as one reflects on the first 20 years of a democratic South Africa it is clear that the situation is, in itself, quite complicated. Yet, it is also clear that it was not just a handful of political activists who paid the exorbitant price for freedom. It was all of us. And some continue to pay the price two decades later.

A single example that highlights for me how divided South Africa still is the Oscar Pistorius case. There is no doubt that he shot and killed his girlfriend; his entire case hinges on whether he knew it was her behind that door or not. The assumption is that, in a country like ours, if it had been a black person who was trying to steal from a vulnerable double amputee, it would have been okay to kill them. The reality is that it was his supermodel girlfriend behind the door and not a stranger trying to break in. None of us were there except the two of them so we'll never know the truth. But as a nation, our stance on the case is based on how we measure the value of human life. It is okay to kill a black thief; we don't need to ask why he opted for the path of stealing or, even more profoundly, to ask what it is about our historical legacy that has led to our country producing this calibre of person.

My parents were destined to be together. Their love was able to withstand many storms, but when my mother speaks of why she eventually left my father after 20 years of being together, her answer is simply: 'I did love him; I'll always love him. But I knew that the man he'd become was eventually going to kill me, and my children would have to grow up as orphans. I couldn't allow that.'

Freedom was not free, and if we're honest, glossing over the facts and enforcing false unity is not the best way to address the injustices of the past. The last 20 years have seen great progress, and the majority of South Africans (black, white, Indian and coloured alike) are good, well-meaning people – people who want a better future for their children. It warms my heart to see the younger generation who do not see colour; their world should not be burdened with ugly pictures of a past we would all rather forget. But as the older generation, it is our duty to ensure that we build a united South Africa that we would be proud to hand down to our children's children.

The ebb and flow of ubuntu: Two decades of democracy, by a half-century citizen

Wayne Duvenage
Civil rights activist

I CANNOT REMEMBER WHEN I first heard the term 'ubuntu' – certainly not in my first 30 years of life. Looking back, my five decades of life in South Africa began in a nation imbued with the antithesis of ubuntu. The minority who held power believed there was no need to be united for a common purpose. Their purpose was skewed to favour the minority of white people, while the majority of citizens were denied the right to be free in the land of their birth, all because of one factor: they were born with a darker skin pigment.

I doubt if Verwoerd, Vorster, Botha and the nationalist clan or, in fact, many white South Africans, had heard the term or understood the concept of ubuntu. It was absent from textbooks and our national psyche.

As a youngster growing up through the 1960s and 1970s in an all-white, middle-class neighbourhood, I was oblivious to the evils of apartheid. The conservative nationalist government did a good job in keeping me (and millions of other white families) blinkered from the evilness of their plan. Life was bliss in suburbia in a rapidly growing industrial town: Newcastle in northern Natal. Our minds were tuned out from the realities of segregated life, especially its impact on those from whom we were separated.

News of the Rivonia Trial, the many deaths and incarceration of Black Consciousness leaders, the 1976 uprisings in distant Soweto, never reached us and even if they did, it was in small doses. The propaganda machine ensured our minds were closed to these issues. This was so effective that few of us had heard of Steve Biko before he died. Instead, we were fed stories of the 'evil black communist machine' trying to invade our land. Ironically, we had little idea of what communism meant – schools had been forbidden to teach anything about it.

There was the odd occasion during my youth that presented encounters that triggered questions and raised my curiosity about forced racial segregation and inequalities. I recall clearly, at the age of 15 I met a kind and gentle man called Said, a person of colour, who worked at a factory managed by my father. As much as I would have liked to openly befriended Said and his family, my father, who was a peaceful and cautious person, suggested I be careful in this regard. The idea was prohibited.

And so it was that I did so in secret, riding my bicycle from our new leafy suburb, aptly named Arbor Park, across to Lennoxton – the poorer suburb just west of the town centre reserved for non-white folk – to meet with Said and his family. This was also my first encounter with Muslim tradition and my mind began to open to the kaleidoscope of our country's diversity. Sharing a meal, I asked about his wife's absence from our discussion at the table and this generated interest in his religious customs. It was a moving experience for me and the meaning of ubuntu began to unconsciously stir within.

Towards the end of my teens, I remember my mother telling me that 'my fortunes and privileges in life had been immorally bestowed due to a racial classification – Caucasian, white or European'. This became the jolt that triggered my realisation of how the colour of my skin gave my family and friends unfair access to the best residential areas, state resources, schools, medical treatment and job security. I don't believe I can ever really comprehend the depth of pain and suffering that people of colour experienced during apartheid.

It was during my days at the University of Natal in the early 1980s, that my conscience was truly awakened to the evil nature of the Nationalist Party system. While it was still forbidden to openly display any sympathy for banned Black Consciousness movements, debates on campus were safe places to learn about and express one's opinions on apartheid. My curiosity and learning gave rise to many late-night debates about the evils of forced segregation.

On entering the work environment, I became more exposed to how preferential education, job protection and racism in general gave whites a clear advantage in job opportunities and promotion in the corporate world. As a young white male manager in the workplace, it was easy to climb the corporate ladder. It was also extremely challenging and difficult to promote people of colour, not only because of the inequality of education and training provided to the oppressed, but worse, because it was not encouraged by senior management at that time. The values and essence of the imagined ubuntu were starting to play out in my mind.

But it would only be in the early 1990s, at the dawning of our new democratic dispensation, when the mixed emotions of elation and anxiety within a nation grappling with the transition to racial equality and sharing, that I discovered the true essence and meaning of the word 'ubuntu'. The realisation of sharing and togetherness for a united common purpose, of prosperity for all and through all, was now better understood. It was uplifting and I had mixed feelings of excitement and trepidation about our dawning democracy.

Personally, I was not oblivious to the fact that challenges would abound, but I sensed that most white folk were confident that the country's infrastructure was sound and that the new leadership, under the incredibly forgiving and humane Madiba, would grasp nation-building with both hands. We had no doubt that the education system needed to be corrected and that we had to find mechanisms for sharing and distributing the national wealth as meaningfully as possible. With the world at our country's feet, investors were banging on the door. Where else would one want to be?

I was in my mid-30s when the nation's first democratic elections took place in 1994 and welcomed the first five years under Nelson Mandela's rule. These were magical years. Fears of a black backlash were quelled by Madiba's qualities of humanity and forgiveness that seemed to permeate the nation. He became the hero to all, uniting a divided nation, even those who had earlier referred to him as a scoundrel and a terrorist. He was ubuntu personified and we got it.

Throughout the first decade of democracy, ubuntu was like a new energy that helped white folk to grapple with the ghosts of the past and the occasional guilt from benefits accrued through apartheid. Madiba's immense courage and leadership reduced racial friction, which was crucial for the nation to undergo a process of healing, redistribution and social development. Hopes for a prosperous future for all were high. Our new democracy seemed to be filled with new energy, new possibilities and a cultural fusion of our diversity.

We all had so much to learn, and learn we did, sometimes with resistance, but often with open arms. I recall diversity-training workshops at work and the impact these had on us all. Each session was filled with tears and anguish as we listened to first-hand accounts of the suffering and pain of poverty, illiteracy, humiliation and hopelessness that apartheid had imposed on our previously disadvantaged colleagues. Fortunately, these sessions also brought some relief and laughter, as we discovered each other's senseless fears and prejudices.

As we entered our second free elections, ubuntu was being fully grasped by the nation. It belonged to all of us. South Africa belonged to all of us.

I sold the few shares I had in the company I worked for. Together with my new partner and future wife, we decided to invest what money we had in a property out of town, to build a family business and keep our capital within the country. We invested all we had in the future of our new democracy, sincere in our belief that our and our children's future was in good hands.

The first decade of our new democracy showed promise, but by 2005 the failings of the education system became evident. Skills required in the workplace were not coming out of our schools and the cracks in a government not in tune with its people's needs began to show. In saying this, one can never denounce the excellent work and strides amid trying times that did deliver houses and basic services to millions of previously disadvantaged families.

The benefits of a hard-fought freedom of association and the ability to elect leaders to govern communities, areas, regions and the nation were immense. But freedom and emancipation is short-lived if the masses remain caught in an eternal trap of poverty. Without good education, our people remain trapped, and it became evident the new South Africa – a decade on – had not provided equal access to good educational facilities, resources and results.

The skewed access to equality in learning, health, welfare and general security was still very much alive, mostly as a legacy of the apartheid system, but the new dispensation was making little headway to address these crucial issues. We had to work harder and leaders had to do more to ensure that every effort went into this initiative. In addition, the state's coffers needed to be well managed to channel resources effectively and mechanisms such as the Black Economic Empowerment required evaluation of their effectiveness.

Moving into the second decade of democracy, as the end of

Mbeki's reign over the ANC drew nigh, the frenzy of civil service nepotism began to impact, with weaker output and poor service delivery. People at all levels of government were very often appointed because of who they knew or were related to, and not necessarily because they were qualified to fill the position. Thousands of older white civil servants struggled with a changing business culture, took their pensions and severance packages and moved on. While some will view this situation as local government losing essential skills and expertise, others will see it as a broom sweeping things clean to bring about the necessary change. I imagine there was a bit of truth in both views, but I also sensed that the true spirit of ubuntu was being eroded though this process.

Sadly though, in such situations, a skills drain in any organisation leaves it weaker. This was masked for a while by the growing investment attracted by our developing economy, but cracks began to show in other areas. Maintenance of existing infrastructure tended to take a back seat and deterioration became evident, more so in rural areas and isolated towns where councils lacked expertise. Cities were spared the degradation for a while, but it did not take long to see these issues reach the major metropolitan areas.

At municipal levels the basic infrastructure of roads, water pipes, sewage pumps, and traffic lights began to crumble, as did administration and other basic services. At a national level, the lights started to go out and large infrastructural development projects were delayed with signs of multi middleman interference in rigged tenders and contracts, resulting in reduced value with higher costs having to be borne by taxpayers.

Throughout the past decade, corruption became rife and 'pigs with their snouts in the trough' became the talk on the street and around the dinner table. Corrupt civil servants ran multiple jobs and were rarely seen in the offices from where they were expected to serve citizens. Tenders were submitted through front companies that won huge contracts for family members and friends. Others were outsourced at excessive, marked-up prices to contractors who could do the job. Nepotism and cronyism permeated most local and regional offices and the cost of government increased exponentially.

Sadly, the one area that society had hoped would help to straighten out the mess, the private sector and, in particular, big business, elected to adopt an attitude of 'joining in'. It was a case of more money to be made and no matter how dirty the game, it was more profitable to wallow in the mud than to be left out.

The spirit of ubuntu in our new democratic landscape was ebbing. It was no longer a case of one's existence and prosperity being because of and with others, but rather a case of prosperity and wealth for a few at the expense of the masses.

Throughout the second decade of democracy, government leaders and many connected to them at a national, provincial or local level, wanted in on the action. The boards of many large businesses made room at the table for those connected to the powers that be, and the 'contract swayers', the 'inside informationers' sat alongside the decision-makers. This gave insight to tender and project opportunities that favoured some companies more than others. Chancellor House, the 'investment arm' of the ruling party, became a major shareholder in many private sector companies, supposedly making the ANC one of the richest political parties in the world.

After the 2009 world economic turmoil, despite going through some belt-tightening exercises, most private sector industries continued to survive far better than their colleagues in other parts of the developed world. But, like frogs in a pot of heating water, they had become accustomed to the growing trouble around them.

'This is Africa,' you would hear them say, when traffic light failures became the norm and crime, rape and murder became just part of the reality of everyday life.

Aside from the odd occasion, when a strong business leader would make some critical comment against the government, big business leadership did not want to raise serious challenges against the establishment, nor did they want be seen to be questioning the ill-gotten gains of the few at the expense of society having to pay more for services. With an attitude of 'We're alright, Jack,' they simply looked the other way and continued to focus on today's profit and share price, effectively stabbing the spirit and heart of ubuntu.

Those who complained were labelled the 'naysayers' or the 'doomsdayers', whose depressing mantras of 'Did you know what happened in our neighbourhood/family/club?' were repeated with monotonous regularity. The plethora of negative news became soul destroying and not conducive to feeling good about our country. The natural reaction to rising negativity is the development of an ostrich-like mentality, when people stop listening as a negative defence mechanism to beat off the depression. 'Let's be positive and look on the bright side,' became the order of the day. But ignoring problems does not make them disappear; it just make us more thick-skinned and helps the rot set in.

Today, 20 years after the birth of our democracy, the spirit of ubuntu has dropped to very low levels. The positive energy from the early days of our democratic transition has largely been wiped out. Tensions along racial lines have begun to flare up and new political parties, such as the EFF, are capitalising on this wave, while the government at all levels is regularly chastised on all fronts for its poor performance.

Many believe the once powerful African National Congress erred in 2007 by electing a poor leader in Jacob Zuma. Declining service delivery and political appointments in strategic positions to protect the connected elite have become blatantly evident through all ranks of government. Whatever happened to the plan that citizens should reap the benefits of good foresight, planning and developmental attitudes by officials who work hard for the people? Why has this notion been replaced by a bloated government, peppered with corrupt officials, high costs and greater inefficiencies, exacerbated by numerous deals and middlemen being enriched at the taxpayers' expense?

The spirit of ubuntu, as exemplified by Madiba at the outset of our new democracy, is missing from the psyche of our current government. It no longer displays the true values of an executive that should be at one with, and in service to, its people.

This lack of respect for the people they serve has seeped deep into the roots of our public service. Government has become a burgeoning, cumbersome entity, inefficiently squandering and mismanaging the taxes it collects. The people are becoming disillusioned and it will take a significant change in the mindset of our country's leadership to change that. What we require is for the civil servant workforce to be significantly reduced, by up to 30%, and the development of a lean and visionary governmental institution that enables business to thrive and create employment. Investment must be seriously encouraged, with taxes ploughed efficiently back into society for the greater good of its people. This is what is supposed to happen, but alas, it will not be so within the mindset of the current leadership.

My personal challenge
In 2010, during my tenure as the chief executive at Avis, and following the tumultuous high of the Soccer World Cup, we witnessed the unfolding of an irrational and relatively evil scheme. The decision to slap a 45-gantry e-tolling mechanism onto our recently upgraded Gauteng urban freeway was grossly flawed and one that I could not ignore. It was clearly designed to suck money out of the motorists within the nation's richest and most populated province of Gauteng. It was fraught with inefficiencies and inconsistencies that didn't make sense.

The Electronic Tolling Company (ETC) joint venture, which had become 85% owned by European-based Kapsch TrafficCom, would be raking in millions of rand in revenue from the South African motorist (over R650 million per annum), along with a host of local 'connected' companies that would supply the multiplicity of services to the tolling entity. In short, we had an R18 billion road upgrade (which cost far more than it should have), being paid for by Gauteng citizens, to the tune of over R100 billion for the next 20 years. Thereafter the tolling would never cease, but instead it would become a 'sacred', immoveable cash cow, partly to ease the burden on the state's coffers but, more worryingly, for numerous entities to profiteer from.

Simply put, the e-tolling plan was not in the best interests of society and, as such, would never attract the high levels of compliance required to get most money collected into paying for the tarmac. To have any hope of settling its long-term debt, SANRAL would have to ratchet-up the tariffs in an endless game of cat and mouse with a defiant public, but in the end, the compliant users (mainly the big corporate accounts) would end up subsidising the growing contingent of the non-compliant.

How would the courts manage the growing prosecutions and how would the credit bureaus react to a growing dilemma of defaulters who had a legitimate argument? Simply put, the e-tolling decision was a farce and needed to be seriously challenged, which was partly why, in July 2012, having spent the past five years at the helm of South Africa's largest and most successful car rental company, I decided it was time to move on and give this challenge some of my personal time and attention.

The Opposition to Urban Tolling Alliance (OUTA) was born in

February 2012, with a team of amazingly good, active citizens and extremely hard-working colleagues. With our talented legal team, we successfully interdicted the launch of e-tolls on 28 April 2012. This was seen as a huge win for society and the start of a process that empowered citizens with knowledge of how shocking the system was. The momentum of South Africa's first large-scale 'tax revolt' was growing and a showdown with the authorities was underway, despite OUTA's decision not to appeal the SCA judgement in October 2013. The jury is out as to whether the e-tolling decision of government will succeed. All indications after the first three months of operation expose a system deep in maladministration, systems challenges and a low e-tag uptake, all of which point to an unviable system in the medium term.

Society's time to challenge
Today, I find myself reflecting on what must be done to get our nation back on track, to restore the true spirit of ubuntu and enable our country to prosper to heights that should be well within our reach. I am also mindful of apartheid's imbalance along race and economic lines that remains so prominent to this day. I also recognise that their involvement in liberating the nation from an ugly past, still enables the ANC to ride high on the support of so many who vote with their heart, despite glaring evidence of government failures. But is the tide turning? Is the notion dawning that liberators in times of change are not necessarily good leaders in times of nation-building? The future of our country's prosperity is precariously poised and much will depend on changing the status quo.

Ultimately though, the seizing of our future and a revival of an ubuntu-driven leadership lies in the hands of society's ability to challenge those in authority, both private and public. Our failure as citizens to hold our leadership to account, outside of elections, is a concern. Our standards and expectations have been dumbed down and diminished and it is time for some introspective visioning, for moral courage and focused leadership to turn things around. It can be done. It must be done!

This is a dream shared by millions of South Africans. Personally, I want my children to live the true spirit of ubuntu, to enjoy the fruits of a safe, healthy and growing nation of citizens in tune with a brighter future for all. Instead, today, our children are oblivious to real peace and freedom from corruption, greed and gross misconduct by civil servants. A young adult of today could be forgiven for thinking 'this is the norm'. Are we fast losing a citizenry committed to standing up and challenging the shockingly poor leadership, the inept behaviour, the overt and brazen corruption and greed?

Conclusion

Today, at the end of two decades of democracy, I sense we have come full circle. We are back to the dark days before Mandela led us into an understanding of the healing power of ubuntu. Not the dark days of race-based segregation and poverty by law, but a diminishing opportunity for knowledge, prosperity and growth. While the setting has changed, we have reverted to a situation of gross neglect by our leaders and a nation falling into despair. I yearn for sanity and inspirational leadership to prevail in this amazing country, at least enough thereof to convince our children to stay here, to feel the pulse of ubuntu rather than seek a life abroad, one that may be richer in stability, safety and service delivery, but poorer in the richness of life that only Africa can provide.

Steve Biko once said: 'In time we will be in a position to bestow on South Africa, the greatest possible gift – a more human face.' I believe he was talking about ubuntu; a person is a person because of other people. Our leaders would do well to remember that a good government is a government that does a great job in serving all the people. Our business leaders would do well to hold our civil servants to account for our taxes they manage, without fear or favour.

Children with disabilities: Musings of a health practitioner turned human rights activist in post-apartheid South Africa

Jean Elphick
Researcher on disabilities

WHEN I STARTED MY CAREER I WAS full of the blind optimism that an idyllic childhood and white, Black-Sash-backing parents could hope to instil. Fresh from UCT, I embarked on my obligatory year of community service – as all post-1998 health professionals are required to do after graduating in South Africa. I was positive about our new 'Rainbow Nation' but, on reflection, hopelessly misinformed. Since then, my outlook has been vastly transformed, as has my professional life. Through exposure to healthcare at the grassroots level in one of the poorest provinces, my eyes were opened to the reality of the challenges that we face in providing essential services to the most vulnerable in our country. Since then, I have experienced various stages of grief and I have felt my resolve harden as my role in the transformation of South Africa has come into focus.

This essay follows my journey of development and my growing passion for addressing the situation faced by people with disabilities in the most forgotten parts of our country. This is not an unbiased account, nor can I profess to have a disability myself. This is, however, a brief account of my views and experiences of working first in health, then in disability, and now in the human rights and development sectors.

To begin my journey: I reported for duty at Madwaleni District Hospital – a deep-rural former-Transkei mission hospital – in January 2007. The hospital is situated two bone-shattering hours down a dirt road off the N2 in the heartland of the Eastern Cape. Interestingly, one of the hospital's outlying clinics was the mission station to which Nelson Mandela is said to have walked as a child from his village of Qunu. Unfortunately, not much has changed since then – the hospital lies in a municipality whose infamous reputation for counterproductive management structures rivals its disastrous child health outcomes.

What began as an obligatory 'year out' of my career, turned out to be a life-changing experience. Journeying along roads to find a place unrecognised by Google maps, with only a cell phone and a small dog for company, I had no idea how the situation and people I would come to meet would profoundly alter my purpose in life.

I had been told not to bother turning up for work in anything less than a 4x4 – that just getting out of the hospital parking would require engaging low-range all-wheel drive! It was not that bad, but the roads were truly terrible and impassable when it rained. Little did I know, that one year later I would sit in on a focus group of mothers of children with disabilities and hear that the single thing we as health professionals could do to improve our services was to get a better road built to the hospital. Physical access and basic infrastructure – concepts overlooked in the Transkei during apartheid – formed just the tip of the iceberg of disabling environmental barriers that persist in South Africa.

Over and above the dearth of infrastructural development in the homeland regions, I encountered a public health disaster area. Infectious diseases spread rampantly: the effects of HIV, TB and epilepsy permeated everyday life. Locals continued to live a largely tribal lifestyle, collecting drinking water from the rivers in which clothes were washed or springs frequented by cows, goats and sheep. In fact, there was hardly any evidence of formal sanitation systems, so water sources were inevitably the ultimate end point for all waste. In addition to the road, running water also became a centre point for my time at the hospital.

I recall a time in the early days when, having finished treating a patient, I took off my gloves, and lathered my hands with antibacterial soap. A minute later I was desperately opening the tap to its limit – much to the amusement of the nurses. There was no water that morning. This became a mounting issue, as eventually there was no water with which to cook, flush toilets, bathe patients or run the hospital's washing machines. Some days we got patients out of bed wrapped in their bed sheet because there were no clean pyjamas to dress them in.

Sometimes we would go running and then bathe in the river, or, more extreme, wash from a bucket of collected water, then hand-wash a few items of clothing, before scooping the water up for use in the toilet cistern. I often feel that these stories may come across as 'war stories' from a time gone by. But they are not – they are tales from a South African hospital in 2007.

After a few months in the area I was tearing my hair out! Yet hundreds of thousands of people had been living in the hospital's vast catchment area, dealing with these situations, since the day they were born. As one can imagine, growing up in an area with scant access to clean running water, bad sanitation and a treacherous hike to the closest healthcare or maternity facility – let alone all the other social determinants of health – gives rise to an overwhelmingly large group of disabled children. For the first time, I was confronted with the terrifying reality of disability in South Africa.

Disability is increasingly articulated as a human rights issue in Africa. Beginning with my first forays into the equality discourse at Madwaleni, I have continued to seek out the stories of those most often hidden and overlooked in our society. In our shining Constitution, disability is explicitly mentioned as being a prohibited ground for unfair discrimination. Our legislative reform and policy development has been trumpeted as being among the most pro-disability and enabling in the world. However, although many of these laws and policies have been enacted for almost 20 years now, I feel that people with disabilities continue to face multiple human rights violations every day.

The issues facing children with disabilities crept up on me slowly. Initially I felt completely ill-equipped to advise mothers who had been caring for their children with complicated multiple disabilities for years. I felt a sense of personal crisis when I gradually started to meet more and more families of children with disabilities: a granny caring for a bright little girl who's writhing body movements were beyond her control; the characterful little boy who lost his vision and gained a hemiplegia as a result of TB meningitis; the beloved daughter with such bad hydrocephalus that I felt ill the first time I met her. These children would come from the far-flung hills – on mothers' backs or at times in wheelbarrows – to see me. Seeking desperately an answer or an improvement.

We attended a monthly workshop for children with disabilities. Everyone would gather and we would attempt to provide some kind of group education – teaching mothers that their children's conditions were medical and not due to their wrongdoing; that epileptic seizures have a neurological rather than a spiritual cause; and, for some, that the prognosis of their child's condition was more or less certain and no amount of traditional medicine or praying was likely to have a curative effect. We also tried to spend time with each child and provide some semblance of a complete rehabilitation service. It was on one of these afternoons, when I was concentrating on one child while 18 others waited for my undivided attention, that a mother arrived with her 18-year-old son on her back.

I cannot remember his name but his face and story will remain with me forever. It was the first time I had met him but his condition left me shocked and soul-searching. Despite his age, he looked no more than six. He was thin, with big eyes and a bigger smile. His body and legs were flexed and rigid as a board, so much so that in the coming months the only way we could find to change his position was to perch him on a massive beanbag. No chair or seating device could accommodate his deformities – believe me – we threw the book at it! He had a broken leg, dislocated wrists, knees and ankles; numerous pressure sores; TB and pneumonia. He had no ID book and received no social grant. Later we received a perplexing call from Elliotdale, the closest town. They had gone to try to apply for documentation and were unsure of how to get fingerprints off him because his hands were so stiff. He could not speak. In spite of all this, he was so alive. He could communicate in a way that went beyond words or gestures. His condition was overwhelming, as was the courage, love and undying dedication displayed by his single mother.

I was running the workshop alone that day, and the day ended before I was able to see everyone in a way that was thorough and satisfactory to me. Somehow the boy and his mother had slipped through the cracks and received the wrong message. This was most likely due to my message being lost in the translation of my broken Xhosa.* Two days later, wracked with guilt, I sent a bakkie† out to find their remote and inaccessible hut. When the driver found their place, it was deserted. It was only on his way back that he came

---

* isiXhosa is one of South Africa's 11 official languages and is widely spoken in the Eastern Cape.
† Bakkie is a South African term describing a pick-up truck or utility vehicle.

across the mother pushing him in a wheelbarrow. They were still on their way home. It had taken them two days to journey home from their hospital visit where I had more or less provided no real help.

It was people like these that fired me with divine discontent. After two years at the hospital, I was at breaking point. I had realised that being a clinician on the ground was not for me. Although the rehabilitation department at Madwaleni was providing services against the odds to everyone – including those with disabilities – I decided that I would be better placed in a broader development role.

It is hard to believe that stories like the ones from the Eastern Cape could become normal or that the lived experiences of children with disabilities could get any worse. In retrospect, though, I feel that at least the children in the Eastern Cape were treated as part of the family and their quirks and atypical behaviours were absorbed by the informal milieu of rural Xhosa life. At the time it seemed to me that the situation could not get any worse for disabled children, but when I started working in the townships around Johannesburg, I was again confronted with a new and shocking scenario.

Despite far better infrastructure – tarred roads all the way to massive hospitals like Bara,* RDP† housing, taps and electricity – the lives and situations facing children with disabilities are saturated with discrimination, marginalisation and a disregard for human dignity. When I started the work I do now, I did a baseline study to try to understand the situation facing children with disabilities in the diverse and distinctive communities of Orange Farm, Alexandra, Diepsloot and inner-city Johannesburg. I compared my findings in Johannesburg with a similar study that I conducted, albeit on a smaller scale, on the Cape Flats. The few months of this study left me an emotional wreck. When I went for trauma counselling, the psychologist shed tears herself when I shared some of the stories I had encountered.

Most shocking to me were the many cases of sexual abuse of disabled children that I encountered. Children and young adults with disabilities make soft targets for abuse: they often spend all day at home instead of going to school like their non-disabled siblings. They may not be able to vocalise their experiences with coherence, fight

---

* Bara is the commonly used abbreviation for the Chris Hani Baragwanath Hospital – a huge, ostensibly fully-equipped tertiary hospital in Soweto near Johannesburg.

† RDP or Reconstruction and Development Programme houses are state-built houses.

off or run away from their abusers. Young girls, particularly those with intellectual impairments, fall easy prey to sexual grooming and exploitation. Most frustrating and disheartening was the reaction that the few cases that were reported received from the police, prosecutors and the courts. Caregivers shared how cases had not been taken seriously, largely because the main witness had a disability. Many victims described how they still encounter the perpetrator in their neighbourhood.

In addition to the obviously appalling safety and security violations, I was also staggered by mothers' accounts of how their children had received their diagnoses; how they had slowly pieced together from all the rushed half-answers they got from doctors, nurses and therapists, that their child would not be what they had hoped and imagined. They described being sent from pillar to post, searching for answers – and all this against the backdrop of the all-encompassing indignity of extreme poverty.

Armed with this experience, I embarked on a journey to look for pragmatic and sustainable solutions. I wanted to do more with my life than treat 15 patients a day in a dysfunctional public hospital or perch in an ivory tower and attempt to describe the situation. At some point I graduated from being a health professional to being a fighter, an activist, a person with her eyes set on a better future for all.

Orange Farm is a sprawling, fairly diffuse township just north of Sebokeng. It costs R36 return in a taxi from there to Bree Street, Johannesburg, so even for the few that have managed to find jobs – and that is very few – it is still a struggle to bring home any real money. The area is wracked by the usual social ills, although in its favour, Orange Farm is home to a set of wonderful people. Just under two years ago I began working in this community with caregivers of children with disabilities – a small group of mothers and grandmothers, and, surprisingly, even one or two grandfathers.

We started off with the basics. This was the first time that any of us had delved into South Africa's Constitution of 1996. We started off by looking at equality and non-discrimination. I was, of course, completely out of my depth. Even getting hold of the Constitution in any official language other than English seemed impossible, leaving us with an often multi-way translation between English, Zulu, Sotho and Tsonga. This being said, explaining why disability was an explicitly forbidden ground for unfair discrimination was easy compared to unpacking the finer nuances of the difference between the other listed grounds. I challenge anyone to attempt to explain the difference between sex and gender and sexual orientation – or worse, religion, conscience and belief – to a room full of traditionally conservative folk, broken-telephone style!

These were humble beginnings. In the four months of our weekly lessons that followed, however, we slowly meted out a clearer idea of what human rights meant to us, and, importantly, what the South African Constitution, laws and policies promise children with disabilities. Our common conclusion in the group was that 'everything comes down to discrimination' for children with disabilities and their families, still, 20 years after the end of apartheid. This realisation formed the motivation for us to establish a self-help group. Following much deliberation on what the group should do, we were able to identify three battles to fight: one was the endemic sexual abuse of children with disabilities; the second was the effectively complete denial of the right to education for children with disabilities; and the final one was to stand up against the discrimination and inequitable treatment of people with disabilities.

Each week we meet on a Friday morning at Arekopaneng Community Centre in the township. It is the best time of my week. At 10:30 am about 20 trusty regulars will come in and find a chair. We sit in a big circle and usually open our meeting with a prayer and our group song – *Sidinga Uthando* (the name of our group which translates to 'all we need is love'). We come up with an agenda and work through the items, translating back and forth among ourselves. Often someone has encountered a problem and shares their experience. Occasionally mothers from neighbouring townships join us. We have started to have guest speakers who teach us new things and answer questions about specific problems encountered by the caregivers. Although I am not a mother of a child with a disability, not even a mother, I resonate with the way the members of our group describe what happens each Friday.

These quotes were shared during some research we conducted recently, and describe what some members get out of our group:

> By the time when you are here in our group, even if you can meet with someone who can try to bring you down, because of this new knowledge and these ideas, they cannot hurt you

or discriminate. It is like we are stronger – we don't hear those words.[*]

When I first came here, I cried tears and everyone came and hugged me. They started talking to me. It was easy for me now, not angry anymore. I treat my child with more calm and understanding. But when you are at home, thinking it is me against the world ... there are people like you who face the very same problems, it's better now, because we come and talk and laugh.[†]

I am relieved that I am not alone.[‡]

I feel love among the mothers.[§]

Immediately after formalising as a group, we set about counting the number of children with disabilities in our township. We gathered as much information as possible. Ages, addresses, whether they had essential currency in the access to services game: diagnoses, assessments, Road to Health cards,[¶] birth certificates. For each child that was short of something, we started looking for ways to get hold of it: educational psychologist assessments, affidavits, case numbers and LSEN[**] letters. For every rape disclosed, we started reporting and following up on the progress of the investigations. We drew up problem statements, attended meetings, wrote letters, stood up at public meetings, filed reports, made submissions, addressed Parliament and sent referral, after referral, after referral.

Although not much time has passed, and, although I am aware of many individual cases wherein we have not succeeded in effectively accessing the services needed, I am starting to feel that we are indeed making inroads. We have seen a rape case through court and we have had the MEC of Education[††] in our province commit to building

---

[*] Focus group, 2 August 2013.
[†] Focus group, 19 April 2013.
[‡] Focus group, 19 April 2013.
[§] Focus group, 2 August 2013.
[¶] Road to Health cards are essential documents used mainly by community clinics to identify children, track their growth and development, and record their vaccinations.
[**] Learners with Special Education Needs.
[††] MEC stands for Member of the Executive Council in South African politics.

a new school for all our children with moderate to severe barriers to learning. We have spoken to over 1 500 people in Orange Farm, Johannesburg and beyond with a message of tolerance, inclusion and equal treatment.

Further, we have begun hosting seminars on child protection issues in the disability sector and have produced groundbreaking academic research on the burgeoning agency exercised by our group of caregivers. A few children have been admitted to schools, and their mothers relate to me their joy at dressing in their uniforms each morning. We are all much more confident about speaking up when we are aware that the rights of our children are being violated.

The programme I have started in Orange Farm is called an empowerment programme, but empowerment is a funny thing. It is said to be both a process and an outcome, an approach and a philosophy. Whatever it is, I feel I have empowered as well as been empowered. Although the implementation gaps and horrors of human rights violations are ever-present, I feel I am no longer in my own crisis about what to do about healing our nation or making a better life for its most vulnerable, marginalised and discarded members.

I continue to witness horrific injustices: children reaching adulthood having never had access to a day's schooling; rapists living with impunity next door to their disabled child victims; and single mothers battling extreme poverty to care for the expensive needs of their disabled children. For those at the bottom end of society, it seems a pipe-dream to live in dignity and enjoy equality. Systemic barriers highlighted by apartheid seem to persist for the disability sector, despite the glorious new laws and policies – theoretically at least – at our fingertips. Yet, in the midst of all this, I feel, more and more, that although the dream of the new South Africa is yet to be realised, there is something I can contribute.

To me, freedom means hope and opportunities

Josephilda Hlophe-Nhlapo

Economist

As I write this diary of episodes in my life, I am in the highest office in the land. I am fortunate enough to be a member of the first secretariat in South Africa to craft the first long-term plan for the Republic. On 24 August, a day before the Marikana tragedy, the National Development Plan was handed over to parliamentarians as elected representatives of the people of South Africa. Hopefully South Africans will rally behind the vision and the plan and make this vision happen. It is good enough I think, but not perfect by any measure; after all, it was produced by mortals, clever ones, but fallible mortals nonetheless.

I am truly excited that I find myself in the highest office of the land charged with ensuring that even in Lower Didimane, my mother's birth place, the promise of the Constitution (prosperity, non-sexism, non-racialism and equity) resonates. That I sit in this office is a miracle indeed; I pinch myself constantly and ask the question, is this real? I, born 314 years after the arrival of Jan van Riebeeck's crew on the Dromedaris, Reijger and Goede Hoop, 187 years after the first wars of resistance, 53 years after the Land Act and 13 years after the Bantu Education Act of 1953, was born of a race and gender that automatically meant I had very few prospects. Yes, this not so little African girl, daughter of Mangaliso who is the son of Mphakamela kaNgayiyane, did not aspire to more than a modest house. That I would acquire at least one degree I knew would happen. Those who know my mother understand that I had no alternative but to go to school.

Yet I dared not hope for more.

My office is in the East Wing, parallel to Robert Sobukwe Street, named after the liberation struggle hero who was so feared by the apartheid regime that he had his own clause in the terms of his sentence and was cast into solitary confinement for longer than any other political prisoner on the Island of Makana. I have often wondered who the original occupant of my office was and whether he (yes, most probably it was a he) ever thought that an African woman would be sitting in that office and in that very chair. My office has ancient furniture. I swear it is the same furniture that officials used as they continued the work Lord Milner and his Kindergarten had started in the Sunnyside offices in 1903. When we work late at night we sometimes jokingly wonder what Verwoerd's ghost feels when he sees us working on complex econometric models, preparing inputs for our black principals. Remember, Verwoerd said that the likes of me could be only hewers of wood and carriers of water.

I grew up in exile. My earliest recollection of life was me quietly hiding in a thicket to try and escape a baboon. We had a neighbour who kept all types of animals, including baboons and snakes. We had enlightened parents, which is why they were not branded as witches but rather seen as neighbours who preferred exotic pets. The baboons would escape from their enclosure now and then. On this particular day, my siblings and I had gone foraging for guavas. The eldest of the foraging party was my ten-year-old brother. On seeing the baboon, they all ran and left me there with the beast. I didn't scream but crawled into a thicket and literally stopped breathing. I didn't have to wait long because my brave mother came brandishing an iron (the big, heavy ones in which one put hot coals) to chase the baboon away. To be honest, I don't think the baboon saw me but from that day on my parents considered me a hero of some sort.

Indeed, living in a foreign country meant we had the strangest upbringing. I have to talk about this because my story is the story of many South Africans who grew up in exile but thrived against all odds. My father was rarely there. He would disappear for months on end. He says he was doing liberation work and who am I to question that? Raising four children alone in a strange land with no relatives around is not easy. My mother coped by allowing her mind to leave her now and again.

On these occasions, instead of sitting down and starving to death or getting sugar daddies to buy us food, my resourceful sisters would borrow money for food from my father's friends on his behalf. I doubt that my father ever repaid his friends but these exiled aunts and uncles knew how to look after their own.

When my sisters thought oBabu'Mhlongo needed a break, the nuns were raided. Those Dominican nuns were a very enlightened bunch, I tell you. One, a Sister 'Evangelist', introduced what I would now call Life Orientation. She taught sex education and explained why our traditional religion is not sinful. She explained that it is only a good ancestor that becomes *Idlozi*. Who then is best placed to intercede for you to the one who has always been there, Umvelinqangi, than someone who knows you? After all, we are the sum total of our ancestors. Yes, those were the days when all adults were parents. We couldn't bunk school because any adult who saw us loitering in a school uniform could scold us or even give us a beating and drag us to school. So, although I had parents who wandered away physically and otherwise, I grew up and certain values were instilled in me. I know the difference between wrong and right. Had things remained the way they were, we would not be talking about the moral regeneration movement or about the values encapsulated in Chapter 15 of the National Development Plan.

Life was different then. There was no TV, and radios ran on batteries and were preserved for listening to Radio Freedom. My house had many books, bought when a library folded in Bremersdorp. My school also had a huge library, stocked with books on all the saints of the Catholic Church, as well as books by Enid Blyton, from Noddy to The Famous Five, as well as Nancy Drew and the Hardy Boys. Everyone in my family read and recited poetry, so much so that by the time I was eight, even though I couldn't speak English yet, I could recite a paragraph from *Macbeth*: 'She should have died hereafter.' Our lives were so boring that we had no option but to go to school. As my brother who left home at 16 to join the ANC in exile always reminds me, I owe him and many others *abadela konke*, a lot. They risked bullets and torture internally, sacrificed their education, and risked malaria for me to be what I am today. I agree with him and to *amadela kufa*, I say respect!

I sometimes forget that to ordinary people in exile still singing *Qinisela Mandela; Qhawe lamaQhawe; Uyokuzwa ngathi masekulungile*, this transition to freedom and democracy was quick. I remember how I got to hear that Mandela was to be released. I was washing the dishes and I looked out the window and there was a student who lived in our garage, brandishing the *Sunday Times*, screaming and wailing like a banshee. I hurried outside thinking that he had attempted to braai himself again. This boy's only possession was a motorbike. One day he was trying to fix it by candlelight and, as many of us know, a flame and petrol don't mix. He became a human torch. I doused the flames by throwing him in a bath I had been running for myself. I then accompanied him on foot, late at night, to hospital. I didn't realise how hurt he was until the next morning, when I saw pieces of flesh in the bath. Anyway, he came back from hospital weeks later. Now you can understand how worried I was when he came out of the garage screaming!

On reading the paper, I, too, started screaming. My mother joined us and soon the whole neighbourhood was screaming and car horns were blaring. The joy was palpable. Aunties who had not spoken to each other for months suddenly hugged and cried; it truly was a wonderful feeling.

Fast-forward to 1996. By then a lot had happened. I had married, had two children, earned a degree in Economics and had even witnessed (physically) the fall of the Berlin Wall in Germany. We came back to South Africa. One of our treasured possessions was a left-hand-drive BMW. One day, my husband was waiting for a former colleague in the centre of Pretoria, when he was waylaid by a white man carrying a gun. Out of the blue, this man told him to get out of the car. My husband, who was petrified, drove off. The man shot until my husband crashed into a concrete barrier and passed out. He woke up not in hospital but in a police cell. The crazy man brandishing a gun turned out to be a plain-clothes policeman who had mistaken my husband for a car thief – how else was a black man supposed to have a European model BMW?

At the police station, no one would believe that it was his car, that he was an engineer and that he could not speak Afrikaans. He called me to tell me he was in jail and, knowing him well, I quickly put down the phone and continued with my meeting. You see, my husband is the type who abides by the law to the T. It was only when he called again that I realised that he meant it. The issue was sorted five days and thousands of rands in lawyers' fees later, but not before he had spent those five days in maximum security prison with hardened criminals, who took his watch, spectacles and shoes in order to protect him from themselves. Strangely enough, the criminals believed him. It was during this time that I understood the importance of the family. My aunts and cousins, paternal and maternal, were physically and emotionally there for me. *Ngiyabonga boXaba boNonkosi nani Zigegede, boNonogombili!*

It was also during this time that my sister, having just returned from exile where she taught at SOMAFCO and worked in the ANC office in London, passed away. This is a loss from which I am yet to recover. She was only 35 years old and I had not seen her for 15 years before seeing her again in England. This tragedy has not made me stronger; I still weep inside. The world would have been a much a better place had she lived! *Lala Ngoxolo Mwelase.*

In 1997–98 I went to further my studies at the Institute of Social Studies in The Hague. I got a scholarship from the European Union. Those who have ever had to prepare to go overseas for a lengthy period will know how hectic the preparations are. They include going for endless medical check-ups, applying for visas and, in my case, assuring my family that my husband would cope with the two children. In Holland, I found lodging with a young family from Bolivia, who had a small son. The poor things could hardly cope and my experience came in handy. I would put the baby on my back and take walks to calm him.

They were my first friends in Holland. Slowly I began to recognise my colleagues and formed friendships with my homies. There was one whom I shall call Lady R. She always came to class well-groomed – two-piece suits, pantyhose and all. She had been a director in some government office in the North West. I assure you, ladies and gentlemen, by the time we had finished the Master's degree, she was wearing socks bought from the market. But again I digress. At about this time I realised that I might be pregnant. I made an appointment and the doctor confirmed that I was not only pregnant but expecting twins.

As someone who always did the right thing, I reported the pregnancy to both the school and the scholarship representative. The school congratulated me and said they hoped that the pregnancy would not interfere with my studies and I promised it wouldn't. The scholarship people, on the other hand, called me and handed me a one-way ticket home. I asked why and they said it was because I had fallen pregnant before I came to Holland. I said yes, I could only have fallen pregnant at home because that was where my husband was. They said I was not medically insured for a pregnancy. My husband's medical aid sent a letter confirming that I was medically insured wherever I was because my husband worked for a multinational company. The scholarship office said that they still wanted me to go home. They were withdrawing their scholarship. So I gave up and packed. I remember well, it was a Thursday. Mr M came to find out why I was not in class and on finding me packing asked why. I explained. He literally said, 'Stop packing,' and left the room. Before I knew it the entire institute was toyi-toying, yes toyi-toying, outside the school against the scholarship organisation. Petitions were signed. Even Ms EB, a white South African who had attended Potchefstroom University, was an active member of the campaign. The school lawyers joined in and I hear my case was discussed even in Brussels. All of this took about three to four months and all along I was supposed to be continuing with my studies and passing while the sword of Damocles was hanging over my university career. I longed for home, for someone to tell me it was not a sin to be pregnant and that they looked forward to the baby. I missed my babies, Menzi and Nokukhanya. Hey, I even missed my boss, Mama Sindi, and my colleagues.

I appreciated the campaign very much because I loved schooling and still do. How can I not? My maternal granny would tell us all the time how my mother was the first girl *kulali yakhe* to complete form five with distinctions and get herself to university at Wits and then Roma in Lesotho. My father would say he got himself through school by selling sweets and modelling himself on Dr Jacob Mfaniselwa, a distant relative who was the first black South African man to have two PhDs. But the lack of privacy became a bit too much. Visitors would trickle in at all hours of the day. With each visit I would have to tell my story again. The most frequent question was: 'How could you fall pregnant knowing you have a scholarship?' I wish I could have had an answer to that. I still don't. Africans from as far as Rotterdam and Amsterdam would come over and offer to cook for me or bring me food.

One such friend was a Zimbabwean who had a partner called Rob. Poor Rob would be made to cook, buy me ice cream and anything else my friend desired for me. I remember her saying, 'Rob, we Africans prefer sadza, cook her sadza'; 'Rob don't put too much spice, it is not too good for the baby.' Lady R would grab me physically in the corridors and declare that I was anaemic and cook me liver. It really was a stressful time for me but eventually the case was sorted and I was allowed to stay at school provided I did not stay a week more than expected. I am still grateful for what the school and my fellow pupils did for me.

I was so exhausted emotionally; I just wanted to come home. A few days later I went into premature labour. One twin had died in my womb. The other remained in intensive care for a long time. [I stayed home a month more than I had envisaged. Both my mother and my mother-in-law refused to let me take the baby back to school 'lest the white people kill this one too'. You should have heard them talk: 'What else would you expect *ngamabhunu kakade?*' My sister-in-law agreed to look after my baby, who was literally as long as the palm of my hand and weighed about one and a half kilograms.

The good news, dear reader, is that this year she is doing Grade 10 and received the sacrament of confirmation. For those not familiar with strange Catholic rights and rituals, this means she became an adult in the eyes of the church. Why do I tell you this very personal story? It illustrates the power of solidarity and the audacity of hope. Had Mr M, Lady R, Ms EB (South Africans), Monica from Bolivia and Ms E from Namibia not started a 'She is not going anywhere; a pregnancy is not sin campaign' against the might of the scholarship organisation, I would be telling a different story.

I came back from Holland and started my job with the Southern African Catholic Bishops' Conference, Development and Welfare Agency. In this job I met many unsung heroes who, with minimal resources, were trying to feed the poor in their parishes and run early childhood development centres. These development activists, many of them ordinary men and women, were fired up by the liberation theology of constructing a just world here on Earth. I wonder if that fire still exists. I know my parish, the St Vincent de Paul Society, still gives monthly food parcels to the poor and has adopted the kindergarten in a poorer part of the neighbourhood.

The most notable happening at that time in 1996, besides the massive debates on how the church should respond to the HIV and AIDS pandemic, was the visit from the then minister of defence to explain to the conference the virtues of the arms deal. Of course, he was asked whether investing so much in arms was wise when we had such huge social backlogs. We were told that although we didn't face any imminent threat we had to protect our oceans from being depleted by foreign fishing vessels.

In 2000 I joined the Congress of South African Trade Unions

(Cosatu). I was appointed as social policy coordinator. It is this federation that taught me to speak up and to fear no one. I was a mouse hammered into subservience by sociopathic teachers. Let me digress to explain something that still scars my psyche 40 years later. We had school assembly every day. The teachers would stand in front on a raised platform and we would be on the ground in lines by class.

I was a short, plump child because my mother breastfed me until my siblings were so embarrassed about it that they told me that if I looked at my mother in that way again I would grow donkey ears. I believed them and that is how from one day to the next I stopped breastfeeding. Being short, plump and terribly myopic, I always wanted to be in the front of the class. Anyway, the short of it is that the teacher, Mrs Z, beat us when we were about seven years old until she drew blood because she had concluded that we had peeked under her dress. We were told why we were beaten only after the fact. Apparently we were declared *peekers* because we were in the front below the dais. Believe me, I was so naïve then that I wouldn't have peeked because then I truly believed that all panties were made of flannel and were green, blue or maroon.

At Cosatu my incredible shyness was banished forever. I remember my boss ZV and Dr NM would encourage me by saying, 'You cannot let 2 million workers down. Remember the 2 million members of Cosatu and the rest of the working class are behind you. You are their only hope.' With that calling I was ready to face all of hell's demons. I remember one day I debated at the Alliance summit on the social proposals of Cosatu, which included the Basic Income Grant. I was alone against many people, so much so that the now ambassador of some country in the East said, 'Comrades, you are being unfair, all of you against her, hear her out!' This is because all my other Cosatu comrades had rushed off to the Economy group. Remember, it was at the height of GEAR and the Anti-privatisation Campaign. The affirmation from my bosses unleashed the tiger in me. This is important and is a request for all bosses to affirm and mentor young bright sparks. Mentoring, affirming and talking about a greater cause enabled this grey mouse to agree to represent organised labour at a global level and speak at a United Nations panel during the World Summit on Sustainable Development against the privatisation of water provision. Were it not for the positive reinforcement I received from my bosses, I strongly believe I would have remained a mouse.

In 2003, my teenage son stole my car and disappeared. I remember I was in Cape Town. I got a frantic call from my husband. We did not know it then but he had been stealing the car so often that he could drive. We imagined him under a truck dying somewhere. I took the next plane home. When I got home, he was already there. I gave him a piece of my mind, after which he said, 'Mama, it's not as if you care. The only things you care about are the 2 million workers and the Basic Income Grant.' As a young parent, I didn't know then how manipulative children are. But be that as it may, I introspected and realised that I enjoyed my job too much to the detriment of my children. I decided to quit.

I conclude my diary entry with the hope that these happenings in my life will inspire other African girls. I enjoy my work at the Presidency. I can immerse myself in it because the children are now older. Yes, I can say the new dispensation has been extremely good to me – to us. Many more people have access to schools, health services, electricity and water. The fruits of democracy are very visible. South Africa has been able to hold eight elections that were considered to be free and fair. The Independent Electoral Commission has become a centre of excellence and, in November 2011, received the first prize from the Centre for Public Service Innovation (CPSI) for its e-Procurement system in the category Innovative Use of Information Communication Technology for Effective Service Delivery.

I have been successful beyond my imaginings. I have crossed many oceans. This African girl who sold lemons to neighbours who had lemon trees in order to eat, has breathed the same air as President Obama, three South African presidents and many other heads of state. I am able to provide my family with three meals a day; I am able to pay university fees for my children and the children of relatives; I am able to provide decent shelter and food for my ancient mother. But what is most important to her is that I am able to take her to church every Sunday. Yes, I am fortunate indeed.

However, we dare not be complacent. Inequality is huge. As everyone agrees, the face of the poor is still largely African. We still have to 'emancipate ourselves from mental slavery'. We are still products of our past.

I'll tell you two amusing anecdotes.

One day I travelled to a neighbouring country, but I hadn't realised that because I travel alot there was no space left in the passport for the immigration officer's stamp. She said, 'I have just turned back a white woman with the same challenge as yours, *bowungubani ke wena.*' I was not going to insist anyway because, as a civil servant, I must not encourage another civil servant to do anything against the law. I turned back.

My sister tells a funnier anecdote. She went into a well-known supermarket. The cooked food and fresh cakes smell and looked inviting but, unfortunately, not only to humans but also to flies. So she alerted the staff and suggested that they cover the food. Their prompt response was, '*Hayibo waze wazenza ngcono, ngisho abelungu imbala bayathenga lapha* and they don't complain. What is your problem?'

However, a not so funny incident happened at my workplace. I was told that if you are an African woman and you don't want your boss to complain about the quality of your work, get a white male colleague to submit it as his own. It works like a charm. Try it!

My liberation, my reality

Kanya Kali
Young lawyer

I WAS BORN IN 1987 IN THE FORMER capital of the Transkei, Umthatha. Some call it Mthatha, but that's a story for another day. I don't really remember much from my early days, although I've heard that I was extremely dark in complexion, quiet and very shy. It honestly boggles me when people say they remember events from when they were three years old. I mean, really?

I went to preschool in Ntseshe in the Eastern Cape, where my home is. One of my most vivid memories from this time is of a friend and I hiding behind *onomaweni* (aloes), trying to bunk school. Pretty bold for five-year-olds, I must say, but I've never really been one to draw inside the lines. In those days aloes grew everywhere, we didn't need to plant them. Our parents used the plants to *cima* us (induce diarrhoea to rid the body of 'toxins'). I also remember going to another pre-primary school, but this time in Comfivaba, another rural area in the Eastern Cape, but this memory is a bit blurry.

Before I continue on my journey from oblivion to my current reality, perhaps I should start at the beginning, where the seed of my existence was planted. A dashing young man by the name of Winard Vumile Kali met an exceedingly gorgeous woman, Nosandla Pheliwe Electra Toyi, in vibey Soweto, while she was there on holiday. These are my parents. My dad was a policeman back then and my mom either a nurse or a teacher. She ventured into both professions in an order I'm failing to recall. My dad fell madly in love with her. At the peak of the new romance, he decided to move back with her to the Eastern Cape. They became entrepreneurs and my mother gave birth to six stunning girls and one handsome boy. It's no secret, however, that they had six girls trying to conceive more boys – fate just didn't allow it.

When we were still very young our parents shipped us off to stay with my mother's sister, 'Mama', in Cofimvaba. Yes, we called our aunt 'Mama' and our mother '*Makazi*', meaning aunt. It happens. My friend also refers to her mother as *Makazi*.

I remember on my mother's 40th birthday we decided we were going to start calling her Mama but, as the Xhosa say, '*isiqhelo siyayoyisa ingqondo*'. We inevitably failed dismally at this attempt but to try to fail is better than to fail to try. Mama was very strict. Everyone knew her for that. She would pinch us hard and spank all the kids who tried to steal peaches from the garden. I remember once my sister banged the door. Mama decided to bang her head against the wall so that she would feel how the door felt when she banged it. Let's just say she was a practical woman. She was a warrior and she was the one that caused my parents to be such great entrepreneurs. She was a hard worker, so whenever she was around, you had to look as though you were doing something. When she came home from work in the evenings, we all had to pick up a broom, cook or get water from the tank, whatever, as long as we were busy. Her influence is most probably one of the drivers of my success to date; her lessons about hard work and practicality have helped me jump many hurdles and taught me how to deal with what was to come on my journey to my current reality.

After our stay in Cofimvaba, which I called 'cough no more' (I have no clue why I called it that, I think I just copied my older siblings), I went to school in Willowvale, a small town in the Eastern Cape, not too far from the beach. It was a missionary school named Valley Dawn Christian School, so you'll understand why we had chapel every morning. It was a good solid Christian foundation. The majority of the teachers were from the United States of America. We loved them and they loved us. I spent all my preparatory years there. We lived in the hostel, which consisted of one big room for all the girls and another for all the boys. It was fun. I have such great memories from those years. Blissful ignorance!

I cannot honestly say that I remember experiencing racism at these young ages. I guess it is because I lived in the Transkei, which was independent from South Africa. I do, however, remember that when we went to East London in South Africa, we would have to stop at the Kei Bridge and have our passports stamped. It was normal for me, but I didn't know the significance of it. I didn't even notice that it was only black people that had to do this. I was young I guess, oblivious.

Finally in 1990, Nelson Mandela was released from prison. In 1994, black people voted and we had a black president. It sounds very victorious and unforgettable but, unfortunately, none of this triumph resonates well enough within my memory to allow me to recall either my emotions or the celebratory events of that 'new freedom'. One reason for this lack of recall was that I was still in Willowvale at the time and we did not discuss politics there. After all, I was just seven years old. This was the turning point of all our lives – our destinies were rightfully returned to us. It was a time for new dreams and new hope for the future. All the doors were suddenly opened, but this had very little impact on a young mind who never knew they were closed to begin with.

In 1996, my parents bought a house in East London, in a suburb called Selborne. My siblings and I moved there and the girls were enrolled at Clarendon High School for Girls and my brother at Selborne College. These schools are well known for excellence – my parents wanted the best for us. I remember going to Grade 4 orientation. When my friends and I look back I looked like a rural kid. My dress was horrible and my hair said that I was rural and, basically, not a cool kid. I am as little bothered by that now as I was then. Making friends in primary school was relatively challenging because I wasn't that popular. I didn't really make white friends but we spoke now and again. I assumed we would have nothing in common. I don't think I really thought about this, nor did I intentionally link it to the lack of common pigmentation. I just didn't and I was okay with it.

High school was confusing for me: trying to keep up with being a cool kid, studying and extramurals for the string of badges that we all wanted. I was not a cool kid but I hung around with them. I studied hard and my name is even on the honours board. Extramurals were my favourite because I received colours for them. This meant that my blazer no longer looked like the other scholars' – it had a special trim. I made more friends in high school and even a white friend. Yes, we joked and laughed with a number of the other white girls, but there is only one that I consider my friend to this day. We have not seen each other for years but when we chat, we understand each other so well.

There was an incident back in high school when there was a party. I think this is when I started to remove my blinkers. One of the

Selborne boys hosted it. He was white. We had just finished putting on a play at the Guild Theatre and we wanted to have a party, so we thought we would join them instead of having our own party somewhere else. By 'we' I am referring to a small group of black boys and girls from the drama team. When we arrived at the white boy's home, his parents closed the gate. They said it was full, or something like that. Right of admission reserved. Well, so to speak. My white friend was inside and I remember thinking, 'Why isn't she saying anything? Why isn't she fighting for us?'

As I grew older I understood the situation she was in. She was a white girl, with white friends and parents around. It would have been too difficult for her to defy them all. At the end of the day, she had to live with them. It would have also been difficult for me if the situation had been turned around. That is what being human means: putting yourself in the position of another sometimes. Anyway, I got over it quickly.

Generally, throughout high school, even though I had realised that we were different and that there were issues, I still mostly thought we were all fine and pretty much equal, except for the odd occasion here and there. I didn't hate white people – my neighbours were white on both sides. I did note that there were more English than Afrikaans speakers in East London though. Nonetheless, life went on. I did well in high school but I just missed the distinction that I wanted.

Just before I went to university, my mother fell horribly ill. In fact she was ill during my whole matric year. It was not easy, but luckily by that time Mama had also bought a house in Selborne and my sisters and dad were always around. By the time it came for me to leave for university, I could see that her health was deteriorating, which made it even harder for me to leave. The day I left, I cried uncontrollably, just hoping that my mother would be alive when I came back. I left for Johannesburg and my sister fetched me. We bought everything I needed and we headed for the University of Johannesburg. I was in Amper Daar Residence. Almost all the residences there had Afrikaans names. I didn't really care about that though. We had orientation, I'm sure for a good month. In the middle of that month, my sister and cousin invited my brother and me for dinner. He was in another residence, Oppirief. That day they broke the news to us that my mom had passed away. I was numb. I don't really want to divulge much about that time in my life. I remember when she was sick and she realised that my dad would have to take care of us alone, she told me to apply for NAFSAS, a government-funded education loan. I did and I got it and it paid for both my degrees.

Initially, I barely thought about my residence life filled with Afrikaans traditions, neither did I think of the freedom that had allowed me to not only attend this university but receive the funds to do so as well. As time went by though, it became a bit harder to ignore. When we were juniors we had to share rooms. Not one single white girl shared a room with a black girl in my year. I didn't really care though. Then I realised that subjects were being taught in English and Afrikaans only. This meant that Afrikaans students were given preferential treatment. English is a universal language, but not Afrikaans, so I did not understand why Afrikaans students then had such options, which we were denied. But I also got over that. It was actually the first time that I had been around so many Afrikaans speakers. They are crazy, those guys – well, some of them – but fun, too, if they liked you. University exposed me to so much.

Back home we thought that foreign blacks were Ghanaians. When I met Congolese, Gabonese, Nigerians, Cameroonese and others, I was taken aback. I even studied French for a while. It was very refreshing for me. I also met some very sweet Afrikaans guys – cool guys that enjoyed hearing my views on life and arguing with me. It used to get heated. Nonetheless we were all there for one reason. Education.

The first time I graduated I remember thinking how I wished my mom was there. Of course Mama being there helped because one always dreams of both parents being present at such moments.

I got my education and started looking for a job. In a country where black females are supposedly sought-after, it sure did take me a long time to get article training, let alone a job – contrary to what many white people might think today. I started looking the year before my final year. I thought maybe having a BCom degree as well as an LLB would get me somewhere – but no. I decided not to waste my newly acquired, considerably substantial and valuable knowledge by doing nothing, so I started volunteering at an NGO and they ended up employing me for two months. It felt like I was wasting time; I guess I was feeling defeated, unchallenged and dissatisfied. I even resorted to looking for call-centre jobs. As a young adult who felt the pressure and hunger for success, it became increasingly difficult to still be dependent on my father, so I tried by all means to ask very little of him. He had seen me graduate twice, yet I didn't seem to be 'bearing any fruit', so to speak. I know he didn't mind, but still it wasn't good, perhaps due to my own pride and, to some extent, shame.

The government jobs were the worst. You do not even know whether they received the application or not – no response whatsoever, even if the job suited you perfectly. I understand they received thousands of applications, but I believe they should capture these and at least have the decency to SMS or email the unsuccessful candidates. If they cannot, they must outsource that department. I'm sure I applied for about 15 positions there, even positions for which I was overqualified but willing to take. Nothing. Nada. Zilch. That's when one wonders, how does one get into a job in the new South Africa – the land of possibilities? I was feeling tied up with empty promises and suffocating with frustration. I started to question my freedom.

After volunteering at the NGO, I started to look for articles training rigorously again. I went for an interview. It didn't work out. I went for another interview. They called me the next Monday and I got the job. I was ecstatic. I called my sisters and my dad. It meant the end of my dad supporting me. I realised during this time that white supremacy still existed and they did not even try to hide it. The firm I worked in is a black-owned firm but we obviously had to interact with other entities. Some of my friends also worked for the big companies and, in some of these, racism was not even subtle. My friends realised that, being black, they would not be invited to certain functions or allocated certain positions. I also know of positions for which I had better qualifications than my white colleagues but they got the job. Race was finally featuring in my life, in my thoughts and in my reasoning.

My whole life I have never had a problem with white people and even when certain incidents happened, I got over them. But I started to question the state of my country, where we had come from and the possibility of a prosperous future for us. I analysed the opinions around me. I finally opened my eyes and ears and embraced the current discussions on everything from black empowerment to economic freedom and this 'white genocide' that some white people felt was happening. When I heard them saying, 'This is racism against white people', I realised that they did not comprehend the extent to which black people were disadvantaged and how that situation still affects them.

I sometime wish that white people could experience racism so that they would see what it means. Is that my rage talking? Trevor Noah, the comedian, used a very good example. He said that apartheid was like cutting the majority of people's legs off for decades and leaving the others to walk. Then you decide to give the majority blades like Oscar Pistorius and expect them to just start running immediately with no training or headstart whatsoever. That is still putting them in a similar situation: disadvantage. One honestly cannot expect these people to get up and run like the ones who started walking and running at a young age.

I may have grown up aware of very little of what apartheid was like but as time went by and through the different seasons in my life, my eyes were slowly opened to where our country had come from and the extent of the damage caused by the 'sickness' of racial differentiation, socially and economically. Right now, liberated and all, I do feel like the government might not be doing what they promised to do. Or not doing enough. Or not doing it fast enough or well enough. Currently, I feel a deep frustration with the freedom we have achieved. I suppose it is difficult to accept that the damage to our society and our respective lives will take much longer than two decades to undo but at times it feels like we will never get there.

The despair of my current situation and that of many of my peers who are in similar situations blurs the vision of a bright and better future for us all. Having said that, I do recognise that we have come a long way and I hope that we will find a way to take even greater strides towards the beautiful dream that our parents and great grandparents fought for. To this I chose to dedicate my life, to assist and to fight any way I can towards realising the dream of our struggle heroes, for us and for this beautiful country.

Freedom: An intergenerational cause

Wandile Kasibe
Scholar

Tales of freedom

'THE NEW DISPENSATION CAME TO symbolise the promise of freedom and multiple beginnings: individually and collectively, 27 April 1994 was an invitation to envision ourselves differently than we had up until that point'.[*]

If I had been born elsewhere, in a different place and context, far away from the teargas canisters and gunshots that claimed the innocent lives of many black people whose only 'crime' was to be born black in the country of their forebears, my life would have turned out differently. But we don't choose the context into which we are born and 'we cannot choose our parents'[†] either. We can only change the circumstances of our present and our place in society, thus creating sane choices in an insane and racially divided world. It is only because of the vigour of the collective cause and intergenerational agency that today I am able to reflect on what democracy means to me.

Our arrival to 1994 was an outcome of many sacrifices made bravely by generations of struggle heroes and heroines that came before us, who faced heavy imperialist munitions with arrows, assegais, stones, pens and ideas. Our democratic narrative will never be complete without reflecting on them. We are who we are because of the sacrifices of those who came before us, and many who are still among us today. It is within this context, that I have entitled this reflection, 'Freedom: An intergenerational cause'.

I wish to connect and reconnect myself through a simple vernacular, to the 'heart' of the continuous struggle for social and historical

---

[*] Gqola, PD. 2010. *What is Slavery to Me? Postcolonial/Slave Memory in Post-Apartheid South Africa.* Johannesburg: Wits University Press, pp. 1–2.

[†] Bradford, PV & Blume, H. 1992. *Ota Benga: The Pygmy in the Zoo.* New York: St Martin's Press, p. xiv.

justice, passed on from one generation to the next, from my parents' generation to my own. This essay could be understood as a personal journey travelled within South Africa's rich polysemous narrative, rather than a political analysis of the political complexities of our current body politic. Indeed, South Africa's 20 years of democracy is only the beginning and most work still lies ahead.

Reflecting on 20 years of democracy from the battlefield of a democratic political victory to me reaffirms the understanding that we are, in our diversity, a part of a bigger picture, whose meaningful puzzles lie in the truthful assembly of the continuum of the past and present to create a collective future.

When I go into the inner resources of my own being, I begin to understand that my being born 468 years after the Khoi–De Almeida confrontation of 1510,* 319 years since the first Khoi–Dutch confrontation of 1659,† 199 years since the frontier wars in the Eastern Cape, 18 years after the Sharpeville massacre, 14 years after Nelson Mandela (aah! Dalibhunga‡) and the Rivonia trialists were banished to life imprisonment on Robben Island, two years after the 'big bang' of 1976 and a year after the terrible death of Steve Bantu Bonke Biko, is all part of what I have become. I understand that I have inherited their cause for justice and that I now assume my role in the tapestry of our country's unfolding history.

At the very heart of my interconnectedness with the struggles of my forebears, I now see a simple truth – our history and transition could not have happened in any other way and it happened the way it did so that the continuum of intergenerational agency against injustice of any form is forever encoded in the DNA of our collective consciousness. And that we are obliged to take an individual and collective pledge never to perpetuate the evil against which our heroes and heroines, both sung and unsung, fought.

Our democracy did not arise out of nowhere, but came into fruition as an outcome of our country's 'Aluta Continuum'. My particular place in this continuity could be understood as follows: I came of age through the burning fires of the 1980s and during the last stand of apartheid in the late 1990s. Just like any other black

---

* The full-blown confrontation that took place between the Khoi and Francisco de Almeida, Viceroy of Portugal in 1510.
† The earliest confrontation that took place between the Khoi and the Dutch in 1659.
‡ Nelson Mandela's royal name, meaning 'he who creates a council'.

child, I was born into a system where my 'blackness' was associated with evil and was an anathema that had to be expunged from the narrative of our country's rich history.

I was delivered into a despised and humiliated race, by parents whose lives and dreams were involuntarily strangulated by a pass book or 'dompas'. The dompas was the everyday intrusion of apartheid into the lives of its African bearers. To talk of 'liberation diaries' is to remember my parents' untold struggles and sacrifices, interwoven through my upbringing in the dusty and rough streets of the place in which I was born, Mdantsane,* the sprawling black township located a few kilometres from East London.

Your story of freedom is mine too

Diaries, memoirs and memories are interwoven to create the critical processes of our collective national identity. However, we don't always like what we remember. That which we are trying to forget always remains with us. I remember that 23 years ago, I lost a father on 28 February 1991, whose untimely departure continues to shape my political philosophy into democracy and beyond.

I remember how in the early years of democracy in 2001, 10 years after my father's death, I found his dompas among documents that were hidden, locked in his drawer. To me this was the most sentimental moment, perhaps the very moment at which I got to understand the deeper psychological complexities of the processes that led to our country's democracy.

Seven years into democracy, I sat there in the dark room of his partially furnished house, that had developed cracks and peeling paint on the walls due to neglect, wondering whether my father had left the documents for me to discover and how they had managed to escape from disappearing into the black hole of history. Here I was holding a symbol of the lack of democracy, which my father never lived to see end and yet his dream of freedom has been passed on to me. I wondered why this book survived and why my father never burnt it as a protest, but I am grateful that I could hold it in my hands and have tangible evidence of our people's dispossession.

Though I may never fully understand the gravity of the relationship my father had with his pass book, two decades into democracy, I feel

---

* Mdantsane is the second-biggest black township in South Africa after Soweto.

that I have inherited his struggle and the continuous struggles of his generation for equality and a better life for all, thus I am part of his story and he of mine. In my veins I carry the blood and imprint of a man whose life was determined by a book. His shattered voice and ambivalence is carefully observed by Bloke Modisane in his compelling autobiography, *Blame Me on History*:

> The pass or the Reference Book is a life of its own, a kind of indestructible monster; its relationship to the African is one of an indecent intimacy, it controls his entire life, strangulates his ambition; it is his physical life. Only the Reference Book can claim a registered letter or cash a Money Order; it is the Reference Book which gets married, the marriage ceremony might very well be conducted as something like this: 'Do you, Reference No. 947067, take Reference Book No. 649707 as your lawfully documented wife?' ... It is the Reference Book which states that the bearer may be employed where, when and how long...[*]

What is interesting here is what seems to be the fact that the pass book was more important than my father's life. It became a replacement for his soul, because without the pass book, my father never existed in the eyes of the apartheid law. In his generation, this book used to speak on behalf of its bearer (my father) and was a tool of corroboration for his existence and without the book, he was 'an illegal' and, technically, non-existent. This was his condition.

I speak, here, of a man to whom I am bound by the continuum of grief, a pain passed on through generations of our ancestors' struggles. A man who now cannot speak for himself. One whose pain has been inculcated in me, so that when I look at the pass book, I see it not merely as a pass or reference book, but as a 'living' 'intergenerational object', which tells the story of my father and that of me and my family, through time past and perhaps present. As much as I decry the censorship experience the book represents, I also embrace the book because of the life and soul it carries, the person it tries to represent – my father.

On the stamped pages of pass books is embedded the historical

---

[*] Modisane, B. 1963. *Blame Me on History*. Johannesburg: AD Donker, p. 307–308.

narrative of the scattering and censorship of my people, tried and tested by intergenerational manmade pain, but who were determined to move on, nevertheless. In their road to democracy, they changed the course of history and stood for a democratic idea whose time had come. These liberation diaries, which celebrate the dawn of democracy, are indebted to their courageous centuries-long struggle against injustice. We are bound to them by our collective grief, as they were bound to the pursuit of freedom.

In 1994, when the nation went to the polls to vote for a new democratic government, I had just turned 16. Years prior to this, I had already seen many heinous crimes being committed against humanity, during and after the State of Emergency in 1985. Like any other black child at the time, in the daytime I could never escape the terrible sound of helicopters that hovered above our rooftops, and I could not escape the terror of night with police raids undertaken to eliminate our uncles and aunts, who had been stigmatised as 'terrorists' and enemies of the state because of their quest for freedom, our freedom. We were confined to the psychological and physical battlefields, subjected to continuous dehumanisation by those who regarded themselves as the leaders of humankind.

It was through those harsh conditions that I learnt about politics and why there is a need for democracy and a right to human dignity. The then government continually reminded me that I harboured a pigmentation of the 'defeated race'. I had, like my peers, developed a loathing for a government that negated my human rights long before I was even born, so that by the time I came into this world, I would be born into a category of chattels meant for exploitation and servitude.

At the age of 10, the only contribution I could bring to the collective struggle against apartheid was to join a crowd of protesters and stand on the streets to face guns with stones. I disregarded the man-made category of servitude to which I was condemned, attending community meetings and rallies organised by the African National Congress's (ANC) branch in Mdantsane NU2. Around the same time, my political persona began to form at candlelight political meetings held at Encotsheni Secondary School hall, Elwandisa Primary School soccer pitch and during street patrols aimed at bringing about socio-political order. It was here that the joint political will of the ANC and Pan Africanist Congress (PAC) instilled in us a greater sense of self-determination and freedom, and captured our collective imagination. Political protests were an open university in which our collective imagination and urgency of the then 'now' was captured.

It was around this time that I also learnt about Umkhonto weSizwe (MK) and Upoqo, the military wings of the two political parties. Later, my older friends went underground to join the military wings, in preparation for the then imminent confrontation between blacks and whites in apartheid South Africa. I was too young to go to the trenches so, instead, I participated in the consumer boycotts and bus boycotts, and joined the Congress of South African Students (COSAS), a period during which I first witnessed people being burnt alive for being accused of collaborating with the apartheid system.* I have lived and surpassed the reign of the then Prime puppet Minister, Chief Kaiser Matanzima, who ruled in the former Bantustan called Transkei and Lennox Sebe in the Ciskei, after who followed the 1992 Bisho massacre instigated under the leadership of Brigadier Oupa Joshua Gqozo.

My hopes of a freer South Africa were shattered when Uncle Chris Hani was assassinated in Boksburg on 10 April 1993, a year before the dawn of democracy and freedom in South Africa. There was thick silence and it felt as if the progress of time had stopped and that our doom was upon us. We were confined between grief and anger and the terrible decision that would determine our future: should we avenge Uncle Chris or swallow our grief for the benefit of future generations? These were the questions that kept us in our numbness. The country was on the brink of a civil war, out of which it was clear that only few would survive. It was through this fragility and the then pending civil war instigated by the right-wing Afrikaner Broederbond† that the true courage of our nation, its commitment to peaceful resolutions and African diplomacy, was tested.

Nelson Mandela stood up in a nationally televised address and called for the nation to find a peaceful resolution to what seemed to be an inevitable tragedy saying, 'Tonight I am reaching out to every single South African, black and white, from the very depths of my being',‡ and he reminded us that there can be no truer courage

---

* This term was used to refer to the apartheid government.
† An Afrikaner movement founded in 1879 by a Dutch Reformed minister from Paarl, SJ du Toit (please see Marq de Villiers. 1987. *White Tribe Dreaming: Apartheid Bitter Roots as Witnessed by Eight Generations of an Afrikaner Family*. New York: Viking, p. 176.
‡ Nelson Mandela, African National Congress, 'Television address to the nation by ANC

than a people who resolve their differences through dialogue and diplomacy.

Memory and the struggle against forgetting

It is through these compelling words and the collective will of the people to become the champions of their destiny that the nation miraculously went through to the elections of 1994.

And who can forget the euphoria that preceded the inauguration of Nelson Mandela as the first democratically elected president, who in his inauguration uttered these words:

> the time for the healing of the wounds has come, the moment to bridge the chasms that divide us has come ... we pledge ourselves to liberate all our people from the continuing bondage of poverty, deprivation, suffering, gender and other discrimination ... We commit ourselves to the construction of a complete, just and lasting peace ... We enter into a covenant that we shall build a society in which all South Africans, both black and white, will be able to walk tall without any fear in their hearts assured of their inalienable right to human dignity...*

And that:

> Never! Never! And never again shall it be that this beautiful land will again experience the oppression of one by another and suffer the indignity of being the skunk of the world...'†

With the gravity of these words our fledgling democracy began, and bravely endured through the schisms of our political transition into the second decade of our democracy. As if he had personally received an epiphany, Mandela held our country's fragile balances, advocating peace, nation-building and reconciliation, aah! Dalibhunga.

The 1994 transition and the new political order was, to me,

President Nelson Mandela on the Assassination of Chris Hani'. Available at: www.anc.org.za/show.php?id=4304 (accessed 5 March 2014).
* Nelson Mandela. Statement of Nelson Mandela at his Inauguration as President. Available at: www.anc.org.za/show.php?id=3132 (accessed 1 October 2013).
† Ibid.

a rebirth of freedom, and a triumphant victory over all that had been fought for since the arrival of Western colonising forces on the African continent, particularly in the southern plains. It was an answer to soothe the cries and bring solace to the countless generations of desolate souls destroyed by the men of the West. And it also represented a moment at which we had to reflect on our agonies, so as to mobilise ourselves not to repeat them in the future; as George Santayana observes, 'those who cannot remember the past are condemned to repeat it.'* And part of this reflection and healing of wounds in our new democracy was the establishment of the Truth and Reconciliation Commission (TRC), chaired by His Grace Archbishop Desmond Mpilo Tutu after the dawn of democracy.

I was there at the hearings of the TRC, held at East London City Hall. I saw Archbishop Tutu break down when the silenced stories from our bygone years were finally spoken, entering the bloodstream of our country's body politic. When he drowned in tears, we cried with him too, shocked and heavily burdened by the terrible crimes committed on our people. I interviewed Mrs Mohapi, because I was doing academic research on the TRC at the time. Her husband's story and many other victims' have lingered on into the heart of our democracy. As Don Mattera wrote, we had 'held back our tears [and] suspended our pain… [because] the darkness was [very] deep'.†

In the Eastern Cape it was Raymond Mhlaba (Oom Ray), the first premier of the province under Mandela's administration, who led us into a sustainable transition and through the most difficult times. Sadly, I don't hear much about Oom Ray; his name, however, has not been forgotten. Yet it is the struggle heroes such as Oom Ray, Nelson Mandela, Walter Sisulu, Oliver Tambo, Govan Mbeki (Oom Gov), Mama Winnie Mandela, Bram Fischer, Father Beyers Naudé, Helen Joseph, Joe Slovo, Ruth First, Ahmed Kathrada and … the list is endless. These are people who we must learn from as future leaders.

The values they held created this democracy, but to realise it will require a continuity of cause and shared wisdom. The post-1994 scenario has brought about a number of future prospects and challenges for the nation, particularly for young people. It is often

---

* Santayana, G. 1905. *Life of Reason: Reason in Common Sense*. New York: Scribner's, p. 284.
† Mattera, D. 1986. Steve Biko in *Exiles Within: An Anthology of Poetry*. Writers' Forum, p. 37.

said that young people are the future of every nation and society. One wonders, however, what happens when that future is being dismembered from the agency and struggle for social justice of its forebears. In the African context, stories and former deeds have been passed on from one generation to another through oral history and intergenerational conversations. It is this form of empowerment that has helped preserve our culture, heritage and narrative, thus adding value to our cultural heritage and sense of place.

When stories stop being told, the gap between the older and younger generations widens – our wisdom is lost. When we lose that connection between the young and the old, the streams of history are dammed and cannot flow strongly into the future. As the Yoruba proverb says: 'When an elder dies, it is as if an entire library has burnt down'.*

There is always sadness and a sense of anxiety when one contemplates what really happens when elders leave no stories or sense of guidance to the younger generation.

In South Africa this feeling of a communication breakdown between the older generation and younger generation has, since 1994, been the most important underlying factor – among many others – for young people's apathy and lack of confidence in their own contribution to society.

Be that as it may, it is, however, undoubtedly true, that South Africa is much better off than it was before 1994. Its competitive economy and socio-cultural and political influence on the African continent and in global politics are some indicators, among many, that could be taken into consideration. Our reconciliatory approach to conflicts still remains a beacon of hope to many post-conflict societies that seek peaceful resolutions to complex confrontations that pose a threat to the sanctity of life. Its pivotal role in championing African diplomacy, through its contributions in the Organisation of African Unity (OAU), now the African Union (AU), and the United Nations (UN) is undisputed.

These milestones and others similar to these, cannot, however, be seen as suggesting that South Africa has no challenges to overcome and that the 'post-apartheid' project has now reached its zenith. As

---

* The Metropolitan Museum of Art, Heroic Africans: Legendary leaders, Iconic Sculptures Available at: www.metmuseum.org/en/exhibitions/listings/2011/heroic-africans-legend-ary-leaders-iconic-sculptures/pageantry-and-ritual-the-akan (accessed 30 October 2013).

a matter of fact, the country finds itself at a difficult crossroads, confronted by simple but difficult questions: what does democracy mean to its citizens? What does it mean to the majority of people whose lives are still languishing on the margins of society, as the poorest of the poor?

What does it mean to the children who find themselves born into a continuous cycle of abject poverty and deprivation? What does it mean to that young person whose dream was shattered, because he or she had no money to pay school fees in order to lay a strong foundation for his or her future? What does it mean to the families of the mineworkers who were shot and killed at Marikana for simply standing up for their constitutional rights? What does democracy mean to Andries Tatane's family – also a victim of police brutality at a service delivery protest – and many who bear the deep physical and psychological scars from their advocacy for social justice? What does it really mean to those who have been censored from expressing their deepest concerns about the unfolding of the current political dispensation? Who will take the current political vanguards to task, if dissenting voices are shattered, we might also ask.

What about the ugly face of xenophobic hate crimes targeted at foreign nationals of African descent? As Kofi Annan said, 'national sovereignty [cannot be used] as a shield behind which we brutalise our own'.* It is these realities and others similar to these that should confront our consciousness to ask the basic question about the state of our nationhood in a democratic dispensation. And, further to this, we also need to ask the question: what can we do to salvage the situation?

Looking ahead

Our nation faces these new and evolving challenges, which push us, yet again, to new limits, thus testing our pursuit of the creation of a freer and more just society for all. It is in finding practical solutions together to these hard-hitting problems, that we can ensure citizens the inalienable rights to security and human liberties, as enshrined in our Constitution and Bill of Rights. It is this process of creating a society and a sustainable system where 'everything falls back

---

* Kofi Annan at One Young World 2012. Speech followed by Q&A. Available at: www.youtube.com/watch?v=f67KY6-KI0Q (accessed 2 October 2013).

unfailingly into truth',* that we can regain our noble cause, and be a nation that takes good care of its own citizens and those of the globalising world.

We must ask the most difficult and uncomfortable questions about our collective morality and point out what appears to be moral decay and prevent the planting of corrupting seeds, which lead to a culture of impunity, tribalism, sexism, racism, xenophobia and other ills that are eating away the fibre of our society, thus plunging the nation into an impasse.

As a nation of great people, nothing can deter us from realising the dream of our forebears. As Biko said:

> we have set out on a quest for true humanity, and somewhere on the distant horizon we can see the glittering prize ... [and that] in time we shall be in a position to bestow upon South Africa the greatest gift possible – a much more human face.†

As we gaze upon the vistas from the mountain-tops, 20 years on and beyond, we need to remember the words of Ben Okri:

> No one can dwell on a mountain-top long; the air there is too pure and unreal. The value of mountain-tops is not to live on them but to see from them. To see into the magic and difficult distances, to see something of the great journey still ahead; to see, in short, the seven mountains that are hidden when we climb. It may be only once that a people have such a vision.
>
> Maybe very, very great nations have such a vision a few times, and each time they do they affect a profound renewal in their history and take a quantum leap in their development. Most nations never glimpse the mountain-top at all; never sense the vastness and the greatness of the gritty glory that lies ahead of them in the seven mountains each concealed behind the other.'‡

---

* Baudrillard, J. (1997). *Fragments: Cool Memories III, 1990–1995* translated by Emily Agar. London & New York: Verso, p. 7.

† Biko, S. 2002. *I Write What I Like: Selected Writings*. Chicago, IL: University of Chicago Press.

‡ Okri, B. 13th Annual Steve Biko Memorial lecture held at the University of Cape Town on 12 September 2013. Available at: www.iol.co.za/capetimes/full-speech-ben-okri-honours-biko-1.1382746#.Ul6_hFODTUM (accessed 13 September 2013).

Twenty years of democracy is only the beginning of the work that still lies ahead. It is a moment for the nation to renew its strength in making democracy a realisable dream for all who live in it. The truer realisation of democracy is when people regain their dignity by having direct access to the ownership of land, mineral resources and the means of production. It is when our aspirations to a better life are rekindled through the creation of better opportunities that ensures self-sustainability.

For us to achieve this noble cause, we (people, government and business) need to double our efforts to find ways in which the continuous project of democracy can be translated to basic human needs: food, shelter, sanitation, good health and education for all. For there is no society that can survive without these essentials. It is only when people have food on the table, when children are no longer taught in mud schools and share classrooms with animals and sleep in the gutters of the slums, or grow up amid the swelling smells of the townships' open drains and poor sanitation, that democracy can have a truer meaning for all of our people.

My democratic South Africa, my country, my freedom

Bheki Khumalo

Communications executive

STOKED AT HEARING ON THE RADIO about Zahara's latest album, I had to savour and build on that moment. So I slotted in a visit to the nearest music store to purchase *Phendula*. Fascinating was the fact that this, but her second offering, reached platinum within hours. I played this album ad nauseam, especially one song about our sadly ailing and ageing titan of struggle, Nelson Mandela. True to my confessed penchant for occasional excess, bordering on obsession, I played it non-stop for nearly four days. In a bittersweet and nostalgic odyssey, I drove through the vast, ever-expanding informal settlements in what is now ironically named Winnie Mandela.

That is next to my place in Tembisa. I lived there once. I know those ever-mushrooming shacks, testimony to our housing challenge and the need to cope with all sorts of migrants seeking refuge in our country. The place is sandwiched in the modern metropolis of Midrand, festooned, as it is, with ever-expanding gated communities. In stark contrast, the original township of Tembisa is still characterised mainly by the overcrowded four-roomed houses – those little boxes, or Unos. These Unos (derogatory term for the smaller post-apartheid RDP houses) are companions to the informal settlements that seem to spring up just about anywhere.

These new sprawls have scant regard even for democratic municipal bylaws or planning. Water and electricity are filched via illegal feeder connections, some home bonds, not far from Winnie Mandela, remain unpaid, as communities ask themselves the reasonable question, why have they missed out on economic advance since democracy? And why are so many RDP houses badly constructed? That is urgent and unfinished business of the second phase of the democratic dispensation, now opening before us all.

Driving through these areas, my mind rolled back to 2005 when I

102

went for an interview at Siemens for my second stint at the company. I had left earlier to join national government as spokesperson to my former Fort Hare rector and then Minister of Education, Professor Sibusiso Bengu, and later his successor Professor Kader Asmal and finally President Thabo Mbeki.

The then CEO of Siemens, Dr Klaas Doring, a German expatriate and strong supporter of democratic South Africa, took me outside his offices and pointed out the striking scene with his pen literally shaking, his eyes glowing and full of optimism. We surveyed the original Midrand area that had grown so exponentially and quickly, standing as it does pinioned between Johannesburg and Pretoria.

Doring observed that never since his arrival in South Africa a decade previously had he seen this scale of development, with its majestic office parks and other structures such as housing and commercial development. The noisy, multi-lane highway bisecting Midrand gave passing cars a grandstand view of progress since 1994.

Driving past Busy Corner (a shisinyama just outside Tembisa) daily, invaded by throngs of youths and the middle classes escaping from the now desolate suburbs, I immediately remembered that when I joined Umkhonto weSizwe in 1986, our dead-letter-box (the place where we hid our arms caches) was concealed in the then vacant land that now constitutes Ivory Park.

My commander, Thabiso Radebe, had told us that when the ANC took over this place would be transformed into the non-racial modern city envisaged in the Freedom Charter.

Such defining moments occupied my mind as I listened to Zahara's unbelievable rendition. In it, people's poet Mzwakhe Mbuli (let's leave aside criticism of Mbuli, inter alia, for his poetry, since it served us so well in United Democratic Front days), constantly reminds us not to betray the promise of Madiba's 1994 victory, and to continue to build a successful non-racial South Africa.

In this, there are echoes of the wisdom behind adulation accorded by bards and sages to other nation-builders in history. One's mind wanders from Bolívar to Atatürk, from Giap to Lenin, from Gandhi to Nehru, from Lincoln to King – and so powerfully from King, at last, to a kinsman once but dreamt of, black President Barack Obama.

The mind wanders on to our own continent – and our special African heroes and martyrs, like Kwame Nkrumah, Patrice

Lumumba, and Jomo Kenyatta. Then we think of the South African greats, the Luthulis and Tambos, and suchlike, who inspire us today. And standing tall, above so many of the illustrious global figures, is our beloved Madiba.

This Mbuli exhortation was not new. Another artist, Mbongeni Ngema, famous for the world-acclaimed *Sarafina!* had warned us in *Township Fever*, written in the turbulent 80s, about the need for maximum unity in defending liberation.

He does this through a character writing to his young wife Tonko, whom he married just before the strike that landed him in prison and on death row. He called on the comrades in the townships not to betray the struggle after liberation. This reminder is particularly apt today.

These moments amid music took me back to three decades earlier. I recall 20 October 1979 vividly. I was at primary school in Tembisa where I gambolled with friends waiting patiently for the World Boxing Association's heavyweight title fight between a white Afrikaner, Gerrie Coetzee, and an African American, John Tate.

The government wanted the fight so badly that they relaxed apartheid laws and allowed blacks into Loftus Versfeld: a bastion and temple of Afrikanerdom. Blacks had come to the stadium before, not as spectators, of course, but as 'natives' restricted to cleaning the stands and tending the grass. This time there was a sprinkling of blacks, a tiny part of the 81 000 mainly white spectators in an event that had attracted the biggest crowd for a boxing event in more than 50 years.

After the initial expectations were aroused, the SABC baulked and decided not to show the fight live, only doing so a few days later. That 'sprinkling' at the fight clearly packed its own punch, maybe a slim symbol of majority rule to come. For me that fight, more than anything else pre-1994, reflected graphically the scale of racial animosity and distance that marked life under apartheid. Let all, including the once-privileged, be warned never to hanker back to those horrific days.

Jon Qwelane once described in an article how blacks had blindly supported John Tate and urged him to '*moer* the *baas*', and how the Afrikaners who made up the majority of the people who watched the fight encouraged Coetzee to '*donner* the "kaffir"'. To crown it all, Tate, an African American, was a 'kaffir' purely on the basis of the colour of his skin, yet through-and-through a Yank.

Tate was, after all, a hero of all black South Africa since he defeated symbols of white supremacy Kallie Knoetze and Coetzee (though Tate lost the title five months later and Coetzee finally won it in 1983!).

In fact, Madiba's act of showing common cause with, and defending, the Springbok emblem, wearing Francois Pienaar's number 6 shirt when we won the Rugby World Cup on home ground, demonstrated the power of sport in uniting our people across the colour line – as US scholar WEB Du Bois had foreshadowed at the turn of the previous century.

It was under Madiba and Tambo's leadership that the ANC correctly read the balance of forces typified by its decision, criticised as a sell out by other black liberation movements, to jettison the more appealing option of continued armed struggle in favour of a negotiated and peaceful transition to democracy. This saved our country from the abyss.

It averted the tragedies of the kind that had prompted Roméo Dallaire, the Canadian senator, humanitarian, author and retired general who led the UN mission after the Rwandan genocide, to retort, paraphrased, that he now believes God does exist because in Rwanda he shook hands with the devil. The exemplar Mandela shook hands with all South Africans on that pivotal rugby occasion.

The first thing I was exposed to in the period after 1994 was local government. Contrary to RW Johnson's assertion that post 1994 ANC leadership would keep missing meetings through such trivial excuses as forgetfulness, we nevertheless ran efficient and effective local government. We were pioneers of the post 1994 experiment, working at the grassroots where delivery was paramount and experience elusive.

Let us not forget that the 'punctual' ones lived in times of engineered terror for blacks. It is an affront to good sense and intelligence to seek to draw conclusions that imply an equivalence.

Yet, if we are to summon a bit of hindsight, we were sometimes outwitted by those with long experience in governance, albeit one-sided. Paradoxically we were to learn even from the National Party (NP) something about governing a city, combining Tembisa and Kempton Park, now non-racially.

Lessons of the time compelled us, despite our despicable past, to begin to find – and to learn – from one another. That is the subliminal message of the past 20 years. We moved towards becoming 'united in our diversity', as the Preamble to the Constitution puts it.

As local leaders of the ANC we resisted, even though we could have and were expected to have, the temptation to appoint the comrades into administrative positions without the requisite qualifications and/or experience.

What we wisely did then was to identify comrades with appropriate qualifications and promise. We were not shy of making some of them deputies of the white administrators we found in the Tembisa-Kempton Municipality. We actually reflected the demographics of our country in the new entity called the Kyalami Metropolitan Council. Most of these comrades have developed into the finest administrators running Ekurhuleni Metropolitan Municipality.

Even as we engaged in the most serious tasks of our lives, as I remember, the then leader of the National Party caucus, the late Haan Eybers, wearing a cartoon tie, made an unforgettable comment. We were passing the first ANC budget in 1996. It was correctly designed to effect transformation in the allocation of funds. He told council we were passing a Mickey Mouse budget similar to the Popeye in his tie. The cap indeed fitted the Nationalists' own era of minority power.

We need to encourage our kids, black and white, to aspire, as they should, to gain technical and academic qualifications knowing they stand a chance in a government entity or anywhere else. We need to encourage them to stand on their own two feet, as Steve Biko would remind us were he alive today.

We need to exercise power with caution and restraint – and a sense of responsibility. Such admirable qualities seem to elude a few dominant cliques eager for power at all costs. The good governance approach can help to improve service delivery and stem the tide of protests in many traditional strongholds of my life-long organisation, the ANC.

In 2001, shortly after the opening of the school term and after being on television and radio quite a bit as spokesperson for Professor Asmal, I applied for a job as chief director and spokesperson to the then deputy president, Jacob Zuma. He was a fellow 'homeboy', from Nkandla in KZN, where I had lived for four years. I was unsuccessful. However, the panel recommended me – no doubt supported by Tony Heard, then special adviser to Essop Pahad – for consideration for the job of spokesperson to the president, at the junior rank of director.

I remember walking into Professor Asmal's office, chuffed to tell him about that, for me, auspicious development. A man short in stature but strong on convictions, he rose to his barely five feet. at his desk, and laughed in disbelief. In his half-Irish way, he uttered words to this effect: 'Who do you think you are to think you can work for President Mbeki, a man with scant regard for other people, a cold person who will never take you seriously and who will sideline you.'

This was somewhat deflating.

Asmal seemed to forget that he saw me for the first time at the provincial conference of the ANC where I was at ease in engaging in complex theoretical debates to an extent that he asked my name and gave me his business card, having asked if I could work for him as his spokesperson. This explains the act of fate where he found me in education, a portfolio which I held until I became spokesperson to the president.

I told him that I was nevertheless determined to take up the job offer with the president. I remembered ruefully that when President Mbeki, then ANC director of international relations, came to Fort Hare (I was SRC vice president) I had told him that the leadership of our movement, the ANC, was living in Cloud Cuckoo Land if it thought that the NP would voluntarily give up power. Yet, it did, sharing in the Government of National Unity at first, until FW de Klerk's precipitate withdrawal.

When two weeks passed without my even having met the president, I started regretting having joined the Presidency. Asmal's words came back to haunt me. On the face of it, the Asmal judgement seemed correct. At least, until Zamikhaya Maseti, then director in Mbeki's office, introduced me to the president. What Mbeki said, in the studied cordiality that was his hallmark – and while wearing a somewhat strange yellowish suit – disarmed me totally and ended my incipient feelings of prejudice.

He said with a typical lack of emotion, 'This is the man I usually see on television and hear on the radio… and I have appointed you spokesperson so you can go back to your job.'

That was the end of the meeting, and I tore into my work with a mix of realism, energy and idealism. Often it meant flying by the seat of my pants.

I was given a remarkably free hand in my role of spokesperson. That was liberation. It bred a sense of responsibility. It accorded the necessary seniority and scope in a not easy job – spokesperson to an intellectual, a much-misunderstood man, but one of African destiny, Thabo Mbeki.

The issue of government handling media at that time is now the subject of many books. I will do one myself in the fullness of time and give an account of the professionalisation of government communications and how we handled two most arguably difficult issues of the Mbeki years, excruciating HIV and AIDS and almost intractable Zimbabwe, both of which attracted lightning plus thunderbolts.

Since 1994, I have followed with great interest the twists and turns in the trajectory of government's service delivery track record in all areas of our society. Our struggle against apartheid was designed to forge human dignity for the majority and to create a democratic society based on equity, non-racialism and non-sexism. Indeed, it was a struggle against social exclusion, violence and the systemic violation of human and civil rights. It was freedom in action.

Space limitations do not permit a comprehensive assessment of the successes and shortcomings of government's track record in addressing all the social ills we faced during the first two decades of democratic rule.

It is incumbent on all South Africans to offer insights into the vast question, where should our economy be going? Here are some of my thoughts. We have always believed that the key to addressing what Minister Susan Shabangu calls the evil triplets of unemployment, poverty and inequality afflicting our society lies in improving the performance of our economy.

To craft an appropriate economic model to help cure the malaise afflicting our society, the ANC traversed the globe in search of a 'best practice' development model. We examined a number of development models underpinning successful economies, including the ones that were followed by the Asian tigers (South Korea, Malaysia, Thailand and Indonesia) and the 'Celtic tiger' (Ireland), which at one stage was a star performer averaging an annual gross domestic product growth of 9.3% for the period 1994 to 2000.

Building on the experiences of other countries and using the fundamental principles embodied in the post-1994 first national plan (the Reconstruction and Development Programme), we all sought to reconstruct and develop the post-apartheid society. We engaged in subsequent policy initiatives and programmes designed to stabilise the macro-economic environment and to spur economic prosperity. Such efforts included the Growth, Employment and Redistribution Strategy (GEAR), the Accelerated and Shared Growth Initiative of South Africa (ASGISA) and, later on, the New Growth Path (NGP).

At the core of all these initiatives is the realisation that sustained, inclusive and job-creating economic growth is essential to reduce poverty, stimulate employment and improve the living and material conditions of all South Africans.

While the country has made remarkable progress in these critical areas since 1994, there is evidence that a great deal of work still needs to be done to create the non-racial, non-sexist, prosperous society envisaged in the Freedom Charter and the Constitution of South Africa.

Needless to say, there has been a significant and rapid advance of blacks into the middle and upper strata of our society. But there is consensus that the 'social dividend' of our two decades of democratic rule has not been shared equally.

The day-to-day experiences and tangible opportunities for South Africans still differ markedly, with massive inequalities between the poor, who are still mostly black, and the rich, who are still mostly white, best described in President Mbeki's unfairly criticised and apt two nations thesis. Blacks are still excluded from the economic mainstream and this exclusion finds stark expression in the high rates of unemployment, despite the approximately 6 million net new jobs created since 1994.

Over the past decade, the labour market absorption rate has fallen to uniquely low levels compared to international norms. This is not pointing in the right direction as the labour market participation rate for black people is 15 to 20 points below average. As the diagnostic report of the National Planning Commission pointed out, 50% of young people are unemployed.

We urgently need to rescue our troubled economy to increase the labour market participation rate for black people. According to the International Monetary Fund, the country's real gross domestic product growth has since 2009 averaged 3% compared with 5% and 3.7% for emerging markets and commodity-exporting countries respectively.

The required rates of growth for our economy cannot be achieved by government initiatives alone. Government, in partnership with business and labour, needs to work towards fixing the constraints and investment hurdles in order to facilitate rapid economic growth and, ultimately, job creation.

There is need to foster a social compact so that South Africa can achieve growth rates in excess of the 5% of gross domestic product desired to make a serious dent on unemployment. Our social dialogue institution, the National Economic Development and Labour Council (NEDLAC), needs to be properly capacitated and strengthened to play a leading role in this regard.

We need to rekindle the courage of the kind that was shown by the Mandela government to turn the economy around. Shortly after 1994, Madiba visited various world capitals, and he was received as a cult-like-figure.

At the time, on the home front during the early years of Mandela's presidency, the economy was in a crisis, with even public sector debt ballooning out of control; GDP growth lagging; inflation, critical for bringing down interest rates, was in the 10s and even 20s; and more importantly, the country's national foreign reserves were in the negative.

We had a net open forex position that exceeded US$25 billion. In those heydays of forex volatility, we were adding to our national liability up to US$1.0 billion per day. We were going broke, fast.

We had arguably inherited a slag heap in the early 1990s, and it took time to turn this around. By 2001, the government public debt was among the lowest when compared with its peers. As these obstacles were being systematically removed government's credibility grew over time. SA's credit ratings improved, economic growth picked up and by 2004 our GDP had grown by 5.5%.

My time with Mbeki saw this turnaround steadily and impressively executed. We need the courage of our convictions to return to those gilt-edged if not golden years of prudent fiscal management by the ANC, an organisation that was not initially trusted by the markets. Remember how the markets reacted to the appointment of Trevor Manuel as the country's first black finance minister because of the ANC's previous left-leaning policy positions.

Our economy needs to be globally competitive for us to achieve the required rates of gross domestic product growth. In particular, we have to address the cost of capital (debt or equity) that remains higher than that of our major competitors; to continue to fix our education system, which is the foundation for creating human capital; and to streamline the mining regulatory system, one that that costs the economy billions of rands due to delays once mining rights are issued.

The need to introduce a one-stop shop licensing process cannot be overemphasised.

We need to take bold measures, as we did between 2004 and 2007, by comprehensively tackling the budget deficit that has a negative effect on the extension of the comprehensive social security system, which now reaches more than 15 million people. We would do well to ask 'what happens to a dream deferred?', to borrow Mbeki's favourite reference to Langston Hughes's poem 'Harlem'.

In this vein, Hughes alludes to the plight of black African Americans whose dreams of emancipation had sagged, rotted and festered into troubled inner cities like Harlem.

Mbeki was referring, in our context, in Mark Gevisser's words, to 'the crisis of expectation of black South Africans awaiting liberation and who now found themselves often with less even than they had before, and thus on the brink of dangerous explosion.'

To respond to this threat we need, among other things, to ensure that we do not lose the portfolio investment inflows on which we depend to pay for an excess of imports over exports to stop the further slide of our currency and to prevent rising inflation. Done correctly these steps may result in shielding us from further downgrades by rating agencies so that we can continue to attract further investments in our economy.

As Frans Cronje, CEO of the SA Institute of Race Relations pointed out recently, we need to end the unnecessary bitter ideological fight between what he calls modern versions of the *verligtes* and the *verkramptes*. We would do well to remember the adage 'when two elephants fight it is the grass that suffers.'

Iraj Abedian, a progressive economist, put it equally well when he told the 2013 Mining Lekgotla that the mining industry stakeholders are shooting themselves in the proverbial foot. This was because of the South African tendency to argue among ourselves and start a conversation from needlessly extreme vantages, which invariably results in huge reputational damage by the time the solution is found.

This syndrome was reflected graphically by the debate regarding proposed changes to the MPRDA.

The sector and the country want clear, decisive and agreed upon ideas on policy and implementation. All stakeholders must assist to this end, and not take positions where everyone goes down like rats in a bag. That threatens our hard-won new democracy at its very base.

As Professor Asmal used to say, democracy, once gained, has to be deepened. It arrives as a babe, not an adult. It has to grow, and be free to grow. My organisation, the ANC, has on balance, done well in deepening our democracy, despite the shocks that, from time to time, we might suffer, particularly in such a conflictual party-political environment, and in a country where fierce differences of opinion are endemic.

Change is the one thing that is endemic. This is a reality that ancient philosopher Heraclitus of Ephesus knew was and always will be with us. 'Nothing endures but change' he observed as long as 2 600 years ago. He illustrated this with his famous remark: 'You could not step twice into the same river; for other waters are ever flowing on to you.' Heraclitus knew that life, and politics, indeed all those things we think to be permanent, move on.

So, we have made a good start, with glitches. Let us improve on that record as new decades dawn. Let us, inspired by Madiba, work in collaboration – all races, all faiths, all South Africans, together. We have it within ourselves to achieve success, given the NDP's clear 2030 vision, and given the inspiration drawn from our own history of triumphant struggle.

To be young and hopeful in a democratic society

Sakhiwe Kokela
Intern and post-graduate student

I COULDN'T HAVE SEEN THIS COMING, one couldn't have, and the government didn't either. We never expected this tragedy of illicit drug use after South Africa became a democracy in 1994. Unfortunately, although the ANC-led government sought to upgrade society, since 1994 there has been an issue of excessive illicit drug use among the youth. This is a serious concern for parents, guardians and the government. So what went wrong?

Some in society believe that the rise in illicit drug use among the youth is a consequence of democracy. But why should democracy be the central cause of illicit drug use? Some parents and guardians base their argument on the fact that illicit drug use was not as much of a problem pre-1994 as it is in the current situation with the youth having grown up in a democracy.

It is vital to highlight people's criticisms of democracy and for their perspectives to be heard, as we are about to celebrate 20 years of freedom. It is also important to clear up misunderstandings that make people sceptical about democracy. In this essay, I underline some of the causes of drug use, outcomes and the recently introduced risky drug, woonga. This is aimed at supporting youth and making them aware before they trash their lives and pollute the environment through illicit drug use. Finally, I discuss my own experiences in fighting illicit drug use.

The highlights of democratic admittance
After the 1994 general elections, South Africa became a democracy. Undeniably, South Africans were ecstatic about this after the discriminatory apartheid system. Humanitarian leaders and self-developed youth steadily battled to create a peaceful environment marked by democracy and the principles of freedom and equality.

Democracy set high expectations for the government to realise equality and alleviate poverty. People expected the government to free society from oppression and allow free speech, to implement fair laws to protect citizens, to enhance the living standards of the disadvantaged, and to create a peaceful environment in which people could interact freely and effectively to strive for development. This implies that government should interact, communicate with and consult with society for the effective implementation of democracy and development.

Unfortunately, the current unexpected tragedy of illicit drug use is gradually disrupting interaction between society and government. Illicit drug use does not correlate with what society and government expected after the attainment of democracy.

Criticism of democracy within the society

This criticism of democracy emanates mostly from the older generation – parents, guardians and caregivers. This group generally considers itself to be the 'moral generation' and they make comparisons between the South African lifestyle before 1994 and after 1994. Their comparisons are as follows.

Prior to 1994 there was no alarming issue of illicit drug use; back then individuals were thoughtful. Prior to 1994, youth grew up respecting their elders and fellow human beings. They took note of what their parents said and received proper guidance concerning life – parents knew that young people are not capable of guiding themselves. Parents had to develop young people's maturity for later life. This implies that the moral generation self-developed – that they were capable of building the future society through the upcoming generation. They were assertive men and women, strong enough to secure peace in society. Lending their ears to their elders was the supreme strategy that monitored their behaviour and made them conscious of themselves so they could conquer unwanted tendencies that tempted them to destroy their wellbeing, so they lived long. They were hard and smart workers as they sought to take care of elderly parents and the younger generation. Illicit drug use was never an issue during the moral generation's youthful phase.

In contrast, the generation freed by democracy continuously eradicates their consciousness of self. Democracy has given the current youth the wrong impression of what real freedom is and the use of illicit drugs is the result of the 'excessive freedom' claimed by the current youth. Freedom has caused unending conflicts between and isolation of parents and their children. Therefore the current youth are labelled the 'immoral generation' or the born-frees. The born-frees independently get guidance from random individuals and then they discover themselves in situations that disrupt their existence. Illicit drug use reduces the lifespan of the born-frees. This has caused violence and dull relationships within families.

Various South African artists have expressed criticism of democracy and youth behaviour through their songs. Among them are traditional artists such as Phuzekhemisi Mnyandu from the Zulu tribe and Nothembi Mkhwebane from the Ndebele tribe. They express the view that freedom altered the youth's attitudes from positive to negative. These artists ultimately advise born-frees, via their songs, to consider a proper lifestyle.

Criticism of democracy is driven by the outcomes of unnecessary illicit drug consumption in South Africa. Various scholars who focus on the current youth lifestyle substantiate the perspective of democratic criticism. For example, Peltzer et al asserts, 'Globalization has facilitated the introduction of potent addictive drugs such as heroin, cocaine and ecstasy in South Africa'.[*] In this case, freedom permitted individuals to globally interact. Legget notes that 'prior to 1994, many of the street drugs such as cocaine and heroin were not readily available in society'[†]. The title of a paper by Athi Nxusani, 'Born-free! But Dying Young: Post-Mortem of Youth and Democracy in South Africa'[‡] is telling.

Jones highlights the following about illicit drug use in South Africa: 'lifetime estimates for cannabis use among school-going youth are 13%, followed by 12% for inhalant use, 12% for over-the-counter or prescription drugs, 7% each for mandrax (methaqualone), cocaine and club drugs, and 6% for heroine.'[§] In 2011 Lucy Holborn

---

[*] Peltzer, K. Ramlagan, S. Johnson, BD & Mafuya PN. 2010. 'The Use of Illicit Drug and treatment in South Africa: A review'. Available at: www.ncbi.nlm.nih.gov/pmc/articles/PMC3010753/ (accessed 5 March 2014).

[†] See Legget, T. On Drugs, Sex Work, and HIV in Three South African Cities. Available at: www.sahealthinfo.org/admodule/drugs.htm (accessed 28 February 2014).

[‡] Nxusani, A. 2013. 'Born-free! But Dying Young: Post-mortem of Youth and Democracy in South Africa'. Academia.

[§] Jones, PC. 2013. Claimed that 1 in 3 South Africans are Drug Users Based on a Flawed Survey. Available at: www.africacheck.org/reports/flawed-survey-claims-a-third-of-south-africans-are-drug-users// (accessed 28 February 2014).

stated, 'Drugs and alcohol seem to be easily accessible to many young people. Nearly a third of 12- to 14-year-olds said they had easy access to marijuana and 8% had easy access to crack cocaine'*. These statistics represent an increase in consumption of illicit drugs by the youth. Recently South African communities have experienced shocking outcomes brought about by the recent drug, woonga.

Woonga generates dreadful outcomes within society

The outcomes of illicit drug use are known by most people within society. Individuals who engage in illicit drug use experience poor self-esteem, depression, anxiety and a lack of motivation, among other things. The outcomes for woonga are similar to any drug but much worse. This recent drug is used mostly by young people, in cities, townships, villages and in rural areas. Woonga is a mixture of heroine, detergent, rat poison and antiretroviral drugs (ARVs). It is also sometimes called nyaope. Young people who consume this drug ultimately regard the streets, malls and parks as their comfort zones. This is generally the result of disputes between them (the victims of woonga) and their parents/guardians. Woonga users usually form groups in their comfort zones. They design strategies to successfully persuade people to part with their cash to feed their addiction. Young people who consume woonga gradually lose their consciousness of self and self-respect. Woonga is a relatively cheap drug but is nevertheless costly to those who cannot afford it.

Most South Africans are aware of the tendencies of illicit drug users. The question is: what happens when drug addicts are unsuccessful in obtaining sufficient cash to pay for their drug addiction? Crime becomes the only way to get money. Woonga users' families, relatives, neighbours and communities, and society itself suffer from the consequences of crime and this establishes a sense of fear within society. The environment becomes unpleasant for all inhabitants because violence becomes an issue. Woonga turns young people into zombies so the impact on society can exceed that of HIV and AIDS. Victims of this drug remove themselves from societal activities and live their own strange street lifestyle. Woonga

---

* Holborn, L. 2011. 'Nearly 50 000 School Girls Fall Pregnant in One Year: Why the Odds are Ttacked Against South Africa's Young People's Succeeding'. Available at: www.moneyweb. co.za/moneyweb-soapbox/nearly-50-000-school-girls-fall-pregnant-in-one-ye?sn=2009+De-tail (accessed 28 February 2014).

steadily paralyses the aspirations of young people and could have a disastrous effect on South Africa's future and affect all aspects of its development. Rich McEachran's investigation into woonga that: 'Nyaope is a killer. In my eyes, the situation is worse than the current unemployment, HIV and AIDS crises put together.'* Woonga will facilitate greater destruction within society than any other drug that has existed prior in South Africa. Society can be affected in the following ways by drugs:

Sports
Young people generally dominate in the field of sports. Sports impact positively on economic development, enhance the societal image and create employment. Sports activities maintain good social interactions among individuals and reduce crime statistics. Victims of woonga do not engage in any sports activities. Victims engage in group activities to develop the best strategies to feed their next addiction period. Participation in sport enables the discovery of new talent among young people and this will increasingly fade. Capable individuals will be unable to realise their abilities because of the tragedy of illicit drug use.

Education
Any illicit drug use has a negative impact on education. Government has spent a considerable portion of the budget on education. SouthAfrica.info highlighted the following: 'Spending on education has increased tremendously in the post-apartheid era. In 1994, the government spent R31.8 billion on education. By 2006, this had risen to R92.1 billion – 17.8% of total government spending. At roughly 5% of national GDP, South Africa's rate of investment in education is among the highest in the world.† Education remains the way to close the inequality gap within society. The effects of woonga have had a terrifying impact on both male and female learners and will result in increasing dropout rates. Victims of this drug consider education to be a low priority. Currently, there is a shortage of skills in South

---

* McEachran, R. 2013. 'In South Africa, a deadly new drug is made with HIV medication'. Available at: www.theatlantic.com/international/archive/2013/08/in-south-africa-a-deadly-new-drug-is-made-with-hiv-medications/278865/ (accessed 28 February 2014).
† SouthAfrican.Info. 2013. 'A huge investment in education'. Available at: www.southafrica.info/about/social/govteducation.htm (accessed 28 February 2014).

Africa and illicit drug use is contributing to this. Education reduces poverty, therefore woonga or any other illicit drug will heighten the rate of poverty.

Health
As mentioned earlier, woonga comprises a mixture of ARVs and other deadly substances. South Africans have a high rate of HIV and AIDS. The government has sought to aid society and provide free ARVs to those with HIV and AIDS. However, the victims of woonga mug HIV and AIDS patients to obtain their ARVs. This creates a terrifying scenario: HIV and AIDS patients fear fetching their ARVs from local clinics in case they are mugged. A healthy society contributes to effective economic production. When the health status of individuals deteriorates, the social context becomes weak. And woonga affects the health of its consumers. Woonga victims find it a challenge to consume healthy food and eat mostly junk food, such as snacks, sweets and fizzy drinks. Bread remains their staple food so their health deteriorates. Young girls turn to prostitution to feed their habits while boys commit all sorts of crime. Woonga users ultimately perish as a result of lengthy consumption.

Can illicit drug use among our youth be attributed to democracy?
In this section I do not intend to judge or resist society's criticism of democracy. The purpose is to highlight the essence of democracy within society and between government and society. I hope it will assist to ease quarrels and scepticism concerning the essence of democracy within society. Democratic principles are aimed at emphasising good interaction among citizens. Democracy means that an individual should be free without infringing upon the freedom of others. This denotes that individual rights must be respected and protected by the state. The rule of law is a central feature of democracy. Individual rights are protected by the rule of law enshrined in Chapter 3 of the South African Constitution. The rule of law condemns the use of illicit drugs. Therefore democracy aims to free individuals from unnecessary oppression. Democracy assists to enhance society through development. Blaming democracy for society's ills undermines individual rights and the development of the country.

Many born-frees misinterpret the essence of the freedom brought about by democracy and do not take responsibility for their actions. This implies that users of illicit drug do not know how to exercise their given freedom and this leads to 'negative freedom'. Democracy should not be blamed for the misdemeanours of youth. The blame for illicit drug use should fall squarely on the shoulders of the youth and be totally detached from democratic values.

A wake-up call for the born-frees

On 16 June 1976, self-developed youth united in the struggle for freedom in South Africa. They paid a heavy price to liberate the country from undemocratic rule and laid the way for the freedom that the born-frees now enjoy. Are the current youth progressively failing the spirit of the generation of 'moral' youth? The moral youth attached their actions to democratic principles that benefitted all. The born-frees need to discover strategies to preserve our great environment for the next generation and move away from a progressively careless lifestyle.

Illicit drug use destroys the aspirations of individuals and creates an unpleasant environment for the next generation. It is heart-breaking to see girls falling pregnant at an early age and engaging in prostitution and boys committing a variety of crimes as a result of illicit drug use. If this continues, the next generation will be raised by violent, irresponsible and egotistic parents, who will be unable to provide adequate care and guidance. This reckless lifestyle, driven by illicit drug use, will cause confusion and terror in the coming generation. Luckily, the current youth are supported by government, who have implemented national strategies to fight illicit drug use. However, some drug addicts do not respond effectively to measures aimed at getting them off illicit drugs.

Non-governmental organisations (NGOs) play a vital role in the fight against social ills, including drug addiction. The media also has a role to play in alerting young people of the risks involved in taking drugs and drawing their attention to the terrible outcomes of drug addiction and how this has destroyed the aspirations of some of our celebrities. Academics also have a role in the fight against illicit drug use among youth. Their published articles, books and journals provide the government and the media with vital information regarding drug use. However, the missing factor in this fight against drugs is the youth.

Securing South Africa's future

The youth cannot expect the government, NGOs and academics to provide all the solutions and solve their issues. The current youth have to take responsibility for their own actions and come up with their own strategies for self-development. In this case, self-development among the youth can assist government to meet social development aspirations. Self-development of individuals does not equate to doing favours for government; it is safeguarding one's existence.

Today's youth are tomorrow's parents. Central requirements for being a parent are discipline and the capability to inspire the new generation. South Africa is a developing state and we need the current youth to advance its future development.

Youth should inspire one another and encourage self-development. This will create altruism within society, which, in turn, will preserve a decent environment. Youth must discourage the use of drugs within their social groups and encourage self-awareness and conscious decision-making. They must take responsibility for their own actions and act rationally. Youth should not be an extra burden on society – South Africa has so much else to focus on, such as development and the eradication of poverty and disease.

We need effective, practical strategies to fight this scourge of drug addiction. If we ignore the problem, there will be a tragedy in the future. The current youth have to stand firm against drugs and secure South Africa's future.

Lead by example: Changing tragedy to strategy

In any democratic state, citizens expect peace. Peace does not originate from the oxygen we breathe. Only individuals can create and secure peace within society. Illicit drug use creates the opposite of peace – crime, violence, anxiety and tragedy. I do not intend to criticise the already existing tragedy but to discover strategies that will effectively diminish it. We have to, in order to preserve our current democracy. The state needs citizens who are capable of solving societal ills through appropriate strategies.

This is my story.

I am still young and I, like all youth, am exposed to and experience youthful thoughts. I discovered the right direction through aligning myself with influential individuals. Fortunately, influential individuals are mostly welcoming and ready to make good moves. I decided to use my critical judgement before deciding to join them. These influential individuals aimed to plant incentives among leaners in the South African schools so it was a decent group to join.

I grew up in KwaMhlanga in Mpumalanga, where the issue of illicit drug use was not alarming – it was a tragedy in cities and suburbs rather. Joining influential individuals from Seidet School Projects (SEISPRO) and the Foundation for Ethical Youth Leadership (FEYL) was inspiring. Both SEISPRO and FEYL are based at the University of Pretoria, and are facilitated by remarkable youth. It was time for the crew from both organisations and me to assist government through youth development.

During our voyage, various communities highlighted terrifying issues brought about by illicit drug use. Elders blamed democracy. They said that the youth had acquired excessive freedom and that they undermined the elders' supervision. They acted as they wished and had no direction.

These communities were astonished about our youth incentives to sustain youth development. However, this is how it is supposed to be in a democratic system – finding strategies to eradicate suffering in others. Through our programmes, the majority of the youth from various communities got inspired and began to consider education as key.

Planting incentives within society became a chain when others joined our youth development journey. We consider ourselves to be the go-getters and go-givers. We provide incentives to acquire knowledge through education instead of using illicit drugs. The go-getters and go-givers strategy has inspired teachers in various communities. Inspired young people join the go-giver and go-getter strategy when they enroll at the university. However, this does not imply that the go-getter and go-giver strategy exists only at the tertiary education level. This strategy can be used wherever one engages with individuals within society. The purpose is to change the journey of spreading illicit drugs to the journey of spreading positive incentives within society.

This go-getter and go-giver strategy will assist those who are sceptical about democracy to regain their trust in it. It convinces people that democracy is a suitable system for society if its principles are considered properly. It also proves that the current youth can embark on expanding development and discouraging illicit drug use.

Hopefully, the tragedy of illicit drug use will gradually fade. Our strategic journey is aimed at creating a peaceful environment for current and future generations.

Concluding remarks

Illicit drug use among the youth has caused people to be sceptical about and critical of democracy. These people are confusing individual choice and behaviour with democracy. Human behaviour can create either peace or disaster within society. Democracy maintains peace within society if considered appropriately. Young people who consume illicit drug pollute the environment by committing crime and violence, and this threatens the freedom of others. Changing tragedy to strategy can rebuild illicit drug users' lives in various communities. Democracy practiced well stabilises the relationship between society and government and keeps our society safe for current and future generations.

Twenty years for women cadres in diplomacy

Nomfanelo Kota

Government communicator

Introduction

EVEN DURING THOSE DARK DAYS OF apartheid when all odds were stacked against the majority of our people, I knew that I would be a diplomat one day, to represent my country at the United Nations, like Oliver Reginald Tambo. It is now 31 January 2013, as I board the plane back to South Africa with my children, Litha and Chioma, having completed a two-year stint as South Africa's communicator in the United Nations Security Council (UNSC) and I bid farewell to New York, a place I called home for 27 months.

So, when the editor wrote to me about the *Liberation Diaries,* commemorating two decades of our liberation, I thought about my passion, diplomacy, and the role the women of our country continue to play in this arena. I realised that dreams can be fulfilled, thanks to a great movement, the African National Congress, which ensured that a daughter of working-class folk ended up representing her country in the global premier political organisation, the UNSC. But it was not always like this.

Before 1994, it was hard to even imagine that our organisation would be filled with diplomats from all walks of life, including its top echelons.

Former President Thabo Mbeki, addressing the Conference of the Corporate Council on Africa in April 1997 in Chantilly, Virginia, said that, 'It is not given to every generation that it should be present during, and participate in, the act of creation. I believe that ours is privileged to occupy such historic space.'

Thus, the women who have been at the forefront of our diplomatic trenches, true to their God-given nature, participated in the birthing of our new nation on the global front. As frontline troopers, they told and are telling the world about South Africa and her story of victory over adversity, from 1994.

Joining the Department of Foreign Affairs in August 2002, after serving in Luthuli House, was the best decision of my life. I met exceptional human beings from all walks of life. A sense of unity brought them together. They had to produce something new out of Africa, regardless of their various political affiliations and different historical backgrounds. In the world, they had to represent one country, South Africa.

My immediate boss, Minister Nkosazana Clarice Dlamini-Zuma, who took over the reins of power in 1999 and addressed various diplomatic forums, such as Heads of Mission Conferences all over the world, used to proudly state that being a South African diplomat was one of the easiest tasks in the world: we were a new country, we no longer had to lie and defend the indefensible, and we no longer had to carry the yoke of apartheid and its brutality on our shoulders.

Writing this liberation story took me to the annals of our history. I came across a book entitled *A Diplomat's Story: Apartheid and Beyond 1969–1998*, written by a certain Pieter Wolvaardt in 1999, who served in the diplomatic corps from 1969–98. On page 246 there is a photograph of South African ambassadors meeting in Pretoria in September 1995. In the sea of men, I could pick out about eight women. Among those I could recognise was Thuthukile Skweyiya, formerly Mazibuko, who used to be the Deputy Director-General at the Foreign Service Institute in Pretoria. She also later served as our ambassador in Paris and has recently returned home after providing support to her husband, High Commissioner Zola Skweyiya.

In the same photograph, in the fourth row, there are four women but I could recognise only one of them: Dr Lindiwe Mabuza, who was South Africa's first democratic representative to the Federal Republic of Germany from 1995–99. She also served as our High Commissioner to the United Kingdom of Great Britain and Northern Ireland.

In the fifth row, I could see Ambassador Barbara Masekela, who used to be our representative in Washington DC. I think she followed immediately after Professor Franklin Sonn, who used to be the Director-General in the Presidency during former President Nelson Mandela's tenure from 1994–99. With sis Barbara, as we used to call her as young activists, I could see our current Minister of International Relations and Corporations, Maite Nkoana-

Mashabane, one of the youngest at the time. When the picture was taken in September 1995, she was approaching her 32nd birthday. Next to her was Uncle Billy Modise, now retired, who used to be our Chief of State Protocol during former President Mbeki's tenure. In the back row, there is a white woman I cannot recognise.

I have started this essay in this manner to reflect on the type of diplomatic corps we took over in 1994. At the time, the first Minister of Foreign Affairs, under President Mandela, was Alfred Nzo, a veteran freedom fighter and former secretary general of the African National Congress. (Sadly, very little has been written about his tenure in the diplomatic arena.)

My story seeks to draw attention to the role women have played in the diplomatic corps and how we should continue to make massive victories in this arena. International mobilisation has always been key to our struggle. The international community was mobilised to impose economic sanctions, and cultural and sporting boycotts as tenets of the struggle. Women played a critical role on the international stage in the struggle, both at home and in exile, albeit in a supportive role.

A 2007 publication by the then Department of Foreign Affairs, almost 12 years after that first Heads of Mission Conference in 1995, showcases our representatives in the world. President Mandela, who served only one term as sitting president, passed over the baton to President Thabo Mbeki, under whose leadership women advanced not just in numbers but qualitatively, too. We had our first woman Minister of Foreign Affairs, Dr Nkosazana Dlamini-Zuma, who led the charge and who had been the Minister of Health in President Mandela's Cabinet. The bright, young and energetic Dr Ayanda Ntsaluba was the Director-General during Dr Dlamini-Zuma's tenure. Most of our Heads of Mission official photographs reflected a new dynamic era in which women featured prominently in strategic missions, not only in their numbers but also in the responsibilities assigned to them.

For instance, the consolidation of the African Agenda, which is a cornerstone of our foreign policy, is premised on the idea that Africa must come first in our endeavours globally. As part of this prioritisation of Africa, our diplomats at the time included veteran activist and community leader from Kimberley in the Northern Cape, Eunice Gabatlhaolwe Komane, who was our High Commissioner in

125

Botswana. She was a nursing sister by profession and was the former MEC for Safety and Security in the Northern Cape. The Southern African Development Community (SADC) headquarters are also based in Botswana.

SADC

In Mozambique, our sister country, we had the dynamic stalwart, High Commissioner Thandi Lujabe-Rankoe, who had previously served in Tanzania (1995–1999), as well as in Botswana (1999–2002). Sis Thandi, as we fondly refer to her, had lived almost all over the world. She spent the better part of the 1960s in Cairo, Egypt, working for the ANC. She has published several books: *Child Labour in Africa*, published by UNESCO in 1997; an ANC history booklet from 1912–91 published in Oslo, Sweden, in 1991; and *A Dream Fulfilled: Memoirs of a South African Diplomat*, published in 2006. Sis Thandi was succeeded by another dynamic ANC cadre in Mozambique, current ANC Deputy Secretary general Jessie Duarte. In Malawi, still within the SADC, we had High Commissioner Tsheole, a member of Parliament for ten years before she joined the diplomatic corps. A schoolteacher and university lecturer by profession, Tsheole also served in Cameroon.

In Namibia, Mavivi Myakayaka-Manzini who for many years led the ANC's International Relations Committee, now sits behind our flag in Windhoek, Namibia. A gender activist and fierce debater, Ambassador Myakayaka-Manzini continues to fight injustice whenever and wherever it raises its ugly head. I was blessed to have her as one of my mentors in my formative years in the youth and student movement. We have debated, long into the night, many urgent and pressing matters in our domain, such as the self-determination of Western Sahara and the cause of the people of Palestine.

In Senegal, West Africa, we had Ambassador Thembisile Majola-Embalo, a child of the struggle and someone with a solid background in intelligence matters. She also has a Master's degree in Civil Engineering and a flair for foreign languages.

North Africa

In Egypt, we had Ambassador Sonto Kudjoe, who had served in Sweden as an ambassador from 2002–06. A graduate of Kishinev State University, she had served in the South African Secret Service as

Director: Research and Analysis on Africa from 1998–2000, as well as Chief Director: Africa Multilateral at the Department of Foreign Affairs from 2000 to 2002. An expert in security matters, she was once the deputy CEO of NIPILAR and after serving as Deputy Director-General: Africa Multilateral, our president appointed her as the new Director-General for State Security Services, making her the first woman in almost 20 years of our democracy to occupy this senior position.

Of course, as I share these snippets about the women deployed in our foreign service to build our relations, it is worth mentioning that one of the strategic missions we have is in Tunisia. This is headed by Nonceba Losi, a former combatant of Umkhonto weSizwe, who was forced into exile by the brutal apartheid regime at the tender age of 16. A nurse by profession, trained in Sweden, her forays during the dark days of apartheid saw her deployed in Zimbabwe and in Zambia where the ANC headquarters was. After coming back into the country, she joined the South African National Defence Force and worked for its Military Intelligence Unit. Later she joined the Department of Foreign Affairs as Director: State Protocol and before she took over as the ambassador in Tunis, where the African Development Bank is located, she was the Deputy Chief of State Protocol and often provided support to both former President Thabo Mbeki and our current President Jacob Zuma.

It is important to note that at the helm of these appointments over the past 20 years were very capable women who were able to take our foreign policy engagements to new heights.

Our strategic interventions within the BRICS nations

From 2004 to 2008, in the formative stages of BRICS, we had Ambassador Lindiwe Zulu in Brasilia, the federal capital of Brazil. Brazil in Latin America is a strategic country for South Africa. With similar economic and social challenges, both countries play a critical role in the development agenda in their respective regions, the SADC and MERCOSUR. Zulu went there armed with a Master's degree in Journalism from the Patrice Lumumba University in Moscow and fluent in Russian. She was experienced and had served in various communications: she was Speaker of the Gauteng Legislature from 1994–99 and was Special Adviser to Dlamini-Zuma when she was the Minister of Foreign Affairs from 2000–01. She also headed the

Chief Directorate for West and Central Africa in the Department of Foreign Affairs between 2001 and 2003.

I remember arriving with Minister Dlamini-Zuma in Brasilia at almost midnight and finding the airport lounge full of the entire corps of African ambassadors, some very senior in years, who had waited for our chartered aircraft to land. This does not happen every day and in the seven years I worked with Minister Dlamini-Zuma as her Director for Public Diplomacy, Media Relations and sometimes brought in as speechwriter, this was a first for me. It showed me how deeply Africans feel about one another. Ubuntu!

During President Luiz Inácio Lula da Silva's first term in office, particular attention was paid to Brazil's foreign policy on Africa. As we lobbied for South Africa to host the FIFA World Cup in 2010, Brazil, as a former host, was consulted to share its technical expertise, both politically and logistically. The burden of organising such logistics fell in the hands of Zulu.

Today, as President Zuma's International Relations Adviser, she continues to provide support to the president on major engagements on the global front and in many multilateral initiatives, such as the UN, G20, BRICS and SADC. Ambassador Zulu was also one of President Zuma's Special Envoys on Zimbabwe and has been directly linked to supporting the implementation of the Global Political Agreement in Zimbabwe.

However, after the recent presidential elections in Zimbabwe, the Movement for Democratic Change (MDC) is no longer part of the Government of National Unity. In controversy surrounding some of the comments made on behalf of the SADC during the process leading up to the elections, Ambassador Zulu displayed her courage and tenacity in dealing with fragile political matters.

It is worth noting though that based on the significance we attach to the BRICS strategic initiative, it might be proper to deploy more women in the BRICS nations as ambassadors, consul generals and high commissioners.

I will now look at some of our deployments in the multilateral arena. Under Deputy Director-General Ambassador Nozipho Mxakato-Diseko, many brainy and diligent, several young women have been posted in the multilateral arena, such as Bongiwe Qwabe, who is now our Deputy High Commissioner in the United Kingdom. Her previous position was as South Africa's political coordinator in our first stint as an elected non-permanent member of the UNSC during 2007–2008.

Minister-Counsellor Qwabe led the charge, supporting Ambassador Dumisani Khumalo, who served in our New York Mission as ambassador for almost ten years. Ambassador Dumisani Khumalo had taken over from our first ambassador, Josiah Jele, who served under Minister Alfred Nzo.

Serving as political coordinator for one's country is no mean feat as you become the leading person for your country on substantive matters such as negotiating resolutions; advising the ambassador on the nuances of country statements; drafting our responses to various items on the agenda of the UNSC on a daily basis; and going through each and every colleague's statement at the Mission before they land on the ambassador's desk. I worked directly with Minister-Counsellor Qwabe on the public diplomacy side while based at head office. By the time I led our communications endeavours in the Mission during our second stint as an elected non-permanent member at the UNSC between 2011 and 2012, I had a privileged glimpse of what the task entailed. The Mission in New York was a pressure cooker during both stints for 730 days covering the two-year tenure.

It is still a matter of pride to see Bongiwe in the official photographs of the UN as the only female political coordinator during our first stint in the 15-member UNSC.

I am equally pleased, though, that in our embassy in Paris, where UNESCO is based, we have had three women consecutively as ambassadors: Mary Sibanda-Thusi and Thuthukile Skweyiya, and Dolana Msimanga who also served as our ambassador in Denmark after serving as Deputy President Jacob Zuma's adviser before he became president.

Like London, we were fortunate to have had two women high commissioners, Cheryl Carolus, who was Deputy Secretary general of the ANC when Cyril Ramaphosa was the Secretary General of the ANC under President Mandela, and Dr Lindiwe Mabuza.

Geneva

As one of our strategic missions in Geneva, the Permanent Mission of South Africa is accredited to the United Nations and other international organisations and deals with an array of disciplines that interact with one another and have a global impact. These include: human rights, humanitarian affairs, migration, refugee-related issues, trade and development, health, labour, environment, disarmament, telecommunications and intellectual property rights.

Some of the major international organisations based in Geneva include the Human Rights Council, the UN High Commission for Refugees (UNHCR), the joint UN Programme on HIV and AIDS (UNAIDS), the World Health Organization (WHO), the International Labour Organization (ILO), the Red Cross and the International Conference on Disarmament.

During 2005–2008, Ambassador Glaudine Jacoba Mtshali led our charge. Ambassador Mtshali, a medical doctor by profession and a soft-spoken yet effective diplomat, had previously served a stint as Consul-General to the West Coast based in Los Angeles and was also our Health Attaché in the United States and Canada from 1999–2002.

Currently, Ambassador Abdul Minty heads the Mission, one of our experienced diplomats, especially on disarmament issues, assisted by an able technocrat, Ms Ncumisa Notutela, who also served both in New York and as a director in the UN at head office. Young, vibrant and experienced, this is the type of talent we must nurture so that we can build solid diplomats to sit behind the South African flag.

Cuba

I cannot conclude the essay without speaking about Cuba. The first time I visited this beautiful island of revolutionaries, Fidel Castro, Martí and the Granma, was in about 1998 with our current Minister of Sport and Recreation, Fikile Mbalula. We were deployed by the ANC to attend a political school as newly elected office bearers in the secretary general's office of the ANC Youth League and were looking forward to being hosted by our ambassador, John Nkadimeng, one of the Rivonia trialists. I had learnt about him as a teenage activist during the mid-1980s. Unfortunately, on our arrival in Cuba, Ambassador Nkadimeng was not in town. Ambassador Lenin Shope, who was a number two at the mission at the time, hosted us, together with his wife, Nosithembele Tumse Shope. On that maiden visit, I often teased Fikile Mbalula about having his neck permanently craned looking at the beautiful Cuban women.

At the time of our visit, Nomalanga Mkhize, the daughter the

Treasurer-General of the ANC was also in town, a high school student then. I took her under my wing and attended several of President Fidel Castro's speeches with her. Today, she is Dr Nomalanga Mkhize, a PhD graduate from Rhodes University. She comments in our public discourse with much confidence and intelligence and is the epitome of what happens when young people are groomed into politics from an early age. Her progress also makes one appreciate more the importance of mentoring young women to play leading roles in the future.

Turning back to diplomacy, one woman leader who served as ambassador in Cuba and who continues to be a torchbearer and trailblazer for generations of younger women is Ambassador Thenjiwe Mtintso. Sis Thenji, as most of us know her, was a student at the University of Fort Hare in the year I was born, 1972, and was later expelled for political reasons. A Black Consciousness Movement product, she worked as a journalist for the *Daily Dispatch* in the heyday of apartheid from 1974–1976. An Umkhonto weSizwe commander, she led our combatants in Uganda and one of the documentaries about the history of the ANC shows her in combat alongside Commander in Chief Nelson Mandela, shortly after he was released from jail in 1990. After Cuba she also served as our ambassador in Italy and is now based in Bulgaria.

As deputy to the ANC's secretary general, Kgalema Motlanthe, our current deputy president, sis Thenji mentored many younger generations of women within the ANC and in the broader society. Many, like Febe Potgieter-Gqubule, Vuyiswa Tulelo, Kholeka Mqulwana, Nomusa Dube and me, are now serving in different positions of responsibility in our government and in the international relations field.

Trials and tribulations: Low points and high points

The ascendancy of former Deputy President Phumzile Mlambo-Ngcuka to United Nations Women as its executive director, former Minister Geraldine Fraser-Moleketi to the Development Bank in Tunis as its gender envoy and Navi Pillay in the Human Rights Commission are some of the key highpoints of our 20-year journey.

Of course, Dr Dlamini-Zuma led the charge as the first woman to occupy the Office of the African Union (OAU) as chairperson last year – a first for an African woman since the inception of the

OAU/AU. Almost 51 years after the founding of the continental Pan Africanist Women's Organisation (PAWO), women in our country are shedding the 'second-class citizen status' they have occupied for many years.

What assisted most of these women is the wisdom shared by earlier generations who occupied those positions. Diplomacy is a cut-throat business, totally unfriendly to women in their roles as mothers, spouses and partners in their families. Diplomats love talking and meetings, especially at the UN, can go on and on with little attention given to the many other roles women play. Fortunately, some support is provided by the state to serving ambassadors, high commissioners, and others in the missions.

However, for women to thrive, the system needs to be revolutionised. Family responsibilities should not be seen as peripheral but, rather, our work should be planned to integrate family life with the role of diplomacy wherever women are deployed. Of course, when you enter the UN headquarters in New York on 1st Ave and 42nd Street, you notice that many junior staffers are women. When you proceed to the canteen during lunch, you still see women. But when high-level meetings are held, especially in September during the General Assembly sessions, the people who sit behind their countries' flags are predominantly male. This needs to change. However, I am glad that South Africa, compared to many other countries, has made major strides in this regard. We need to consolidate our gains further.

Dealing with expectations

There is a new breed of diplomat in the Department of International Relations: young, energetic, politically savvy, highly educated and unburdened by our horrible past. They have expertise in trade, finance, economics, climate change, post-conflict reconstruction, gender studies and sustainable development issues. This is the corps that will shape the future. They still have a lot to give and will be there when we realise the African Union's dream. We cannot miss our opportunity to nurture and develop them so that they can take on the reins of diplomacy one day.

The face of diplomacy in the world is changing – it is becoming younger. Those who have extensive experience must be brought in to pass on their reservoir of knowledge in a systematic way through our Foreign Service Institute. These women should continue to learn from those who have walked these corridors before – women like Sheila Sisulu at the World Food Programme, the late Goodwill Ambassador Mama Miriam Makeba, the UN Ambassador on the Fight Against Malaria, Yvonne Chaka-Chaka, as well as Charlize Theron.

Coming full circle: My diary of liberation in corporate South Africa

Khanyisile Kweyama

CEO of Anglo-American Corporation SA

MY APPOINTMENT AS EXECUTIVE DIRECTOR of Anglo American South Africa, the representative of Anglo American plc was hailed widely as a major appointment for the company in South Africa. I was the first black female, in fact the first female, to hold this position in South Africa. My predecessors had all been male, white and black. My election a few months later as vice president of the Chamber of Mines South Africa further demonstrated that the mining industry was making the necessary changes to effect transformation in mining.

The mining industry has lived under the dark shadow of the legacy that is associated with the migrant labour system – a system that singlehandedly, over a period of almost 100 years, caused the largest destruction of the family structure in South Africa. Typically, black males were recruited by TEBA on behalf of the mining companies to work in Johannesburg, eGoli, the Place of Gold. In search of a livelihood and a better life, these men left their rural villages in the Eastern Cape, Natal and as far afield as Mozambique, Lesotho, Malawi and Zimbabwe, and took the long train journey to Johannesburg.

As a young girl growing up in Atteridgeville, west of Pretoria, the capital of South Africa, my father used to let us listen to the banned songs of Hugh Masekela, Miriam Makeba, Caiphus Semenya and Letta Mbulu. Many of them lamented the life of black miners in South Africa; lamented the long periods of absence from their loved ones; lamented the fact that their families never knew whether they would return home alive or in a coffin. Yet they remained ever hopeful that one day they would be reunited.

On his return from an exchange trip to the USA in 1972, my father smuggled several books, music tapes and records into the country. Among these was a banned photography book by Ernest

Cole, *House of Bondage* – a pictoral depiction of life in South Africa. Prominence is given to mine workers starting work in the gold mines. There were photographs of workers being stripped and being given physical examinations by the mine doctors – standing in a row, stripped, with their hands up in the air and legs wide apart for the physical examination. Others were of the all-male hostels where men slept in dormitories, squeezed in like sardines, sharing sleeping accommodation and toilets with no partitions between them. Sadly, this book was either lost or stolen from our home. But many years later, in 2009, I obtained one of the last of two copies on Amazon.com. Two years later I joined the Anglo American group of companies.

Flashback

I first came to Anglo American in 1992 during the CODESA negotiations, when I was employed by the Consultative Business Movement (CBM) as an assistant to the National Programmes' director. CBM was part of the secretariat that ran the administration of the negotiations at the World Trade Centre in Kempton Park. Over a period of one and a half years, we were to spend days and evenings, often late into the night, in that centre and forum that led to the birth of the democracy of this country. Many years later I was to head Anglo American in South Africa.

On 21 September 2013, sitting outside the South African Embassy in the Washington DC heat – 19 years and five months since freedom day on 27 April 1994 – I was taken back to the 1980s and our weekly Saturday pilgrimages to the South African Embassy to protest and march. I was transported back to the cars hooting outside the embassy and the protesters walking the pavements chanting *'Bush and Botha you can't hide – we charge you with genocide'*.

Looking up at the covered statute of Tata Nelson Mandela, I reminisced about the first day I set eyes on him, walking out of Victor Verster Prison on 11 February.

A young couple in their twenties hurried around preparing their townhouse for the many visitors that were going to descend on their home in the next few days, programme planning, constantly on the phone with the ANC office and other ANC members in the Washington area, New York and as far afield as Atlanta, Florida and Michigan all coming to Washington for D-Day. What was all the fuss about? Don't you know Nelson and Winnie Mandela were coming to Washington? *Halala!* This was the moment we had all been waiting for, the moment we had dreamt about all our youth. Sometimes in our despair we gave up on the dream of ever seeing him come out alive – it seemed too distant and unrealistic. But that day, 11 February, we all huddled in front of our televisions at 4:00 am East Coast time to be among the first to see him walk out of Victor Verster and we were filled with anxiety, excitement, curiosity and dozens of other emotions. At last, we would finally see him in the flesh, albeit on television; at last, we could start the countdown to returning home. That moment was watched by millions of viewers all over the world.

We practiced songs that we were going to sing as he stepped out of the plane. Yes! We were going to meet him at the *door* of the plane. Special clearance had been obtained for the Welcome Mandela Committee members in Washington DC to be right there when he stepped off Donald Trump's private jet from New York. Nothing had been spared to ensure the comfort of our leader as he made the journey to meet the folk in Washington DC – his supporters, his people, the cadres who had been living their young lives working and preparing for this great moment. This signified the true liberation day for us. We had seen him walk out of prison on TV; we had seen him address the first rally at FNB Stadium; we had seen him greet the neighbours outside his home in Vilakazi Street in Orlando West, Soweto; we had eagerly followed his first visit to HQ in Lusaka; and now he was coming to us! He had selected Washington DC as one of the stops in his international homecoming tour. What an honour! What a privilege!

Then it was time to drive to the airport, the motorcade hooting, us waving ANC flags, pictures of our leaders, he was free! We are free! Because of him, our nation is free! We had gone from motorcades protesting outside the embassy to motorcades rushing to meet him. We had come full circle!

Then the Trump jet landed, the stairs rolled out of the plane, the door swung open and there he was, tall and majestic – he had to bend to come through the doorway. There were tears, screams, ululating, we all broke into song. He had arrived; he was alive; we could touch him, see him. It had not been in vain. We lived to see him in the flesh.

I left home at a tender age, abandoning the pre-med studies that my parents wanted for me. I crossed the border into Swaziland and leapt off the train at Piggs Peak, tearing the knees of my blue jeans, because I was afraid the train would go back to South Africa with me on it – back to possible arrest, detention and the horror of prison that every young black South African knew about or had experienced. I would rather jump from a moving train than risk that! I walked from Piggs Peak to Mbabane, catching a few lifts along the way, and then walking on again. I had no idea how long it would take but I hummed *Siyaya ePitoli* to keep me focused on the long winding road ahead and take away my stress. Then I saw them on the horizon – the buildings of Mbabane. I had arrived. I was safe. I was alive.

'How many times do I have to write this biography?' I ask my handlers.

'Until we tell you it's okay.'

I later found out it was to check if there were any inconsistencies – any sign that you were not a genuine cadre. That maybe, just maybe, you were there to infiltrate. 'We cannot be too careful, you know?' Three weeks of living in a flat with nothing to do – maybe a little walk outside the door to get some fresh air, but never out into the street. 'You cannot expose this location with your presence. Strangers get noticed very quickly.' Finally: 'You have been cleared; you are legitimate; we have checked with comrades back home and they have vouched for you. Welcome to the ANC! You shall henceforth be called Palesa.' I was part of the flower recruits. I never asked why 'flower' – you didn't ask questions. You accept what you were told – a soldier follows instructions. The discipline began: rules, regulations, strategies, tactics: say them in your sleep. Memorise, chant, repeat, doze off, wake up, memorise, chant, repeat…

This journey would eventually take me to Kenya and then to the USA – to safety, to study, to build a career, to protest every Saturday outside the South African Embassy and wait for that day when I could return home. Felicia Mabuza-Suttle's voice on the podium jars me back to the present moment … yes, I am at the South African Embassy in Washington again, not as a protester this time but as a representative of Anglo American, one of the sponsors that made this 10-foot statue by Madiba possible. As the speeches drag on, Tata's fist emerges from the flag that drapes it. Amandla! Tata has unveiled the symbol of freedom – the clenched fist raised. We are free!

Zindzi Mandela – the little girl whose father was unceremoniously taken away from her for 27 years – speaks about her father. Ambassador Ebrahim Rasool exorcises the South African Embassy in his eloquent address. The young girl who marched throughout the 1980s has returned in 2013 as a mature executive, a leader of Anglo American in South Africa. I have come full circle – 19 years and five months later.

Returning to South Africa in 1990, I found myself thrown into the secretariat of CODESA – yet another opportunity to contribute to shaping our democracy. My venture into the corporate world at BMW was affirmative action gone wrong. Then on to Nokusa Promotions, then KTK HR Solutions. Later, I was an executive in male-dominated executive committees. I was a young black female with a desire to change the corporate world, to shape the emergence of practitioners. We didn't call it BEE then. Now it is called Broad-Based Black Economic Empowerment. Did we succeed? Have we achieved a truly representative workforce?

Serving on the Commission for Employment Equity (CEE) I see the statistics say we have not – not yet uhuru! Every CEE annual report has the same message – not yet uhuru in the boardroom. Some companies are better than others at managing the change process. The journey to become head of Anglo American in South Africa has been one of lessons and experiences – both good and bad!

For many years, women were forbidden from working in underground positions at mining companies. The National Union of Mineworkers (NUM) battled for years for the right of women to work in technical and other roles underground. Indeed, it was a victory for gender empowerment in the mining industry. What a tragedy it was when I visited one of our mines after a young woman was attacked underground in Rustenburg and eventually died of her injuries. What a blow to gender empowerment.

A few months later, a woman was appointed to head Anglo American South Africa. Indeed, the female's journey through the corporate world has been a mixture of successes and setbacks along the way. Contrast the appointment of Cynthia Carroll as the first female CEO of a major mining company with the daily sexual harassment of women underground and indeed in offices all over the country.

Conclusion

Are we any better off as females in the corporate world 20 years into our democracy? Am I better off as a female in the corporate world, in the mining sector, in the largest mining company in South Africa?

Depending on where you stand on the social ladder, your level of consciousness and appreciation of weight of transformation against the backdrop of the legacy of apartheid, the answer to these questions would either be affirmative or negative. Yet as conscientious observers we should honestly assert that indeed women in South Africa are in a better position (socially, economically and politically) today, compared to 1994. Even the act of writing this story, knowing full well that I will face neither jail nor banishment for a critical commentary on the body politic of South Africa, bears testament to that fact.

I am not the only woman who has a good story to tell. Many others have struggled but eventually broken the glass ceiling, inside and outside the workplace. If we truly are spread this democratic dividend to countless other women, we bear the responsibility of creating more spaces for growth and development, for affirmation and recognition. After all, as this and many other stories in this book assert, an investment in women always yield higher benefits for their children and families. If we create sufficient circles of support, we will guarantee that many more women 'come full circle', hopefully a key message that this essay advances.

The meaning of freedom: Of doubt, achievement and hope

David Maimela

Former SASCO president and researcher

Introduction

AND SO 20 YEARS ON, SOUTH AFRICA is politically free and is painstakingly building a democracy and, hopefully, a just society. Understandably and quite justifiably, most of the reflections on this historic milestone will focus on the official works of the state and its agencies to enable all of us to understand material progress. And so government itself and other institutions, such as research institutes, rating agencies and organised interests, will, without doubt, take time to reflect on South Africa's 20 years of freedom.

It is possible that the individual human experiences of South Africans may be overshadowed by these high discourses on economic progress or lack thereof, reconstruction and development of infrastructure (bricks and mortar), delivery of public services, building a democratic state based on new values, transforming the state and society, reinstating South Africa in Africa and in the world, and so on.

I believe the experience of freedom and democracy 20 years on cannot be complete without telling the human and individual experience of South Africans.

Lest I be accused of treachery and dishonesty, I want to state upfront that my individual experience of freedom is inextricably linked to the collective national life experience of South Africa as a whole. So, for example, under apartheid some basic amenities were reserved for white suburbs and if they were provided in black townships they were of inferior quality or difficult to access. The dawn of freedom in 1994 meant that, by law, there should be no disparities and therefore, theoretically, I qualify for better services.

My reflections on 20 years of freedom are based on multiple identities and experiences. I am writing as a young person, as a black person, as a man, as a person who originated from a working-class background, as a recent member of the so-called 'black middle strata' and, above all, as a South African. Politically, because I was born in 1982, I am also writing as a person who has had a longer experience of a democratic South Africa than an apartheid one. Of my 31 years, I lived 11 years under apartheid, of which I can remember only the transition years from 1990–94 and, of course, 20 years as a politically free South African.

For me, I reflect on 20 years of freedom with feelings of doubt, achievement and hope. In my reflections, I intend to tackle issues that fall under three interrelated broad themes: first, democratic rights and, in a sense, political rights; second, the political economy of David Maimela; and, finally, culture and the making of my personal freedom. In the end, I hope to express my definitive views about freedom and ponder the future.

Freedom of expression and the formative and transitional taste of freedom

Of the rights enshrined in the Constitution (Act 108 of 1996), none is as enjoyable, practical and liveable as the freedom of expression. For me, freedom of expression refers to three interrelated rights: the right to vote, the right or the freedom of association and the right to say what I like and to write what I like. I enjoy and exercise these rights in different contexts and with different identities.

These contexts and identities refer to my role as a young political activist in society, as a student and developing writer, as a son who had a relationship with his father in a family setting. I lived and continue to live these rights almost daily through these contexts and identities.

I recall as a Congress of South African Students (COSAS) leader and activist in Mpumalanga, a matriculation examination scandal broke out in 1998: thousands of matriculants' final results had been either inflated or deflated. My brother, Cornelius, was directly affected. Among other things, we managed to mobilise current and former students (now legislatively called learners) to march in protest to the provincial head office of education in Nelspruit. Stompie Nkambule, Luthando Shongwe and I, among others, were the leaders. To be able to call for the head of the department, Ms Faith Sithole, to resign and incur no legal, political or personal adverse consequences was quite liberating. In fact, we went further and called for the protection of the affected students' right to education, so that those already admitted to further and higher education institutions were not prejudiced due to maladministration.

In the end, a mechanism to protect the students, mainly through entrance exams, was devised and Ms Faith Sithole either resigned or was fired; either way, she took the fall for the scandal. My brother, who had obtained a full exemption (university entry), was downgraded to a standard pass. The situation was a baptism of fire for me, and for the first time, four years into democracy, there I was in a collective of student leaders publicly and bravely exercising our right to association and freedom of expression and, to date, no security agency or administrative officials have been set upon us to persecute us in anyway.

In the early 1990s, COSAS and other progressive formations finally won the struggle against corporal punishment in schools. Indeed, in 1996, the South African Schools Act outlawed corporal punishment in schools. This Act was built, in part, on *The Children's Charter of South Africa of 1992*, which constituted part of a developing comprehensive regime on the protection of the rights of children, in which I participated. We formed regional structures of the National Children's Rights Committee (NCRC) in Mpumalanga in 1999–2000. And later, of course, the Child Protection Act of 2005 was enacted.

This children's rights regime had implications for the South African family and, in my case, the relationship between my father and me. As I was increasingly becoming aware and active in students' and children's rights issues, my father was going about being the normal strict, sjamboking and old-school parent that he was. He allowed no *rights talk* under his roof. His parenting style often clashed with the law and the children's rights regime. I recall him saying, 'The rights of Mandela will be enjoyed in the streets, not in my house'.

So, whereas the new children of the democratic transition were growing within the democratic and human rights regime, our parents were basically holding onto the traditional old ways of raising children, the ways in which they grew up themselves. This constituted a struggle on the home front between the new and the old. The quest for the new to be born was met with the resistance of the old to contain and oppose the birth of the new.

As a generation growing up under a changed and changing society, we had a contradictory identity: conformists and rebels all at once. As conformists, we abided by the draconian rules of the family, mainly the father: the patriarch. But as rebels, we maintained that our voices must be heard. We succeeded more in the school setting and failed on the home front. No doubt, my father's mantra reigned: 'The rights of Mandela will be enjoyed in the streets, not in my house'.

Even today, the debate continues over whether parents have a right to 'spank' their sometimes naughty children. It has become a political, moral and legal question. Can the state determine how parents should, in the privacy of their homes, raise their children? In other words, can parents be trusted with the responsibility to protect and care for their children, including advancing their rights? Who knows what is best for children? The scourge of child and women abuse – a deeply patriarchal issue – further complicates these questions.

Of course, these rights are enjoyed and exercised within the confines of the complementary and contradictory relationship between the law and culture. And, as Herbert Marcuse would argue, 'The rule of law, no matter how restricted, is still infinitely safer than rule above or without law.'[*]

In reference to the thesis of Paulo Freire, can the parent learn from the child? Can the learner teach the teacher and can the teacher learn from the learner?

> The teacher talks about reality as if it were motionless, static, compartmentalized, and predictable. Or else he expounds on a topic completely alien to the existential experience of the students… Education thus becomes an act of depositing, in which the students are the depositories and the teacher is the depositor. Instead of communicating, the teacher issues communiques and makes deposits, which the students patiently receive, memorize and repeat.[†]

In a nutshell, both children and parents struggle with the changes

---

[*] Marcuse, H. 1964. *One-Dimensional Man*, London: Routledge, p. 36.
[†] Freire, P. 1970. *Pedagogy of the Oppressed*, New York: Herder and Herder, p. 71–72.

brought about by the transition to a democratic society. The new Constitution, which introduced a new human rights culture, has proven to be both a burden and a blessing. But even in the absence of a democratic Constitution and human rights, the relations between parents and children have always been mediated by cultural norms of sorts and these have changed over time, and, in the process, have brought many contradictions to this natural relationship. There has never been a moment where this and other relationships were not governed by norms and standards that have evolved in a social-relations context.

Politically, to be able to vote for a political party of my choice is indeed liberating. The fortunate position I hold is that of a conscious voter – a politically educated voter. Since my first vote in 2004, I have had the privilege of combining both critical rationality and sentiment to make my electoral choice. I have the ability to make a rational choice on the basis of policies that a contesting political party presents to me, but I also vote sentimentally because of my political party association.

Going into the third decade of freedom, new political and societal challenges are emerging and will undoubtedly impact on the coexistence of rationality and sentiment in my electoral choices. I consider this to be perfectly healthy within me and in a democratic society. I have a right to doubt myself and others – lest I become dead alive. To be in a position to understand the power of one vote is quite amazing and self-fulfilling. To have the right to vote and add my individual voice to policy direction and the future of my country is something I cherish.

The political economy of David Maimela

So, what then is my political-economic reality and how has it evolved to impact on my life and shape who I am today and who I am becoming?

Although there has been remarkable progress in the provision of public services and the rise of the so-called 'black middle strata', the pace and quality of change in South Africa has been disappointing for the majority of the African population, mainly due to structural bottlenecks. For instance, in a family of four children, I am the first and only member to receive a university education, which is considered to be a sign of socio-economic progress and an enabler to access better life opportunities and, consequently, improve one's standard of living. The rest of the family members still experience, in varied ways, a standard of living that I can refer to as *poor but not dire,* thanks to remittances from me, state social grants and other social protections.

I have always confronted this question: how is it that one person – me – could hope to succeed and break out of poverty whereas it seems as if my siblings had neither the courage to hope nor the will to succeed?

The answer is perhaps two-fold. Firstly, I have always seen myself as an optimistic person who has always had self-belief in everything I have done. Most of us in our community did not repeat grades except in dire circumstances, such as going without regular meals, irregular employment of parents and, at times, living in a child-headed household. My parents and teachers have always instilled in us discipline and a love for education. I recall that we never had Christmas clothes or parties but always had the full school uniform in January each year. In one year in high school, I was nominated as one of the best-dressed students but the title went to my fellow classmate, Mthandazo Nxumalo.

Secondly, my political education has made it possible for me to see possibilities and, more importantly, build social capital and networks, which neither my siblings nor many of my peers have done.

My late brother Simon Maimela had similar social capital, which came as a result of being one of the most revered footballers in Mpumalanga, playing from primary school up to the semi-professional Vodacom League. Unlike me, however, he was not as consistently disciplined and, perhaps, was not as aggressively hopeful as I am. And yet at the same time, he faced different life and social pressures to me. As a result, his football talent, higher grades at school and social capital did not stand him in good stead and he was unsuccessful in realising his full potential, and his life stopped at the age of 31.

I want to suggest that it was here that I got to experience the intersection and coexistence of continuity and change. Whereas the new democratic space has opened opportunities for us to thrive the legacies of apartheid are holding some back. Generational poverty, broken families, unfortunate geographic location, and a lack of access to information and other infrastructure are great disablers.

Therefore, I want to argue that material conditions and the skewed structural nature of society can weigh heavily on the life of youngsters in the democratic South Africa to the extent that even the best among us do not realise their greatest potential. For instance, since primary school, I had the privilege of sharing a classroom with many A-grade students and yet some did not even make it to university; others could not get the financial-aid required to pursue their studies. In part, this is how increasing inequality between the races is produced and reproduced. I must note, however, that these students, carried by hope, determination and discipline, have not really fallen by the wayside of progress. But having been given better opportunities, they would be occupying top positions in today's South Africa as scientists, astronauts, accountants, teachers, doctors, lawyers, and successful businessmen and -women.

So, in the end, social stratification can really impact one's social mobility. Some succeed easily due to better opportunities, while others succeed against many odds, such as a lack of access to equal opportunities. The latter is rare and the former is common.

The struggle against cultural domination
As my material conditions of existence change for the better and I enter the ranks of the so-called 'black middle strata', I graduate from worrying about the basic necessities of life. The combination of this new status and my political education allows me to question how I am seen by others and, indeed, how I define myself as a South African, and, yes, as an African.

The question of who determines culture – ideas, beliefs, lifestyle, symbols, identity, language, values and norms – is as fundamental today as it was in the past. The colonisers understood that the colonisation process would not be complete without cultural domination and, as a consequence, Africans were made to believe that what is European is universal and, in our case, legal racism was used to determine who was human and who was not.

A number of examples typifying the struggle for self-definition come to mind. For instance, I find it unacceptable that there are bylaws prohibiting slaughtering an animal in my home yet when you live in the suburbs, neighbours (usually white and clearly a cultural majority) can disturb your right to cultural belief by setting police on you, simply because slaughtering a goat or a sheep is defined by them as 'animal cruelty'. Is there a kind way to kill an animal?

Poverty, ignorance and disease are killing many blacks daily in South Africa and yet there is no overwhelming outcry from a cultural majority (whites) to stop 'human cruelty'. Why is that? Is it because animal life is more important than human life?

Some of our fellow South Africans from the Far East who have been naturalised as citizens enjoy delicacies made from all sorts of 'pets'. Their humanity, culture and socialisation have made this possible; it is who they are and, as the saying goes, 'you are what you eat'. However, in democratic South Africa such cultures are frowned upon, isolated and outlawed just because to be human is to be European and to be un-European is to be savage.

Some of us have stopped cooking *mala mogodu* (tripe) just because the smell from the pot would be offensive to our white neighbours and it is considered backward to do so. Instead, we display our love of unhealthy fast foods from McDonald's, KFC or the nearest pizza place. At the same time, some of our people in townships see the opportunity to stay in suburbs as freedom and progress. Indeed, others are quite happy, once they settle in suburbs, to assimilate into white culture; they see this as expanding their freedom and opportunity.

Due to the legacies of apartheid, our identity as Africans is defined, written and told by literary scholars steeped in the prejudicial education that sought to define us as subjects of history and not makers of history and masters of our destiny. This is despite the fact that the struggle against colonialism was a process to reclaim our humanity, define ourselves and master our destiny. In our history books, this triumphant struggle to rehumanise ourselves – and those who oppressed us – does not receive adequate attention.

Those of us in the research space daily encounter a 'whiteness' that does not consider ideas from Africa, Latin America, the Caribbean or Asia as worthy of recognition, citing or using. This is why I have chosen to be a student for life, so that I can act as an agent to transform our culture and ensure that all cultures are given equal status under the sun.

Final thoughts
In this essay, I have sought to discuss three broad themes: democratic rights, my political economy and the struggle for cultural freedom. For

me, these three themes are interrelated. To the extent that I exercise my democratic rights, I do so within a given political economy, which can either be enabling or disabling, in the instance that it is disabling, my agency becomes important. The issue and theme of culture and access to opportunity illustrates the contradictory nature of change and the possibilities for self-realisation. Whereas I can use the democratic space to advance myself and others, I do so conscious of the fact that the odds are stacked against me – mine is not a life of easy access. Living in the suburbs has meant a different quality of life and yet it also means I have a choice: either submit to white culture or defy it. And I must say, in most instances, I choose to defy it and this is why I have moved from one suburb to another in search of myself in my own country. The question arises: should South African life be like suburban life or township life or a combination of both in a manner that appreciates the intercultural differences of a diverse society where all cultures and identities are treated equally?

This brings me to the false concept of 'born-frees'. I have always believed in the concept of 'total emancipation', where all shackles of oppression and exploitation are dismantled. So, to the extent that I speak of formal political freedom and 'enablers' thereof, I am free. But to the extent that I speak of 'disablers', I am not completely free and, therefore, *a luta continua* towards total emancipation. As a consequence, I am not a 'born-free' and neither are the youths born in 1994, the children of Mandela. The concept of 'born-frees' is ahistorical and misleading because it seeks to build a wall between the past and present realities, which are dialectically linked.

To me, freedom means to be fully human again, to live life and fulfil our cultural and creative rights without which we cannot know who we are. Freedom means being free from begging or struggling for basic human needs. I do not think human beings are meant to spend their lives on Earth struggling to live life. We are supposed to use nature to realise our full potential and talents in a manner that says we have not only existed but lived. And I believe for the majority of South Africans this is a goal they ought to work towards and achieve. But first, we all need to be enabled to realise our disablers and free ourselves from them. In other words, we need to be free to know what freedom is and how to pursue it.

In the end, freedom means being free to be fully human. To see yourself and be treated as a human being with equal rights and responsibilities. The right to be able to live your life free from oppression and exploitation. Indeed, to have human dignity. At a basic level it means freedom to live, have shelter, have food, have clothes and have access to education and information to exercise your responsibility to improve yourself, others and the world you live in.

With the death of President Mandela, the future beckons with some fundamental questions and tasks:

- No matter what we think of them, Mandela's generation cannot be faulted for their efforts to lead the struggle for freedom and delivering the freedom we enjoy today. In terms of the future waiting for us on the horizon, what should we do to advance the cause of freedom? Are we capable of changing our circumstances for the better, as the Mandela generation did?
- Are we worthy inheritors of their revolutionary legacy as freedom fighters? Can we lay claim to be born of their blood?

History recognises women and men, young and old, who in their lifetimes sought to change society systemically to improve the human condition. These men and women have, through their ideas and actions, sought to understand their own reality and the changes taking place in their times, and have sought to bring about a new reality.

That is what awaits us. Freedom is both a gift and a burden. Freedom was never free!

Realising a forbidden dream:
What freedom means to me

Penelope Makgati
Intern and post-graduate student

IT WAS THE REALISATION OF A dream that was once forbidden. It was the start of a new chapter in a book that was once deemed unthinkable. It was the source of a family's pride and joy. It was the pioneering act never before conceived. It was an epoch that was never to have a place in history. It was what I call the mother of experiences.

And this is the tale of an experience of mine that unfolded during 2013, the eve of our country's 20th year of democracy and the centenary of the Union Buildings. This tale will reveal why this act was so extraordinary, and the hopes and dreams birthed from this experience.

I once heard a saying that goes like this: 'Everyone wants to hear about the glory but nobody wants to hear about the story.' I think that there is so much truth in this. With that said, this is my cue to tell you how I came to work at the Union Buildings. Before you protest, let me assure you that this will not be a boring history lesson. On the contrary, I think it will leave you mentally and emotionally satisfied.

It all began during a period of waiting and great anticipation on my part. I was feeling disillusioned and fed up, to say the least, with how slow my life was going. Every morning I got up for my new job of 'standing' in the unemployment line with the rest of the 25.6% of jobless South Africans. Through each passing day I prayed for just one call to attend an interview. All the while I kept a glimmer of hope alive that I would receive *that* call from the Presidency. When the three-month deadline after the submission of my applications had finally lapsed, I conceded defeat. However, the little nagging voice within would not let me simply give up just like that. So I mustered up enough courage to call and enquire whether all the interviews had been completed. The woman who answered the phone confirmed that they had. As I put the phone down I decided to close this chapter of my journey and move on with my life.

Truth be told, I was not really expecting much from what seemed like a gambling affair. Here I was, an applicant in a sea of thousands of hopefuls who had also seen the internship advertisements in a national newspaper. Looking at it like this, I figured that it was almost like playing the lottery and this time was not my winning ticket.

The days after that were monotonous cycles of job hunting and freelancing here and there. I would come up with various dreams I wanted to fulfil, then I would return to the drawing board once again. Then, one fine day in May, an unknown number popped up on my phone. I answered the call and could not believe my ears. I recall asking the gentleman if perhaps he had called me accidently. This was after hearing that he was from the Presidency. I explained that I had called after the three-month deadline and had been told that the interviews had been completed. However, this gentleman was convinced that I was the person he intended to call and he invited me to an interview.

After the call, I was overwhelmed with mixed emotions. I pinched myself to make sure that I was not dreaming and realised that I truly had just been invited for an interview at the Union Buildings. Despite this being six months after the cut-off date. I even thought that it might have been a prank call, but this was dispelled by a confirmation email telling me that the interview would be held in three days' time. The email also mentioned that I would have to write a test. This was all happening so quickly!

Needless to say, on the day of the interview I donned my finest version of a formal outfit. It was a day of firsts for me: my first train ride to Pretoria and certainly my very first trip to the Union Buildings. Despite the bouts of excitement and the ball of nerves in my stomach, I knew that this could be a step closer to fulfilling my dreams.

The Gautrain was lightning fast and provided enough distractions as we left Johannesburg behind. When we finally reached the last station, I was a little unsure about getting to the bus terminal, but I simply followed the throngs of business people ahead of me. Thankfully, in the bus I met a kind lady who offered to tell me when we had arrived. The breathtaking sight of the Union Buildings required no introduction. Seeing it with my own eyes removed any doubts I might have held about its sheer grandeur and I stared at it in awe, like a child. That was short-lived as I quickly snapped back to reality and became the young professional I aimed to be.

I didn't realise that a steep 'long walk to freedom' awaited me. Thank goodness the kind woman from the bus advised me to swap my patent-leather heels for a pair of flat pumps. This little bit of wisdom saved me. Along the way, the woman told me that she had worked at the Presidency for the past decade. We spoke about her family. She told me she had lived and studied in Europe and the United States of America during her parents' years of exile. She was very impressive, but her warm smile and quiet demeanour spoke of her humility despite being so well travelled. My short interaction with her left me with a calm sense of someone who epitomised the African essence of 'botho' or 'ubuntu', which she evidently held dear to her no matter how far she had travelled.

To my surprise we had already reached the top of the stairs and found ourselves at the entrance to the majestic Union Buildings and I was once again awestruck. The patient lady once more brought me down to Earth by gently telling me to swap my flat shoes for my high heels, which I did and then boldly walked across the zebra crossing. I have to admit that at that moment I felt as though I had just been crowned Miss South Africa and was walking on the catwalk instead. I was overcome with an indescribable sense of patriotism and could not have felt more proudly South African than I did in those few minutes.

At the reception, the police told me where I had to go for the interview. However, I had taken it upon myself to be an early bird, so I had quite a bit of time to kill. I was given directions to the nearest shop where I could get something to drink since the walk had left me feeling rather thirsty. It was a lovely little walk to the shop and I had time to do some sightseeing, looking at the various embassies on either side of the road.

My walk back was not as smooth, however, given the steep incline. I decided that there was a lesson to be learnt from this part of my journey. It almost signified the long and arduous road to freedom in the regime change of our country from its hurtful and lonely apartheid past to a more inclusive democratic future. This glorious future was mine at that very moment. Here I could stand and embrace the embassies of 186 countries; I was in the capital city with more diplomatic representation than any other except Washington,

DC. This would have been unthinkable during the days of apartheid, when South Africa was rendered a pariah state and was the petulant stepchild of the international community.

It only truly dawns upon me now how great the gains of democracy have been for our country and, much closer to home, for me, as a young black woman afforded the opportunity to forge a career for myself. This memory of the proverbial walk up the mountain to the highest point in our capital city reminds me to be cognisant of those who came before me, who fought for me to have the right to freely take this walk. If I take a moment to page through history, I realise that it was exactly 100 years ago, in 1913, that the very first women's march against carrying pass books took place, in the city of Bloemfontein. I don't think that it is a coincidence that the march took place on the same day that I would be born many years later. And here I am, walking up the same path along which a multiracial group of courageous women marched against carrying pass books in 1956. Perhaps it also means that my walk will have its own place in history, even if it never finds a place in the great history books.

Once I finally reached the peak I was rewarded with that breath-taking view of the entire city of Pretoria. If such a thing as love at first sight exists, I would contend that it can be love at second sight too. The gardens are so immaculately manicured and the streets are squeaky clean. Upon my arrival back at reception I met another young woman who was also there for the same interview and we exchanged polite greetings and smiles in a warm and friendly South African manner. One of the guards walked us towards the West Wing. He asked us if it was our first visit to the Union Buildings. Clearly my marvelling must have given me away. The other woman said that she was actually here on the day that Mr Nelson Mandela was inaugurated as the first president of a democratic South Africa in 1994. She confessed that she does not remember much because she was very young at the time.

This revelation confirmed to me that she, too, had her own story and place in the history of our country's journey to democracy. The guard mentioned that he was also in awe of the place when he started working there. Just like that, another penny dropped for me as I realised that the three of us strangers were tied ever so intricately together in this moment because of our country's dawn of democracy. What a beautiful commonality we shared and yet this was the very intricacy the apartheid system sought to break by bringing separation to the people of this soil.

The interview
Our arrival at the West Wing was met with the golden inscriptions 'The Presidency' on the left and *'Die Presidensie'* on the right. This was a sure reminder that we were at the highest echelon of authority in our country. Once we had been through another security check, we were ushered into the waiting room where we met with the other two candidates. We introduced ourselves and started chatting. The wait added to the intensity of the moment until, finally, we were called to a rotation of the verbal and written components of the interview. To say that it was the most challenging interview I had undergone ever is a definite understatement. I had to think on my feet like I had never done before. The most interesting part was the verbal component. The fact that it took place in the suite of the deputy president was enough of a 'wow factor' for me and added just a tad to my nervousness. I will never forget how kind and gracious everyone who walked past me was. As I sat waiting for my turn in the grand corridor I was showered with more good luck messages and assuring smiles than I had ever received. Although these did not stop my heart from feeling like it would beat right out of my chest.

Despite it being a Friday everyone there was dressed in full formal attire. I figured that they really meant business. When my turn finally came, I was ushered into a boardroom with an all-male panel of four; I was literally the only skirt at the table. I had a fleeting thought of how democracy had the potential to bring about change in terms of gender equality at this table. The main interviewer greeted me and apologised for the fact that there was no other female representation present. I think that my head spun a little when he mentioned that they had received 300 applications for this particular post, which they narrowed down to 30, and finally shortlisted the four of us.

However, he emphasised that they would be hiring only *one* person for the job. If I thought that the competition was tough during the first round, well then I certainly had to think again. True to form, this round was also very difficult. I truly felt as though I was in a one-woman show. By the end of that long day I had so much on my mind. Even if I never returned, that day's memories and lessons would have been worth cherishing for a lifetime.

A month and a half of waiting went by with no word from them. Each day and night I waited for *that* call. I decided that even bad news was better than no news at all. My hopes were lifted for a time when they called and asked me to submit more information. When a long period of silence followed, I resigned myself to leaving my fate in God's hands.

The call

Then one day I received a call, and not just any call. It was *that* call – that much anticipated one. I finally received the news that I had got the job. In a moment of utter shock, I asked the gentleman whether he was pulling my leg. He laughed a little and confirmed that he was indeed serious. I honestly felt as though I had won some grand prize. I shared this news with only a select group of people, who had been praying for me throughout what seemed like an endless season of waiting. Only once I had signed on the dotted line a few days later did I make it public to everyone else via email. To my surprise, some of my family members cried. It was as though that little email had gone viral from the reactions of joy I received.

My first few weeks on the job still felt surreal. The most surreal moment was when I first met the deputy president. I do not consider myself to be a groupie but that day I certainly felt as though I had a groupie moment.

I believe that I have learnt some of the best life lessons yet from this internship. If anything, it has been my living metaphor of our country's democratic journey. The mere fact that I, a young black woman, am able to work at the Presidency is a miracle in itself given that once upon a time, being a black woman was seen to be the biggest burden. I am proud that our democracy has enabled and empowered not only black women, but women in general. However, I am also very aware that utopia has not yet been reached in a mere 19 years. As we inch ever closer to the 20-year mark, I am constantly reminded of the hurdles we continue to encounter as a society. I see the hurt and hopelessness in the eyes of the many children orphaned and abandoned due to AIDS. The disappointments of the jobless and educated youth are as real to me as the many who keep waiting for better tomorrows. The levels of violence and crime that almost imprison the free in their own homes, through fear of being the next negative statistic, are a threat to our democracy.

The challenges we continue to face are also a testament to the resilience of our people and their strong will to not remain downtrodden. Personally, it is the influence of my maternal grandmother, Florence Manamela Makgati, that has taught me the value of a good work ethic and to never give up. My grandmother, or Mma Rainy as she is affectionately known in her community, has been a pillar of strength not only as the matriarch of our family but also as a community leader. She has donned many hats in her life and has been a mother and grandmother to more than her own nine children. Her compassion knows no bounds, as she started a crèche, free of charge, for the children of the Mazista community in North West. She did not stop there, after being widowed in 1994 and losing one of her sons to an untimely death in 2006, she was elected as a ward councillor. This proved just how adamant she was to take on any challenge. She was one of the oldest members of the community, yet not even age could deter this strong woman. She went on to successfully serve her full tenure of five years as a tough yet compassionate councillor.

I was very encouraged by my grandmother's no-nonsense attitude and big heart for social justice. Here was a woman who had been a herd girl and a domestic worker, who had had limited opportunities to pursue a formal education, but still she chose to rise above all these obstacles.

As Maya Angelou, the American poet and author of the book *I Know Why the Caged Bird Sings* (1969), teaches us:

> We must always be intolerant of ignorance but understanding of illiteracy; that some people, who were unable to go to school, are more educated and more intelligent than college professors, and ... that we should listen carefully to what ordinary people have for generations called 'mother-wit' because in those homely sayings is couched the collective wisdom of generations.

My grandmother undoubtedly possesses the 'mother-wit' spoken of here and I have been privileged enough to reap from this. I know that although my grandmother did not have the opportunity to receive the education I did, she ensured that her children had the best so they could do the same for their children. So I do not take lightly the opportunities that have come my way. Living in a democratic country has also afforded me the quality education and employment that my grandmother could only have dreamt of while growing up under the apartheid regime.

The legacies of the past, unfortunately, continue to haunt the present democratic era. This was evident in the difficulties my grandmother faced as a councillor. One sad case in particular was the shooting and killing of four black people in the informal settlement of Skierlik in 2008. The perpetrator of the crimes was the then 18-year-old Johan Nel from the neighbouring town of Swartruggens.

This tragic incident made headlines nationally and it shocked the Rainbow Nation to its core. It is tragic incidents such as these that leave a tear in the social fabric of our country. This illustrates how much of a long way there is still to travel in the post-apartheid era. It is the responsibility of individuals and the government to ensure that real and positive change is witnessed by all. It all truly begins with quiet self-leadership.

I realised the sheer strength that lies in a gentle and self-controlled leader the day I met the deputy president, Mr Kgalema Motlanthe. It went something like this:

It was so surreal.

I'm still trying to take it all in.

I was the only female at the table.

There were five of us in total.

I sat right next to him.

He epitomises the *consummate gentleman*!

He took my hand into both of his upon greeting me.

Hugged me, to which I was taken aback.

Then he said the words, 'Welcome, my dear,' in that compassionate fatherly manner.

We listened to jazz in the background.

Despite the good ambiance I could not shake off the shadow of the fact that the very same day marked the tragic anniversary of the Marikana shootings. The television displayed the politics of commemoration that took place as the various parties wanted to claim the event as their own.

This claimant paled in comparison to Mr Mandela's three days of lying in state. I had never witnessed so many people in one place than at that time. It was humbling to see fellow South Africans come and pay their last respects. However, what we are to remember is that we walk in the footsteps of Mandela and are charged with the responsibility of making our country a better place for future generations. May we not betray the gains of our hard-fought liberation.

While reminiscing on this moment during the train ride home, I remembered these words: 'She dined with queens and kings but she never forgot what was in her own fridge.'

God brought me here and I will not forget the journey he has travelled with me thus far.

Conclusion

The lessons that I have learnt during this short period, attest to the fact that democracy has been playing itself out throughout my life. The experience of this internship is merely a chapter from a long tale, not only of my own life but also that of South Africa's. I count myself privileged to have my personal story woven into the tapestry of this nation's story about attaining freedom. I am also aware that there is still a long way to go to achieve a truly better life for all. This means that the future should look far brighter than the present. Engaging the youth on matters of unemployment and where they fit into the country is a start. The current buzz word on the streets is the National Development Plan; ordinary South Africans should be discussing this and deciding for themselves if they see the benefits of it and a prosperous future. The bottom line is that we need to take charge of our freedom and allow it to work for us. I for one am ready to embrace democracy not just for myself but for my fellow South Africans too. Here's to the next 20 years.

The black middle class: Food for thought on goodness and greed

Evan Mantzaris
Academic

WHEN I CALLED MY UNCLE IN Kuilsriver and told him I wanted to do a doctorate at the University of Cape Town, his first question was, 'Why now son? All the Greeks are flying back to the Motherland. They are scared. Don't you read what's happening in Soweto?' 'That's why I want to come, uncle,' was my answer.

It was late 1976 when I made the call and I did not expect him to understand. He was not a political being in the strict sense of the word. He was a 7–Eleven cafe owner in Cape Town. His first claim to fame in the Greek community was that he was the first Greek child to be baptised in Saint Georgi's, the newly-built Greek Orthodox Church in Mountain Road, Woodstock, in Cape Town in 1905. His second was that one of the most frequent customers in his modest cafe was one Chris Heunis, a leading National Party politician and Minister of Home Affairs for many years. Having such well-connected uncles, it was not difficult for a political renegade like me to secure a student visa.

My Uncle Kyriakos was three years old in 1906 when the Greek and black cigarette makers went on a wage strike against Polikanski, the biggest cigarette manufacturer in Cape Town. He told me he remembered it very vividly. Typical Mantzaris!

South Africa has been exceptional to me in almost all aspects: personally, politically, intellectually and socially (let us not go into the financial part – depressing). It opened my eyes to things I had hardly experienced: naked racism, state brutality, temporary imprisonment, immense material wealth and even more extreme poverty, but also deep and lasting friendships, outright opportunism and betrayal, the flourishing of mediocrity and laziness, the kingdoms of arrogance, affection, love and forgiveness (without forgetting the suspensions with full pay).

I have travelled throughout this stunning reality called South Africa a few times, from the richness of Limpopo to the deepness of Jozini and from the historical ruins of the Northern Province to the ancient myths of the Lusikisiki forest in the Eastern Cape (or what is left of it). I was never bred to be a hard- or soft-core nationalist, but my love for South Africa and its people is as deep as my affection for everything that makes me grow as a person, a citizen and a human being.

For me, the stark realities awaiting us during the transition started with the celebrations for the victory of the 1995 Rugby World Cup led by the most revered president in the world's political history. The victory was of significance, but I am still amazed at how many millions of people who celebrated the event are ignorant of the fact that, in the same year, a man named Jerry Skosana scored an equally historic goal, crowning the legendary Orlando Pirates FC as Pan-African champions. At least we did celebrate this victory in Lamontville, the home of a man called Bheki.

Ah! Lamontville, daughter of my sorrow, home of the poor and the Mpisanes! Memories; double standards; skewed memory; Rainbow Nation; all of the above or none?

The most popular TV show in Lamont in those days was *Who Wants to be a Millionaire?* It was more popular than *Generations* and *Laduma* put together. When the boys were on a high they used to shout loudly, like the heroic days of the 1983–1987 and beyond, 'Who wants to be a millionaire?' In fact, the question on everyone's lips was (and still is), who doesn't want to be a millionaire?

It is puzzling, therefore, that no serious published and established sociologist, psychologist, anthropologist or economist seems to have tried to dissect scientifically the dialectical/logical/rational/evident relationship between the ever-increasing expansion of the black African middle class and corruption. The May 2013 final report of the Unilever Institute of Strategic Marketing says the black middle class is now 4.2 million strong, up from 1.7 million in 2004. It has been called by marketers an 'emerging class' and is a boon to the growing economy.

I strongly feel that, despite the fact that I have a great admiration for the Unilever Institute, I did some of my own research, and I discovered something really staggering, empirically speaking that is: in one of her responses to a relevant question in Parliament, the Honourable Minister Lindiwe Sisulu provided the empirical answer to Unilever's statistical discovery: South Africa has 34 ministers, 33 deputy ministers, 159 directors-generals, 642 deputy directors-general, 2 501 chief directors and 7 782 directors. During the first quarter of 2013, 44 000 public servants were appointed, bringing their number to 3.07 million, or 22.6% of the total labour force in the country. This is close to the total number of the 'emerging class'.

It is not difficult to assume that a large majority of the members of the new emerging class are involved in mental (as opposed to manual) labour. They are, thus, well educated, skilled and experienced enough to deal with the challenges of their profession. They are the government's new public management 'knowledge capital'.

Yet, according to the latest Report of the Auditor-General, public services spent nationally on consultants R102 billion from 2008 to 2011.

The rest in the emerging class are most likely entrepreneurs, or those who aspire to join the ranks of this strongly supported social entity. They have had, and still have, ample supporters, such as the National Development Youth Agency (NYDA), Umsobomvu Youth Fund before them, commercial banks, Department of Trade and Industry (DTI) agencies, Development Bank, municipal managers, directors-general, mayors, heads of procurement and supply-chain logistics. In fact, the sky is the limit.

Talking about millions, it has been admitted that the Unilever Institute is a top-class unit and the University of Cape Town (UCT) is in the 500 top universities in the world, according to the Shanghai rating scales, read by the country's vice chancellors and their personal assistants before they find their place in the pre-paid extravagantly priced advertisements in the Friday and Sunday weeklies (with the exception of the *Sunday World* and the *Sunday Sun*).

In fact, one of the country's universities declared in a full-page advertisement in the Friday and Sunday weekly press that it was 'voted' the No. 1 university on the African continent. A major achievement one would say, above UCT, Stellenbosch, Wits, Pretoria, Walter Sisulu and Unisa. One could assume that these full-page advertisements were truly justified and rubber-stamped by the university's council, as its businesswoman chair's signature was evident at the bottom of the page.

Then, three months later, when some 'official' rating results were announced, the same university was placed fifth in the country. One would expect silence and quiet, even shame, but no. This university placed new advertisements celebrating its excellence. What can one call such actions? Double standards? Misplaced grandeur? A high degree of self-satisfaction or, perhaps, corruption?

I say it all depends on what angle one uses to balance and weight things. In 2005, while I was doing research in a district municipality it was discovered that in a labour force of 260, 46 were operating in an acting capacity, some of them for over three or four years. A few of them were in senior positions. One thinks, well, it happens. However, when one discovers that all were receivers of an 'acting allowance' fluctuating between R6 000 and R14 000 per month (hopefully taxed), one's thoughts change and the questions come up fast and furious: Does it pay to be in an active capacity? How much? Is it legal? What do the municipality's legal eagles say? Nothing, perhaps because they are there in an 'acting' capacity? What would the DA say? Perhaps nothing because a number of these acting administrators are their members. Finally, what about the municipal manager and the chief financial officer? They are also acting.

This might sound like a Loyiso Gola midnight performance, but it happens and is well-documented. To study corruption one needs to know the essence of sociology. It is not really necessary to study the subject because I have met enough people in all walks of life that have a very deep understanding of the sociological and political, as well as the financial, dimensions of corruption.

Such knowledge and understanding is as easy as an Economics 1 student understanding the theft of billions of British pounds in the 'Libor scam'. Some of the 91 Libor banks colluded in lying about the rates they were obtaining, thus manipulating not only the Libor rate but also all derivative contracts and the credit rates for businesses and families alike. This went on for years. Barclays, Citigroup, JP Morgan Chase, Bank of America, Deutsche Bank, HSBC, Credit Suisse, UBS, Société Generalé, Credit Agricole and the Royal Bank of Scotland were involved in criminal behaviour, resulting in millions of families being issued mortgages at incorrect rates. Many had to leave their homes, while others were evicted because they could not pay artificially manipulated interest rates. And once again the authorities charged with overseeing the operation of the markets turned a blind eye to this crime. No one has been prosecuted; instead they are glorified by the BBC, CNN, The Voice of America and Sky News.

Yet, after the US sub-prime financial crisis in 2007 and the crises in Greece and Cyprus, it was not the poor victims of corruption, fraud and greed that were taken care of after the respective 'bail-outs'. It was the perpetrators, the banks that were recapitalised in the name of 'development'. People were not bailed out, the banks were.

In our case, the gogo in Madadeni is most likely to be ignorant of the 'Big Five' collusion in the construction tenders or the 'bread syndicate conspiracy' of some years ago when the corrupt companies made billions by colluding in the price fixing, or the King's case, or the Fidentia tragicomedy, or JCI, or African Dawn, or Alliance Mining, or Tigon (which authorities have been trying to prosecute), or Pinnacle Point, or a wide variety of pyramid schemes.

However, the gogo can explain how a senior municipal councillor can drive around in a new Mercedes Compressor or marry six wives at one time (before he gets suspended for corrupt practices). When Marx wrote in *On the Jewish Question*, 'Who is the God? Money', little did he know that 20 years after the historic first democratic elections in South Africa, the dictum could be changed to: 'Who is the God? Cash!' Cash is god in such transactions for a number of reasons but primarily because one's salary is taxed – cash just changes hands.

Sections of South Africa's emerging black middle class are asking for more – more from the government, more from the service providers and more from the companies that market to them, not necessarily in that order.

It is very interesting to note that it is only the public services that face the wrath and ridicule of the press, even when untested, speculative, false and derogatory 'reports' fill columns upon columns so the press can boost its decreasing revenue base. The billions upon billions of rands gained as a result of corrupt practices are accompanied by a half-hearted apology: 'Sorry, we were wrong', and the loss of 5% of the giant profits as a monetary compensation. No punishment, no trial, no jail. There are so many beautiful anti-corruption laws, regulations, international agreements signed, but still those who committed the sins associated with the dictum of 'maximisation of profits' (by any means necessary), mostly go unnoticed, unpunished, free to hit again, following religiously the immortal words of Michael Douglas's Gordon Gekko in the movie *Wall Street*: 'Greed is good.'

Those who vilify the greed and corruption of the public servants seem to reserve their venom for public media forums, popular blogs and radio stations. They seem forgetful of the wise dictum, 'it takes two to tango', as almost every single corruption case is based on the insidious 'exchange value' of the 'private–public partnership' at work. The 'private' equation of the partnerships is equally, if not more, guilty of corruption and, in the final analysis, is more likely to 'escape' the law if (or when) the political or administrative partner is suspended with full pay and resigns after waiting two years for a disciplinary inquiry to begin or gets another similar job in some other department, municipality or state entity.

Some researchers and analysts have blamed the problems facing all layers of government structures on the 'administrative–political conundrum'. Of course, it is a major problem in many entities, but it all depends on the way in which one looks at it.

Recent empirical evidence, however, points to the fact that this is not the case, at least in some cases. The 'fights' between a municipal manager, one or two (or more) senior councillors and/or the mayor depend, in most instances, on power relations – but not always.

Take the case of a large municipality that, on more than one occasion, has won the prestigious award as the 'best run municipality in the country'. In a recent report it emerged that in the same municipality there were ten councillors who operated companies that conducted business with the municipality, in contravention of the Code of Conduct for Councillors and the Municipal Systems Act. The mayor unlawfully influenced a tender for a waste volume reduction plant at a landfill site worth R3 billion; the municipal manager contravened the Prevention and Combating of Corrupt Activities Act by not reporting fraudulent and corrupt activities contained in an official report; seven contracts of senior managers reporting directly to the city manager were not renewed but they continued to be employed at the municipality in contravention of section 57 of Act 32; three contractors involved in a R24 million housing rehabilitation programme were issued with appointment letters even before they submitted appropriate documents, and 161 municipal employees were doing direct business with the municipality.

The latest report of the Auditor-General of South Africa indicated, among other things, that 50% of Free State government tenders were issued to government employees or families of politicians; municipal officials and their families have pocketed more than R800 million of taxpayers' money through the awarding of tenders at various municipalities around the country; and only 13 municipalities in the whole country have 'good books'.

These are possibly instances that prompted the country's president to say on 26 June 2012: 'We must cleanse ourselves of alien tendencies. Among the ills we must eliminate are corruption, abuse of power and lack of discipline, that are contrasting with the party's historic values of selflessness, honesty and sacrifice.'

Related to corruption are the brutal killings of senior political cadres and honest officials and activists who have paid with their lives for their honesty and struggle against greed, fraud and avarice.

The case of Moss Phakoe in North West is a case in point. He compiled a dossier on corruption related to the outsourcing of a municipality-owned resort and handed it to then Minister of Cooperative Governance. The then mayor was implicated in the corruption and Phakoe was killed a few days after blowing the whistle. The mayor was recently convicted of the murder, along with his bodyguard, an MK veteran. Despite his being convicted and jailed in Rooigrond Prison in Mafikeng, it has been reported and not disputed that the mayor was still receiving a monthly salary of R357 000.

The fact that Phakoe was a cadre of a liberation movement was not the reason for his untimely death – what killed him was that he was an honest cadre – a whistle-blowing cadre.

In the whistle-blower pantheon of dead that should serve as a reminder to everyone, one needs to acknowledge the assassinations that took place in Mbombela municipality in Mpumalanga, where former Mbombela speaker, Jimmy Mohlala, and provincial official, Samuel Mpatlanyane, were both gunned down in 2009 after they sought to expose collusion between political leaders and construction industry players in the building of the Mbombela Stadium.

On many occasions it has become evident that access to political power is no longer an end in itself, but has been transformed into a money-making scheme of pyramid proportions, where the battle for political power and the battle for money are sides of the same coin – inextricably linked. Political power leads to avarice and access to money – the new God.

These realities in South Africa today confirm almost to the last iota Marx's treatise of corruption to be found in his *Economic and Philosophical Manuscripts of 1844*, in which he described the ways in which money and its pursuit distorts men and women. He described how material wealth possesses humans and turns their strengths into weaknesses, and assets into liabilities. Money constitutes a profound form or instrument of untruth, he wrote. It is the ultimate deceiver, the greatest liar, for it has the capacity to transform that which is, into that which is not, and vice versa. In the case of corruption, however, money is the great instrument of truth, at least potentially. It is the most tangible sign of some ill-gotten gain, of some illicit or criminal activity. That is why its possessor must go to such lengths to hide it, by hoarding or laundering it. Or only accept cash for services.

In South Africa today, the state is the midwife through which large sections of the middle class are born and the state becomes the main access point through which corrupt public officials and greedy entrepreneurs find fertile soil to grow their wishes for a better life for themselves and their families.

Throughout the years I have been a very regular reader of South African Communist Party (SACP) literature, even from the time of the *African Communist*, which was filled with the wisdom of legendary theorists and practitioners, such as Comrade Mzala, Peter Mayibuye and Dialego. In those days and more recently no one has paid attention to the significant warnings on corruption by one of the leaders of the Russian Revolution. One of Lenin's classics, *State and Revolution*, pays serious attention to the potential and historical feature of 'the direct corruption of officials' in capitalist societies, prophesying, in one way or another, the same in a post-revolutionary Russia.

Of course, such positions can be understood because after the collapse of the Provisional Government in 1917, the Communist Party, following its ascendancy to power, saw its membership increasing dramatically and party discipline diminishing, especially among state officials. Simultaneously, the first signs of corruption and greed became evident in the process. Such realities led Lenin to declare publicly, to both the party and society at large, that bureaucracy and corruption would threaten the future of the first socialist experiment.

Now, that particular work has been understood and misunderstood by many, including many South African members, theorists and leaders of the SACP. I have not detected among their writings quotes from Lenin's final works, the *Testament* and *Better Fewer, But Better*. In these, the fear of existing and impeding corruption are evident, together with a number of suggested important steps to fix corruption, such as the empowerment of the state planning committee's legislative powers, the changing of the nationalities policy that had been implemented by Stalin, and more democratisation.

These steps, coupled with the adoption of the New Economic Policy, show Lenin's commitment to toning down some of his earlier, more radical ideas. This, because he was ready and eager to fight corruption, which, in *Better Fewer, But Better*, is described as follows: 'We have been bustling for five years trying to improve our state apparatus, but it has been mere bustle, which has proved useless in these five years, or even futile, or even harmful.'

The South African revolution has produced an ever-increasing, predominantly black African middle class and has simultaneously widened inequalities. This has been acknowledged by key government figures, as well as in the product of the blood, sweat and tears of around 30 wise and highly-educated persons who produced the long and detailed, as well as contested, National Development Plan (NDP), now rubber-stamped by Cabinet and the ruling party as official policy. Chapter 14 of the massive document has some blueprint solutions on corruption.

Yet the government did enact and implement 16 laws, official rules and regulations, and introduce 17 widely diversified institutions to fight corruption, including Chapter 9 entities. These are extremely detailed and thorough. The NDP accepts that they have not worked. No reasons are provided.

The South African transition and the theory and practice of the National Democratic Revolution are still going through a process, if we still believe the May 1968 theorists' powerful slogan, 'be realistic, strive for the impossible'. This transition has been given a variety of names – the 'deferred revolution', the 'first transition', the 'second transition', the 'second phase of the transition' and some others of secondary importance.

The transition has led to two distinct but interrelated realities: an emerging new class of public service professional and existing and aspirant entrepreneurs, and a dissipation of national consciousness that is much deeper and more painful than celebrating Bafana

Bafana's Bongani Khumalo's second goal against France in the 2010 World Cup, but then defending it for 28 minutes instead of attacking for a third goal that would have led us to the second round.

The prophets of the African revolutions, from Thomas Sankara to Oliver Tambo and from Patrice Lumumba to Samora Machel, are gone. Most cadres in the new generations of the emerging classes cannot even spell their names, let alone learn their lessons. The late Claude Ake's 1978 prophetic *Revolutionary Pressures in Africa* is out of print, but second-hand copies are available through Amazon.com. It is worth a read.

One of its key conclusions is: The revolution will be televised (as in Polokwane and Mangaung).

Looking back to understand the present and the future

Ntongela Masilela
Bangkok-based scholar

Backdrop

THIS OCCASION OF THE 20TH ANNIVERSARY of the first democratic elections in 1994, which brought into being majority rule for the first time in the history of the nation, under the leadership of the African National Congress (and its associated partners) and Nelson Mandela (in partnership with formidable intellectuals and outstanding political leaders), gives me an opportunity to reflect on my unforgettable awakening when I returned to the country for the first time in 2004 since my departure with my mother and three younger brothers in 1962 to join my father in 'voluntary exile' in Los Angeles.

While I could have returned in February 1990 when Nelson Mandela (1918–2013) was released from a 27-year political imprisonment and all the national political organisations were unbanned, my 42-year absence can be partly explainable by my wish to justify my extended absence, as a 'child of exiles', by educating myself about the nation's intellectual and cultural heritage.

This hopefully unending acquisition of knowledge through reading and analysis led me to the idea of the New African Movement. Although this concept of an *alternative* cultural and intellectual paradigm of the constitutive or constituted nature of South Africanness – in opposition to the hegemonic one that had been imposed by segregationist and apartheid regimes – was the outcome of the archival research I had started in Los Angeles in 1995, it really began with the extended conversations I had had with major South African writers between the 1970s and 1990s, such as Mazisi Kunene (1930–2006) in Los Angeles, (West) Berlin and London, with Lewis Nkosi (1936–2010) in Warsaw, Seattle and Basel, and with Ezekiel Mphahlele (1919–2008) in Denver, Los Angeles and Lebowakgomo.

What came as a shocking *revelation* to me on my first visit in 2004 was being informed that the Soweto Uprising of 1976 had originated and was concentrated in Orlando West, specifically at Orlando West High. I had played there when I was 10 and 12 in the late 1950s and early 1960s on the site of the Hector Pietersen Museum at 8288 Maseko Street (located at the spot where Hector Pietersen was killed by the military forces of apartheid) now adjacent to Uncle Tom's Hall. I also learnt that students from Thulasizwe Primary School, where I had studied in the early 1960s, had participated in this historic event that completely changed South African history.

Formative years

For nearly 30 years, I had assumed that the Soweto Uprising had occurred in the Mofolo and Moroka and Jabavu areas of Soweto, which in my youthful recollection were relatively poor areas, so as an adult I presumed that this is where a revolution would foment. Certainly not Orlando West, which even in my youth I could see was a middle class area by apartheid standards, distinct from Pimville, which in those days was an evidently poverty-stricken area because it was a slum filled with shacks. Of course, Orlando West itself could not compare to Dube, which was comparatively palatial – this was clear even to an 11-year-old boy. By 2004 the class distinction between Orlando West and Dube was not so drastic because history had changed many things by then.

Two observations are in order here: although the New African Movement was already online by 2004, I posted it only after seven years of debating whether it was of any importance to my country and deserving of being posted; the encounter with my youthful history instructed me that one does know one's history in a visceral way. Although I had presumed until my homecoming that this project was predominantly an intellectual and historical exercise, this confrontation with my boyhood history led me to an awareness that it was also historically *experiential* in that I had seen the Manhattan Brothers, the Ink Spots, and Dorothy Masuka (1935–) perform at Uncle Tom's Hall, and they were all part of the Sophiatown Renaissance, the last intellectual constellation of the New African Movement. But I had also witnessed the making of the New African Movement through the appropriation of New Negro modernity in the United States. What I had understood in adulthood to be a purely theoretical study turned out to embedded in my boyhood experiences.

Even though I'm still somewhat surprised that the Soweto Uprising sprang from my boyhood neighbourhood, when one examines the political, cultural and intellectual geography of the 1950s, within a five-kilometre radius of Uncle Tom's Hall (named after the anti-slavery novel *Uncle Tom's Cabin* [1852] by the American novelist Harriet Beecher Stowe), one notices the names of the major figures of the New African Movement who resided here. On the same block as my old home at 8273 Maseko Street, the corner house belonged to Ezekiel Mphahlele; in the same street but on the other side of the major road from Orlando West to Orlando East, lived Zephania Lekoane Mothopeng (1913–90) – three or four streets down from my house. In the direction of Orlando East, was the house of Nelson (1918–2013) and Winnie Mandela (1934–) on Vilakazi Street.

Later, after we had gone to the United States, Bishop Desmond Tutu (1931–) also took up residence on Vilakazi Street. Which other street in Africa, or for that matter in the word, has produced two Nobel Peace Prize winners? Across another major road going to Orlando East from Orlando West was the residence of Walter (1912–2003) and Albertina Sisulu (1918–2011) in Phomolong.

Across several major roads in Mzimhlope was the residence of Lillian Ngoyi (1911–80). In Dube across the hill separating it from Orlando West was the new residence of Alfred Bitini Xuma (1893–1962), who practically singlehandedly revolutionised the political imagination of the African National Congress in the years 1940 to 1949, but tragically ran afoul of the radical demands on the newly formed African National Congress Youth League (ANCYL).

Although for sure other major figures who resided in Orlando West have been unintentionally elided in this quick listing, an inescapable conclusion seems to emerge: in the 1950s, while Sophiatown was the centre of the cultural maelstrom of New African modernity, Orlando West was arguably, especially conjointly with Orlando East – the central political mind of this newly emergent modernity. This characterisation of Orlando West would seem to be confirmed by it having incubated the 1976 Soweto Uprising – which indicated that the interregnum, as presciently postulated by Nadine Gordimer (1924–) in a *New York Review of Books* article (January 1983), would be coming to an end much quicker than many had anticipated expected.

Induction in the New African Movement

As indicated earlier, it was only later in Los Angeles, after my 2004 first visit home, that I realised, when I was conceptually constructing the ideational notion of the New African Movement from archival materials, that what I had seen on the stage in Uncle Tom's Hall with my *own eyes* and heard with my *own ears* in the 1950s was a major narrative of South African cultural history: the transmission lines of modernistic experiences through musical forms. Practically every boy or girl, even as young as ten or 12, in Soweto, particularly in Orlando West, knew that you had to look in the direction of New York in order to move with the times or be hip, not in the direction of Paris, let alone London.

The sneakers one craved on Eloff Street or the film *The Street With No Name* (1948) with Richard Widmark, told us that one had to reside in the United States in order to move with the times: the Sophiatown Renaissance reinforced this message. *

Given the possible simultaneity between the founding of the ANCYL in 1944 and the residences of the Sisulus and the Mandelas in Orlando West, albeit in different zones, retrospectively it makes sense that this part of Soweto was to be the centre of the coalescence of dynamic political forces that three decades later exploded in the form of the Soweto Uprising. Given also that the principal ideologue Anton Lembede (1914–1947) of the Youth League lived in Orlando East, not too far from Donaldson Community Centre, where some of its meetings took place, lends plausibility – which was to seem logical after the events of 1976 – that these two zones were the centrifugal centre of the metaphysical forces of African nationalism that had seemingly been defeated in the tragedy of the Sharpeville massacre of 1960.

Not more than 15 minutes from the Mandelas' home was the residence of Zeph Mothopeng, who was one of the principal founders of the Pan Africanist Congress (PAC) in 1959. I remember

---

* In parenthesis: two recent brilliant books, Pascale Casanova's *The World Republic of Letters* (2004) and Alain Badiou's *The Adventure of French Philosophy* (2012), convincingly argue, respectively, that Paris was the capital of the whole world in the 19th and 20th centuries in arbitrating matters of cultural modernity, and that French philosophy in the second half of the 20th century can be compared to only two other periods in the history of Western culture – the ancient Greek philosophers from Parmenides to Aristotle and the German Enlightenment from Immanuel Kant to Karl Marx.

the short distance between the Mothopengs' (Mrs Mothopeng was a good friend of my mother's before our departure) and the Mandelas' from my happy boyhood days in Soweto. The founding of the Pan Africanist Congress and the African National Congress Youth League was a new permutation and reconfiguration of African nationalism that originated from the launching of the manifesto of the Ethiopian Movement by Bishop Mangena Maake Mokone (1851–1930) in 1892.

The Ethiopian Movement, which founded African (black) Christian Churches separate from European (white) Christian Churches, created the first major ideological split between those Africans who endorsed it, like James Dwane (1848–1915) and Isaac Williams Wauchope (1845–1917), and those who opposed it, such as John Langalibalele Dube (1871–1946) and John Tengo Jabavu (1859–1921). Although Ethiopianism was historic in articulating the elementary forms of African nationalism (Africanism), this African philosophy of modernity was subsequently postulated in a form of binarism: of *exclusivity* versus *inclusivity*. This ideological conflict was one of the major political dramas of South African history in the 20th century: the defeat of the Marxism of *revolutionary modernisers* by the exclusive nationalism of the *conservative modernisers* in the 1930s; the defeat of Josiah Tshangana Gumede (1873–1947) for the leadership of the ANC by Pixley ka Isaka Seme (1880–1951) (founder of the organisation) in this decade; the founding of the ANCYL in 1944; the prolonged exchange of brilliant, but very bitter, letters between Albert Luthuli (1898–1967) and Jordan Kush Ngubane (1917–1985) in the pages of *Indian Opinion* in 1956; the splintering of the PAC from the ANC in 1959; the founding of the Black Consciousness Movement (BCM) by Steve Bantu Biko (1946–1977) in 1972; and the recurrent expulsions of Africanists from the ANC during the 'exile period' or interregnum period', were all part of this singular narrative.

In my beloved Orlando West neighbourhood, the houses of Mandela and Mothopeng were spatially close to each other but philosophically and politically they were distant and unbridgeable; perhaps it was on Robben Island that a rapprochement was made possible. This whole dialectical conflict between the exclusive and the inclusive has momentarily been put into historical closure by the historic elections of 1994, in which the ANC won 66% of the popular vote and the PAC only 3%. But is this closure real?

The one person who retrospectively represents for me the cultural splendour of Orlando West in those bygone days of the 1950s is Ezekiel Mphahlele. Since he left South Africa with his family for Nigeria in September 1957 in self-imposed exile because of his uncompromising opposition to the introduction of Bantu Education, I must have been aware of him between the ages of eight and nine years, given that I was born on 9 December 1948. What I remember most about Mphahlele in those days is that, like my father, he always wore a white shirt with a tie. My father, Albert Magija Masilela (1912–1968), was as an industrial sociology researcher for the Anglo American Corporation, having obtained a BA degree from Fort Hare University sometime in the 1940s.

My father left South Africa for the United States in 1958 on the invitation of Melville Herskovits to pursue further studies at Northwestern University in Evanston, Illinois. He subsequently moved to the University of California in Los Angeles (UCLA) to pursue doctoral studies. My mother and three younger brothers joined him in 1962. Upon his obtaining his doctorate in 1965, the whole family moved to Nairobi, Kenya. In Nairobi my father renewed his friendship with Mphahlele, who had moved there from Paris in 1963. The two exiled families interacted closely for a year before the Mphahleles moved to the University of Denver in 1966 in order for Mphahlele to pursue a doctoral degree. He subsequently taught at that university and later moved to teach at the University of Pennsylvania, where he met the brilliant African American literary scholar, Houston A. Baker. In 1969 I returned to UCLA to pursue my university studies. Having obtained my doctoral degree in Sociology in 1977, in 1979 I returned to Kenya to rejoin my mother and brothers.

But back to my perception and 'understanding' of the great man in Orlando West in the 1950s. As indicated earlier, though by the age of nine I was aware of the distinctiveness that Mphahlele symbolised and represented on Maseko Street a few years before the cataclysmic events of 1960, for obvious reasons I was not aware that his immaculateness and demeanour represented a particular articulation of *modernity*. An appreciative article written at this time by Can Themba (1924–1967), just before Mphahlele departed to Nigeria, celebrated his achievement of obtaining, through correspondence, an MA degree from the University of South Africa (Unisa) as an indication of both his scholarly seriousness and the literary culture of modernity that he exemplified ('Zeke past Bachelor of Arts!', *Drum*, September 1957).

Although Mphahlele's first autobiography, *Down Second Avenue* (1959), is rightly recognised as a classic achievement because of its existential and experiential portrayal of the searing effects of segregation and apartheid, it is in his second memoir, *Afrika My Music* (1984), that he displays the complex nature of his literary intellectual formation. He mentions his obligatory familiarity with English literary culture from Dryden and Milton to Thackeray and Auden, which was expected of ex-colonial British subjects and, therefore, *all* South Africans who reached a particular education level, before Bantu education did catastrophic damage to African people. But what held him spellbound was his synthesis of different national literary traditions: the Spanish tradition of Cervantes, the Russian tradition of Dostoevsky, Chekhov and Gorky, and the American literary tradition of Faulkner, Wright and Hughes (with blues, jazz and spirituals thrown in for a specific flavour).

The mystical splendour of Mphahlele, that for me sparkled Maseko Street in my boyhood days, was the outcome of a major encounter in South African history of which I was to become aware 40 years later: the rapprochement of *New Negro modernity* and *New African modernity* in an attempt to dislodge the hegemonic form of *European modernity*. This was the central history of the New African Movement in South Africa. Mphahlele was one of the last literary representatives of this historical encounter.

This is the reason in a chapter devoted to his critical writings in *The Historical Figures of the New African Movement Volume One* (2013), I characterise him as 'the Last New African intellectual of the New African Movement'. Mphahlele has been so constant for decades in my imagination that my recent publication, *An Outline of the New African Movement in South Africa* (2013), is, in fact, an unintended homage to his *The African Image* (1962).

Although I still possess *real* memories of Orlando West before my departure for Los Angeles at the age of 13 in 1962, I have practically no memories of the township in which I was born – Kliptown. But before I close off on my beloved Orlando West, I should mention a passion it imparted to me that has remained permanent – soccer.

Over the last 20 years, be it in Los Angeles or here in Bangkok, Thailand, where I moved in 2012 in my retirement, I have seen some outstanding games broadcast live from the English Premier League, the Bundesliga (Germany), La Liga (Spain) or, for that matter, the Champions League knockout stages, but none can compare to the game I saw between the Mzimhlophe Aces and the 'Alexander' Hungry Lions that was played either in 1960 or 1961 at the playground adjacent to the Phefeni Railway Station, at the intersection of Orlando West, Phomolong and Phefeni. I supported the Mzimhlophe Aces who were trailing 3–0 at half time. Within 20 minutes of the second half, Aces scored four goals and won the game!

Looking back, looking forward

I have never been so happy in my life except perhaps when the ANC won the first elections in 1994 or upon the birth of my two daughters. Two outstanding matches I have seen in recent years were in Latin America: in the Bras Brasileirão Cup Final between São Paulo and Internacional in Brazil; and in the Primera Division between San Lorenzo and River Plate in Argentine. Despite this international experience of watching matches, my two favourite teams still remain those from my boyhood days of the late 1950s: the Moroka Swallows with the unforgettable Diffa and the Orlando Pirates with the inimitable Scaramouche. I favoured the former because I thought it consisted of gentlemen, no doubt because it reflected my African middle-class values, while possessing a jaundiced view of the latter because I thought of them as ruffians and tsotsis from the lumpen class. This *culture of the body* for me always went hand in hand with the *culture of the mind* as exemplified by Ezekiel Mphahlele.

Recalling that I was born in Kliptown returns me to the culture of the mind, since it was in this township that the Freedom Charter of the ANC was formulated and endorsed by the oppressed people of South Africa in 1955. The idea of the Freedom Charter, which gave central guidance to the new South African Constitution that made the democratic order of 1994 possible, was proposed by ZK Matthews (1901–68) immediately following the Defiance Campaign of 1952 in order to establish the process of political continuity through unending resistance. Though ZK Matthews is not much mentioned today in the annals of South African intellectual history, he was held in high regard by members of the Zulu Intellectuals of the 1940s, such as HIE Dhlomo and Jordan Ngubane, who praised his political and intellectual acumen in the 1940s and 1950s, respectively, in *Ilanga lase Natal* and in the *Indian Opinion*.

This acclamation is partly due to the fact that he achieved several 'first things' among the New African intellectuals of the New African Movement. He was one of the first two Africans to graduate from the University of Fort Hare four years after its founding in 1916. He was the first black South African to obtain an MA from Yale University for a remarkable thesis entitled 'Bantu Law and Western Civilisation in South Africa: A Study in the Clash of Cultures' (1934), a document that deserves to be published in book form, even now, 80 years after its initial presentation.

He was the first African scholar to be offered a visiting professorship in an American institution of higher learning at Cooper's Union in New York City in the 1950s. Lastly, he was the first United Nations ambassador for the newly independent Botswana in 1966. As though these achievements were not sufficient, he exemplified other inimitable attainments: on receiving his first degree he went to teach at Adam's College in Natal and, together with his colleague there Albert Luthuli, taught the then erstwhile students, Anton Lembede and Jordan Ngubane. He replaced the retiring DDT Jabavu (1880–1959) in the 1940s as Professor of African Languages at Fort Hare. Like Ezekiel Mphahlele, who resigned from his position as teacher at Orlando East High in the 1950s when Bantu education was promulgated, ZK Matthews resigned his professorship. Like other New African intellectuals, such as Clement Martyn Doke ([1893–1980] *Trekking in South Central Africa, 1913–1919*, 1993), Helen Joseph ([1905–95] *Side by Side*, 1986), Naboth Mokgatle (*The Autobiography of an Unknown South African*, 1971), Maggie Resha ([1932–2003] *'Mangoana o Tsoara Thipa ka Bohaleng/My Life in the Struggle*, 1991), Bloke Modisane ([1924–86] *Blame Me on History*, 1962), Ellen Kuzwayo ([1914–2006] *Call Me a Woman*, 1985), Frieda Bokwe Matthews ([1905–96] *Remembrances*, 1995), Gonarathnam 'Kesaveloo' Goonam ([1906–98] *Coolie Doctor*, 1991), ZK Matthews wrote an engaging autobiography, which was published posthumously (*Freedom For My People*, 1981).

The real question for us today, 20 years after the attainment of freedom in South Africa is why, politically and epistemologically, was the *biographical form* prevalent in the post-interregnum period whereas, during the New African Movement and in the aftermath of its defeat in 1960 by the apartheid state, the *autobiographical form* was dominant and hegemonic? It would seem that this historical preference for the biographical form in our time is a clear indication of the existence of a triumphalist consciousness, which is an indirect indication that the *politics of liberation* have superseded the *culture of liberation*. In other words, illegitimately, *representation* has triumphed over *creativity* in relation to the *subject* with possible dire consequences for the future of our country.

Talking democracy: Collective and individual imaginations of 20 years of political activism in a democratic society

Bandile Masuku

Gynaecologist

ON 27 APRIL 2014, SOUTH AFRICA will be celebrating exactly 20 years since the institution of its democracy. Given this milestone, there are bound to be reflections from various quarters, locally and internationally, on the substantive advances that the country has made in these two decades. Some of these reflections will be commissioned by the state, academic institutions, research institutes and the like, necessarily to satisfy the curiosity of many people about our democracy and in order to seek solutions to some of our present challenges. In contributing to these reviews, I have elected to give personal reflections on my impressions of these 20 years of democracy, premising this on the five years before 1994.

I joined active politics in 1989, through the Soweto Students' Congress (SOSCO), as a learner at Sekano Ntoane Senior Secondary School. I attended my first meeting in Vuwani Secondary School in Chiawelo. This was during the heyday of the so-called Twilight Generation, a title referring to the militant youth in townships around South Africa, who passionately heeded the 1985 call made by then ANC President OR Tambo on 8 January to make South Africa ungovernable. During this period we were always surrounded by political activism of one form or another.

My brother, Siphiwe Mgcina, a leader of SOSCO at the time, and the stories of the well-known Ndzanga family, with whom my parents had a great relationship, had the greatest political influence on me. The attack and assassination of Bartholomew Hlapane on 16 December 1986, my grandmother's next-door neighbour and an ANC leader in the Transvaal during the 1950s and 1960s, who later turned state witness in the Rivonia Trial, alerted me to the volatile political situation around me three years before my decision to join active politics. During this period, the central theme that governed our political engagements was related to seeking the best militant means through which we could weaken the institutions of apartheid governance, isolate the collaborating councillors of the time, as well as sabotage public building and institutions. All of this was premised on the understanding that this would lead to an eventual retreat by the apartheid state and its security forces, and thereby create conditions for 'people's power', namely, a democratic government of the people by the people.

Given the volatility of the situation, we had to organise clandestine meetings, where we first gathered at a meeting point then moved to the actual venue of the meeting when all security had been cleared. Our meetings were focused on immediate campaigns and we spent little or no time in reflecting on what we thought our longed-for democratic state would look like. However, our collective imagination was captured by the ideals of the Congress movement that spoke of a government of the people by the people, a non-racial, non-sexist, democratic and prosperous society in which all citizens would have equal rights and opportunities protected by the state. These progressive notions provoked a profound idealism in me, like it did in many others, which made all threats of detention and assault by the police worth daring.

Later, in 1989, we welcomed back the Rivonia trialists, who were released from prison after serving 26 years. These were Walter Sisulu, Ahmed Kathrada, Elias Motsoaledi, Wilton Mkwayi and Andrew Mlangeni – the mythical and towering figures that inspired our commitment to that noble struggle against apartheid repression. I was blessed to be among the crowd marshals in the welcoming rally held at FNB Stadium. We could now get the sense that freedom was around the corner, although we had not really engaged with the question of what exactly we thought this new democratic society would look like, let alone how its administrative, judicial, legislative, cultural and social institutions would function.

The unbanning of the ANC and the release of Nelson Mandela happened in February 1990, about the time I was doing Standard 9. This was a momentous and groundbreaking period for the whole liberation struggle and a breathtaking experience for me – and probably for all in my generation. If anything, democracy was now on the horizon as we witnessed the flocking back of numbers of our heroic township fellows who had gone off to exile to join Umkhonto weSizwe (MK).

This period also signified the beginning of a terrible long journey to political freedom – just as we had naïvely imagined that freedom was about to be simply announced. The period was characterised by the increased violence between the African National Congress (ANC) and the state-sponsored Inkatha, now known as Inkatha Freedom Party, where scores of people were maimed and murdered in KwaZulu-Natal and Gauteng. Led by the Zulu nationalist, Chief Mangosuthu Buthelezi, Inkatha consisted mostly of hostel dwellers in Gauteng, who led a series of vicious attacks on township residents as they were perceived to be ANC supporters.

At the time I was elected to lead COSAS in Soweto, which we relaunched in 1991 in Pietermaritzburg. I served in the executive as a Pioneer Organiser responsible for recruiting members from higher primary schools. I was also doing my matric, which I later passed without gaining university entrance. This was due largely to the demanding tasks of organising for COSAS and thus having to study late into the night with a great friend of mine, Siphiwe Edwin Mthandi – a trade we called 'cross-nighting'. This 'cross-nighting' created a bond between us that later involved our families because we were like brothers.

In the midst of this political turmoil and with this black-on-black violence threatening the very possibility of our leap to democracy, I had to grapple with the personal predicament of having to repeat my matric. I opted to do this in 1992 in an attempt to gain a university entrance pass because I had intended to do engineering or medicine at university. At the same time, I was committed to my role as an organiser for COSAS since it was a critical feature of our lives as the youth to be engaged in this effort of delivering democracy in our country. This decision created some tension at home because my older sister was arguing that I should be enrolled in a private school or in a Model C school in town, thereby distancing me from the political activism that was increasingly becoming dangerous in the township. As a leader of COSAS, I knew that I would be viewed as a sell-out if I acceded to my sister's insistence, so I protested and remained in the township school.

That year, 1992, I was elected to be the first secretary of COSAS's newly established Soweto Zone. This is the year when a national campaign was initiated against paying exam fees. As COSAS Soweto, we led the campaign even when our national leadership had called it off. This got us into trouble with the leadership of the ANC because they were trying to quell the fires that were flaring up all over our townships at the same time as the CODESA negotiations were taking place.

The strategic tension that emerged around this time was related to our militant political culture in COSAS and the moderating concept of negotiations that the ANC leadership was impressing on the whole Congress movement. Despite the fact that we had no coherent conception of what our democratic transition would look like, plus the Inkatha-led violence, our collective imagination still held that the route should be militant and that leaders of the apartheid state had no moral legitimacy to even participate in the formation of our future democracy. I had even gone as far as imagining nothing short of a militant overthrow of the apartheid state – at that time I regarded myself as a fearless militant and radical.

The contradiction that can exist between theory and practice visited us when we had to consider the possibility of a democratic society that would emerge out of a negotiated settlement with the oppressor class, whose relationship to us had been of oppressor and oppressed – jailor and prisoner, hunter and hunted, aggressor and victim. Having committed ourselves to the Congress doctrine of non-racialism, we had to negotiate its practice with the entrenched bitterness we had against white people.

I passed my matric again in 1992, and when my name appeared on the newspapers there was no indication that I had obtained a university entrance. This was disappointing, as the whole point of repeating was not met. When I received my results, I discovered that my English marks were 'pending', meaning that the department had withheld my marks because of a suspicion that I had cheated. Ultimately, it emerged that I had received a good mark, which meant that I had passed my matric with a university entrance. This came with relief and excitement for all the comrades in COSAS and the ANC Youth League (ANCYL).

Parallel to all this I was involved in the process of the re-establishment of the ANCYL, of which I was elected as Secretary of Student Affairs for a Senaoane branch in 1991. During this period, the South African Youth Congress (SAYCO) and the ANCYL in

Senaoane were involved in a deadly feud with a gang of car thieves, after one of our comrades killed one of their thugs. The thugs retaliated by kidnapping and killing a comrade known as Spider. This was one of the scariest moments in my life as a young activist because my life was in danger from both the thugs and the security police that were still detaining comrades.

I registered and begun my academic life on the first of April 1993 following the intervention by the ANCYL through comrade Parks Mankahlana, undertaking to give me a bursary to study. I enrolled for a BSc at the Medical University of South Africa (Medunsa) late into the academic year. I didn't even get space in the residences and I was then compelled to stay in the nearby township of Mabopane that was part of the Bophuthatswana homeland.

On 10 April 1993, ten days after my registration, comrade Chris Hani was assassinated outside his house in Boksburg, a suburb that was historically Afrikaans and home to hard right-wingers and racists. This brought the country close to civil war as the racial tension and hatred heightened. Not even the storming of the World Trade Centre by the AWB or the killing of AWB commandoes by soldiers of Bophuthatswana during the overthrowing of President Lucas Mangope could push the country so close to turmoil as the assassination of comrade Chris did.

It was President Mandela who diffused the tension and the threat of the civil war in the country with his address to the nation that was broadcast by all SABC stations. All this was happening as the ANC and the apartheid government were engaged in negotiations that had reached deadlock over the date of the general elections. All this intensity led to the announcement that 27 April 1994 would be the date of our first democratic elections in which all South Africans of all races voted together and in which the ANC won a majority.

Already by now there were ensuing debates about the 'size and shape' of the democratic state that we were going to build, in light of some strategic concessions that had been made at the CODESA negotiations. These debates began before 1994, and immediately after the elections, the Congress movement had to grapple, for the first time, with the real challenges of assembling a state. The core questions of the 'size and shape' debate were related to the huge tasks facing the new government to reorganise South African society, invest in social capital and restructure our productive (economic) assets in order to achieve maximum deracialisation of our political economy.

I joined the South African Students' Congress (SASCO) in 1994, a year after enrolling at Medunsa. SASCO was a highly intellectual environment as opposed to the more militant platform of COSAS, where I had cut my teeth on Congress movement politics. I was elected onto the SRC in 1995 through SASCO and had the opportunity to meet President Nelson Mandela and the then Deputy President Thabo Mbeki in 1996. We were attending a SAUSRC meeting, a national body of university SRCs that handled national policy coordination. It was an exciting moment, both because of the stature of these two comrades in our liberation struggle and the wealth of wisdom they shared with us regarding the notions of nation-building, reconstruction and development, and the general tasks of social transformation and governance.

Around this period, as earlier stated, the debates within the alliance were heating up. All of these debates were pursued within the context of a ridiculously huge budget deficit that was inherited from the apartheid government and in light of the negative international sentiment regarding the capacity of a black government to carry the tasks of governance. It was around 1996 that these tensions over policy choices tightened up, especially within the ANC-led alliance. All of this notwithstanding, there was agreement about the presence of the state in the allocation of economic assets, in the restructuring of the economy and the creation of a social security net. This was in defiance of the internationally hegemonic notion of a state that had no role in economic development. However, all of us had full recognition of the progress we had made in stabilising our political situation in a manner that had eliminated all elements of counterrevolution and political violence. Regression to any form of civil war was not a central concern that boggled our minds as a country.

Our imprints in global political affairs were becoming visible, more so following the election of President Thabo Mbeki in 1999 as state president. South Africa emerged as a central driver of the African Renaissance vision, among its core principles being the dictum of 'African solutions to African problems'. Already the ANC government had managed to preside over a consistent trend of upward economic growth that lasted well into the global economic crisis of 2008. This saw the emergence of black middle and upper classes. Social services like sanitation, housing, road infrastructure and social grants were incrementally provided in order to avoid a collapse into poverty by our people.

However, the Zimbabwean situation around the early 2000s revealed something about our new democratic society. Although we had successfully entrenched a shared vision of a democratic country, we had mostly racialised divisions on our strategic allegiance towards Africa. It was very common for white South Africans (journalists, public intellectuals and ordinary citizens) to have doubts about our government's handling of the situation. Of course, these doubts were detectable even among our black editors. This lack of strategic coherence around our African policy still exists, even today.

I was elected as deputy president of SASCO in 2002 and later catapulted into the seat of president by tragic circumstances, following the death of our president, comrade Siphiwe Zuma, in a car accident. I was president of SASCO till 2004, following my re-election in 2003. SASCO had led an engaged militant campaign for the democratic transformation of higher education in South Africa as part of the broad democratic discourse.

We were confronted with institutionalised racism in the historically white institutions that presented every possible stumbling block against the democratisation of higher education and the deracialisation of staff, academia and student enrolment. Our campaigns also sought to galvanise government's attention to the need for strategic policy initiatives that would facilitate this transformation in order to thoroughly democratise the systems of human capital production. These included the need for the recapitalisation of the under-resourced, former black universities and technikons in order to increase their productive capacity by modernising their technical capacity and infrastructure. Battles over the nature of curriculum content in order to reflect the sentiments of our democratic vision were also there.

As if in a parallelogram, our commonly shared appreciation of a stabilising political system and democratic institutions was combined with soaring disagreements over social and economic policies. Despite the commonly understood strategic tasks of the democratic project, there was not much consensus around which policy choices were appropriate in order to accelerate social transformation. Particularly within the ANC-led alliance, these policy divergences were the result of varying interpretations of the global situation and the extent to which there is existing room for manoeuvre to do things differently to what was globally policed by Western powers, like the United States, and institutions such as the World Bank and the International Monetary Fund (IMF). Debates around HIV gained traction around 2004, with our government acquiring a label internationally as 'AIDS denialists'. This was in response to some questions they had posed regarding our conceptual understanding of the HI virus and the resultant syndrome AIDS. At the centre of this debate was the drug Nevirapine that is no longer used in any treatment of HIV and AIDS. This followed the recognition that it had contributed to many deaths of pregnant mothers because of its toxic nature, much to the vindication of our government's earlier contentions.

As a senior medical student I felt that this debate was closer to me than, I would say, many of my comrades in SASCO and the Congress movement broadly. The debate was not simply a question of public health policy and social policy choices relating to the provision of medication. It extended to scientific medical themes that would be the basis upon which social and public health policy choices would have to be rooted. Without venturing into my stand on either side of the debates at the time, it is worth noting that history has brought us full circle, with the current Minister of Health, Dr Aaron Motsoaledi, battling it out with international pharmaceutical companies.

I have been a practising medical doctor for almost ten years, having commenced with my internship in 2005. I have served as coordinator of the ANC NEC Health and Education subcommittee. My medical knowledge and grasp of strategic political questions relating to social classes acting within our political economy and globally have given me an advantage in reflecting on these matters of public health. It is a positive development to notice that there is greater appreciation, both within the ruling ANC and society at large, that debates of public health policy and the related matters of rolling out medication are directly related to the complex dynamics of the local and global political economy.

South Africa is going to hold our fifth general elections in May 2014 since the 1994 democratic elections. The three general elections between the 1994 inaugural elections and the coming 2014 elections have successively passed a decisive vote of confidence on our democracy and its institutions. Instances of violence because of political or racial intolerance are so rare that they do not pose a potential threat to our democratic order, as was the case before and immediately after 1994. I must concede that the presence of many opposition parties, some emerging as breakaways from the ruling party, are an affirmation of a progressive culture of political tolerance and an entrenched right to freedom of association. As a result, our political spectrum is rapidly diversifying, carrying outfits of the ultra-left to the right-wing, yet without the threat of collapsing our democratic order and constitutionalism. In this light, I believe that we have done very well in creating a democracy of which we are rightly proud. The present situation does capture the collective imagination we had as young activists and my individual idealism at the time also has actual representation in modern South Africa.

Despite the fact that we have normalised social and race relations, we still have to attend to some systemic weaknesses. It is common cause that poverty and underdevelopment are still racialised. I would suggest that this requires that all progressive social forces must consider a radical approach to understanding systemic trappings and to entertain the possibility of pursuing an unorthodox trajectory of restructuring our productive (economic) assets. The persistence of these systemic trappings and their retention of racialised inequality and underdeveloped create a platform for all manner of inflammatory and demagogic political currents to seek relevance at the expense of our common good as South Africans.

Expressions of community engagement in a new democracy

Lawrence Matemba
Social policy analyst

Introduction

THE DAWN OF A NEW DEMOCRACY in South Africa in 1994 gave hope to a new way of community engagement based on a system of public representation. However, the experiences of community engagement in the early 1990s in Thembalihle (Vrede) in the Free State and in the early 2000s in KwaMpumuza (Pietermaritzburg) in KwaZulu-Natal point us to some of the areas that still need to be worked on in order to strengthen further our young democracy.

The reflections presented in this paper are personal observations and experiences of micro-foundations (individuals, processes, and structure; and interactions within and across components) that, once disturbed or challenged, cease to act as authoritative guidelines for social behaviour. Not only have I observed manifestations of these dynamics in the form of disturbance to stability and order in social life, but also, tragically, fundamental alterations to social structure. More concerning is that if such phenomena are unchecked and allowed to get out of control, it may destroy the fundamental provisions in the Constitution, namely the functioning of the system of public representation and its attendant aspects of democracy and justice. What may appear on the surface as a community dynamic in the form of, for example, a clash between Christianity and traditional culture or protest action, as we will reflect on later, has shaped society to be what it is today, nearly 20 years since 1994.

In order to remain within the confines of the intentions of the editor of this collection, I have adopted a micro-foundations approach, which necessarily focuses on collective phenomena that need explanation, specifically the creation and development, and the reproduction and management of collective constructs, such as protest action, in the exercise and pursuit of the democratic provisions

188

adopted in 1994 and enshrined in the Constitution. This reflection is best suited to a micro-foundations approach because it proffers that primarily the explanations of these collective phenomena requires consideration of lower-level entities, such as individuals or processes, and their interactions.

Another important element concerns the lens through which I view these issues: I am a naturalised citizen who arrived in South Africa in 1991 and has spent some 22 years in the country, 19 of these post democracy. Acquiring nationality by naturalisation, as opposed to traditional means based on either *jus soli* ('right of the territory') or on *jus sanguinis* ('right of blood'), involves taking an oath or a pledge of allegiance to honour, respect and abide by the Constitution. In this case, I made a concerted effort – perhaps unlike someone who acquires nationality through traditional means – to consciously reflect on and know more about my new home country. I take nothing for granted.

Community protest action at Thembalihle

When I arrived in South Africa for the first time in February 1991, I observed how the local community of Thembalihle Township in Vrede in the Free State expressed its views on a number of issues affecting it. I had come to South Africa to pursue the second phase of my training for priesthood in the Catholic Church and was based at St Conrad Noviciate, located on the outskirts of the Vrede and the beginning of the township.

Some few weeks before my first arrival in Vrede, there had been disturbances within the community because the congregation of this Catholic parish was unhappy with the resident parish priest at the time. I am given to understand that efforts had been made to resolve the situation in the weeks earlier, to no avail.

This first experience at Vrede was somehow shocking for me because it was the first time that I had encountered a community that had challenged its parish priest in the way it did, namely, using very strong language accompanied by threats of a physical nature. I have to admit that having travelled to many parts of Africa, I was shocked when presented with this kind of reaction. This is not to say that priests cannot be challenged per se, but that this should be done within certain boundaries.

I witnessed a second incident some two months after my arrival at Vrede in which the community of Thembalihle boycotted shops owned and run by white people in Vrede. One lunchtime a fellow novice and I decided to take a walk into town to buy a few toiletries. Unbeknown to us, anyone from Thembalihle seen to be buying items from the boycotted shops were not looked upon kindly by the community. In fact, a few months later, I witnessed an incident where someone was beaten up and the items that he was suspected of buying were trashed.

While the two incidents presented here may not appear abnormal in the context of the days of apartheid, I must admit that for someone new to the country, I found these acts and other similar ones, shocking and, indeed, traumatic.

The observation that there is a marked increase in the intensity of protests due to unhappiness with the levels of service delivery is quite correct. However, perhaps behind this increase is the very fact that democracy has made it possible for various formations of society, such as communities and organised labour, to be able to organise and express themselves in whatever manner they see fit.

Although more expensive and generally beyond the reach of the majority of ordinary citizens, those that are able to afford it are beginning to turn to the courts to enforce their rights. This is because in post-apartheid South Africa, the Constitution provides arguably the most favourable textual framework in the world for pursuing such claims, with its ringing commitment to achieving social justice; improving the quality of life of all; an equality clause designed to achieve equality of outcomes (substantive equality); provisions explicitly mandating land restitution and reform; a generous panoply of socio-economic rights; the application of rights, not only against the state, but also against private parties that violate rights; and the wide remedial powers of the courts to strike down legislation and policy that is inconsistent with the Constitution, and to grant just and equitable relief. This is arguably a totally different experience from that prior to 1994.

While in many countries democracy is defined in a narrow sense to mean participation in elections in the main and, occasionally, through the legislative process, one can only admire the lengths to which the courts in South Africa have jealously guarded the participation of society in their own affairs. On numerous occasions, one observes the courts endorsing various forms of citizen participation in the processes that give meaning to rights, such as designing and implementing social programmes and legislation. To give an example, in the case of *Doctors for Life International v The Speaker of the National Assembly and Others* (CCT12/05) [2006], the Constitutional Court required public participation in legislative processes, holding that such participation promotes the 'civic dignity' of citizens, enhances government accountability, increases the legitimacy and effectiveness of legislation, and serves as 'a counterweight to secret lobbying and influence peddling'.

To conclude this section, my experience thus far is that engagement has the potential to contribute towards the resolution of disputes and to increased understanding and sympathetic care if both sides are willing to participate in the process. The mechanisms of procedural fairness and meaningful engagement (despite all their limitations) also have rich potential to give meaning to rights from the bottom up. There is much fruitful work to be done in designing participatory mechanisms within all spheres of government, as well as the private sector, that afford marginalised communities a meaningful voice in decisions that affect their socio-economic wellbeing. At the end of the day, the survival of our constitutional democracy depends on building capable, accountable and responsive institutions and organisations.

Perceived clash between African tradition and Christianity

Staying in Vrede from February 1991 to February 1992, reflecting mostly on my calling to religious life and priesthood helped me to learn a few things with regard to traditions, culture and language in South Africa. In the inter-actionist line of argument, my stay helped me to understand how individuals and the community as a whole, in cases where well-established social order and stability are challenged, save face or affirm themselves; in ethnomethodology, how they negotiate and improvise to make sense of and legitimate processes of compliance and acceptance. Hence, I started to develop an interest in how individuals and the community to which they belonged, *behaved* rather than how they chose, planned or determined their response.

Moving from the premise that everyday reasoning requires individuals to negotiate rules and procedures flexibly and reflexively to assure themselves and others around them that their behaviour is sensible, I observed that sustaining social interaction is the 'basic security system' of the self. It was interesting to note how the community crafted a distinction between the public face and backstage reality, overlooked or avoided anomalies, minimised discordant signals, and decoupled formal procedures and structures from everyday work as steps to maintain the assumption that it was acting appropriately.

What I described in the previous paragraph stood me in good stead to set the scene for the second phase of my training, this time in philosophy and theological studies in Pietermaritzburg, KwaZulu-Natal (1993–97). This period is characterised by a strong focus on pastoral work influenced, in the main, by the encyclical letter, *Redemptoris Missio* (Encyclical on the permanent validity of the Church's missionary mandate) of Pope John Paul II; postconcilar writing of Pope Paul VI's apostolic exhortation, *Evangelii Nuntiandi* (Evangelisation in the Modern World); and *Ad Gentes* (the Second Vatican Council's Decree on the Missionary Activity of the Church).

The biggest shock of the second phase of my training was the clash I witnessed between a local chief, who had in the earlier years received and accepted Catholicism but later denounced it because it challenged his practice of marrying more than one wife. Some aspects of this experience are captured in my thesis for a Master's dissertation, which was later published in *Diversity in Africa: The Coming of Age of a Continent,* edited by Kurt April and Marylou Shockley (2006, Palgrave Macmillan).

To understand the historical origins of the clash, it is important to first follow the development of the parish of St Vincent's, because, as we shall see, the clash contributed to the development of the parish. Like many other Catholic parishes, St Vincent's, located at KwaMpumuza – a semi-urban location on the outskirts of Pietermaritzburg – started out as an outstation of St Albert's Parish, Esigodini, another semi-urban locality in the vicinity. This is evident in the following account of one of the interviewee's (Mgoza, 2003) early years as a child:

I was born in 1931, yes, in this same place of Mpumuza 1. However, it was only two years later, that is, in 1933 that I was baptised at St Albert's Parish – that parish in Esigodini. We all used to go there for the celebration of the Eucharist, even though it was very far for most of us.

With the passage of time, the outstation of St Albert's, which is now St Augustine's at Machibisa, grew in population. This necessitated that St Augustine's be raised to full parish status. According to Mgoza (2003), this development meant that the people of Mpumuza had to be divided with regard to the parish to which they belonged. When St Augustine's at Machibisa became a full parish, all those people from around Ama-sixties (one of the wards of Mpumuza 1) and Ashdown started to associate themselves with St Augustine's because it was geographically close to Ama-sixties. A dedicated parishioner who later became a catechist, and also helped in the establishment of St Vincent's, was Mr Colonelius Shange. In addition, it meant that all those people from the south-western side of Mpumuza 1 area continue to associate themselves with St Albert's Parish at Esigodini.

During a period, which an interviewee, Mhlongo (2003) referred to only as the 1950s, people were forcefully removed from the Ama-sixties area, that is, from the south-eastern ward, into the area where St Vincent's Parish building is located now. It is not clear why the removal was carried out. However, another interviewee, Dingane (2003), was of the strong opinion that the chief who lives about two kilometres to the north of the location of St Vincent's ordered all his people to live around him as the population there was sparse.

What were the consequences of this decision of the chief for the parishioners? First of all, it meant that all the population from Ama-sixties drifted away from St Augustine's parish. In the second place, it meant that there was now quite a sizeable population around the centre of Mpumuza 1. As a result, there arose a need for the Catholic community at Mpumuza 1 to start organising its church activities locally, that is, in Mpumuza 1 itself. It was during this period of forced removal and its aftermath, that discussions were held about changing the outstation of St Augustine (now St Vincent's Parish), into a parish.

Among those removed from Ama-sixties were strong and dedicated people like Petros Nyandu, Julia Mntambo, Victoria Nene and Elizabeth Zondi (Mgoza, 2003):

> These were probably the strongest pillars of the present St Vincent's. They used to visit the sick and pray for them. They always reported to the 'father' that is, the parish priest at

Machibisa whenever somebody was sick and therefore needed the services of a priest.

Where was the catechist then? As is often the case, is it those who carry duties such as those performed by the four people mentioned above? The answer to this question is that the catechist stayed at Ashdown and was, therefore, not affected by the removal. Even though none of my interviewees remembered exactly when St Vincent's officially became an outstation of St Augustine's, the three names of Mrs Sithole, Mr Petros Nyandu and Mr Raphael Madonda were mentioned as those who were sent to the chief to ask for a place of worship:

> Initially, the chief was reluctant to the introduction of the Catholic faith, and any type of faith for that matter. However, in 1961 the chief gave permission to the introduction of the Catholic faith in his area. To that effect, Mrs Victoria Nene donated her house as a place of worship. This house was a traditionally Zulu grass-thatched house (Mtolo, 2003).

With the official recognition of the outstation at Mpumuza 1, a number of developments took place. In the first place, the Parish Priest of St Augustine's, Fr Ngubane, appointed his assistant, Fr Mkhize, to the outstation. It is said that Fr Mkhize now celebrated the Eucharist more often than ever before at this outstation. The local chief was converted to the Catholic faith and the Eucharist was celebrated once every three months at his home. Furthermore, the chief had a place of honour in the church building. In addition, the Catholic Church was the only one allowed to carry out any religious activity in the area.

The traditional Zulu grass-thatched house that was donated was becoming too small as the population was growing. In addition, the building was no longer viable since it leaked during the rainy season. Therefore, to address these problems, a bigger church had to be built. Here again, Mr Colonelius Shange (2003), the catechist, was instrumental, as an interviewee narrates:

> Our catechist used to travel all the way from Ashdown everyday to come to build the new church. It was constructed from mud

building blocks. Unlike the previous building, this new one was bigger. It had a sacristy and one spare room.

One other development in the life of the outstation during this period was its naming (Buthelezi, 2004):

What happened as far as the origin of the naming of St Vincent's is concerned can be traced to the fact that the catechist and other members of the parish belonged to the Society of Vincent de Paul. This association also existed at St Augustine's, at St Albert's and at St Mary's in the city of Pietermaritzburg, a whites-only parish at the time. It was this association of Vincent de Paul at St Mary's that donated windows and the roof for the new church building at KwaMpumuza. Subsequently, the new church building was named St Vincent's in gratitude to the donations made by the association of Vincent de Paul.

Another new development that was to have a major impact on St Vincent's was the coming of the Spiritans (Congregation of the Holy Spirit) to St Joseph's Theological Institute at CEDARA, near Howick in 1985. According to one of the interviewees, who later became the parish priest of St Vincent's (Sibeko, 1996), the Spiritans were initially looking for a place to build a house of studies for their students, who would be attending lectures at St Joseph's. After negotiating with Archbishop Denis Hurley of the Archdiocese of Durban, the Spiritans were offered some place on the outskirts, to the west of Pietermaritzburg, just on the boundary with Mpumuza 1. Here, the idea was that the Spiritans would minister at St Vincent's. Consequently, in 1987 the Laval House of Studies was officially opened.

After the ordination of the first Spiritan to the priesthood in March 1989, Fr Michael Sibeko, CSSp was appointed to work in Zimbabwe. However, he had to wait for almost a year before his work permit was approved. Meanwhile, he ministered at St Vincent's. It was during this period that the present St Vincent's Church was built at its present site – a site somehow in the centre of Mpumuza 1.

The years 1990 and 1991 are remarkable in the history of the development of St Vincent's Parish for a number of reasons. First of all, Archbishop Denis Hurley, the Archbishop of Durban, officially opened St Vincent's Parish on 29 October 1990. This was remarkable, indeed, because it was a sign of the autonomy and growth of the parish. Secondly, 1990 and 1991 were the years when violence in the Mpumuza 1 area was at its worst. In fact, one interviewee (Mgoza, 2003) suggested that it was because of this violence that St Vincent's was built. However, it is difficult to believe that St Vincent's could be built because of violence alone. Here, one would do well to remember that big decisions like erecting a church building are not taken in a hurry – funds have to be raised and there must be a likelihood of a parish priest, for instance. All other informants interviewed pointed to the fact that it was due to the increase in membership of the parish that there arose a need for a new church building.

However, an interviewee (Mhlongo, 2003) alluded to the fact that, on the one hand, the parishes of St Albert's and St Augustine's were no longer accessible to the people of Mpumuza 1 as these parishes are situated in African National Congress (ANC) aligned areas, whereas St Vincent's is located in an Inkatha Freedom Party stronghold. On the other hand, membership and church attendance at St Vincent's increased dramatically. Violence also impacted St Vincent's in the sense that some people were not sure whether or not to go to church. 'It was a time when one just had to sit at home and listen to the radio; to be updated on the development of events in the area' (Mhlongo, 2003).

Furthermore, the years 1990 and 1991 were remarkable in the development of St Vincent's because Fr Michael Sibeko, CSSp, the longest serving parish priest at St Vincent's thus far, was to be replaced by a new German parish priest. The new parish priest brought some changes in the parish. Instead of bringing Holy Communion to the elderly as the custom had been previously, he collected them from their homes and brought them to church to celebrate Mass together (telephonic interview with Gibis, 2000). In addition, while he continued celebrating Mass at the chief's place once every three months, he introduced catechetical lessons in the area of the chief's residence. It was at this time that the new parish priest learnt that the chief had three wives.

One interviewee confided that the new German parish priest asked the chief to terminate his marriage with the other two wives because Catholic Canon Law did not allow it. By then, the chief's first wife was already baptised and received communion in the Catholic

Church. A problem surfaced when the chief's third wife enrolled for catechetical lessons for baptism. The new parish priest refused to baptise the chief's third wife and instructed the chief to leave the second and third wives. This clashed with Zulu custom, as it is this third wife who is supposed to give birth to the son who will succeed to the throne. This is obviously a complex issue – an issue in which a custom clashes with Canon Law.

The manner in which the new parish priest dealt with this issue illustrates his lack of understanding of the local culture, as one interviewee puts it (Mkhize, 2000):

> The new parish priest refused to baptise the chief's third wife, stopped the old and established tradition of celebrating Mass at the chief's place once every three months. This was an insult to the chief. He is our chief and we are under his authority. He has to be respected because we are living on his land. If the chief divorces his third wife, who is going to give birth to the future chief then? Doesn't the new priest know that the chief can decide to terminate the Catholic Church here?

The quotation above shows just how much authority the chief has on the affairs in his territory. Indeed, the same informant made the point that as a result of this stand-off between the chief and the new parish priest, the relations between them (including the parish as a whole) went sour. It is alleged that immediately after this dispute, the chief reduced the amount of land that was allocated for the development of parish projects, including that of the crèche. The interviewee even physically pointed out the original boundaries of the parish.

To illustrate the extent to which the relationship went sour, the chief once stormed into the church during the celebration of the Eucharistic demanding that his people leave to attend his meeting. He also wrote letters to two former parish priests demanding that he should have his people anytime he wants them, whether on a Sunday or on any other day (Mgoza, 2003).

In 1995, the new parish priest built a hall in the church premises, despite the state of the bad relationship between them. He explains what he had in mind when he decided to build the hall (Gibis, 2003):

> There are lots of activities that take place in that parish. I can

mention activities like concerts, meetings, wedding parties, etc. We cannot have them in the church. It is not right. Moreover, the community of KwaMpumuza does not have even a single hall. So I thought that the hall might help in such instances. It is for the whole community as long as it is booked in good time and that the intended activity does not go beyond five o'clock in the afternoon.

Conclusion

Reflecting on one's experience of the new South Africa post 1994 using a micro-foundations approach reveals very interesting dynamics in community life. It would appear that for many communities, stability is maintained by rules, norms, beliefs, convictions and worldview as located in tradition and culture. It is institutions such as outlined here that still guide attitude and behaviour in the majority of cases. While being sensitive to these institutions and the role they play, through policy and legislation, the Constitution has become the primary guide and source for community stability. However, communities are yet to internalise the Constitution. This will take time and possibly generations.

Simple expectations, complex transitions: The story of two decades of democracy

Nozipho Mbanjwa

CNBC Africa presenter of Beyond Markets

I'M ON THE LEDGE. BALANCING precariously on the awkwardness of 29 going on 30. This does mean that for most of my life I have lived in a democratic South Africa. It also means that I have patches of memory from my childhood during the time of apartheid. In a bizarre way, this unbalanced overlap of two worlds has served its purpose. As memories do, those of my childhood, however nostalgic they remain, continue to fade with time, but hardships that my family had to endure loom large and serve as a defiant reminder of what life was. Of course, the stories from my parents and others who took on the apartheid regime remain a chilling memory and somewhat a warning of what a 'white-ruled' South Africa was like.

I don't think that this is unusual for any black person born in the mid-eighties with no significant family-name collateral to draw on. Our memories shape our outlook of South Africa 20 years into democracy. We don't suffer from a historical disconnect and maybe our frameworks of thought are too deeply immersed. We are our history.

My most vivid memory that staggers to life at the mention of the word 'apartheid' is quite dramatic. I can almost feel the heat of the flames on my back as I clung to my dad's back as we fled the fire that was engulfing our home, again. The ANC and IFP violence, an offshoot of the apartheid regime, terrorised the province and the people. Our homes were torched. Our fathers and brothers were hunted. Our mothers and sisters were raped.

My expectations of a democratic South Africa are uncomplicated. I expect democracy to translate into freedom. Personal freedom. Economic freedom. Political freedom. Just being. Democracy has failed to live up to my expectations. So, do I toss the baby out with the bath water? Absolutely not! But we keep working on getting the baby as squeaky clean as possible – scrubbing, refining, polishing.

My first real encounter with democracy was in 1994. I got to change schools. I had been smuggled into a school for coloured children for the first three years of schooling. My fair skintone and my quick take to the English language – dripping with a coloured accent – served its deceitful purpose. For three years I was Bridget Victor. Bridget is my second name and Victor is my father's second name and together they replaced Nozipho Mbanjwa. In January 1994 I received the news that I would be going to a 'white' school and that although I had to keep my second name as my first I would be able to use my surname. This was democracy but this was not freedom. I learnt to lose my coloured accent. It wasn't appropriate. I learnt to curl my tongue and round off my words and to speak through my nose. I learnt to be white. This was the only way to make it in this new world.

Admittedly, at that age I didn't fully understand the nuances of these democratic transitions. If anything, I thought it was a lot of fuss over nothing. Learning to change the way I speak and how to 'be white' was simply adaptation. I was a child. I was happy. The only real differences was in the depth of my parent's pockets relative to those of the parents of other kids. Going to a white school meant doing white things and white things were expensive. I quickly learnt to feign indifference no matter how much I wanted to try out, for example, being on the canoe team because, at the end of the day, my parents would not be able to afford the canoe that I'd need to compete. So I participated where my limbs were all I needed: long distance running, netball and basketball.

I excelled at academics and that bought me the social capital that made me acceptable. I was that bright black girl that white parents wanted to be seen to have taken an interest in. So I got invited to the parties and the braais and even a sleep-over party. That's when I really understood how different my life was. That's when I realised that Mandela still had a lot of work to do. The homes were like nothing I had ever seen before. Each person had their own bedroom – up to four bedrooms in one house! They had swimming pools and big television sets and fridges that I thought I could get lost in. We were still far from being free.

In 1998, I graduated to secondary school and we kept with the tradition of the white school. By then, these schools had been renamed as former Model C schools. I still don't know what the C stands for but I knew that I was lucky to be able to go to one of these schools.

Mind you, it was not from any relative wealth on the part of parents. My father had worked in a shoe factory for as long as I could remember. My mother was, and still is, an entrepreneur. She sold everything that could turn a profit, from alcohol and fruit to cooked meals. you name it and she sold it, and got me into these fancy schools. I don't want to belabour the point about our poverty simply because this was the norm for many of us. Growing up poor in South Africa is not a 'story' any more. Black people are poor in South Africa. We could get into the semantics about the affluent black minority but that's where it ends. The vast majority of black people remain in poverty.

The school I entered in 1998 was a single-sex school and one that was determined to align itself with the new democratic dispensation. It was modelled on equal opportunity; they tried their best to use academic ability, the willingness to learn and the willingness to try as the only differentiators. It was not easy to have real conversations about apartheid and the new-found democracy. At 14 years old, it was difficult for us to even articulate what these things meant to us. Watching the movie *Sarafina!* for the first time at age 15, as part of our history syllabus, left me with a great sense of unease, anger, and disappointment. I remember that many of us in the class started crying. Both black and white. I can't speak for the white kids, but I cried because I was mad at the injustices of the past. I was uneasy about the feelings running through me and how they would influence the way I interacted with my friends from then on, and I was disappointed that after everything that my parents had gone through, we were still the underdogs. But there was a sense of optimism and hope that we were in a better place and that we were working through the kinks.

By the age of 18, I think I had covered a lot of ground personally. I had a greater sense of self. I reverted back to my full birth name: Nozipho Mbanjwa. When I took the decision to go to university in a traditionally Afrikaans city, I heard the warnings about going into the heart of racism but I wanted to be close to the diplomatic core and so Pretoria it was. I quickly learnt the two-facedness of the human spirit. Within the sanctuary of the academic corridors, my peers were my friends. We all struggled with Microeconomics, we loved Politics of Africa, we shared the same awkwardness when we took on South African Politics 101 and we all bunked Computer Literacy. We were all 19-year-olds wanting to fit in, wanting to do well and wanting to be cool. This was a marked difference from our interactions outside the university walls.

To augment the little that my parents could contribute, I worked. I tutored and I was a waitress at a local Portuguese restaurant. My white 'friends' would frequent the restaurant with their families. This is where the black and white could not be underplayed. When they were with their families, steeped in the socialisation, values, customs and traditions that make up white (Afrikaans) families, they were on opposite sides of the fence. The academic strands that held us together in lecture halls had no place there. We were people from different sides of a war, both steadfast in our belief that we were more deserving of this country, and both blinded by the rage of the past and our immediate experiences. It was during this time, while waiting tables, that I think I learnt so much about the aspirations of the black person and the will of the white person to keep those aspirations as unreachable as possible.

I would get irritated when black families came in because, by and large, they did not understand the concept of tipping. This was a detail that we are still learning. So, although the conversation would be camaraderie and it felt like being among family, the smiles for tips would not pay my rent or buy my textbooks. I was well versed in the 10% rule. I learnt not to care that my classmates would pretend not to know me as they spent what could easily have been my father's salary on lunch. I learnt to serve them with a smile and keep offering more items on the menu to get a healthy 10% tip.

I can't say that it was my decision not to hate white people – that would be giving myself too much credit. I chose to look forward and focus on where I was going and play the game in the here and now, if need be. When I reached my third year and took a class of 120 students as a junior lecturer, the majority of them white, I began to appreciate that the tide was turning. Freedom was near.

Completing my undergraduate degree and then moving onto a postgraduate degree unveiled professional opportunities. Yes, it is true that one of democracy's most tangible benefits is education. It brings some degree of balance to the skewed scales. I have never feared white people. I have never had reason to. Envied them, maybe. When I completed my first two degrees, I considered myself as capable as anyone and understood that any limitations I experienced would be self-induced.

I got an opportunity to do my Master's degree in London at the School of Oriental and African Studies. It was an eye-opening experience for me. I remember walking into the allocated accommodation with at least a hundred other 20-somethings from all over the world. I gravitated towards a girl with a broad smile and solid kindness about her – Oksana Kemp. Sana, as she was commonly known, was Ukrainian but had assumed British citizenship. We became fast friends. At our first encounter I remarked that this year was going to be interesting given that I seemed to be the only black person and the only African in the group of 100 or so. She shrugged nonchalantly and said that she hadn't noticed. This was a life-changing moment for me. I realised then that we are self-defined and that the categories and classifications to which we adhere are our own constructs. This is the freedom I expect from democracy. It's being able to unshackle even the cognitive and emotional binds that constrain us from defining or even redefining our own agency.

I came back and continued my work in South Africa. At that stage I was working as an intern in the Office of the Deputy President – something that would not even have been in the realm of possibility in the past. This is another thing that democracy ought to do. I'm not sure what to call it; others would say, where there is a will, democracy must make a way.

Through the early years of my career after the Presidency, I can confidently say that for a handful of black people, democracy has allowed us to leapfrog. But these great leaps have left many behind and even seen others fall into greater disadvantage.

As a young woman, my social impediments are still intact. Unmarried and without children at 29, my social standing within my black community is in question. Interestingly, my parents seem to be the ones succumbing to the pressures more than me. They, too, will learn that democracy is also about personal choices. They will get a son-in-law and maybe two grandkids when the phantom husband and I choose.

As I reflect on my life story and whether the notion of democracy has lived up to my expectations, it's difficult to give one resounding answer. I prefer to think about a collage of memories, opportunities, setbacks, obstacles and prospects. The backdrop is solid. There was a South Africa before 1994 and a South Africa after 1994. Those distinctions in history are deep troughs that slice our lives into the before and after. Government policies have played a strong and forceful role in pushing back the gatekeepers and creating opportunities that people of colour could once not even have dreamt about. Perhaps, in other areas we have been slow off the mark. When I look at the glint of the silver and grey skyscrapers that jostle for space in the Sandton business district, I get a sense of optimism. When I drive less than five kilometres away from the skyscrapers towards the periphery of Sandton, I encounter the township that teeters on the brink of poverty, unemployment and disease. Democracy still has a long way to go.

But this collage is not only littered with these glaring disparities. Some of the colours have seeped into each other and new hues and tones are coming to the fore. And I see this every day: mothers and fathers with multiracial babies, blue eyes with a head of dark, tightly coiled curls. I think this is beautiful. But it also comes with its own headaches. We need to guard against losing the original essence of the people by holding onto our languages and keeping our culture and heritage whole.

In my view, democracy needs more time.

As I put the final touches to this self-portrait, the architect and symbol of South Africa's democracy, Nelson Mandela, lies in state at the Union Buildings. Since the passing of Madiba, debates about whether we have been able to uphold his legacy have been many and intense, inevitably. Thankfully, I feel that the foundations for a strong and active democracy are in place. This is no fragile state. South Africa's democracy, even at a youthful 19 years, is strong, stable, and I may go as far as to say solid. This is not to suggest that the country does not have its challenges. This is not to suggest that I am blind to the political leadership vacuum. But I am of the view that there is no such thing as a perfect democracy. We are a democracy in progress. Though our expectations remain simple, the transitions continue to be complex.

In search of ubuntu: A political philosopher's view of democratic South Africa

Thaddeus Metz

South African-American Professor of Ubuntu

I WRITE AS AN HONORARY SOUTH African, someone born in the US, but who has had an interest in the country for a long while and has lived here for 13 of the 20 years since the transition to democracy. In the 1980s, as a teenager, I helped to organise protests in Des Moines, Iowa to push banks to divest themselves of Kruger Rands, and then I supported the divestment movement at universities, as well as followed, with delight, the process by which Congress overrode President Reagan's veto of legislation that imposed economic sanctions on South Africa.

My interest in South Africa has not been merely negative, in the sense of wanting to see a patently unjust system of racism and autocracy abolished. It has also been positive, a matter of hoping for some approaches from Mzansi to culture, society and the state that would be different from typical Western and Eastern dynamics. I am a political philosopher who has long been disenchanted with the centralised authoritarianism characteristic of the East and the fiercely competitive and instrumentalist models often found in the West. In the early to mid-1990s, I looked to South Africa for the proverbial 'third alternative' that would foster more cooperative, participatory and communal relationships and organisations, ones that would produce more cultured, egalitarian and meaningful ways of life.

In the vernacular, I have been hoping to see more ubuntu in South Africa's institutions than had been present in the two dominant socio-politico-economic models across the world in the 20th century. I haven't been expecting utopia from the past 20 years of democracy; I've just wanted something new to come out of Africa. In this essay I recount my experience of learning that it is not always forthcoming, at least not as quickly as I would have liked. However, I conclude by indicating that the promise remains, suggesting several concrete and attractive ways that South Africa could apply traditional values of ubuntu to a contemporary setting.

Welcome to Johannesburg: Africans, Americans

I first arrived in South Africa in 1999, when I was a young lecturer in philosophy based in St Louis, Missouri. At that time there was an African American rapper from St Louis, Nelly, who was making it big. As I stepped off the plane in Johannesburg, I did not know what to expect as I entered the airport. Oh, I knew not to expect lions – after all, knowing some detailed history of the country is what persuaded the Durban woman after whom I was in hot pursuit to spend time talking to me at a Halloween party in St Louis. But I didn't know how the Joburg airport would be decorated, which sort of food and drink would be on offer, what people would be wearing, that sort of thing. I certainly was not expecting to hear Nelly as the airport's choice of background music. But guess whose voice was blaring out of the speaker on the ceiling as I entered the building.

Part of me was happy to hear my hometown singer getting some play in a major city about a 20-hour plane flight away. I felt at home. But I shouldn't have been able to feel quite so at home. I, an American white guy, should not have had my life so easily recreated here, without any effort, let alone intention, on my part. Another part of me was sad for South Africa, and continues to be.

One promising thing about post-apartheid South Africa has been its opportunity to blend the Western and the African, to create new mixes, styles and relationships in ways that tie its diverse populations together. No single extant culture has it all. America has onion rings, jazz and great universities, but also strip malls, an inadequate amount of paid holiday for workers and Miley Cyrus. South Africa has the ethic of ubuntu, Ladysmith Black Mambazo and the TRC, but also grotesque inequality, poor public transport and the occasional muti killing. As humanity moves forward, various civilisations should, ideally, reflect on themselves, learn from one another, and fashion the good, the true and the beautiful in ways that, while growing out of a given locale, speak to fundamentally human themes.

Too often, I think, South Africa has messed up its chances to mix

– Nelly as its welcome to visitors coming from abroad and citizens returning home being a case in point. It has not been all bad, of course. Lebo Mathosa, Mandoza and Freshlyground are great. And at the Rosebank Mall in Johannesburg, management allowed people to write messages on a wall in honour of an ailing Nelson Mandela. There, I encountered, 'Get better Mandizzle. If it wasn't for you I wouldn't be on a date with a white girl right now.' Here, the appeal to African American slang is adapted to a South African context in a bottom-up, creative, political, funny and touching way.

However, on the whole, South Africa has not escaped the strong gravitational pull of the West. Better West than East, I suppose, but better still would have been more South, as I explain.

East and West: The two elephants

One of the two major types of society in the post-war era was exemplified by the Soviet Union and China. They used extreme coercion to advance a specific conception of how to live, centred on the realisation of a political agenda or a vision of human nature. The state took control of the means of production and employed them in the way that a small group of unelected bureaucrats thought best. They stifled ideas that could have competed with their programmes, and killed, jailed or exiled those who they judged to be disinclined to support their ideology. Some states continue to adopt a similar strategy, enforcing a single, narrowly interpreted religion and punishing those deemed to have flouted it with, for example, whippings for alcohol possession, beheadings for apostasy and hangings for homosexuality.

In the cases of the authoritarian regimes of the previous century, violence and other severe practices ultimately did little good as far as bringing about the desired goal, instead causing mass starvation, large-scale warfare and, more day-to-day, lives full of fear and frustration and devoid of much wealth. And more contemporary forms of state coercion, while more limited, are still usually ineffective. Punishment and threats of it are unlikely to change people's attitudes, while keeping silent about one's views merely to avoid punishment is unlikely to impart meaning to anyone's life, neither the one threatened nor the one threatening.

On the other hand, there have been liberal societies in Western Europe, North America and Australasia where the state has largely aimed for neutrality with respect to how its residents live. The state has sought mainly to enforce people's rights to choose their own ways of life, regardless of whether they are pious, virtuous, meaningful, healthy or not. Instead of expressing support for one particular way of life, this sort of state has protected people's civil liberties and provided financial and other resources, such as healthcare and education, that would be useful for achieving whatever goals people might elect to adopt. It has allowed the means of production to be privately owned and deployed to promote profit by buying people's labour-power, making products and then selling them on an open market.

Although the liberal societies avoided the disasters that befell the totalitarian ones, their residents are not living as well as they could be. People feel alienated from the political process, their participation reduced to a miniscule vote once every few years or, alternately, expanded to a disproportionately huge share of influence on politics in the forms of corporate lobbying and threatening to relocate to tax havens.

The unemployed feel that they are failing to contribute to society and to support their families, while the employed think they are working too much on activities they do not find important. Typical jobs are organised so as to maximise outputs (sales, responses to clients) and minimise costs (salaries, time), which require workers to conform to assembly-line models of production.

When workers get home from their isolating drives, they are exhausted and unable to do much more (after having sorted out the kids) than watch television or play on their iPads. The rich are surrounded by material objects but often lack human connection, while the poor find themselves without the resources to acquire, say, education, artistic supplies or sporting equipment.

In general, people in the West suffer from lives of boredom, loneliness, isolation, neurosis, depression, alcoholism, addiction, conformity, adaptation, passivity, aimlessness, manipulation, repetitiveness, ugliness, separation from natural beauty and a lack of wisdom (trenchantly captured by critical theorists such as Erich Fromm and Guy Debord).

Neither society has been maximally attractive considered in itself – but then the post-war era was all the worse for the two giants having fought and also sought to expand and replicate themselves.

Invasion, annexation, colonialism, imperialism and proxy wars were the name of the game. As the old African saying goes, when two elephants fight, it is the grass that suffers.

A third way, in principle

In lieu of both models, I, and many others on the left, have sought a 'third way': roughly, a society with more community, creativity and, more generally, human excellence. It would be a matter of the state adopting policies designed to promote meaning and flourishing in people's lives, but with a minimal use of coercion. Instead of radically narrowing residents' options in light of a monolithic conception of how best to live, and instead of refraining from acting for the sake of people's good and leaving citizens utterly to their own devices when it comes to how to live, a state could seek to guide people's decision-making towards a variety of value-rich behaviours, albeit without substantial punishment and threats.

For example, a state could: offer rewards; provide incentives; warn of risks; inform about goods; educate the young in certain ways; obtain pre-commitments from people to adopt certain practices; adopt 'facilitative' law that would give people legal options, such as marriage; make opportunities available; and use 'nudges' such as making bad choices harder for people to make, but not forbidding them (on this, see *Nudge*, Richard Thaler and Cass Sunstein). It could also use coercion in ways that close some doors but do not force people to go through a single door, so to speak. Here, the state might prohibit television broadcasts during, say, Saturday mornings, with the expectation, but not requirement, that people would spend more time together as a family or engage in hobbies (an approach suggested by André Gorz long ago).

Such policies would, arguably, deal with human freedom in the right way. Substantial meaning or excellence cannot accrue if people are forced into a certain way of life that they would otherwise not choose, and yet people often need help from the state in order to uphold ways of life that they themselves are likely to recognise as desirable. To enrich people's lives, a state could enable them to pursue the good, the true and the beautiful.

And it could also do so in participative ways. Although direct democracy is a tall order in large territories and urban environments, other forms of collective decision-making could be practiced that would be more attractive than either having no vote and being controlled by a small political party, or merely voting once every few years for distant representatives. For instance, imagine a state whose officials routinely consulted with civil society organisations, engaged in 'town hall meetings' and publicised their plans on television and other media, actively encouraging feedback from the populace via SMS and the web before implementing.

The road still not travelled
In the 1990s, South Africa looked as though it might carve out a new kind of society, in the direction of the sort of ideal I have sketched. The Constitution was constructed in response to substantial input, not merely from political parties, but also thousands of individual citizens; the Constitution explicitly counted indigenous customs as law to be considered alongside parliamentary statute; the first elected government was one of national unity; the beginnings of an inclusive South African identity stirred, especially with Nelson Mandela's support of the Springboks; the TRC was a novel and inspirational approach, grounded on sub-Saharan mores, to dealing with political crimes in a way that aimed to heal broken relationships; and the state established bodies such as the Commission for Gender Equality, the Moral Regeneration Movement and the National Heritage Council.

However, these approaches did not continue much towards the end of the 20th century or at least they did not blossom in salient ways in the 21st. Formally segregated facilities are gone and interracial relationships are on the rise, but racial divisions have deepened. There is neither enough goodwill between races, nor enough of a sense of togetherness among them. One cannot expect every day to feel like it did on the first day of the Soccer World Cup, when a garage attendant told me, 'Jesus better not come today because no one would pay attention'. However, the spirit of the country these days feels like one in which people are out to hang onto and secure as much as they can for themselves and their respective groups.

In addition, the style of governance post-Mandela, both with respect to the ANC and the government, has been widely perceived to be fairly closed to different viewpoints. Democracy is real, a patent gain over the apartheid era. And yet togetherness is missing, with the ANC routinely taking advantage of its majority in legislatures and executive positions to push through laws and policies that lack broad consensus, as well as to appoint administrators and managers on a cadre basis. People generally feel out of touch from the government – not even officials at the municipal level do a good job of responding to queries from residents. And people are streaming to the courts, NGOs, the media and other outlets to complain and seek relief because their impression is that the government will not hear them out and give them a fair shake.

The underclass is secure with an enormous state-funded grant programme for some quarter of the population, and the upper and middle classes now include black folk. However, healthcare, education and services in general are extremely poorly managed, even if they cover many more people now; attempts at land reform have been unsuccessful, with little land transferred and with the Minister of Rural Development and Land Reform indicating in 2010 that more than 90% of the land so far transferred to blacks was lying unproductive; unemployment is among the highest in the world, with millions of people remaining idle and scavenging; and there is substantial skewing of public resources towards private interests.

The major cities are overrun by cars, such that those with them are often stuck in deadlock and those without them spend lots of time waiting for transport by taxi, bus and train. And with regard to culture one routinely gets: Steven Seagal and other American 'B' movies on television; KFC, McDonald's and similar fast-food outlets; the blight of constant advertising and the annoyance of unexpected sales calls; colonial-style hotels that evince nothing of Africa; malls that, in terms of atmosphere, organisation and store content, feature little that one could not find randomly in the West; and Nelly on the airport sound system.

In short, the country of South Africa has moved thousands of kilometres in a Western direction (but with a large chunk of inefficiency).

The next 20 years for South Africa: More of a 'third way' in practice?
As a political philosopher, I cannot predict South Africa's path between now and 2034, but I can close by making some recommendations about how I think it should develop. Just look at that Freedom Charter! Just look at that Constitution! South Africa has dared to pursue big goals. I have some more to suggest, which

involve refurbishing for a modern context instances in which pre-colonial sub-Saharan societies exhibited ubuntu. I submit that these projects would not take a lot of money or even many complex skills. Or, let me put this way: if the government could host such a smoothly run World Cup – complete with new trains and stadiums – then it could implement programmes such as the following.

Sharing labour

In many traditional African societies, it has been common for people to help one another harvest their fields. Instead of those living on the land being solely responsible for gathering up the produce from it, all those who had harvesting to do would collectively move from field to field to help one another. In southern Africa, such cooperative farming is often called *letsema*. How might such a practice be realised in today's South Africa?

One way might be if the government were to ask everyone in society to lend a hand to help improve education and then coordinated their contributions. Of course, the state should do what it can to fund and otherwise improve public education as usual, but it could also organise the efforts of many other, private agents. It might ask: construction companies to put up some rooms that would serve as a school library; wealthier individuals with extra books to donate some to the libraries, taking the time to collect from their neighbourhoods; and retired persons to volunteer their time to run these libraries. And it could widely publicise, on the Internet, radio and television, a list of who has contributed and how, indicating to society how far it has come towards its goal of X number of new libraries and how far it has yet to go.

A state that mobilised a wide array of actors to help achieve a common goal in this way would: improve social cohesion; enable people to give their time and other resources towards a concrete goal; and, of course, help to improve students' education.

Sharing power and ideas

According to the sub-Saharan proverb, if you want to go fast, go alone, but if you want to go far, go together. Or as Steve Biko remarked of Africans, 'we are prepared to have a much slower progress in an effort to make sure that all of us are marching to the same tune'. In the political sphere among many indigenous black peoples, this sort of orientation has been manifest in the form of consensus seeking. It has been common for societies to elect (usually male) elders who are expected to come to a unanimous agreement about what should be done and then for chiefs usually to defer to their judgement. Another political instance of the inclination to walk together has been for small-scale societies to make decisions affecting the group consequent to giving all adult members the opportunity to voice their opinion. How to bring such practices into the 21st century?

Some would suggest changing the Constitution to require parliamentarians to come to consensus in order to ratify legislation, fascinatingly advocated by several African political philosophers (including Kwasi Wiredu and South Africa's own Mogobe Ramose). More practically, the dominant political majority of our time, the ANC, could be less opportunistic with regard to the power it has legally secured. It could make appointments based much more on qualifications, including integrity, and much less on party membership and patronage. It could also appoint more persons to Cabinet who are not ANC members, as well as meaningfully engage with those likely to be affected by proposals as well as with experts who are not part of government. Working together, South Africans could do more!

Sharing space and children

Nuclear families, let alone single-parent households, are a bad idea. Rearing children is too big a job to be done by one or two adults, especially when life in a modern economy often requires labour to be undertaken on the job market. If it takes a village to rear a child, a village should be created. What if a state designed housing so that a dozen or so units formed a collective compound reserved for those with children and those interested in supporting them?

Perhaps the units form a circle, so that the middle is a play area for children, on which all could keep an eye. Maybe the compound requires a certain balance in terms of the genders and ages of its residents, and it might favour some women with children who have suffered abuse and need shelter. A few of the residents could stay home to watch over the younger children during the day and be financially supported by others who work outside the compound. Suppose there is a collective area where all children do their homework, or there is a compound rule that no one may play outside until their homework is done or that television broadcasts are turned off between 4:30 and 7:00 pm. Parents might meet together every two weeks to talk about parenting issues or matters of collective concern, or listen to social workers and child psychologists. Wouldn't this attempt to extend families be a social experiment worth conducting?

Sharing opportunities

According to Walter Sisulu's understanding of ubuntu (as related to Johann Broodryk in an interview), if you have two cows and the milk of the first cow is enough for your own consumption, you are expected to donate the milk of the second cow to your underprivileged brother. Similar practices abound among indigenous Africans, where, for instance, those with many cows would donate one to a recently married couple to help them get started. How might this type of giving guide South Africans, particularly those with wealth and power, beyond them paying taxes and donating the odd bit of change to beggars at crossroads?

Here are three ideas. First, white farmers could decide to impart skills to black people and to transfer a certain percentage of fertile land to those with the demonstrable ability to make use of it. Current agricultural associations would be sufficient to coordinate such a redress programme; state supervision would not be necessary. Surely this is how AfriForum should be keeping busy.

Second, businesses could lend a hand to unsuccessful job applicants. For instance, they could provide a brief indication to candidates about why they were not hired and offer constructive advice on how to make themselves more competitive. Of course, it would not be feasible to do this in cases where there are several hundred applicants. But it could be done for those shortlisted or some other subset of the pool.

Third, and finally, governments, businesses and other organisations could go out of their way to provide chances for local artists to display their work. I encountered a Zulu poet at the opening of an academic centre and a Xhosa musician at a book launch, and both gave powerful, memorable performances (and if I could remember their names, I would plug them here). Who stepping off a plane in Joburg wants to be greeted with Nelly? Hear me, Airports Company South Africa – not even the fellow from St Louis!

Twenty years of youth advancement in a free and democratic South Africa

Bongani Mkongi

Former Member of Parliament

IN APRIL 1988, THE AFRICA FUND in association with the American Committee on Africa concluded in their bulletin that:

> It is clear that the youth of South Africa is one of the key groups in the struggle against apartheid. Because of their crucial role in opposing apartheid as well as their relentless commitment to this fight, they have historically and will continue to be one of the most heavily repressed groups within South African society. There is no doubt that the militancy and energy of South Africa's young people will make them instrumental in the dismantling of apartheid and the forging of a new society for all South Africans.

The history of the youth movement in South Africa is the history of struggle and resilience against the apartheid system that subjected the majority of the population to conditions of abject poverty, underdevelopment and ignorance. We are aware that before the 1994 dispensation, young people in South Africa, especially blacks, played a pivotal role in opposing the policies of apartheid. They were at the forefront in the battle to support the strategic objective of the liberation movements.

Youth is a microcosm of society. Their struggles in South Africa have always been an integral part of the broader struggles of society. In their organised formations they were always reflective of a society they envisaged: a society that is free, democratic, united, non-racial, non-sexist and prosperous.

Dr Saleem Badat in his article adapted from a speech delivered at the launch of his book, *Black Man You are on Your Own*, narrates:

For white South Africans the 1960s were generally a time of political calm, rising living standards, prosperity and sharing in the sustained economic boom of that period. Some blacks shared in the bounty, those for who the opportunities for the accumulation of wealth, power and privilege through the Bantustan and separate development programme proved irresistible. For most Blacks, however, the aftermath of the 1960 Sharpeville massacre – with the suppression of the African National Congress (ANC) and Pan Africanist Congress (PAC), the repression of radical political activity, detentions, bannings and banishments – was a period of intensified exploitation, extended and tightened social controls, demoralization, fear and enforced and sullen acquiescence.

The youth of South Africa did not escape this reality. They also bore the brunt of apartheid brutality. In order to qualify the above statement, Dr Badat says that:

The black universities gathered together talented students who had survived the rigours and hurdles of black schooling, including the pernicious 'Bantu education'. Notwithstanding their talents, upon graduating black students were still to be condemned to a future of limited socioeconomic opportunities, disenfranchisement, inequality and injustice ... there were few black youth who had not encountered directly the humiliation of white superiority attitudes, while all suffered in some degree the effects of legal discrimination.

Consequently, as we approach the celebrations of 20 years of freedom and democracy in South Africa on 27 April 2014, it is beneficial to pause and take stock of the progress made since 27 April 1994 in addressing the legacy of apartheid colonialism on young people in South Africa and the challenges they face in our country today.

This essay will therefore focus on three strategic and important challenges that face the youth in South Africa and what the ANC government has done to tackle those challenges since assuming power in 1994, namely reducing unemployment, increasing education opportunities and dealing with the health challenges of young people.

Economic status of youth

According to the findings from the 1996 Census, which were publicised by Statistics South Africa in 2001 under the theme 'The Youth of South Africa', after the transition to democracy in 1994, South Africa emerged as a society with inherent problems. The legacy of racial, gender and urban/rural inequality, inherited from the policies of apartheid, had a negative impact on the living conditions of certain sectors of the population. These policies, among others, affected the provision of basic services such as water and electricity, the provision of housing and access to education, healthcare, the provision of sport and recreation facilities, arts and culture as well as employment opportunities.

The 1996 Census paints a bleak picture of the status of youth in South Africa. It reveals that of the 40.6 million people living in South Africa, just over 16.1 million or 40%, were youth between the ages of 14 and 35 years. Nearly four in every five of the youth in our country were Africans, less than 10% were coloured, 10% were white and the remaining 3% were Indian.

The overall unemployment rate for the youth in our country, according to the 1996 Census, was 40.9%. The unemployment rate for economically active youth was higher for females (49.6%) than for males (33%). Unemployment was more intense in non-urban areas (51.3%) than urban areas (35.7%). African youth had the highest unemployment rate of all population groups (50.2%).

More pressing was that 12% of all youth who were not studying in 1996 did not have any formal education. In the 14-year-old group this percentage was higher (52%) than in the age group of 35 years (16%). In the period under review, of the 16.1 million youths, 7.3 million were not economically active, 4.5 million were employed, while 3.1 million were unemployed using the expanded definition.

Of the employed female youth, the largest proportion worked in community, social and personal services (25.3%) followed by private households (20.9%). Of employed male youth, the largest proportion worked in community services (15.7%) followed by manufacturing (15.3%). With regard to occupation, the largest proportion of employed young females had elementary jobs (36%), while the largest proportions of employed young males were craftsmen (23%).

Of the four national groups, African youth had the highest unemployment rate followed by coloured youth. Women, in

217

particular, were highly affected by unemployment. Whereas about half (49.6%) of all female youth who were economically active had been out of work, about 33% of young men were unemployed. Such discrepancies also appeared between the provinces; for example, the Eastern Cape (a former Bantustan) recorded an unemployment rate among youth of 55.6% while the Western Cape recorded 22.3%.

In the final analysis, prospects for a life of quality, particularly in relation to job opportunities and general living standards, remains a major concern in respect of a large proportion of the youth in South Africa, given their low level of education.

This is a synopsis of the great challenge that the democratic government faced when it took over in 1994. Poor living conditions, starting a family at a young age, inadequate education, lack of employment opportunities and high unemployment rates were indicators of poverty. Large proportions of South African youth were living in poverty.

Policy interventions

Historically, young people have tended to feel the burden of marginalisation in many societies across the globe. South African youth faced enormous injustices as a result of apartheid. This lack of opportunities has mobilised the youth in South Africa to fight for social change and social justice throughout the decades.

In order to salvage this sorry state of affairs, after 1994 the ANC government passed many pieces of legislation, including a National Youth Development Policy Framework (NYDPF). This led government to pass the National Youth Commission (NYC) Act 18 of 1996, as amended in 2000, and establish the Umsobomvu Youth Fund (UYF) in 1998 with an aim of creating an enabling environment for youth development.

These strategic interventions were also aimed at promoting the participation of youth in the socio-economic development of South Africa. After the review of the work of the NYC and UYF in 2009, government established the National Youth Development Agency (NYDA), a product of the merger between the NYC and UYF, to accelerate and expand youth development initiatives.

Since 1994 the ANC government has acknowledged that young people are not a homogenous entity. They have different historical, cultural, linguistic and socio-economic backgrounds and they live in varying contemporary circumstance (The Status of Youth Report, 2003). In this regard, due consideration needs to be given to a continuum of youth needs, with appreciation and acknowledgement that the legacy of apartheid has created greater disadvantage and vulnerability among women, rural and young black people (National Youth Commission Report, 2001).

In the past 20 years, as part of the human development strategy, the democratic government has engaged in the process of solidifying the early childhood development sector as the bedrock for positive youth development. This approach was aimed at building constructive citizenry, beginning with the societal development in families and extending through schools and communities to civic, political and economic engagement.

Government has put in place a system in which youth development is viewed within the context of broader community and national development. It put youth development at the centre of the agenda of the state, with safe, nurturing and supportive environments created by families, communities and society in the context of free basic education, a National Student Financial Aid Scheme (NSFAS), the provision of sport and recreational facilities, job creation, skills development, arts and culture, and many more. In doing so, the government has built reciprocal and mutually shaping relationships between young people and their families, schools and communities, through greater investment in parent, teacher and learner participation in educational matters, from school to university, as well as at community level.

Education and employment
As a result, according to the 2011 Census, there is a clear and consistent trend showing that younger people are attaining higher levels of education in South Africa. This implies that more young people are in educational institutions than before 1994. Most of the studies on schooling in South Africa show high levels of enrolment of young people in institutions of learning.

Perry and Arends (2003) revealed that post-apartheid South Africa witnessed an increase in the enrolment of African youth 'with the percentage of youth (aged 20 to 34 years) with matriculation increasing from 23.6 per cent in 1996 to 29.7 per cent in 2001'. This trend was also witnessed in the enrolment in higher education and further education and training institutions. According to Subotzky (2003), African enrolment in higher education enrolments increased fourfold, from 97 485 (29% of total enrolments) in 1988 to 368 289 (60% of total enrolments) in 2000.

These changes in the educational levels of Africans and youth have major implications for the growth of the economically active population and, therefore, for employment rates among young South Africans.

The Status of Youth Report (2003) noted that for the older generations, the data showed that men had a consistent advantage in educational levels over women, but that this gap has closed for the youngest (18–30) age group.

The report further argues that in relation to tertiary qualifications, for example, males 61 years and older were twice as likely to graduate than females. However, this gender gap has closed among 18- to 30-year-olds, with a slightly higher percentage of women graduating than men. These changes need to be seen within the context of the enormous growth in educational levels for both men and women. Massive gains in educational levels have been achieved for both young men and women, especially Africans.

Based on the research by the Human Sciences Research Council (HSRC), in 2003 more young women had work. The slightly higher percentage of women in the 18- to 24-year-old age group, who have worked may be an outcome of the application of employment equity policies in the workplace. However, for both males and females, percentages of those who have ever worked exceed 50% only among the 36- to-44-year-old age group, which may suggest that they have had work as youth between 1994 and 2003.

While the 2011 Census report exposes the fact that the majority of people in South Africa who are still at the coalface of unemployment and poverty are young, the report also reveals that unemployment rates generally declined with increasing age. According to the official or narrow definition, unemployment rates between age cohorts 25- to 29-years-olds is 33.7%; 30- to 34-year-olds is 27.4% and 35- to 39-year-olds account for 24.0%.The overall official unemployment rate for young people is estimated at 29.8%.

However, if we use the expanded definition, it changes the picture altogether. Using the expanded definition of unemployment, young people aged 25–29 years account for 42.7%; 30–34 years for 35.8%

and 35–39 years for 32.3%. The overall expanded unemployment rate for young people is therefore estimated at 40.0%.

Whether the 1996 Census report used a narrow definition or an expanded definition to reach a youth unemployment rate of 40.9%, the 2011 Census report reveals that youth unemployment in South Africa has steadily declined to 29.8% when using the narrow definition, and 40.0% when using the expanded definition.

In this regard, it should be noted that South Africa emerged from apartheid colonialism with an economic legacy of relative isolation, and an inward-looking policy regime that had been pursued over a number of decades. The economy embedded racial inequalities in economic assets and access to jobs and social services, and was dependent on primary production and primary exports, despite its relative diversification.

The ANC's approach to the development and support of small business is an example of a comprehensive, integrated national strategy to create full employment. It was born out of the commitment of our government and stakeholders at the Small Business Summit held in 1995. Government reaffirmed the importance of micro-, small and medium-sized enterprises in economic development, especially youth development and participation in the economy. In the same vein, in 1997 the government promulgated a National Small Business Act to pave the way for the establishment of wholesale agencies charged with spearheading a national strategy for developing and promoting small business.

Thus, after the successful Job Summit in 1995, government called for the establishment of the Umsobomvu Youth Fund as well as a Mentorship Scheme and Business Incubation (MSME). It was further emphasised that the South African Youth Council (SAYC), as a civil-society umbrella body of youth, should represent the interests of young people in the National Economic Development and Labour Council (NEDLAC) for such a purpose.

As a result, the International Labour Organization (ILO) regards this intervention in youth unemployment as an example of a comprehensive, integrated national strategy. After the Job Summit, the ILO said:

The relationship to youth employment in South Africa has been more clearly specified. First, the above programmes will be required to indicate targets for youth as beneficiaries. Second, given the difficulties of promoting self-employment among youth, especially the younger ones, the employment framework of South Africa provides for the integration of youth oriented public works and special employment programmes with MSME projects such that they would benefit from each other.

To this end, South Africa has contributed more than R5 billion to these programmes, including direct employment programmes. South Africa uses this approach to integrating public works initiatives targeted at youth and other special labour segments, such as women, rural people and the youth with disabilities. Another initiative to support direct employment-creation programmes includes special employment schemes for young people in the form of the National Youth Service (NYS), and skills-development programmes through institutions such as SAYC, NYDA, the Sector Education and Training Authorities (SETAs) and the revival of Further Education and Training Colleges (FETs). These schemes take advantage of the temporary status of young people as a tenure during which a combination of volunteerism and exposure to training and work is undertaken in a manner that is patriotic, civic, and socially and economically beneficial to the country and the youth.

Health

As was reported in the 1996 Census, young people comprised the majority of people who were HIV positive and this was a threat to the future of South Africa and the strength of our workforce.

President Jacob Zuma unveiled a 'bold plan' for South Africa to accelerate its fight against the HIV and AIDS pandemic, and tuberculosis and other diseases associated with HIV and AIDS. Prevention was at the heart of this new National Strategic Plan for HIV, Sexually Transmitted Infections (STIs) and Tuberculosis (TB) that aims to reduce new infections by 50% through a holistic approach in a more multi-sectoral response.

This multi-sectoral response included the promotion of sport and recreation programmes, healthy lifestyles, arts and culture, and the fight against substance and alcohol abuse, violence against women, children, the elderly and people with disabilities.

This strategic and multi-sectoral approach turned the tide against

HIV and AIDS in South Africa. The 2008 survey conducted by the Human Sciences Research Council (HSRC) and the Medical Research Council (MRC) indicates that HIV prevalence has decreased among young people in South Africa between the ages of 15 and 24 years from 10.3% in 2005 to 8.6% in 2008.

In order to qualify this statement the reports goes further to suggest that HIV and AIDS prevalence at a national level has decreased among children aged two to 14 years from 5.6% to 2.5%. For the 15- to 20-year-olds, it was found that there was a substantial decrease in incidence in 2008 as compared to 2002 and 2005, in particular among 15- to 19-year-olds.

Indeed, today, South Africa is better than yesterday and tomorrow will be better than today.

However, the 2011 Census report and the National Development Plan (NDP): Vision 2030 indicate that the challenges still facing the majority of young people 'raises some important questions about constraints that youth in our country face in attaining positive human development and a successful transition to adulthood'. The reports indicate that the majority of young people, especially Africans and coloureds, grapple with unemployment, difficulty in finding a job, substance abuse, teenage pregnancy, diseases, taking longer to complete secondary schooling and dropping out at an early age, and economic dependency.

Therefore, government should tighten up the performance monitoring and evaluation of youth development programmes and interventions in all government departments and state organs at local, provincial and national levels. It should review the implementation mechanisms and capacity deficiencies within government departments to put youth development programmes at the centre of their delivery programmes. Civil society and other strategic stakeholders dealing directly and/or indirectly with youth should be assisted by the state to accelerate youth empowerment and development programmes going forward.

Even though South Africa has made significant progress since 1994, enemies of progress will still find it difficult to accept this and will continue to use youth development as contested terrain. This is because 'youth development' is 'a socially constructed concept, and as such is subject to ideological distortions based on power relations in society, vested interests and conceptions of how things ought to be done' (*Umsobomvu Youth Fund,* 2003, p. 39).

By the same token, the Social Transformation Committee of the ANC asserts that:

> The gains recorded [during the past 20 years of democracy and freedom in South Africa] can be partially attributed to gains recorded in the policy arena as facilitated for and delivered by the transformed institutional and delivery mechanisms available to the state.
>
> Some of these policies have seen the achievement of key indicators such as an increase in enrolment in early childhood development institutions, primary and secondary schooling and in institutions of higher learning, decrease in HIV and AIDS incidence among young people in South Africa, improved access to primary healthcare for young women and girls, expansion of beneficiaries in the Child Support Grants, gender parity index as well as the implementation of solidarity based social policies which are aimed at offsetting significant job losses among young people in South Africa.

Conclusion

While the significant progress made by the democratic developmental state from 1994 to 2014 needs to be applauded, it should be borne in mind that this progress was accompanied by the robust engagement and radical contributions of many young people in South Africa through their organised formations.

We must commend the work and contribution of successive generations of young cadres who were at the helm of the SAYC, NYC and NYDA, including cadres in the Progressive Youth Alliance, present and past. We must also thank the previous generations of youth in South Africa and elsewhere that fought tirelessly for the realisation of a united, non-racial, non-sexist, democratic South Africa.

References

African National Congress Social Transformation Committee discussion document for the ANC National Conference. Mangaung, 2012.

African Fund in association with the American Committee on Africa, The Struggle of Youth in South Africa: 1988.

Saleem, B. 2009 *Black Man You are on Your Own*. Steve Biko Foundation: STE Publishers.

Human Sciences Research Council in association with the Medical Research Council (MRC), A Turning Tide Among Teenagers? 2009.

International Labour Organization (ILO), Recent Economic Reform in Selected African Countries; Successes and Failures. 2002.

National Planning Commission. 2012. National Development: Vision 2030.

National Youth Commission. 2002. National Youth Policy Framework.

Perry, H & Arends, F. 2003. Public Schooling, in *Human Resources Development Review 2003: Education, Employment and Skills in South Africa*. HSRC, Cape Town: HSRC Press.

Sudotzky, G 2003. Public Higher Education, in *Human Resources Development Review 2003: Education, Employment and Skills in South Africa*. HSRC, Cape Town: HSRC Press.

Statistics South Africa (StatsSA). 2001. Selected Findings From Census '96.

StatsSA, 2011 Census Report. 2012.

Umsobomvu Youth Fund. 2003. The Status of Youth Report.

United Nations Development Programme, Achieve Universal Primary Education Report (MDGs).

Finding love in a democracy: Our story of living in a free society

Toivo and Setumo Mohapi
Young professionals

DEAR HUSBAND

While the world was experiencing pain, hurt and anger, we fell in love in a country called South Africa. While the Elders, led by Archbishop Desmond Tutu, prepared themselves for their mission to Sudan to address the conflict and human suffering in Darfur, we chose to stay at home and pray for them. While our politics were experiencing turbulence, we created our new foundation.

In the mist of this, we found time to fall in love. We came from two different worlds and yet our liberation, led by our forefathers, brought us peace and stability. I always wondered if it is okay to feel at peace while the rest of the world is suffering. How does one liberate oneself when the world is experiencing an economic crisis? In South Africa, our real GDP growth fell from 5.5% in 2007 to 3.7% in 2008. Many young South Africans find themselves unemployed. Currently our unemployment rate is estimated to be 25% and huge inequalities still exist. For instance, there are huge income inequalities – the richest 20% of the population earn 70% of the income while the poorest 10% get less than 0.6%. The mean income for an African is R777.46, the median is R406.95, while for white South Africans the mean is R7 645.58 and the median is R5 331.61, and coloureds and Asians are in-between.

Liberation seems to come at a price. Dr Pallo Jordan once stated that 'uprooting the legacy of national oppression and delivering on the promise of liberation has not been easy. But there is a slowly emerging consensus that the eradication of poverty should be the priority item on our national agenda.'* If liberation is about a state of mind, how do we ensure that our love does not feel oppressed? Or

---

* Ruth First Lecture, 28 August 2000.

226

should we rather use our love to liberate others? If we had to test our love against the philosophies of liberation, would we survive? If we subscribe to the philosophy that argues that liberation is about the 'universal discourse of truth, as opposed to claims that it can only be an expression of a particular people, or class, within a particular culture' (as Douglas Kellner noted in his critical thinking review paper titled 'Critical Theory, Poststructuralism, and the Philosophy of Liberation'*), we should admit that our love is yet to enter this discourse, which deconstructs the definition of liberation, as argued by Enrique Dussel's philosophy of liberation ('The Philosophy of Liberation: The Postmodern Debate, and Latin American Studies', 2008).

Today marks our 5th anniversary of marriage. I am happy with the journey we have travelled. Our country is in the process of building a nation that will allow our children and their children to truly enjoy the fruits of democracy. We can proudly state that South Africa is a nation in transition. Our social cohesion outcomes, such as sharing common values, creating social order and control, our commitment to social solidarity and reducing wealth disparities, and the creation of social networks and social capital have demonstrated that South Africa is committed to the process of nation-building.

Our history of racism has left many scars, although South Africa still manages to evolve positively. Issues of race, class, identity and leadership continue to be areas of contestation. Our society has reached a point at which we are starting to understand and/or deal with the nature and feasibility of social cohesion and accept multicultural practices, belief systems and intercultural communication. These issues take time and, like our marriage, they require patience. Thanks to our Constitution, this transitional process is respected and shared. 'South Africa belongs to all who live in it'. Imagine if we lived during the time of the 1913 Land Act and the 1903 African Native Affairs Commission? Would we be together? Yes, I think we would have been together. However, I doubt that we would have received the level of education we have achieved today and our house and home would have been a dream. Our spiritual and emotional wellbeing would have been compromised.

Today, South Africa's flagship advantages continue to shine.

---

* pages.gseis.ucla.edu/faculty/kellner/essays/criticaltheorypoststructuralism.pdf.

Globally we are ranked:
- 1st in legal rights;
- 1st in regulation of security exchange;
- 1st in efficacy of corporate boards;
- 1st in strength of auditing and reporting standards;
- 2nd in availability of financial services; and
- 8th in effectiveness of anti-monopoly policies.

We, as a nation, have produced a National Development Plan that puts all South Africans on a path towards attaining the common vision of eliminating poverty and reducing inequality by 2030. This plan is founded on six pillars:

- Mobilisation of all South Africans;
- Active engagement of citizens in their own development;
- Expansion of the economy and making growth inclusive;
- Building of key capabilities (human, physical and institutional);
- Building a capable and developmental state; and
- Fostering strong leadership throughout society.

I love the fact that we have taken a collective decision to become active citizens. Our contribution to the plan has started the process of liberating others. The plan presents South Africans with opportunities that will allow them to become agents in their own development. We acknowledge all the hard work our government has done since 1994. We welcome the 3 million new homes that were built. We understand the importance of providing social assistance to the 15 million grant beneficiaries. We celebrate efforts made to ensure that every South African has access to education, and we will work with our government to improve the quality of education in our country. More can be done but alone government will not be able to deliver a better life for all. We have a responsibility to assist.

The unfortunate aspect of debating our liberation is that we are bound to reflect on issues related to political domination, matters of equality and social differentiation. As I write to you, affirmative action and Broad-Based Black Economic Empowerment (BBBEE) is at the centre of the equity debate in South Africa. For instance, income dynamics have played a complex role since 1994 and the income of skilled people and those with assets has increased a lot.

Similarly, those in the upper middle class have benefitted from rising real salaries. Social grants have benefitted the poorest, especially those in the bottom third of the income spectrum. Furthermore, low-skilled workers feel stiff competition from foreign migrants, keeping salaries low in many informal sectors, including domestic work. As a result, people in the third quintile have not seen their incomes grow very much and it is these people who cannot find regular, stable employment. It is often people in the middle that are most disenchanted and feel most marginalised. These people constitute the 'middle' in terms of income spectrum in South Africa but they are not regarded as 'middle class' in conventional parlance. They might be working poor or underemployed or township residents who survive through a family benefactor. They are also not the poorest of the poor.

When a Grade 8 pupil assaulted his teacher, we found ourselves reflecting on our role as parents. When some learners received awards for being the top provincial contestant for maths, we found ourselves congratulating them in the comfort of our home. While the ANC retains its control in the Tlokwe by-elections in North West, we called upon all South Africans to register, vote and exercise their democratic right in the 2014 national and provincial elections. While we read the crime statistics, we pray for the victims of crimes. While I pen my thoughts, I remember the journey we have travelled.

I love you
Toivo

DEAR WIFE
You write so well and put our present and past in context. I often wonder how we would have coped if we had been this age not too long ago and had dared to express ourselves like this. Would we have had to cut our ties with our kids, to see them only when they had their own children? As you know, I spend a lot of time thinking about the father that I never knew. It is a private pain that I share only with you.

This freedom to express ourselves is exciting. Every day we see our kids outstrip us as they work our tablets and phones, playing their games and downloading their apps. We take it for granted that our kids have access to the same technologies as other kids around the world, as soon as these become available. We forget that our parents could hardly listen to a radio or watch television, even if they were freely available around the world. We take it for granted that what we see as an opportunity to connect our children to the world, to prepare them to participate fully in the global economy and society, was seen as way to poison minds and souls not that long ago.

In 1993, the Independent Broadcasting Authority was created. This was the beginning of the end of a very strange era. The beginning of the beginning of what we now consider to be normal: we can write and publish our stories freely; call each other on our phones whenever we want to; share photographs of the first lost teeth of our kids as soon as this happens; communities can create and disseminate their stories through their community broadcasting services; the public broadcasters can keep us informed to enable us to express ourselves, with our votes; and entrepreneurs can also express themselves freely.

Perhaps we take the creation of this institution for granted. Every morning before work we have a choice of so many television stations to bring us up to speed with events in the world around us. In our cars on the way to work we have a choice of more than 20 radio stations to listen to and we appreciate, perhaps without being explicit, the achievement of our democracy. We should continue to worry though about our brothers and sisters who still struggle to express themselves fully in spite of the opportunities. What is the freedom of expression if the means of expression are not available? What does it mean for this fundamental right, if some of us still cannot afford to make simple telephone calls as we celebrate the fact that before the dawn of our democracy there were no mobile telephone services and now we have so many? When will these people be able to participate in the global social networks and access the global knowledge base? When will they contribute to the global economy?

It is a tough one, my dear, and, of course, these are questions that we ask ourselves every day when we think about our kids. We are fortunate, I must say, that at least the country has a roadmap for solutions to these tough questions. Indeed, for the sake of our children, let us continue to put our energies behind the National Development Plan.

Where do we draw strength from to turn up every day and to be part of the daily spin? Every day chips away pieces of our bodies, our minds and our spirits. What happens when we don't replenish ourselves? We perish faster than we should – this is a fact of life. I must say that I am lucky though to have you. Every day, no matter whether in happiness or sadness, your presence replenishes my life, my soul and my spirit. You are my strength. We are also Africans and we draw strength from our environment and heritage; our stories weave elegantly through our families, our communities, our environment, our histories, our dreams and aspirations. Indeed, in the middle of this complex and unkind world, our heritage has created a complex reservoir of strength and we survive. Thabo Mbeki once said in his 'I am an African' speech:

> I owe my being to the hills and the valleys, the mountains and the glades, the rivers, the deserts, the trees, the flowers, the seas and the ever-changing seasons that define the face of our native land. My body has frozen in our frosts and in our latter day snows. It has thawed in the warmth of our sunshine and melted in the heat of the midday sun. The crack and the rumble of the summer thunders, lashed by startling lightening, have been a cause both of trembling and of hope… The dramatic shapes of the [landscape] have … been panels of the set on the natural stage on which we act out the foolish deeds of the theatre of our day.

We must take care of each other; we must take care of our environment; we must take care of our heritage. We did not create any of these and we owe it to our children to preserve what we found and guarantee them a future.

Tomorrow, we are going to one more of our kids' concerts. They will all be singing and dancing proudly, oblivious of the bigger world around them. They will not know how lucky they are. They are too young to understand that that their songs of innocence were preceded and enabled by songs of liberation. That while we clap and shout 'bravo' at the end of each session, not too long ago, songs were followed up by *klaps* and screams of pain and suffering. But we will teach them these things so that they take nothing for granted about their future, so that they respect fully the sacrifices made by the ones who came before them.

I love you
Setumo

DEAR CHILDREN

We are so fortunate to have our children in our lives. When you read this letter you may wonder why are we reflecting or what the big fuss is about. Our journey with both of you began in 2008, but the real journey of your future started with our liberation in 1994. Andimba Toivo ya Toivo wished us well. The day we celebrated our union he said, 'I am happy to be here. This is a special occasion for this child and I hope they grow old together and set a good example to their children.' This open letter came at a time when we remembered these words. We asked ourselves if indeed we are setting a good example for you. If we are, what have we done? Are we fulfilling our constitutional mandate of ensuring that all your basic needs are taken care of? How can we as parents assist you to develop as caring human beings who are not selfish? It is important that we collectively, as a family, contribute to eradicating poverty and reducing inequality. The ills of poverty are hampering our developmental path.

Like so many other countries before us, so many other children before you, the journey to this future was complex. You now enjoy the simplicity of its results; you walk into your small class at school and your best friend gives you a hug and your teacher sees you as a talent to be developed. You experience the world as it should be but it was not always like this. You must, therefore, always remember the period between 1990 and 1994, when the power of righteousness and the spirit of perseverance triumphed over the natural weakness of evil. That was a time when your elders wrote a chapter in the book of humanity and clearly demonstrated that, at its core, South Africa is a nation committed to peace and sustainability. Collectively we are continuously negotiating our developmental path. One day you will find yourselves debating this terminology. In the meantime, we ask you to engage with Chapter 13 of the National Development Plan.

As your parents we will encourage you to work towards building a cohesive nation. Your task is far greater than ours. We have ensured that the fundamental democratic institutions are in place but your efforts are fundamental for growth and development. These institutions are there to protect you and guide you through this democracy we have fought for. You have a responsibility to protect these institutions and to ensure that they are used to serve the people and not individuals with egocentric interests.

Today our nation has lost a father. He emerged from prison with anger and yet taught us – and the rest of the world – the meaning of healing, forgiveness and reconciliation. He reminded the world that 'no one is born hating another person because of the colour of his skin, or his background or his religion. People learn to hate, and if they learn to hate, they can be taught to love, for love comes more naturally to the human heart than its opposite.' You must not only learn about his life, his tragedies and triumphs, but you must also learn the ideals for which he stood and suffered.

As you go through your lives, you will soon realise that knowledge on its own is not enough. Application is just as important. You will soon learn that your daily actions, the way you treat your neighbours, the way you talk to strangers, the way you react to adversity are also part and parcel of life; they give shape, texture and smell to the lives we live. You must, therefore, live the ideals that the great man stood for. You will be challenged, though perhaps not as much as those who came before you, to create your future, and you must persevere. Your experiences will be unique and different for both of you. You must accept and celebrate diversity; cherish what you are made of and don't worry about who you could have been. Don't be envious of what you don't have or look down on those who don't have what you have. Enjoy diversity because it is, in fact, the fuel of life.

You must draw on the life and spirit of the great man, and the lives and dreams of the great men and women from whom he drew his own strength and humanity. You will then succeed in your lives. You will then fulfil your potential and create a future for the new generation.

We love you
Mom and Dad

Nationalism in post-apartheid South Africa: Observations

Dan Tlhabane Motaung

Researcher

The true test of a civilization is not the census, nor the
size of the cities, nor the crops – no, but the kind of man
the country turns out.
(Ralph Waldo Emerson, essayist, 1803–82)

Eppur si muove. (And yet it moves.)
(Galileo Galilei, 1564–1642)

Introduction

IF I WERE TO SHARE WITH A MARTIAN visitor my personal experiences
about the notion of post-apartheid nationalism in South Africa after
20 years of democracy, I would contend that while our constitutional
democracy is the bedrock of self-evident civic nationalism, at a
deeper level we have not yet extricated ourselves from the mould of
mutually inimical ethnic nationalism into which history cast us.

Despite the occasional national euphoria spawned by sporting
activities and numerous other conscious attempts by state and civil
society, South Africa has not, as yet, seen the merging of historically
constructed, fissured identities into an indissoluble whole. A long
shadow cast by our odious history of racial oppression still dominates
our social landscape. To be sure, mainstream society, which is
reflective of the spectrum of South Africans, does coalesce around the
core constitutional values that define post-apartheid democracy. This
mainstream society is the overwhelming majority of South Africans
of all descriptions and backgrounds who owe their allegiance to the
vision of a united, non-racial, non-sexist, just and prosperous society.
Yet even within mainstream society much still, both in material and
social terms, suggests that national reconciliation cohered society
together but left intact the inherited historical consciousness that

defines our moral universes.

For purposes of throwing more light on this conversation, it is useful to give a notional definition of both civic and ethnic nationalisms, since my aim is to show how the past ineluctably provides the individual with a conceptual framework for the perception of current reality and their place within it.

Civic nationalism sees a nation as a voluntary association of people enjoying and sharing equal political rights. Such a group of people volitionally espouses similar political procedures, seeing itself in political terms as a political entity. By implication, civic nationalism is all-inclusive in that it enforces uniformity while valorising the will of the people as *quid pro quo* for the existence of the state. Our system of constitutional democracy resonates with civic nationalism. At the core of civic nationalism is the imperative for the state to be based on the will of the people, without which it loses legitimacy.

On the other hand, ethnic nationalism departs from an essentialist basis, contending that nations are hereditary connections of people. The central theme of ethnic nationalism is that 'nations are defined by a shared heritage, which usually includes a common language, a common faith, and a common ethnic ancestry'.* By definition, ethnic nationalism is discriminatory since it is ethnically exclusive, emphasising the primacy of common ethnic ancestry. While culture and language are also important elements of ethnic nationalism, on their own they are neither necessary nor sufficient conditions because nationalism based on culture and language can also easily incorporate non-natives through the process of assimilation. This explains the continued exclusion of coloured people from the Afrikaner fold, even though they have a shared language and, to some extent, the Christian religion.

The former prime minister of the United Kingdom, Winston Churchill, hit the nail on the head when he noted that 'the farther backward you can look, the farther forward you can see'. Nowhere is this perceptive observation truer than in this South African context, where evolution of ethnic self-consciousness, which owes its creation to the ideological designs of the colonial powers, goes as far back as (and is therefore incomprehensible without) the beginnings of

---

* Muller JZ, 2008, *Us and Them* in Current Issue 501 Mar/Apr 2008 en.wikipedia.org/wiki/ etnic_nationalism.

colonialism and its philosophical underpinnings.

What makes this ethnic nationalism particularly disturbing is that it is not just some historical happenstance but the inexorable outcome of a noxious dogma that worked on the human mind by instilling notions of racialism and creating fear of 'the other' in the dominant community. It worked out easily, just as in the case of slavery, where the ideology of racism assuaged the conscience of the slave-master by depicting the slave as a beast of burden who needed European guidance for his own edification.

As the innately propulsive impulse of ethnic nationalism, racism permeated the lived experience of all of us. It inflected social institutions and was reflected in the cultural expressions that made up the daily grind, influencing the outlook of individuals.

What I think accentuated the subtle existence of opposing nationalisms in post-apartheid South Africa is the attempt to correct this historical injustice visited on black people since the moment colonialism took root in the soil of this land. This imperative to address the past is a *sine qua non* for the realisation of a truly just and democratic South Africa is proving to be a knotty task. As measures to correct the said injustices kick into action, some South Africans begin to show signs of growing unease.

The white working class, especially among the Afrikaner section of society, equally resented such corrective measures as affirmative action and Broad-Based Black Economic Empowerment (BBBEE). The perception often expressed subtly, even by some sections of the mainstream society, is that corrective measures – the imperatives of empowering those historically disadvantaged – are reverse discrimination. One wonders whether years of systematic subjection to racial indoctrination through socialisation had been so strong as to numb the senses of those who benefitted from the court of white privilege that they could deny their victims the right to be affirmed.

More baffling is that among the ranks of those who frown upon correcting past injustices are sections of the white or Afrikaner intelligentsia – the very beneficiaries of the past unjust system! It is also worth noting that one never comes across a reasoned rejection of present corrective measures on the grounds that they are ill-conceived; rather, it is the very grounds for corrective past injustices that is questioned.

Two prominent examples that touch both the white and black sections of mainstream society are cases in point. The singing contest *Idols*, shown on DStv, typifies the fragmented soul of our nation. Throughout its existence, except in the year 2012, winning the contest had always been the prerogative, of the white section of society. Now it should be borne in mind that, until recently, many black people could not afford to purchase a decent television set, never mind a monthly subscription to such services as DStv.

With this background in mind, more that 50% of the viewership of DStv were people other than black Africans. This gave white people a voting advantage over blacks when it came to voting for the winning contestant. It is therefore no coincidence that, since its onset in 2004, whites have always won the *Icons* contest. I am sure that no sane person could believe that a singing contest could be won by one section of society consistently for a period of more than five years in a heterogeneous nation such as South Africa. It simply does not make sense at all.

Then along came the year 2012, when one Khaya from KwaZulu-Natal swept to victory in a historic win that broke new ground. Once again, Khaya's win further goes to show the extent to which mainstream South African society has failed to wean itself off ethnic nationalism. During the final rounds of the contest, Khaya received a blaze of publicity and support from many black people, especially from the province of KwaZulu-Natal. People were urged to call again and again in order to ensure his victory. I can assure you that about 90% of those callers were black Africans.

Contrast this scenario with the events of the 2014 National Sports Awards presented by the Department of Sports. Once again, voting by the public was the system of selecting winners in all categories up for grabs, including the overall winner, the South African Athlete of the Year. During this event, broadcast live on the SABC, it was clear that the South African swimming sensation, Chad le Clos, had been head and shoulders above all and sundry. Such had been his performance that one could even submit that had there been a world sports award, including all sporting codes, Le Clos would easily have been among the top three from whom the ultimate winner was to be selected.

Yet, once again, Le Clos was beaten for a six by the footballing star, Itumeleng Khune, who had an outstanding year on the national front, helping his team Kaizer Chiefs to win a double, the league and an ABSA Cup.

Head to head though, it was clear that Le Clos' achievement was on another level as he had made a splash in the global arena.

On both occasions, voters voted with their hearts and not their minds, goaded by the shared ethnic affinity, the primordial attraction to one's kin, as well as the general historical background that pre-inclined the social impulses in particular directions.

I would say that the implications of this simple act of ethnic predilections are troubling. For one thing, we can extrapolate that there are many unknown cases where both black and white South Africans act in racial ways that go against the grain of our constitutional values but also the ongoing attempts to forge social cohesion in South Africa.

This would also explain the all too frequent resistance to affirmative action and other means to address the historical injustices suffered by black South Africans. One can then also ask the logical question: if society is still largely fissured, as demonstrated by the above examples, and corrective measures to assuage the historical pain suffered by a significant segment of society are seen as reverse racism and so on, does the historically advantaged section of society acknowledge the historical injustice suffered by black people, Africans in particular?

As such, two ugly blemishes continue to mar the face of post-apartheid South Africa in ways reminiscent of past social domination – the economy and culture. Race is profoundly implicated in the class system. As a social force, the class system constitutes the power–knowledge nexus manifested in the possession of the means of cultural representation. Possession of resources enables a social group to access high-level education, thus locating it in the global mainstream through immersion in dominant knowledge systems and the production of ideas, as well as control of technology, the driver of modernity. In sum, social class determines the conditions that enable self-reproduction and thus self-perpetuation.

That there is a causality between our present and our past is clear and all thinking people would be hard put to deny the dominance of this feature of our history and its consequential effect on the current historical period in South Africa.

The ineluctable conclusion from this history is that the perculiar nature of our past must necessarily dictate ways and means of uprooting the historical conditions with which our nation is faced. It cannot be anyhow. Any half-hearted or ill-conceived measures will come short under the combined weight of the continued race/class nexus. Of course, if unchecked with time, the inability to reduce socio-economic disparities will pose a mortal threat to the social fabric and political stability. In all sincerity one would have thought that this straightforward historical understanding would be all the more compelling grounds for the collective assault on this tangled web of racial legacy.

However, this is not the case, at least not among some sections of the liberal establishment. What one reads off this social attitude to our historical conditions is the wilful blindness to acknowledge the scope of the social devastation confronting us. Instead, the tables are turned so that those seeking to extirpate the odious presence of the past on the current historical period are, in turn, accused of reverse discrimination.

A case in point in this regard is the reported tension that gripped the South African official opposition, the Democratic Alliance, recently. In this saga, it is reported that the party was largely divided into two racial camps, over support for the policy on Black Economic Empowerment, a government programme meant to launch the formerly disadvantaged into the mainstream economy, and other policies meant to redress past injustices. While the one side of the debate moved to acknowledge past racial injustices and their implications for the current policy of redress, the other side stridently advocated a policy of racial blindness. In this line of thought, all races are purportedly equal, as entailed in the Constitution, and there is no need to hark back to the past.

While the first side does not go far enough in proposing radical policies commensurate with the extent of the job at hand, it is completely baffling that a modern liberal party could even imagine that in a country such as South Africa one could avert one's eyes from history. Insensitive and almost short of denying the effects of past injustices in our country, this brand of liberalism has been the most pronounced since the onset of democracy in 1994, but has been somewhat attenuated by Helen Zille, the current leader of the party.

With patrician certainty, we are also admonished against state intervention in the economic arena and, instead, advised to let the impersonal force of the market play its role to correct the past and grow the economy. Inherently tendentious, this argument is riddled with flawed historical assumptions. Further, by dint of its rugged intellectual tradition, meaning, in effect, its control of the cultural means of expression, this segment is able to map out and shape public discourse in high-flying terms, in ways that give lie to their numerical insignificance. With a sleight of hand, whites are depicted as 'new blacks' who are at the receiving end of unfair racial discrimination at the hands of 'black government'. Parenthetically, note that government is made out to be 'a black government' and not, as it should be, 'a democratic government'.

It baffles the mind that this liberal commentariat, while acknowledging apartheid racial inequalities, fails to go as far as acknowledging that our past set the course of action of the post-apartheid state. Boldly confronting issues of race, as imposed by apartheid on the present democratic space, is the *sine qua non* for bringing about justice in the socio-economic domain.

The mind boggles, too, at the failure of South African liberalism to acknowledge the nature of the apartheid system, which was antithetical to the core tenets of the liberal tradition. Many writers have shown that the racially uneven patterns of economic distribution during apartheid remain indefensible, even in liberal terms. In *Why Race Matters*, Michael MacDonald posits an argument that casts post-apartheid South Africa in lucid terms, especially if we are to appreciate the historical imperatives that dictate the policies that the democratic state has to pursue.

In sum, his contention is that in normal liberal democratic societies there is a univeral agreement that there exists the 'public' and the 'private' space, between which a distinction must be drawn. The public space entails equality of citizens, while the private space reflects inequality among citizens because of the inevitable consequence of freedom. The argument further states that in liberal democracies 'equality in the public realm – in citizenship and under the law – provides important justification for inequality in other realms, notably the economic'. MacDonald goes on to argue that 'equality under the law performs the indispensable service for liberal democrats of proving that economic inequality is legitimate, that it is the by-product of freedom and equal opportunity'.

Against this background of liberal societies, the democratic state faced historically anomalous socio-economic conditions when it assumed power, since South Africa's racially defined economic inequalities were just that – racial inequalities – and, hence, could find no justification in legal and political equality, as do liberal societies elsewhere.

South Africa's economic inequalities are the result of deliberately racist policies derived from the philosophy of white supremacy. The usual justification for inequalities attributed to liberal democratic discourse of meritocracy comes unstuck in the context of the South African historical trajectory.

In consequence, this logic of apartheid, which departs from the liberal social conditions that underlie class structure in normal capitalist economies, singularly predisposes the democratic state to pursue policies that are responsive to this history.

Equally dishonest is the sentenious line about minimising the role of the state in the economy so that the markets on their own can grow the economy, pull the majority out of poverty and thereby narrow the economic chasm. Devoid of historical consiousness and above social realities, the markets on their own could not be conducive to social justice. Inversely, markets would be best suited for those for whom history has been a quoin of vantage, such as those who benefitted from apartheid. Markets do not take into account the unfair advantage between the players because they are but impersonal commercial processes embodying forces of supply and demand.

While rooted in the rational-liberal paradigm, this view about less government interference or intervention – as the case may be – patently fails the test of history in South Africa. Implicitly or explicitly, liberalism acquiesced to the legitimating ideology of the apartheid state, which rode roughshod over defining liberal values of equality and freedom.

So it amounts to rank hypocrisy to expect the democratic state to take a back seat, yielding to market forces to address the legacy of inequality generated through the abuse of state and government to priviledge one section of society in the first place.

Whereas the liberal tradition seeks to separate the state, government and society, so that the state is the sovereign to which society owes unqualified allegiance, and, in turn, their liberty and equality as citizens, apartheid could not meet this objective because of its inherent racist impulse.

Instead, the state, the sovereign, and the government – the administrative bureaucracy presiding over the state apparatus – consciously employed state power to advance racial interests, to the detriment of the rest of society. The accumulated results of these decades of entrenched racial interests and the deliberate policy of disempowerment of the rest of society are manifested in today's legacy of racial inequality in all societal respects. It is, therefore, not only in the interests of justice but also in the interests of all the people of our country, that, within reason and the constitutional framework, the state assumes an interventionist role to eradicate this historical injustice.

Post-apartheid South Africa may be a democratic society where equality and liberty are constitutionally guaranteed, but it still faces a historical deficiency in the form of racial inequality that cannot be solved through means other than the state. Apartheid was no historical contingency. If the South African liberal tradition cannot grasp this factuality, it is possibly because it can't help its untruthfulness.

Going forward
Unless South Africa manages to bring about full social emancipation, whereby all South Africans, all ethnic groups in South Africa, enjoy the material comforts of life, ethnic nationalism will not wither away on its own. Worsening global economic conditions, which have impinged on South Africa negatively, can only exacerbate simmering ethnic tension in society. History has already proven that depressed economic conditions tend to accentuate ethnic consciousness, as fascism has shown. When things are tough, the notion of a nation reverts back to its atavistic form, as derived from its Latin etymology, meaning 'a breed of people or racial group'.

Whether Afrikaner nationalism expressed in the rubric of conservatism or English nationalism manifested in liberal ideology, or even African nationalism antithetically constituted as it opposes colonial legacy, nationalism needs to be all-inclusive and colour blind, strengthening on the back of a growing economy that accommodates the aspirations of all.

While economic progress will go a long way towards undermining poverty as the incubator of political pathologies, we need to wean our society off the hovering legacy of past divisions, expressed in ethnic exclusivism. For this, the intellectual apparatus bears the responsibility. A new form of intellectualism is needed to recast our public discourse and cultural socialisation across the spectrum, while seeding the idea of indivisible South Africanness.

The intelligentsia will do well to acknowledge the damage history has done to a particular section of society and stop insinuating that Africans indirectly owe colonialism a debt of gratitude for modernisation. Insidious to the core, this line of thinking not only misleads current generations into thinking that colonial damage was minimal after all, but it also helps to perpetuate the pain of the victims.

Some white people wax defensive whenever the topic of white racism is brought up. A common defensive tactic is to talk about black racism as if it were an equivalent moral evil – as if black racism were anywhere nearly as much of a problem for white people as white racism is for blacks. While black racism is real and our country needs to be careful of African nationalism that seeks to justify economic material accumulation in the name of history (and this is a subject on its own), black racism, where it appears, does not suggest a systematic pattern with the potency to disempower a particular people as a group. In addition, while black racism should never be indulged (racism is a virus that must be exterminated all round), it is unconscionable to use it as an excuse to avoid dealing with white racism, embedded in power structures of society.

Equally, there needs to be an acknowledgement that undoing the damage caused by colonialism and apartheid does not constitute reverse racism – it is the right thing to do. Accusing former victims of reverse racism, when the accusers are themselves beneficiaries of the past, is rank hypocrisy bordering on denialism. It is a fallacy of the first degree to seek to burden black Africans with the aftermath of historical designs that had sought to turn them into objects. It is only when an all-inclusive nationalism arises, steeped in civic nationalist sentiments, that South Africa can be truly non-racial!

My democracy village: An odyssey of suffering to dignity

Moloto Mothapo
ANC Caucus spokesperson

GA-MAJA IS A SEMI-MOUNTAINOUS VILLAGE situated at the foot of the imposing Mogodumo Mountain, approximately 30 kilometres outside of Polokwane in Limpopo. The village's name originates from that of the reigning royal family, Maja, under whose chieftaincy the area has existed for ages. This is a village that approximately 5 000 residents call home. If it could tell a story, it would be one of generations of young activists who left behind their motherly warmth to join the anti-apartheid struggle for liberation; it would tell of peasant resistance and the glorious struggle against an illegitimate and repressive regime that robbed people of their basic human rights; it would tell of a village that bore the brutal brunt of apartheid and colonialism; it would tell a story of generations of poverty and destitution; and it would also tell a story of children robbed of a decent and healthy family life by the apartheid migrant labour system and repressive apartheid legislation.

This village has seen it all: the blustery political storms of the apartheid era, the freezing downpour of economic hardships and the destructive tornadoes of white-perpetrated violence against defenceless people. Today, this village still stands firm, defiant and proud – a remarkable testimony to the human spirit and its triumph over adversity.

I was born in this village more than three decades ago to a migrant labourer and a housewife – a family narrative shared by millions of rural families across South Africa. Under such circumstances, wives and children saw their husbands and fathers only once or twice a year. Heartbreaking stories abound of men, both young and old, who left families in search of greener pastures in Johannesburg and never returned – thanks to the murderous apartheid security police. Therefore, not only did apartheid bring poverty, deprivation and destitution to this village, it also left many families in a state of psychological disrepair and abandonment.

As a young boy growing up under such conditions, I was never under any illusion that life would be a bed of roses. Poverty and destitution were palpable everywhere: you could smell it, see it, hear it and feel it. The effect of apartheid manifested itself in all areas of our daily lives. Access by Africans to basic services, such as electricity, clean water, decent housing, sanitation, quality basic education and decent road infrastructure, was a pipe dream.

The government's *Development Indicators 2012*, published by the Presidency, sums up the narrative:

> Apartheid deliberately sought to prevent many African households access to basic household items that would improve their overall living standards. For many African households, access to television, telephone, washing machine or being able to shop at a supermarket or trying to obtain insurance and other financial products was simply not accessible before 1994.

For the majority of villagers, things that are today regarded as common, such as access to a television, were luxuries that could be afforded by only a handful of households. As youngsters, we would often assemble weekly at a house that had a television and, for a small fee, we could watch the next episode of a Sotho SABC drama (such as *Bophelo Ke Semphekgo* and *Lesilo Rula*) or a Soweto soccer derby. There was no electricity, and therefore those who acquired television sets had the added burden of also securing a car battery or a petrol-operated generator. To keep the television operating did not come cheap either. TV owners had to dig deep into their pockets to recharge the battery in town about 30 kilometres away, using very scarce and expensive transport. As a result, even those who had TVs hardly watched them.

Things such as access to, or affordability of, a television set might appear insignificant in the broader scheme of things, but they are among the indicators used to measure the population's living standards. Today, as we mark the 20th anniversary of freedom, there has been significant improvement in the material conditions of the lives of millions of South Africans. The democratic government has worked hard to provide decent basic services to millions and roll back the frontiers of poverty, inequality and underdevelopment. Census 2011 shows that the proportion of households with a television increased from 53.8% in 2001 to 65.5% in 2007 and to 74.5% in 2011. Limpopo, which is home to 10.4% of the population, has registered an increase in television ownership from 39.8% in 2001 to 70.9% in 2011. Gone are the days when the entire community would assemble weekly in certain homes to watch television. This improvement in living conditions can also be seen in the national increase in access to household goods such as refrigerators (68.4%), radios (67.5%), computers (21.4%), the Internet (35.2%) and mobile phones (88.9%).

As children growing up in a poverty-stricken community in which households were headed by unemployed women who rarely saw their husbands due to the apartheid migrant labour system, we would enthusiastically await our grandparents' paltry old-age grants, which came once every three months. Although African pensioners received their grants once every three months, they were ridiculously tiny compared to what their white counterparts received monthly. These meagre grants were hardly ever used for their intended personal care, but supported extended families.

They would buy each family a chicken, a delicacy that many villagers would taste only once in a blue moon or whenever there was a wedding in the community. Despite the fact that the 'day of pay' (as it was colloquially called) came only four times a year (if at all), everyone celebrated and appreciated these times. For us children, and probably many in the community, each of those days meant a special moment in which we would sleep on ballooned bellies after feasting on a slaughtered chicken and mounds of pap. The days represented a pleasant momentary distraction from the daily life of poverty and deprivation.

However, things are different now. Since this government came into power 20 years ago, it has introduced numerous types of grants for the poor and indigent, regardless of race and on a monthly basis. Whereas less than 3 million people received grants prior to 1994, today over 1 million people receive government social support such as the old age grant, war veterans' grant, disability grant, foster child grant and child support grant. In Limpopo, 55.16% of the population benefit from social grants. Today, all social grant beneficiaries are paid equally and monthly, regardless of race, colour or creed. Before

1994, pensioners used to support children from extended (poor) families, today over 11.5 million children receive monthly child dependency, foster child and child support grants from government. Government has increased the budget for social assistance annually in an attempt to keep up with inflation. This has significantly enhanced millions of households' income.

Under apartheid, South Africa's economic make-up was racially skewed: Africans were poorly paid, and suffered racial discrimination and harassment in the workplace. The migrant labour system was more of a curse than an economic opportunity for African labourers and their families. White workers were paid ten times more than Africans for doing the same work. Repressive labour legislation, harassment and systematic onslaught on trade unions, and the banning of formal political activities meant Africans toiled under inhumane conditions for slave wages and enjoyed neither labour rights nor human rights. Our primary school principal would, whenever she meted out corporal punishment to us, remind us that '*botatago lena ba raga ke maburu kua makgoweng gore le kgone go ithuta*' (your fathers are being kicked by the Boers in Johannesburg in order for you to be educated). No father would ever admit to being kicked around at work by a white boss young enough to be his son. But I could easily deduce from my father's usage of phrases such as '*ek sal jou donner*' whenever he unleashed his own fatherly discipline, that this must have been said to him.

Our fathers had this inexplicable sense of anger, disenchantment and aloofness. They toiled under the most excruciating conditions, endured regular physical abuse from their white *baases*, spent months, even years away from their loved ones, and at the end got paid a pittance, not even enough to put their children through basic education. They worked and lived under poor conditions until they became too old and frail to continue working. Then they would be sent back home to die, with nothing to show for the many years of hard labour. This is a common life story experienced by many men and their families in my village.

Our government has worked hard to reinstate the dignity of African men and African families through the creation of quality jobs, ensuring workers are paid equally for the same work and putting in place laws to protect vulnerable workers. According to Frans Cronje, CEO of the South African Institute of Race Relations (SAIRR), despite the poor performance of our labour market, approximately 6 million jobs have been created since 1994. According to the 2011 Census report, this has translated into a substantial increase in the average annual household income in the last 10 years.

The government has introduced laws to protect workers; created machinery to negotiate wages and working conditions; set minimum wages for domestic workers, farm workers, hospitality workers, taxi workers and those in the security sector; and established maximum hours of work for all. Affirmative action laws were also introduced to ensure employment equity and promotion of skills.

Although unemployment is at unacceptable levels, multifaceted government programmes and plans are being put in place to remedy the situation. The National Development Plan (NDP), for instance, plans to create 11 million jobs by 2030 and drastically reduce poverty and inequality.

The migrant labour system still exists but it has been fundamentally transformed. Although job seekers from my village continue to flock to industrialised cities such as Johannesburg for work, our laws go a long way to ensure that they are now paid a living wage and they can either visit their loved ones frequently or live with them closer to work.

Before 1994, workers from Bantustans needed special passes to live and work in Johannesburg. The Transvaal Local Government Commission of 1922 captured the objective of this system thus: 'The native should be allowed to enter the urban areas when he is willing to minister to the needs of the white man, and should depart there from when he ceases so to minister'.

Those who worked or lived 'illegally' in those areas were terrorised, arrested, tortured, banished or even murdered. As a child I witnessed first hand the constant violent morning raids carried out by apartheid security police during visits to my father in Alexandra township. Baton-wielding young white policemen would break down doors, kick African men and frog-march them into a police truck almost naked. Any child seeing a father or uncle, whom they looked up to as a protector and head of the family, being manhandled in that manner is sure to be left with an indelible psychological scar. The abolishment of laws such as the Groups Areas Act of 1950 and the Bantu Homelands Citizenship Act of 1970, which enforced geographical segregation on the basis of race, ensures that a job seeker and his family can now work and live in the cities without fear of harassment, torture or being deported back for not having a pass.

The WHO/UNICEF Joint Monitoring Programme for Water Supply and Sanitation (JMP) recently remarked that lack of access to clean and safe drinking water, which translates into poor hygiene practices, and sickens and kills thousands of children every day, leads to impoverishment and diminished opportunities for thousands more and denies children, particularly girls, education as schools lack decent sanitation facilities. This largely sums up the rural conditions in which some grew up. As a teenager, one experienced first hand the gross inconvenience and the effect the lack of access to clean water had on people's daily lives, including on schooling. At that age, one had to wake in the early hours before going to school to fetch water at a remote communal river or dam, from which livestock also drank. To minimise chances of contracting fatal waterborne diseases, the water would then be boiled and left to cool before drinking.

A typical day in my teenage years in the village was spent fetching water, hewing wood for the fire and schooling. For instance, when we wrote our final matric exams, we would rise at 3:00 am to join a long queue at the newly installed communal water pump, which was several kilometres away, to fetch water before heating it up, bathing and heading off to school. The water pump wasn't the easiest of machines to operate either. We skinny boys always shuddered at the embarrassment of being swung up and down by the force of the machine arm as we applied our entire body weight on it to extract intermittent spurts of water. To fill a 50-litre bucket was an effort and then to push it for kilometres in a wheelbarrow up a hill was nothing short of slavery.

For a full body wash, villagers had to travel kilometres to the nearest stream in order to preserve the scarce water in their homes. Lack of access to clean and safe water created fertile grounds for various ailments and caused unnecessary deaths, making the cruel living conditions under the apartheid regime even more difficult to bear.

Today, households in my village have access to clean running water on their doorsteps while others even have flushing toilets in their houses. All the schools in my village have running water and sanitation facilities. The recent census report shows that Limpopo has registered an increase in the percentage of households with access to piped water, from 35.8% in 1994 to 52.3% in 2011. Nationally, access to clean and safe water in 1994 was at around 60% – translating into a mere 5 million households. Since 1994, the government has ensured that more than 95% of households have access to running water. The NDP's target is that every household must have clean water by 2030. The last 20 years of democracy has restored the dignity of the people in my village, eased their living conditions and reduced their chances of acquiring water-related diseases. Schoolchildren, in particular, are studying under much improved conditions than before.

Another daily chore of the villagers was to hew firewood to cook for their families and warm their households during the winter. Women, in particular, assisted by us teenagers, had to walk long distances to chop wood, then carry neck-breaking bundles of it on their heads – at risk of encountering wild animals, *ditopolane* (murderous kidnappers), rapists and other thugs who hid in the dense vegetation, ready to pounce on vulnerable women and children. It was therefore not only unbearably hard labour, but also very risky. Often one had to go to school, which was also miles away, in a state of extreme exhaustion and excruciating pain resulting from such physical labour.

As schoolchildren, we did our homework and studied by candle or paraffin light; we literally burnt the midnight oil. Lack of access to electricity did not only affect households, but also schools and clinics. The apartheid regime had largely ignored rural electrification, except for commercial white farms. According to the Reconstruction and Development Programme (RDP) document, only 36% of South African households had electricity and about 19 000 black schools (86%) and around 4 000 clinics were without electricity.

Today, households in my village have access to electricity, and clinics, schools and multipurpose centres have been electrified. The school where I passed my matric, for instance, now has computer and science laboratories, and has various other electricity-powered study facilities and equipment. This has boosted the quality of our education and made studying easier. It may even be a contributing factor to the annual increase in the matric pass rate and increased the number of university enrolments from 360 000 in 1994 to 740 000, and increased the number of African students obtaining degrees since 1994 by 269%.

Statistics SA shows that in Limpopo in 2011, the proportion of households using electricity for lighting had increased to 87.3%, for heating it had increased to 45% and for cooking it had increased to 50%. Nationally, close to 10 million South African households (76.5%) have access to electricity. Government is currently constructing several additional power stations in three provinces in its drive to expand access to electricity. One of these, Limpopo's Medupi power station, is set to be one of the largest greenfield coal-fired power stations in the world – producing 4 800 megawatts of power. Life today is much better and convenient than it ever was.

In my village, as in all African communities, children are considered to be a blessing. But under the apartheid conditions of poverty and economic inequality, children became more of a burden than a blessing. Not only did they mean additional family to care for, feed, clothe and educate, but they also imposed an additional burden on poor families to provide more housing space for their growing families. Very few families in my village could afford a decent brick and mortar house so people used materials provided by nature to build their houses. My village, as many others across the country, was populated with hut structures built from stones, mud and wood and completed with a thatch roof and cow-dung flooring. All these materials were freely obtainable from the nearest veld. A decent property brings dignity and peace of mind to its owner, and is a source of pride and success. However, mud huts brought the complete opposite – there can be no dignity and peace in a house that can hardly withstand the vagaries of weather.

For this reason, the RDP directed the government to prioritise the development of a rural housing action plan to roll out decent housing to rural communities such as Ga-Maja village. It noted: 'While recognising that rural incomes are far lower, the democratic government must consider rural housing needs in calculating backlogs, and make provision for gradually improving housing in rural areas.'

Today, a hill's view of my village reveals numerous shiny corrugated-iron-roofed RDP houses the government has built since 1994. Gone are the mud structures as well as the indignity that was associated with them. Mechanisms have also been put in place to ensure that building constructors are held responsible for any potential poor workmanship. Nationally, government has worked hard to reverse the 1.2 million housing backlog it inherited in 1994.

Over 3.28 million houses, housing over 11 million people, have been built in the last 20 years. Government continues to build around 100 000 RDP houses annually and provides housing subsidies to people whose earnings are too high to qualify for RDP houses but too low to afford a house.

Today my village, Ga-Maja, stands proudly, having defied and conquered the historical vagaries of apartheid. This is not only an extraordinary testimony to the human spirit's triumph over adversity, but is also an illustration of remarkable progress driven by a caring democratic government to change the material conditions of all South Africans, particularly the poor.

There is no denying that, despite government's excellent track record since 1994, it still has a lot to do and could do better. Indeed, challenges such as corruption, maladministration and fraud continue to bedevil the government systems, frustrating its ability to deliver on the commitments contained in the Freedom Charter and the RDP. However, for every existing problem, this government has demonstrated a political will and a practical plan to deal with it. South Africa is among very few countries to put in place a comprehensive long-term national plan (the NDP) to make the country a better place to live in.

Some intellectuals and media commentators have inaccurately suggested that service delivery protests are an indication that government is failing at service delivery. Nothing is further from the truth.

The surge in service delivery protests is a by-product of an increase in government's service delivery. SAIRR CEO, Frans Cronje, eloquently describes this phenomenon as 'the curse of rising expectations'. In his article published in the *City Press* of 6 October 2013, Cronje argues:

> a cruel irony for the ANC is that as the proportion of people receiving welfare grows, so the proportion believing government is performing well shrinks. In what is no doubt a disconcerting experience, the party leadership is coming to realise that the more people get welfare and the more houses are built for them and electricity laid on, the faster public opinion is turning against the government. We call this the curse of rising expectations.

People's expectations of government are normally driven by their experience of government's history of delivering services, which then engenders their confidence in its ability to meet their expectations. These experiences are primarily the reason our people continue to have confidence in the ability of their government to deliver more. For a person who grew up with access to basic things such as water, electricity, sanitation, and decent housing and road infrastructure, this story of democracy in my village might sound inconsequential. But for me and my fellow villagers, this has been an extraordinary life-changing story few could have imagined. I can therefore today state without equivocation, that our future is bright.

References

African National Congress. 2009. National Elections Manifesto.

Cronje, H. 2013. 'Policy Battle over the Big Ideas', *City Press*, 6 October.

Department of Performance Monitoring and Evaluation. 2012. Development Indicators.

Eskom. Medupi Power Station Project. Available at: www.eskom.co.za/c/article/1854/home/ (accessed 10 October 2013).

Government of the Republic of South Africa. 1994. The Reconstruction and Development Programme.

Government of the Republic of South Africa. Bantu Homelands Citizenship Act No. 26 of 1970. *Government Gazette*, 9 March 1970. Pretoria: Government Printer.

Magubane, B. 2006. Resistance and Repression in the Bantustans, in *The Road to Democracy in South Africa Volume 2 (1970–1980)*. Pretoria: Unisa Press.

Presidency, National Planning Commission. 2012. National Development Plan 2030.

South African History Online. 2013. The South African Government Passes the Group Areas Act. Available at: www.sahistory.org.za/dated-event/south-african-government-passes-group-areas-act (accessed 14 October 2013).

South African Institute of Race Relations' Social Media Facts Updates. #IRRKnowYourANC 2013. Available at: www.twitter.com/SARaceRelations (accessed 10 October 2013).

Statistics South Africa. 2011. Provinces at a Glance. www.statssa.gov.za/Census2011/Products/Provinces%20at%20a%20glance%2016%20Nov%202012%20corrected.pdf (accessed 17 February 2014).

Statistics South Africa. 2013 Quarterly Labour Force Survey. Available at: www.statssa.gov.za/publications/P0211/P02111stQuarter2013.pdf (accessed 17 February 2014).

United Nations Children's Fund. 2013. Water, Sanitation and Hygiene. Available at: www.unicef.org/wash/ (accessed 10 October 2013).

Excuse me Miss, I'm Khanyi Mbau: The post-apartheid cultural schizophrenia

Zuki Mqolomba

Researcher and writer

THERE IS MORE TO KHANYI MBAU'S story than meets the eye. Khanyi Mbau is not a stranger to us. Truth be told, Khanyi Mbau's story tells our own narrative and class posture in a seemingly (un)changing society. She is the epitome of the coveted life of the black middle class in South Africa, the so-called black diamonds and emerging black elite.

Khanyi's ideals reveal much of what now constitutes our own 'class' character and the new set of value propositions that drive our own interactions with the world. We are Khanyi Mbau, oh yes! She is an honest appraisal of us. Our notions of freedom are captured in the life she attempts to lead – she wants to be as filthy rich. Oh, yes. Let's be honest with ourselves. She mirrors us to varying degrees. Excuse me Miss, I am Khanyi Mbau, broken and still (un)becoming, inside.

South Africa's black middle class has remained a subject of intense preoccupation, both for right and wrong reasons, since 1994. On the one hand, with the sudden rise of the black diamonds post 1994, leading retail houses, financial service institutions and car manufacturers have made deliberate and unapologetic efforts to capture the sudden surge of this new market in a bid to expand their profit shares. On the other hand, the black middle stratum was, and continues to be, seen by white capital as an economic threat: heralded as competition to white privilege and a generation of white elites who continue in their legacy of ruthless entitlement.

Even within our very own political ranks, consideration of the 'revolutionary' role of the emerging African elite continues to be problematised, and correctly so, posing hugely awkward questions about the role of the state in the creation of a privileged class of benefactors. The debate on the creation of the 'black bourgeoisie' has been seen by most to be counter progressive, and rightfully so, as it undermines the very task of changing the class structure of South African society and challenges the very assumption of the non-antagonism of classes within the liberation family.

This descriptive essay focuses on the narrative of the black middle class primarily because it is a class that matters in foretelling the South African story as it continues to unfold. It makes an attempt to give a description of the 'class imagination' of the middle class, particularly its own notions of freedom as it is lived out, in real and imagined ways, sometimes sophisticated and sometimes not. It makes a plea for a change in our social imagination because surely we can do better. We should do better. Society needs us. Surely our understanding of the narrative of the black middle class will determine our imagination of the South Africa of the future. Unless there is a fundamental change in the values that have captured the black middle class, which will leave it indebted, we can never be a non-racial, non-sexist, prosperous and democratic country and continent. Truth, said.

The black middle class matters in South Africa

The narrative of the black middle class also matters in telling and predicting the African National Congress's (ANC) future. Leading ANC policy-maker and NEC member, Joel Netshitenzhe, recently launched a debate about the role of the middle class in shaping the character and nature of the formidable ANC. He has continued to ask very difficult questions about the (un)changing class structure of the ANC as it mimics, and should continue to mirror, society, particularly the class posture of the ANC and its ability to attract or appeal to a populace behaving as is characteristic of its newly inherited class structure.

Netshitenzhe has even gone to the extent of urging the ANC to consider the political implications of the changing class structures as the ANC continues in ardent pursuit of the resolution of social contradictions: a noble pursuit. Even President Obama's recent election campaign trail focused on the importance of the middle class as a stabilising stratum in society, particularly in fuelling economic growth and promoting social cohesion. It is important to note, therefore, that the middle class simultaneously enjoys a historic and a contemporary place in society. The debate on developing a class of emerging black elites therefore simultaneously has its roots embedded in historic and contemporary missions and, in South Africa, is a deliberate attempt to resolve national contradictions as these have been defined in this moment in time.

The debate on the role of the middle class is also borne through struggle and enjoys a historic context, particularly in South Africa. In 1994, the ANC-led government inherited an economy and society that was in a profound structural crisis. The harsh reality is that our political economy is characterised by significant distortions in income distribution and consequent structural distortions in the demand for goods and services, which have resulted in significant economic malaise. The majority of our people continue to be restricted from meaningful participation in the economy. Access to assets, economic opportunities and skills continues to be racially segregated.

The majority of South Africans continue to bear – and disproportionately so – the brunt of poverty, unemployment and underdevelopment. Inequalities in income distribution and low levels of investment have become deeply entrenched. The apartheid system has, therefore, not only prejudiced and disadvantaged black people, but continues to fail us. Racial inequalities therefore remain a foremost development dilemma that needs to be addressed to resolve South Africa's developmental challenges. We need to resolve the debate on transforming the semi-colonial structure of the economy as a matter of urgency. This remains government's most urgent task. Until we undo the racial legacy of apartheid colonialism, we will not be able to meet the socio-economic needs of the country as a whole.

Since 1994, the ANC-led government has undertaken extensive policy reforms in an effort to resolve social contradictions. In 2003, our government came up with Black Economic Empowerment (BEE), intended to transform South Africa's race and gender relations and to deracialise the South African economy. BEE was later changed into Broad-Based Black Economic Empowerment (BBBEE) to bring about significant increases in the numbers of black people that manage, own and control the country's economy, as well as to decrease income inequalities. Much progress has been made towards decolonising the economy. Bearing in mind our history of segregation and apartheid, part of South Africa's democratic success is often, therefore, measured by its ability to grow a strong black middle class.

This is particularly important bearing in mind that the distribution of income in South Africa remains shockingly skewed, to say the least. The poorest 20% of the South African population earns about 2.3% of the national income, while the richest 20% earns about 70% of the income. Needless to say, South Africa's middle class continues to grow as a much needed social buffer. According to the UCT Unilever Institute of Strategic Marketing, the South African middle class has more than doubled over the last eight years, growing from 1.7 million in 2004 to 4.2 million in 2012. South Africa's middle class now comprises 20.4% of the population compared to 10% in 1994. According to the 2012 African Development Bank report, it enjoys 33% share of gross national income. Africa's own middle class (US$4–US$20) has also grown since the 1980s, from 24% to 34% in 2010, and is expected to grow to 42% by 2060. Whether we like it or not, the middle class in South Africa and Africa at large remains an important social stratum.

The middle class generally plays a vital role in society
The middle class as a social stratum enjoys a distinctive place in society for a number of reasons. While the middle class comprises approximately 20% of South Africa's population, the middle class accounts for 50% of the country's taxable income. The black middle class, particularly, provides a much needed social safety net for society's lower echelons by, for instance, supporting large extended families in the form of remittances, income tax and consumption-led growth. Also, a strong middle class has always been a prerequisite for robust entrepreneurship and innovation in emerging economies. South Africa's middle class consumers are worth R180 billion in spending and they create the incentive to conceive, manufacture and sell.

That demand drives business opportunities and spurs investment. Entrepreneurship and invention are also rooted in the middle class and the rise in middle-class worker productivity generates much of our nation's wealth. The middle-class is also an important voice for holding government accountable to its electoral promises of service delivery, such as quality education and public healthcare services, crime and corruption, transport and communications infrastructure, and BBBEE. This is because the middle class is as dependent on public services as the poorest class and, therefore, has as much vested interest in good governance and quality public service delivery as the poor.

The Cosatu e-tolling protests are but one example of the interdependence of the interests of the middle class with the working-class poor – the upper class can easily opt into civic compliance and/or opt out in favour of private services when public services fail them. The black middle class, in particular, has also enjoyed increasing influence over the policy space as South Africa's business elite, as shown by Black Management Forum's increasing role in driving the BBBEE/AA/Transformation agenda in strategic sectors such as mining (for example, the 2004 Mining charter) and the financial services sector (for example, the 2003 Financial Sector Charter).

If President Zuma's aspiration to build a critical mass of black industrialists through government's massive infrastructure programme is to be realised, South Africa's black middle class is likely to take centre stage in our body politic in the coming decades. However, while we must acknowledge the distinctive role of the middle class in society, we also assert that the working class remains the main vanguard of social transformation and this cannot and should not be underestimated.

Social contradiction
Unfortunately, however, South Africa's black middle class is laden with social contradictions, and has its own (wayward) class aspirations. It is a class after its own interests, big on spending money on things it does not always need and not big on saving. StatsSA confirms that consumers knocking on the doors of debt counsellors earn an average salary of R15 000 per month, with about 89% of their disposable income committed to paying off debt. South Africa's household debt currently stands at 75% of disposable income. This class would, therefore, rather be seen in a hot beemer or in a club with a bottle of ridiculously expensive whiskey than reading or enjoying a warm night under a fully paid-off roof. They want to be seen living lavishly as in a 'larger than life' reality show despite the fact that poverty is only a pay cheque away. They continue this unabated spending on things they do not need just so that society can see them in states of temporal (but unreal) prosperity. Aspirations spew out in sordid (un)sophistication – because they must. Better vice than verse. Story of the black middle class, really!

This class is also fragmented and unorganised, fluid, insecure, volatile and often tenuous. It is a seriously conflicted class on the

258

inside. While it faces racism at work, it is the very same class that stands in ardent defence of its white masters to its peril. It climbs up the corporate ladder uttering quiet betrayals in big corporate boardrooms, they, too, saying 'blacks should not have a sense of entitlement', and 'oh no, please, spare us the race card again'; sitting rather laudably, listening sympathetically, in quiet defence with very little defiance. It is conflicted because of its desperate desire to safeguard newly earned privileges, while obliged to equally protect the 'hard-earned' privileges of its master that must continue to dispense it.

We see the random display of conflict at work as the black middle class is forced into deadly compliance in corporate boardrooms in the arrogant face of arrogant racism and male chauvinism; forced to keep quiet or the master removes the bronze spoon from lips wet and dry. The black middle class is conflicted when it must choose between that 'much-earned' holiday in Mauritius and sending remittances back home, *emakhaya,* or sending a child or two to school. It is conflicted when it has to choose between overtime work on a Friday and Saturday evening and ardent involvement in community projects because it has to prove itself all the way to the top – a top guaranteed to only a select few blacks. The black middle-class has to work harder, run faster, jump higher, no matter how little the rewards, at least it's something. The stratum is constantly conflicted – sold to the system; sold by the system; desperate to keep afloat amid inequitable realities.

The stratum is, at worst, parasitic and not innovative, feeding off unproductive patronage, often dispensed by private capital and the state, offering very little in return for its newfound gains, merely maintaining the status quo. BBBEE fronting, the 'travelgate' scandal, Sushi King lifestyles and unproductive 'tenderpreneurship' are but a few examples of a non-progressive middle-class that wants to eat for its own sake without considering its social contribution to society. Each year South Africa loses up to 20% of its procurement budget – R30 billion – to BEE fronting, corruption, fraud and mismanagement at the hands of a parasitic class of people. Contrary to popular belief, the black middle class is not, therefore, naturally predisposed to looking after the class interests of others. At worst, its aspirant class interests are intimately linked to undermining the class interests of others. Unfortunately, very little is said about its particular role in driving social transformation in South Africa.

I confess: I am Khanyi Mbau

So are we not, therefore, the lived expression of her spoken words: 'just because they can't put bread on the table, doesn't mean that I'm not going to eat my croissants and blue cheese, I just like nice things … I'm not here to save the world' (Khanyi Mbau on the *3rd Degree*, SABC 3). Are these not the typical sentiments of our own middle-class, us, the so-called black diamonds who remain indifferent in the face of escalating poverty? Yet we are repulsed when she does it, even as she mimics us, our own class aspirations, the coveted lives of those she sees on shows such as *Top Billing, Desperate Housewives* and *Footballers' Wives*. She believes it is her turn to eat no matter how she climbs up onto the dinner table.

The aspirations of Khanyi Mbau are no different from those of our own, as black diamonds. She is the epitome of what the world generally celebrates, hence she has become a celebrity who commands R35 000 a night for public appearances. Just like Khanyi Mbau, we, too, tend to eat for eating's sake. We forget easily, shunning the social contribution we, too, could make. That tough choice between a bottle of Moët we can hardly afford and starting a grocery club for the elderly? That fine line between the good life and poverty, even though poverty is just a pay cheque away?

Constructive role of the black middle class

I believe that the black middle class/professional class/learned class has a role to play in addressing the triple scourge of poverty, underdevelopment and social exclusion in society, as 'player', 'partner', 'intermediary' and 'enabler'. I believe that we can build a calibre of stratum ready, able and willing to reposition South Africa, and Africa at large, as 'actor', 'propagandist' and 'change agent', as well as build the prerequisite capabilities we need to compete with the rest of the world. The creation of a new generation of a class that is 'creator', 'producer', 'strategist' and '(decision)-maker' is more than just an economic imperative but is a moral requirement. It is an economic solution in keeping not only with the values and principles of equity enshrined in the South African Constitution, but of Africa's broader socio-economic aspirations as well. A strong black middle class is a prerequisite for robust entrepreneurship and innovation in Africa at large.

The black middle class should, therefore, play a more engaged role in helping to build productive capabilities or the prerequisite skills base in order to accelerate the creation of jobs in both the manufacturing and services sectors. Leaders within this class must continue in efforts to invest in education, skills-building and knowledge transfer, particularly in communities that find themselves at the margins, on the outskirts of economic activity. 'Each one, teach one'.

The black middle class constitutes a privileged class, and, by virtue of this, is best placed to appropriate knowledge in ways that improve the quality of life of the communities from where they come. There is no other way. There is no economy without people. There are no societies without people. People are an important part of the equation in driving innovation and societal success. We also know that skills are essential to improve productivity, incomes and access to employment opportunities, particularly for those who are vulnerable to being excluded from the labour market. It is crucially important to maintain, as well as to improve, the responsiveness of the supply side of the labour market.

Not only should the black middle class take the helm in small, medium and micro-sized enterprises (SMMEs) and start-ups but the black middle class should also be actively involved in efforts to promote micro- and small enterprises, as well as community cooperatives, particularly for those who are extremely vulnerable (that is, blacks, youth, women and people with disabilities). Since it is recognised that micro, small-scale and medium-scale enterprises are more employment intensive in their operations, these types of enterprises should receive a much larger share of available investment energy, as should human resources development initiatives. This will provide opportunities for the poor to generate their own income. Emergent black elites, in partnership with government, must revitalise credit/investment/cash injection facilities to revitalise micro- and small-enterprises.

Conclusion

The black middle class must partner with government to come up with strategies to deal with growing informality, underemployment and working poverty that currently characterises our labour market. Informality poses a genuine challenge as it worsens the jobs crisis, as well as weakens enterprise development. It also makes minimum wages less effective, as well as creates and deepens the mismatch between skills and jobs available (especially for the youth about to enter the labour market). These disguised forms of unemployment tend to be aggravating circumstances under a crisis of this nature. The black middle class must partner with government to transform informal work into decent work. Decent work is an essential part of the solution.

The era of socio-technological advancement, advanced communications and globalisation has enhanced our access to information, knowledge communities and other knowledge forms. Today, as a consequence of middle-class innovation, almost 18 million Kenyans can use their mobiles to deposit or transfer money and pay their accounts through M-PESA – compared to 30 million (70%) of Kenya's unbanked population. We should take advantage of new social forms and engage, and actively so, by learning from others and, most importantly, learning by doing.

While the black middle class needs to be organised and autonomous, they must be embedded and organised towards a cohesive nationalist social programme. We need to move towards a new era and build a new pedigree of class that is more proactive, forward-looking, involved and unapologetically sympathetic to the struggles of ordinary South Africans – committed to the poor.

However, there's an even deeper conversation that needs to be had in South Africa. It is the conversation about values: Which values count? Whose values count and why?

How do we relate the basic values of ubuntu to the question(s) of wealth and ownership? Do shared values matter in increasing share value? And if yes, to what extent?

Do we endorse the new values that condone eating sushi off the bodies of naked young women, and getting rich quick, it don't matter how you get there? Do we accept these burgeoning cultural value propositions as our own or do we continue to hold in high esteem the values of old? And if yes, to what extent?

When is 'enough' ever enough, for whom, if ever at all?

So I submit to you that Khanyi Mbau, alongside many other bling-stars, is but a national question: a representation of us as we unbecome, finding ourselves (un)done, (out)done. The curious case of Khanyi Mbau therefore begs genuine engagement, not opportunism for racialism's sake. It begs critical analysis, genuine concern and the opportunity for a national dialogue on values.

At the end of the day *values do matter*. Even a rejection of this statement is a value proposition on its own. *So whose values count? And what do we do about it?*

Has democracy
weakened the family?

Vukani Mthintso

African Union advisor

Introduction

THERE ARE SEVERAL PERMUTATIONS TO what democracy has brought. It is an open secret that those who were tasked with running the state at the dawn of democracy were largely inexperienced in the running of government. However, in utilising some of the characteristics and experience of 30 decades of struggle and three decades of the ANC in exile, the ANC was able to shape its 'developmental state model'. Twenty years after the first democratic elections, this essay traces the roots of these characteristics, which are principally focused on ensuring that the most vulnerable are cared for.

In utilising the prism of one of these vulnerable sectors, that is, children, insight is provided on some of the gains and lost opportunities confronted by the ANC-led government, with some of the pre-democracy policy statements as the barometer of these failures and successes. No doubt, repetitive narratives exist in all spheres of our lives, whether in this important volume, the social media or mainstream media. However very few mix the historic genesis of South African modern-day social policy and its potential implications for children.

Twenty years on, there is an abundance of statistics related to how many jobs have been created, for how long there have been laid water pipes and, most importantly, how the will of the people has reigned supreme. Indeed, the Mass Democratic Movement (MDM) has moved from one of resistance to one of builders of a common destiny, no matter the visible differences in tactics. All these, including these differences, are important portraits and markers of the gains of South Africa's democracy. After all, as Hubert H. Humphrey said in his last public speech, 'the moral test of government is how that government treats those who are in the dawn of life, the children;

those who are in the twilight of life, the elderly; those who are in the shadows of life; the sick, the needy and the handicapped'.

And so, from the onset, the democratic government led by the African National Congress (ANC) assumed a posture of a developmental state, understanding that the welfare of the citizen is cardinal in building a working and viable South Africa. Consequently, on the eve of taking up the reigns of the state, the ANC proclaimed in *Ready to Govern* that the approach to pursing a democratic, equitable and prosperous society was based on 'the belief in the human dignity of all in South Africa [and a belief] in the importance of the family as it is understood within the social and cultural norms in South Africa'.*

Many mistook this to mean that under the ANC in government South Africa would become a welfare state. However, the ANC remains quite conscious that to build aworking developmental state requires the gradual improvement in the welfare of its citizens, until such time that the real and sustainable development of the citizenry is within their individual and collective reach. This pragmatism and realism can be seen in the Constitution, in particular in sections 26, 27, 28 and 29, which recognise the progressive realisation of fundamental social and economic rights, such as healthcare, water, social security and education. In layperson terms, the ANC has the desire to meet all the rights of citizens but it realises that this will take time, given limited resources.

The ANC in exile and models for a new South Africa
Now, to the uninitiated, in the growth and metamorphosis of the ANC, this may seem to be polemics (at most) and propaganda (at its least). However, one would have to find the roots to this outlook in the ANC in exile and home.

For instance, from the 1960s the ANC in exile became accustomed to supplying every family with food and clothing every month. It was also customary that the MDM in South Africa would support families of detained or 'missing' cadres who could no longer contribute to the livelihood of their families through organisations such as the Detainees' Support Committee. Perhaps one important landmark

---

* *Ready to Govern: ANC Policy Guidelines for a Democratic South Africa*, as adopted by the 48 National Conference of the African National Congress, Durban 1991.

to its inherent developmental outlook is the Solomon Mahlangu Freedom College (SOMAFCO) and the surrounding settlement in Mazimbu, Tanzania. From this isolated 250 hectare plot, donated by the Tanzanian government in 1978, the ANC in exile went about the task of weaving together a model of an ideal South Africa.* Cadres received material support, education and basic needs, and, in turn, they would volunteer and provide their labour to building model healthcare, industry, housing, sustainable farming and an integrated social policy model for cadres in the populous surrounding areas.

This settlement was followed by the establishment of Dakawa in 1980. This housed the ANC Development Centre that focused on agriculture, industry, and arts and culture. Perhaps the most relevant (to this article) development, which displayed the intention of the ANC (as an apprentice government in waiting), was the establishment of the Charlotte Maxeke Children's Centre in 1982. In that year's 8 January Statement, ANC President, OR Tambo, said 'the children at the Charlotte Maxeke Crèche must be brought up to play their role as the new men and women that a free South Africa will need'. By the same token, a new South Africa would have to care for its children.

With that a major policy intention was made available for all to see; unless the children were taken care of, there would be no future South Africa. The nature of the Charlotte Maxeke Mother and Child Centre also provides evidence and insight into this outlook. 'Charlottes', as they came to be known, were organised into small family units with 'mothers' assigned to do various tasks for the children, whether it be cooking, teaching or storytelling.† The determined future for South Africa was shaped around looking after the most vulnerable, and shaping society to facilitate for their care, especially where children were concerned. However, although the children and general populous were entitled to basics rights such as food, shelter and education, they, too, had an obligation to contribute to the general wellbeing of the society and towards the liberation of South Africa.

---

* Pethu Serote. 1992. 'Solomon Mahlangu Freedom College: A unique South African educational experience in Tanzania', *Transformation* 20.
† Human Science Research Council. 'The Charlotte Maxeke Children's Centre', *Education in Exile*, Chapter 4. Pretoria: HSRC Press. Available at: www.hsrcpress.ac.za/product. php?productid=1960.

ANC in transition had decades of experience in governance

This cursory history provides a basis for the assertion that although the ANC in 1994 had no experience in government, it had the benefit of over three decades of struggle experience in exile to shape its outlook on governance. This experience, with some of its challenges and limitations, resulted (among other things) in the understanding that the family is the basic unit that shapes societies. This understanding carried the liberation movement for three decades in exile and was to inform its policy and programmatic principles in a democratic South Africa.

In the ANC outlook, family constitutes all those who one loves and those who share a love for the revolution and the total emancipation of South Africa. Such is the strength of this belief, that one can recall fetching members of the movement – with bag in hand and no idea where they would bed – from various airports and train stations wherever one lived. However, one knew that the ANC family led and lived. One was certain of safe passage, perhaps a meal, the possibility of education and the certainty of the satisfaction of most basic needs.

This also complemented the understanding that the ANC is a people's Parliament. Consequently, the family outlook was and remains cardinal. Families and family unity are, in general terms, driven by love. Love is an important ingredient in the development of a child. Love is also an important contributor to the development of the characteristics of any true revolution and revolutionary. Who can forget the chilling words of Solomon Kalushi Mahlangu at the Pretoria gallows in 1979, when he said: 'My blood will nourish the tree that will bear the fruits of freedom. Tell my people that I *love* them. They must continue the fight.'

Indeed, it was el Comandante Ernesto Che Guevara who said: 'At the risk of seeming ridiculous, let me say that the true revolutionary is guided by a great feeling of *love*. It is impossible to think of a genuine revolutionary lacking this quality.'

Sidebar: Democracy weakened the 'family'

Well, let me here just take a sidebar and sound ridiculous: the introduction of democracy to and by a semi-prepared organisation brought with it a loss of love, which in turn destroyed what was the African National Congress family. This character is an important ingredient in bringing shared growth and prosperity to our land.

Democracy, with its conservatory and predatory tendencies, paid back in dividends, back onto our beloved family. The ANC family into which I was born, nurtured and lived was one in which the weakest were protected and nurtured with all the necessary attention. This in the orthodox is not because of the necessity of survival (contrary to popular belief) but because, like elephants, we were taught that the protection of our weakest signals the prosperity and survival of society, which requires a strong and united family.

In exiting my sidebar, I would like to recall that, in this context, the 'family' has attempted to meander with some fortune through a 20-year storm, the epicentre of which can only remind one of Rubisana's adaptation of '*Zimkile iInkomo Magwalandini!*' This prose was also recorded in the 1882 outburst by Isaac Williams Wauchope in response to the freeing of chiefs imprisoned on Robben Island, wherein he asks the question, 'where are the poets and orators today?'

Evaluation benchmarks

In seeking, therefore, not to stutter, I shall measure the ANC government based on its historic genesis, policy intents and how it has treated some of its most vulnerable members of society – its children. Of course, I have chosen love and family as an undertone since they are important for a child's development. Love is also a motivating revolutionary force, which is a requirement for the fulfilment of the objectives set by the National Democratic Revolution, as defined in many policy positions, including *Ready to Govern*. In my view these initial intentions remain some of the most purely developed since the Freedom Charter.

I shall also interspace my brief analysis with measuring to what extent the quality of life of a South African child has regressed or improved in relation to the ANC's experiences in exile. I have taken this benchmark because I believe that there is a plausible reiteration of experiences of the ANC in exile and in government, even though (sadly) there have been missed opportunities for the ANC in government (at least in as far as the purview of this article is concerned). I have also decided to use two of the four initial and basic objectives, as set out in *Ready to Govern*, as barometers because these remain important indicators for dreamers not constrained by government. These objectives are: (1) striving for the rights of all South African [Children]; and (2) overcoming the legacy of inequality and injustice… in a swift, progressive and principled way.[*]

In general terms, the South African developmental state has fared very well in the quantifiable improvement of the quality of life of its citizens, if the above benchmarks have to be utilised.

Measuring the 20 years of democracy against the ANC in exile
There are obvious limitations in trying to utilise the ANC in exile as a barometer to measure 20 years of democracy. An obvious one is that settlements like Mazimbu, with its surrounding community, had about 10 000 'citizens' and South Africa (20 years after democracy) has about 50 million. Another important limitation is that the propensity to foster cohesion and common purpose was more tangible in the ANC in exile, since, after all, most of those who populated the settlements had left home with a common purpose to liberate South Africa. South Africa 20 years after democracy has myriad interests and the common vision is either absent or elusive. With all these and other limitations, it is still possible to isolate key elements and provide an opinion on gained and missed opportunities and lessons.

The ANC in exile was constituted of 'families' of cadres and volunteers who were in service to (and a feeder into) the bigger family, which was populated in over 70 countries. Despite this spread, each and every cadre and, by implication, child was in service and was nurtured for the positive qualities they have the potential to realise. Cadre development was not rhetoric but a reality, which saw attention being paid to each and every child located in these units with their development being horned towards their current and future contributions to the broader society. Every need was fed – three meals a day for every child, even though sometimes the quality was questionable; quality school attendance, even though sometimes there was vociferous debate on the content; clothing on their backs, even though most (if not all the clothes) were second-hand from overseas; quality vocation and recreation, even though some of the most basic tools were lacking. Of all the requirements, children in

---

[*] African National Congress. 1992. *Ready to Govern*. Available at: www.anc.org.za/show. php?id=227.

exile were mostly surrounded by love. Even when biological parents were absent from the settlements, there were plenty of mothers and caregivers. Even though these caregivers were not blood-related, they were struggle-related.

These ties and relations have sadly diminished with every X we have placed on every ballot paper since 1994.

The demands of running a flourishing democracy have seen the strongest prosper more and the weakest comparatively marginally. Many would point to the complexities of governance and the need to focus on the development of the state without fear or favour. The bigger problems of macro-economics and fiscal discipline have seen the number of recorded orphans, according to UNICEF's South Africa: Annual Report 2012, reaching an estimated 3.7 million, with close to 150 000 children believed to be living in child-headed households.* This is about a 29% increase in just the period between 2005 and 2009. In the same period, adoptions decreased by 52% and foster-care grants increased by 72%.†

There are several causes for this. One could be related to the policy choices, which favour a more Eurocentric definition of the family and the incentivisation of foster care as a step towards adoption, with the former having some material support from the state. In advancing this Eurocentric view, the *White Paper on Families* issued by the Department of Social Development defines family as, 'A societal group that is related by blood (kinship), adoption, foster care or the ties of marriage (civil, customary or religious), civil union or cohabitation, and go beyond a particular physical residence.' This, therefore, means that most of those who raised and cared for me, according to our democratic state, have ceased to be my family and, by implication, those who I know little about but with whom I happen to share my lineage are more relevant to me now. To borrow a term more common on Twitter SMH!

Others have pointed to the burden of HIV and AIDS and some adverse economic conditions. The 2008 Department of Social Development's *Review of Children's Access to Employment-based Contributory Social Insurance Benefits* notes that because of the pandemic (among others) '9% of the child population has lost one or

---

* http://www.unicef.org/southafrica/protection_6631.html.
† South African Press Association (SAPA), 'Rising Number of Orphans', *Sowetan*, 9 July 2012.

both parents [with] approximately 630 000 double orphans, 500 000 maternal orphans and 2 000 000 paternal orphans'.*

Whatever the prism utilised, it is abundantly clear that the space for the definition of the African family has been shrunk, with the state offering better support to individuals fitting within its policy-choice option. This is quite different from the ANC definition, which, to a large extent, focused on supporting the household unit as a basis for family support as opposed to defined individuals. This household approach may seem to be a romantic pronunciation, but examples elsewhere exist where society is organised in units that translate to streets that, in turn, translate to ties and villages/suburbs.

Such an example exists in Cuba where Youth Volunteer Social Workers (as led by the Young Communist League of Cuba) have organised themselves to service society with seemingly mundane tasks and the gathering of household information (on a weekly basis) on, for instances, diet and education with a view of landing direct support to families with an emphasis on the total wellbeing of children. It is not my intention here to evaluate the merits or demerits of a capitalist and socialist system, but one has to point out the underlying value systems that promote behaviour in such systems. In general terms, young people in a capitalist system are motivated by self-preservation, as well as individual progress and prosperity. In the converse, the young volunteers of the Young Communist League of Cuba are motivated by selflessness and the national philosophy of '*Patria o Muerte! Venceremo!*' meaning 'Fatherland or death! We will win!' Needless to say, a love of their people and nation is the motivation for their contribution.

Over the past 20 years the South African government has attempted to replicate such models. Initially the Masakhane Programme, which intended 'to create the conditions in which every South African has the opportunity to create a better life', brought water to over 2.5 million people, built 600 clinics and electrified 2 million home in less than four years.† Another such attempt is the voluntary National Youth Service Programme (NYS), which was launched in 2004 with the objective of engaging young people in civic responsibility while

---

* *A Review of Children's Access to Employment-based Contributory Social Insurance Benefits*, United Nations Children's Fund, May 2008.
† Speech by President Mandela during the Masakhane focus week, Bothaville, 14 October 1998.

271

offering them opportunities to gain some work experience. In its first five years, the programme engaged more than 100 000 out of school, unskilled and unemployed young South Africans.

Although it was up to each cluster of governance to isolate the available opportunities, a coordination mechanism existed, which would provide total oversight in all spheres of governance over the programme, principally through the National Youth Commissions, with the Umsobomvu Youth Fund acting as a supporting agent. Programmes such as the Joint Initiative Priority Skills Acquisition (JIPSA) complemented the programme. JIPSA sought, through partnerships with private sector and donor agencies, to skill and channel these volunteers into work opportunities in industry. The NYS was also to be complemented by the Public Works Programme, which was replaced by the Expanded Public Works Programme (EPWP) in 2004. The EPWP, which targets young people (and other groups) with a view to improving service delivery to vulnerable communities, has created just over 4 million work opportunities since 2004.

Interestingly the social cluster focused its efforts on the early childhood development (ECD) and healthcare for the EPWP, while the community works programme took a household level approach. In seeking to advance some of the objectives of the NYS and EPWP, various departments have put in place feeder programmes such as (1) the National Rural Youth Service Corps of the Department of Rural Development and Land Reform, which targets about 10 000 rural youth per annum, (2) the Isibindi Programme which intends to reach over 1.8 million vulnerable children, and (3) various other national and local programmes.

Twenty years on, the ANC-led government can confidently say it has taken its service philosophy and has reached millions of vulnerable individuals and families.

However, the ANC-led government would have done better had it paid attention to the manner in which these households and families experience these services, as well as the consistency and reliability of these services.

These households experience this service in an isolated fashion wherein the total value proposition or benefits are seldom experienced in total. For instance, the social grant receiving 'service delivery' protester may threaten to withdraw their vote because of metred electricity, but they will conveniently forget that their child attends a no-fee school with a feeding scheme. This has to do with how citizens experience 'service' in pockets and the state 'arriving' at the household at varied times with differing messages and delivery modes.

The ANC in exile did not isolate the satisfaction of the need for nutrition from healthcare and education, for instance. The child in Mazimbu experienced all of them simultaneously and consistently. Thus, going forward, there is a need for policy work and attention has to be paid to the delivery architecture, In doing so, attention has to be paid to the total experience and value proposition for each individual household and family. Service has to be to the benefit of these units, with the underlying philosophy of strengthening the family and reaping from the contributions from that family, as was shown by the Mazimbu model. If a family experiences government in totality and consistently, the promotion of cohesion and voluntarism for the common good ought to be less illusive.

Secondly, the millions reached are an important indicator. However, the changing of programmes with the same objectives from Masakhane to EPWP in 20 years makes it difficult to maintain a longitudinal and qualitative view of progress in key areas. The key lesson for the ANC-led government from the ANC in exile is that it is important to maintain consistency in programming, while allowing for tactical evolution of programmes so as to address the ever-changing circumstances confronting the 'family'.

Striving for the rights of all South African children
One area that has been consistent from the ANC-led government is the insistence on children's rights, while also ensuring a progressive realisation of these rights. This rights-based approach has been enshrined in the Constitution, with section 28 specifically being dedicated to children. Other pieces of legislation and policies, such as the Children's Act 38 of 2005 and Child Justice Act 75 of 2008, further protect and determine the qualitative scope and depth of those rights. The joint South African Human Rights Commission (SAHRC) and United Nations Children's Fund (UNICEF) *Review of Equity and Child Rights* notes that:

> Significant progress has been made since the end of apartheid in 1994 in fulfilling the rights of children in South Africa...

New laws, progressive public spending and reorganisation of administrative systems have contributed to accelerating the fulfilment of rights. For example, millions of children are benefiting from the Child Support Grant through the extension of the age of eligibility and an extensive outreach programme by the state. Recent changes in government's response to HIV have also been far reaching, including state provision of treatment for all HIV-infected infants at government-run health facilities, and provision of treatment and care to HIV-positive pregnant women earlier in their pregnancies to prevent new paediatric infections. Near-universal access to primary education has been achieved and government is increasingly focusing on the improvement of the quality of education.[*]

Overcoming the legacy of inequality and injustice

The above report further notes that the eligibility age range for the child support grant was gradually extended, over a period, with it reaching age 18 in 2013. There is ample empirical evidence, that shows that the child support grant positively impacts and benefits the development of a child and directly contributes to the reduction of poverty and vulnerability. The quantitative and qualitative measure (for the African child) are a stark contrast to 1994 data, where in 50 and 40 per 1 000 coloured and Indian beneficiaries, respectively, received the state maintenance grant; 14 per 1 000 whites and only two per 1 000 Africans were grant beneficiaries[†] The SAHRC and UNICEF report also highlights the fact that about 2.8 million (or 15% of all children) have been reached through RDP or state-subsidised dwellings. The cumulative effect was that between 2004 and 2008 child poverty was reduced by 13%.

In general terms, the South African developmental state, in its 20 year existence, has fared very well in the quantifiable improvement of the quality of life of its citizens, especially children.

However, the SAHRC and UNICEF report notes: 'some 2.1 million children eligible for the Child Support Grant were not receiving it 2008' and that 'some 1.7 million children (9 per cent of

---

[*] South African Human Rights Commission, *South Africa's Children: A Review of Equity and Child Rights*, March 2011.

[†] Lund, F. 2008. *Changing Social Policy: The Child Support Grant in South Africa*. Cape Town: HRSC Press.

all children) still live in informal housing such as shacks in backyards or squatter settlements'. The overall effect of this limited access is that 'some 11.9 million children (64 per cent of all children) live in poverty'.*

One of the biggest barriers identified in accessing these services and reversing child poverty is the lack of identification documents and unemployment in the children's families and/or households.

Whereas there has been concerted effort on the part of the state and civil society to ensure mass identity document registration, very little visible work has been undertaken in cross referencing of data on children and beneficiaries of these services and general social protection system. Put in simple terms, the question of how many of the newly registered and beneficiary housing subsidy families are also benefitting from the no-fee schools, primary healthcare, free water and social grants remains elusive to the state. The state is unable to answer the 'price' of the social wage to each household and what the general average or minimum is and should be. This illuminates the point made earlier: the citizens and children are experiencing government services singularly instead of holistically. This is a fundamental contributor to continued inequalities in South Africa and the vexing question of children's living standards.

Conclusion

In looking at the history of the ANC in exile and the first 20 years of the ANC in government, through the eyes of a child, the words of President OR Tambo during the 48th National Congress of the ANC come to mind: 'It is fair to say that on some issues and in some instances we could have put up a better performance than we actually did.' Despite this and because the movement had the capacity and will to handle such contradictions, the family flourished. Like in any family we had our disagreements, but each and every one of those disagreements were directed at ensuring the flourishing of the family with the ultimate goal of delivering a free, prosperous and equal South Africa. This is best exemplified by the 1985 Kabwe Conference wherein President Tambo reflected that:

---

* South African Human Rights Commission, *South Africa's Children: A Review of Equity and Child Rights*, March 2011.

Conference took place against a climate of heightened confrontations between our people on one hand and the regime on the other. Like today, the regime and the South African press sought to create divisions amongst us by resorting to all sorts of schemes including attempts to draw a wedge between the youth and the older generation within the ANC None of these schemes have succeeded.*

The ANC in government has taken account of this rich history and has adopted a rights-based and developmental state approach, at least as far as children are concerned. This has led to the assertion of children's rights principally through the Constitution and legislation. In providing expression to these rights various initiatives, such as the National Youth Service and Social Protection System, have been implemented in the first 20 years of democracy. These programmes have contributed to overcoming the legacy of inequality and injustice in a swift, progressive and principled way.

The challenge over the next 50 years is the deepening of these gains and returning to the fundamental ANC approach of building strong families as a basis of a strong and cohesive society. This will require several steps to be taken. Included in these is the revamping and redesigning of the architecture of the state, such that the citizens in general (and children in particular) in the most vulnerable families experience the state's delivery holistically and to an agreed upon minimum social wage floor that can be progressively realised and surpassed.

Mayibuye!

---

* www.anc.org.za/show.php?id=104.

History will be kind to us for we intend to write it

Mhlengi Wandile Ngcaweni

First-year student

Born-free? What born-free?

Born on 2 May 1994, I was born right in the middle of everything: the elections had just happened on 27 April and the inauguration was on 11 May. I am a first generation 'born-free' – a child born into democracy. This means that we should never have to be disadvantaged on the basis of our race and, in theory, our backgrounds.

What does being a born-free mean to us, you might ask. In truth, being born-free means more in theory than it does in practice. Being born-free means we should never have to suffer the way the past generations suffered; that we can be whatever we want or dream to be; that we can date and be friends with whomever we like, regardless of race; that we can be educated anywhere we want and play any sport we want. Basically, it means that we can do anything we wish to do and that we have rights from birth, which the past generations were fighting to get.

We have a lot of pressure on us as born-frees because we are actually the proof of the success or failure of this democracy. Our success or failures will expose many things about being born post-apartheid and whether it really was a privilege to be born post 1994. Twenty years after democracy we are the proof that everyone has been waiting for to determine how successful our democracy has been.

Firstly, the country has seen how we have lived, how we have gone to school, what our challenges and weaknesses have been as a generation, and we have been criticised greatly for our lifestyles and choices by the older generations and leadership of the country.

Secondly, the country is waiting to see how we, born into a privileged South Africa, are going to perform on the world stage. They are waiting to see what kind of leaders might possibly emerge from a group born in 'almost' total freedom. We graduated from high school in 2012 and our graduation showed us some limitations on the part of government, as some of us have been unable to continue with our studies because there are not enough higher education institutions in South Africa. It is government's fault that a lot of the so-called born-frees will not have opportunities to further their studies.

I can speak only from what I see as an individual born in 1994 and hope that most of the issues I have decided to raise are agreed upon by other born-frees, and that they help the past and coming generations to see things as we see them and realise that change is something we want and will not apologise for.

Dreams and aspirations of our generation

I have been exposed to diverse social circles, different people at school and the general public. I have been able to analyse and determine if indeed we are a successful democracy and, if not, what are we still missing? This is something Nelson Mandela never had the opportunity to do.

All the young men and women I have had the honour of chilling with are paving their own special routes and trying to identify themselves and distinguish themselves as individuals. They want to be intellectuals, entrepreneurs, poets, artists, sportspeople, writers and aspiring philosophers, teachers and professionals – to pursue any field they choose. This social privilege was definitely not normal to someone born in the 1960s but to a child of 1994, now a young adult, this expectation could not be any more normal.

The thing that needs to be realised is that we are a diverse group of open-minded youth and we know a lot about the past, and we have accepted that what happened in the past was not right and the government was unfair. I feel we have played our role in making sure we do not go back to those days; we have played our role in making sure we move forward and do not get stuck in the past.

We have a problem with being reminded constantly about how *special* and *lucky* we are that we are living in complete freedom with all the opportunities available to us. This constant drilling us to remember how lucky we are is not necessarily the best way to make us stay free. Freedom is, after all, ours by right and we should not be made to feel responsible for it.

Do not get me wrong: we are aware of all the sacrifices made earlier, as I have said, but we do not need to be taught to doubt our peers' intentions or be afraid to express our opinions freely and openly just because we fear being labelled. Letting us live together the way we wish would be the best because we are constantly reminded about the past, because some find it necessary to inherit the hate or the grudge, or they simply develop the grudge themselves. Let us live our own lives. We do not find it necessary to fight wars that are not ours to fight as born-frees; the war has been won, but you still find people fighting it.

The past generations are to blame for us not generating new ideas but staying in the past because they are afraid that we will forget or not realise that we have not been completely freed as black people, as Steve Biko would have hoped. We should fight Steve Biko's war individually and collectively and seek to free ourselves and not forever hear about how the black man should do what, how and when, as Biko did. People of the past generation had their own battles and agendas, like winning democracy and getting rid of apartheid. Our battles and agendas are different: to make sure that South Africa realises the prosperity aspect the ruling party aspired to: to building a non-racial, non-sexist, democratic and united South Africa.

Our mandate, our commitment

We are, indeed, a powerful generation but we are still only as strong as our weakest link, caused by circumstances over which we have no power. Well, at least for now. That is the stubborn legacy of apartheid and racism. South Africa will grow and hopefully become a first world country under our generation's leadership. And, believe me, this is what we think we are capable of as the 1994 generation, and this is one of our shared goals for the country.

Both the white and black populations are burdened by racism. We need to start calling it what it is, racism, and not call it something else. The truth is, we experience setbacks where we find white people, when they are under pressure in certain situations, cracking and saying extremely racist statements. We need to realise that these things have been growing inside them and when they are under pressure, they show their 'true colours' and true feelings towards other races. And this is unacceptable! But who said lived and learnt attitudes of superiority can be abandoned within 20 years when they took centuries to form? I have been exposed to racial outbursts from teachers and peers alike, and, shockingly, they think it is acceptable and that they should be forgiven because we have somehow excused them for so long. An example is when a teacher or a coach says 'you people' and then smiles at you as if what they have just said is acceptable. Or when they make jokes about blacks and crime, or about Indians and sandwiches, or about coloureds and gangsterism and where they come from, or about how white people behave.

Sadly, these jokes are also said by my generation and I would say this is one of our weaknesses as a free generation: free from living in a society where racism was sanctioned by law. We are threatening our own freedom and equality because the more these jokes and stereotypes are accepted or these outbursts forgiven, the less we will move forward. I personally have never found these jokes funny or smiled with a teacher who had a racist outbursts.

A good place to see racism is at the top ex-Model C schools. When I was in high school, Jeppe High School to be precise, I saw how black teachers were respected less by students of all races and, sadly, also by their white colleagues, who were open about this lack of respect. The headmaster did nothing to try to unite the teachers, either professionally or socially. Afrikaans and isiZulu were both offered as second languages and English as the first language. I did isiZulu as a second language and had a brilliant isiZulu teacher who knew her work. Her classes had a higher average than the Afrikaans classes but she always taught in one of the worst classrooms in the school and had the worst facilities. The Afrikaans teachers, on the other hand, taught in classrooms that were maintained and they had all the facilities to make their teaching easier.

One would have thought that my isiZulu teacher would have been head of her subject, given that she was the only one who taught it, and very successfully considering the average of her classes. But this was not the case. She had to report to a white teacher who was the moderator – a moderator who couldn't write a single word in isiZulu! These were obvious discriminatory and undermining tactics and the headmaster was evidently fine with us knowing. It showed us black students where we stood. When a headmaster undermines the capabilities of a black teacher like this, how are the students supposed to have faith in and respect for the rest of the black teachers? And how are we supposed to respect any teacher that constantly reminded us how lucky we were to be in a school of that calibre, rich in history, and how we were part of something we would not want to lose because the school's waiting list was full throughout the year.

The social construct of difference

We learn from what we see happening around us, we learn from our parents and we must not underestimate how much we learn from our teachers, even things that are not in the curriculum.

Socially, we as a group have managed to go far in terms of not making friends based on skin colour or background. We see kids of different races being best friends with each other, we date each other and we listen to genres of music that were previously viewed as only being popular with certain races, whatever race we are. After 20 years though, this is not good enough. These interracial activities are practiced by a minority and the parents of this minority are still very judgemental and racist. It is still difficult for us to be 100% comfortable with each other. We might be comfortable to a certain extent, but when you visit your white friend's house and your friend's parents start making uncomfortable jokes, or they offer you food to take home as if you somehow don't eat enough at your home, or they are uncomfortable about leaving you in a room alone and you see that your friend doesn't see anything wrong with what their parents are doing, it is difficult. It is fair to say that I also do not notice when my parents make any white friends racially uncomfortable. My ignorance does not make me innocent and me being best friends with one white person does not make me accepting of all the differences that come with white people.

Dating is a very complex arrangement for us, especially when we date across racial lines. It is still hard to date a religious Indian girl because her Muslim parents expect her to only be around Indian Muslim guys. Well, I guess this is a religious constrain, but I mentioned it here because it happens and is relevant to seeing what else needs to change. White girls have a bigger problem with other races though some do date interracially for experimental reasons. But at least there are more white girls dating interracially than there are white boys. I personally don't have any white male friends that have dated a black girl or even half considered doing so.

Black girls also don't have a very positive outlook on dating interracially; they only tease but they never let anything serious develop. Black guys are simply too suspect with their intentions because they always seem to have a lot of excuses about their preferences. Most of the time these are physical preferences. They have been in this world for only 20 years, so they should not have preferences that apply to race specific when they were born into a racially diverse country. I would blame the older generations for teaching us the wrong way to look at women altogether. Having a preference after 20 years is simply not good enough anymore. If the born-frees are going to be the future, we need to do more across races.

On politics and allegiance

I think that one of the challenges facing the born-frees and the generations following is for us not to be dogmatic about the political parties we support. We should never be 100% ready to vote for a certain political party purely on the basis of history. We must vote for a political party we feel is the best to lead the country forward – into a non-racial, non-sexist, democratic, united and prosperous future.

I feel that most political parties have failed to teach us about real democracy. The leading parties have worked our minds to make us feel indebted to them for the struggle they led, which means that our generation will be confined to political parties merely on the basis of the past, without consideration of the present circumstances facing South Africa. If we are dogmatically aligned to a certain party, like our parents, we will never be able to see the wrongs or rights of that particular party.

What I mean is, it is well and good for us to support the ANC because we come from ANC families and we appreciate the ANC's role in leading the struggle and championing transformation since 1994. However, history alone should not always be the ANC's currency. It will not sell!

We must never be in a position where we feel that no one could be better than who we currently have in power. The born-frees are voting for the first time in May 2014. The votes that will be cast by us will be historic because, again, we will be the first generation born into democracy to vote, we will play our part in keeping democracy going, and we will make a change by selecting people who will have our best interests at heart, in terms of our futures, our wellbeing and the prosperity of South Africa. This is what our votes should mean. The party that wins the elections this year needs to realise that the youth in this country are a force and therefore should be considered when decisions are made. That also means youth development should be the centrepiece of election manifestos.

I feel that one of the things that should not have been scrapped after democracy was the post-matric military service that was compulsory under apartheid. More and more young South Africans are resorting to crime because they have nothing else to do with their time, and they have no way out of the situation they are in even though the government says it is doing the best to build colleges and universities. A matric certificate also doesn't help much because it doesn't equip one with any skills and so it doesn't do justice to a young person looking for a job to keep themselves out of poverty.

Military service would take the youth off the streets and give them something to do. In service they could be taught skills and be put to use where they would gain experience and be taught about the country and how to be united for a common cause. Fewer idle youth on the street or at home could only mean fewer people resorting to crime and doing drugs in their spare time.

Another thing this government needs to be strict on, like the pre-1994 government was, is the number of interns or trainees the big companies recruit on a yearly basis to help train the youth and give them work experience. The companies simply don't take enough young people under their guidance even though the government compensates them for every person they take in through such programmes as learnerships.

Conclusion

'We need to see race as a social construct, not as a biological identity.' This is a Black Consciousness quote I have read. This is one of the ideas we need to embrace as 20-year-old young adults born in 1994 because the problem, as I have attempted to show, is no longer in our minds. We undoubtedly believe in ourselves, whatever our race, and we have, to a large extent, freed ourselves from the racial constructs that made us believe that we are inferior to white people. What we need to do is carry ourselves forward and ask ourselves how we can get out of this quicksand that seems to be pulling us down when we want to move forward. We need to try to pave a solid pathway for the generations that will follow and see what we can do with the inheritance that we have in our hands, as a joint family and no longer a particular race. Trying to teach the older generations more about our socio-economic needs is important but we need to realise that investing in the future is even more important.

I guess you could say that Nelson Mandela was a major investor: he took great risks at a time when all confidence was lost and he tried his very best to make sure that we are secure and valuable. In this way he was ensuring a clear path for the future generations to follow. Well, it is now time for our generation – the one Nelson Mandela invested in – to reach its first bloom 20 years later. Let this happen soon with the help of the generations we are paving the way for. As individuals we shall have our own opinions, regardless of our race or culture or age; we need to make sure that we are informed about everything we do not understand.

Eventually, whatever the confusion carried in this essay, the answer to what democracy means to me, is that our generation is free from the legal strictures of apartheid. Opportunities have opened up, thanks to progressive policies that have transformed our country. However, it is not yet cultural and economic uhuru for some of our citizens. As young people, we must strive to change that so that all South Africans enjoy the democratic dividend. This new struggle should include rebuilding and reasserting youth structures and student representative councils, which have been rendered redundant in many institutions of higher learning.

Post-apartheid social pact and perennial exclusion in a fractured multiracial society

Dumisani Ngcobo

Public servant, social policy focus, KZN

Introduction

THIS IS THE JOURNEY OF AN EDUCATED black African in post-apartheid South Africa under the African National Congress government from 1994 until the present within the social fracture brought about by an exclusive social pact under the Rainbow framework. In this journey I wish to share my almost 20 years' experience of freedom in light of our political and economic expectations, aspirations and outcomes. I have structured my reflections under the following themes:

- What does non-racialism means in the context of race relations?
- What has been the experience with upward mobility – secure jobs – under the Rainbow framework?
- What social protection is there for an unemployed and underemployed liberated person in post-apartheid South Africa?
- What will South Africa look like in 20 years if it recrafts its social pact to include all stakeholders: the unemployed and underemployed workers, employed workers, government and business?

Non-racialism under the Rainbow framework

It is my considered opinion that non-racialism as a concept is based on the negation of the existence of the biological construction of race categories among human beings. Non-racialism has been bequeathed to the 'new' South Africa by the entire liberation movement that includes the African National Congress and its allies, the Pan Africanist Congress and the Black Consciousness Movement. On the one hand, one might argue that, initially, owing to the rampant racial division in the country, the Congress movement subscribed to the notion of multiracialism in which all 'races' were to be included in a free political dispensation.

On the other hand, the Africanist and Black Consciousness strands focused on directly confronting racism. In their broad language, they were 'anti-racist', instead of recognising the existence of multiple races. As Sobukwe put it, we believe in the 'human race' and reject the notion of multiracialism as 'racism multiplied'.

I have spoken about the history of the concept of non-racialism in order to show that the 'Rainbow' construct put forward by Archbishop Emeritus Desmond Tutu, which is the ideological expression, if not foundation, of race relations in post-apartheid South Africa, does not negate the existence of races but rather acknowledges them and promotes their distinct existence. Materially, this translated into the transfer of the race privileges of whites and Indians and the race subjugation of black Africans and many so-called coloureds in the post-apartheid South Africa. However, since at the beginning of post-apartheid South Africa, race and class coincided, ideologues of the new order have been able to escape the charge of continuing racism in a refurbished ideology called Rainbowism. Rainbowism is not anti-racist because that would have meant the overhaul of the inherited economic, cultural, social and political structure in South Africa. It translated into the extension of privileges that were originally a preserve of the whites, to the African, Indian and coloured elites, leaving the majority, particularly unemployed and underemployed Africans, outside the new society. In short, it created a multiracially exclusive society.

The experience of educated black Africans, represented by myself in these reflections, has been a painful journey to integrate with white society/structure on its own terms assimilating its values of crass materialism, elitism, exclusion, classism, consumerism, militarism, sexism and violence. Educated black Africans have been accommodated into white middle-class society, whether as temporary or permanent sojourners (time will tell), only if they accept that the insiders in the new society are whites, Indians, some black Africans and some coloureds, and the outsiders are the black African majority – the historical victims of apartheid colonialism who are unemployed and underemployed.

Therefore the experience of non-racialism under the Rainbow

framework has been the continuation of racism and its economic, cultural and social structure, not vigorous strides towards creating an anti-racist all-inclusive society.

Upward social mobility under the rainbow framework

As I indicated earlier, the new South Africa recognises the existence of mainly four races in the country: whites/Europeans, Indians/Asians, black Africans and coloureds. So upward social mobility has been structured along these lines whereby the state has consciously sought to affirm educated black Africans, Indians and coloureds, women of all races and the differently-abled people through affirmative-action policies and equity acts, although to different degrees.

It is common knowledge that progress in this regard has been achieved more in the public sector than in the private sector for the obvious reasons that black Africans control the first sector, while whites overwhelmingly dominate the latter sector. In other words, there has been upward social mobility for black Africans, Indians and coloureds in the public sector, whereas these corrective policies are being implemented with resistance in the private sector. However, due to the high education level of Indians and white women, these groups have registered a disproportionate advance, even in the private sector, and one can therefore conclude that, judged within the confines of demographics of the country, Indians and white women have been the major beneficiaries of affirmative-action policies and equity acts within both the public and private sectors.

Another constraining aspect for black Africans on upward social mobility is that small companies with fewer than 150 employees are exempt from affirmative-action policies and equity acts. Since small- and medium-sized companies create a substantial number of jobs in the new South Africa – according to the National Development Plan (NDP) they are expected to create 90% of the 11 million projected jobs by 2030 – black Africans will certainly not benefit proportionally to upward mobility. They will receive the same as they have over the past 20 years – the jobs that whites and Indians don't want, the 'indecent jobs', in the language of the trade-union movement. This is the paradox of upward social mobility under the Rainbow framework: instead of proportionally benefitting the historical victims of apartheid colonialism, affirmative-action policies and equity acts have disproportionately benefitted white women and Indians and will continue to do so.

It is my submission that if upward social mobility is to level the playing field, it should be based on the principle of democratic ownership of the South African economy. In a country with arguably, together with the United States and Brazil, the worst history of racism against black Africans, democratic ownership of the economy, in terms of participation in the South African labour market at all levels should have been based on the acceptance of the demographic representation of all 'race' groups in the labour market. In simple words, black Africans should have been represented as per their demographic make-up of the country of their ancestors and not be 'affirmed', as has been the case with their minority counterparts in the United States. Any formula will perpetuate inherited disparities and no one could raise the issue of skills as a hindrance to this basic democratic proposal, since black Africans have enough basic skills to populate any labour-market segment in post-apartheid South Africa proportionate to their demographic make-up of the country.

The table below supports clearly the statements regarding the racialised nature of participation in the labour market. Specifically, this table offers comparative statistics of employment and unemployment per education level and racial categories for the periods 1996 and 2011. Black Africans are the least educated and they are the overwhelming majority in the country but they have the lowest labour-market participation. This, unfortunately, has been their experience in the 20 years of democracy.

Social protection under the rainbow framework social pact

I am educated myself, with a doctorate in Social Policy that I received at the age of 27. I regard this as an achievement considering my background: I am the second of five sons of a tea lady and a manual labourer, whose work history is punctuated with long spells of unemployment and/or redundancy. At the age of 24 I already had a Master's degree. I am not mentioning these facts to boast but as an introduction to my work history.

In spite of my academic achievement at a relatively early age, I only got a permanent decent job at the age of 33. For a decade after receiving my Master's degree, I was either unemployed or held temporary contract jobs or learnerships without benefits. During the intractable years of unemployment, I survived without any income.

I only had access to food, clean water, shelter and clothing through living with my father, who got some financial support from my late elder brother. I struggled to get money to apply for advertised jobs. But what got me through those trying times was the hope that one day, through my higher education and the networks I had generated during my study days and short stints at work, I would land a job.

What about the millions of uneducated black Africans – who have absolutely no access to income and who get food and other bare necessities only through the meagre old-age pensions of their grandparents or child grants or remittances (or, bluntly, through crime) – who have no hope of getting a job in the near future? Life is terrible without direct access to material goods, such as food, water, clothes and housing, but psychologically unbearable without the legitimate and realistic hope of finding a legal means to an income, whether it is a job or a government grant.

This is the sad story of the past 20 years of freedom for more than half of the population of South Africa, 95% of them black Africans, who live a life devoid of dignity and decency because they do not hold a job or receive an income. It is no exaggeration to state that this excruciating experience has visited all classes/groups of black Africans, whether they are graduates, postgraduates or school dropouts on the peripheries of cities or shanty towns and rural areas.

This is not the same as saying that black Africans have been totally helpless in the face of incredible disregard for their social protection. They have tried to exploit the opportunities that have been availed by the emergence of a tender economy in post-apartheid South Africa, only to be frustrated by the fact that tenders, like decent jobs and Black Economic Empowerment deals, are offered largely to the politically connected. This has been the problem of the dominant political party politics in the 'new' South Africa, which has meant that those with access to resources in almost all spheres of the public sector, and some sections of the private sector, belong exclusively to the higher stratum of the dominant political party or the liberation aristocracy, which, as indicated earlier, has embraced the values of their former white colonial masters of self-aggrandisement, classism, elitism and exclusivity.

The lower classes of the minority groups, namely whites and Indians in post-apartheid South Africa, have found their social protection in the jobs offered by small and medium companies in the

Labour market status (expanded) for each education level, 1996 and 2011 (thousand)

1996	Employed	Unemployed	NEA	Total	2011	Employed	Unemployed	NEA*	Total
No schooling	292	388	410	1 090	No schooling	118	139	191	448
Some primary	527	643	932	2 101	Some primary	266	368	459	1 093
Complete primary	286	330	598	1 214	Complete primary	181	251	386	818
Some secondary	1 356	1 343	3 491	6 190	Some secondary	1 957	2 796	4 163	8 916
Complete secondary	1 084	698	758	2 540	Complete secondary	2 435	1 996	1 593	6 024
Tertiary	561	63	83	707	Tertiary	1 065	301	307	1 672
Other	181	73	163	417	Other	26	10	13	49
Total	4 287	3 538	6 435	14 260	Total	6 048	5 861	7 112	19 021

Expanded unemployment rate (%)	1996	2011
No schooling	57.0	54.1
Some primary	55.0	58.0
Complete primary	53.6	58.1
Some secondary	49.8	58.8
Complete secondary	39.2	45.1
Tertiary	10.1	22.0
Other	28.6	27.1
Total	45.2	49.2

Absorption rate (%)	1996	2011
No schooling	26.8	26.3
Some primary	25.1	24.4
Complete primary	23.5	22.1
Some secondary	21.9	21.9
Complete secondary	42.7	40.4
Tertiary	79.4	63.7
Other	43.5	53.5
Total	30.1	31.8

Expanded labour force participation rate (%)	1996	2011
No schooling	62.4	57.3
Some primary	55.6	58.0
Complete primary	50.7	52.8
Some secondary	43.6	53.3
Complete secondary	70.2	73.6
Tertiary	88.2	81.6
Other	60.9	73.4
Total	54.9	62.6

* Not ecomomically active

Labour force expanded	1996 (thousand)	2011 (thousand)	1996 (%)	2011 (%)
No schooling	681	257	8.7	2.2
Some primary	1 169	634	14.9	5.3
Complete primary	616	432	7.9	3.6
Some secondary	2 699	4 753	34.5	39.9
Complete secondary	1 782	4 431	22.8	37.2
Tertiary	624	1 365	8.0	11.5
Other/Unspecified	254	36	3.2	0.3
Total	7 825	11 908	100.0	100.0

Labour market status (expanded) of each population group, 1996 and 2011 (thousands)

1996	Employed	Unemployed	NEA	Total
Black African	2 613	3 170	5 385	11 168
Coloured	628	246	407	1 281
Indian or Asian	189	39	149	378
White	815	61	441	1 317
Other/Unspecified	42	22	53	116
Total	4 288	3 538	6 435	14 261

2011	Employed	Unemployed	NEA	Total
Black African	4 374	5 237	6 081	15 692
Coloured	627	412	502	1 541
Indian or Asian	227	65	153	445
White	744	124	346	1 213
Other/Unspecified	75	23	30	129
Total	6 048	5 861	7 112	19 021

Expanded unemployment rate	1996	2011
Black African	54.8	54.5
Coloured	28.2	39.6
Indian or Asian	17.2	22.3
White	7.0	14.2
Other/ Unspecified	34.2	23.6
Total	45.2	49.2

Absorption rate	1996	2011
Black African	23.4	27.9
Coloured	49.0	40.7
Indian or Asian	50.1	50.9
White	61.9	61.3
Other/ Unspecified	36.0	58.3
Total	30.1	31.8

Expanded labour force participation rate	1996	2011
Black African	51.8	61.2
Coloured	68.3	67.4
Indian or Asian	60.4	65.5
White	66.5	71.5
Other/ Unspecified	54.6	76.4
Total	54.9	62.6

private sector due to the loopholes elaborated upon earlier, which has ensured their disproportionate representation in the labour market.

In reality, it is mainly black Africans and some coloureds that urgently need social protection by the state in the form of income support for the unemployed, from 18 to 60 years of age, who are currently not covered by any form of social security provisions.

How South Africa might look in 20 years' time
It is my considered opinion that the Rainbow framework is so pervasive in the 'new' South Africa, with its accompanying exclusive social pact that benefits its ideologues – the new rulers/elites, both black and white – to the extent that they have a solid interest in keeping it intact and uninterrupted at all costs for the next 20 years. If the multiracial elites have anything to do with it, the Rainbow framework will survive for eternity because it represents/captures brilliantly the elite compromise that the founders of the liberation movement in South Africa had in mind in 1912.

What are the implications of this statement, politically and economically, for the black African majority who are unemployed and underemployed, and other excluded members of the new society? From henceforth, they should organise themselves into an independent, united fighting movement to challenge the state so as to spearhead the crafting of a new social pact, whose constituent members include the organised unemployed and underemployed workers, organised labour, government and business.

Politically, the continuation of the Rainbow framework for the next 20 years means that the majority of black Africans will experience democracy as the democratisation of disempowerment, where they will continue to be the means to an end for the multiracial minority bent on usurping the resources of the country exclusively for itself. The black African majority will continue to be important during electoral periods to give credence and legitimacy to the plunder of resources by avaricious multiracial elites, as has been the case for the past 20 years. However, here lies the dilemma: as they are exhorted to participate, albeit periodically, in the democratic process, the majority of black Africans and other excluded groups in the new society will continue to appreciate the value of electoral politics and how it could change their lives meaningfully – if they could only capture and deploy it for the benefit of their collective underclass through their bona fide representatives in a refurbished democratic system that is truly participatory.

Economically, the continuation of the Rainbow framework within an exclusive social pact will not alter the inherited economic relations and will perpetuate the disproportionate share of national income, participation in the labour market, ownership of the economy and land among the four grossly unequal constituents of the Rainbow framework, namely: whites, Indians and the African and coloured middle classes.

It is my considered opinion that the dominant party in South African politics today, which is the anchor of the Rainbow framework, will continue to be dominant in 2014, but that their continued control of the state afterwards will hinge on the absence of an independent united movement of the excluded, which, through alliances with other parliamentary opposition parties, could put an end to the ANC's factitious rule earlier than generally expected. But my considered projection suggests that the ANC will be in government for the next 20 years up until 2034, when there will be enough voters who had not experienced oppression and discrimination to be the base to vote it out of power.

The new coalition that might usurp power under these projected political conditions will be able to chart a new, truly non-racial, non-sexist and non-classist dispensation if it, together with other stakeholders, crafts a new all-inclusive social pact that will reverse racial polarisation, ethnic strife, class conflict and social cleavages, and arrest rampant corruption and consolidate national reconciliation projects.

Higher education and training 20 years into democracy

Siphelo Ngcwangu
Western Cape activist

The meaning of 27 April 1994

THE DAWN OF DEMOCRACY IN SOUTH Africa on the historic occasion of the first democratic elections on 27 April 1994 signified a momentous break from the past of colonialism and apartheid in which the black majority where systematically marginalised from mainstream economic activities. The various legislations of the apartheid government, including the Bantu Education Act, the Job Reservation Act and a variety of other related legislation, had been systematically devised to protect the interests of the white minority through oppression and brute force on many occasions. It is widely accepted that the democracy we attained in 1994 occurred within a global political economy that was not of our choosing as progressive forces internationally. These developments meant that the African National Congress (ANC) was assuming power in South Africa within the vicissitudes of such global pressures.

The essence of these pressures and contradictions are captured succinctly by ANC intellectual Pallo Jordan,[*] who states:

> What remains unsaid, but should be read between the lines, is that the elections of April 1994 entailed a degree of compromise, some concessions and postponements, many of which took account of the enemy's real strength and untapped power. Others were made to draw to our side of the conflict vacillating class elements and strata who might otherwise have reinforced the ranks of an as yet undefeated enemy. Yet others were made to widen the fissures and cracks within the enemy's

---

[*] See Jordan, P. 1997. 'The National Question in Post 1994 South Africa.' A paper prepared for the ANC National Conference (51st) in Mafikeng, North West Province South Africa.

own ranks and to buy time that would enable us to consolidate the gains made. There were also compromises forced upon us because we could ill-afford to jeopardise the larger prize – majority rule – in pursuance of a few uncertainties.

Our political transition has been characterised by a need to sustain social transformation within the context of a rising neoliberal global agenda, which asserts that developing countries should exercise fiscal prudence, adopt austere macro-economic policies and limit the role of the state in the economy. In the earlier period of our political transition, our government sought to respond to these pressures by adopting policies such as the Growth, Employment and Redistribution (GEAR) strategy, which sought to stabilise the South African economy and address the burden of debt inherited from the apartheid era, while creating the necessary space for further fiscal expansion for social development.

However, the controversy over these policy choices,[*] which is well documented, was mainly due to the replacement of developmentally oriented programmes such as the Reconstruction and Development Programme (RDP), which were developed through popular consensus within a radical socio-economic framework with policies such as GEAR. It is within the context of these domestic and international pressures that I tell my story of how I experienced higher education and training in South Africa as a student, student activist, professional and researcher.

My diary
I matriculated in 1994 from a Roman Catholic school in Port Elizabeth with no specific clarity on what I wanted to study. I had a sense that a field related to politics, law or the economy would suit my interests, although in school my passion was for English and History. I had an interest in professional sport but soon withdrew from competitive soccer due to study commitments. By 1995 I was enrolled at the PE Technikon (now the Nelson Mandela Metropolitan University or NMMU) for a Diploma in Human Resources Management. The technikon model had been presented as a better option, which could

---

[*] See, for instance, Adelzadeh, A. 1996. 'From the RDP to GEAR: The Gradual Embracing of Neo-Liberalism in Economic Policy', *Transformation*, 31.

lead to job opportunities more quickly than a university degree.

I was soon very active in student societies at the PE Technikon and assumed a variety of positions, included being regional deputy chairperson of the South African Students Congress (SASCO) in the Port Elizabeth region, I was subsequently also on the Student Representative Council (SRC) of the PE Technikon as the education and transformation officer. These experiences gave me my first exposure to the unfolding debates about transformation in South African universities, particularly as there were newly introduced democratic university councils and broad transformation forums, which we referred to as 'BTFS'. These were soon changed to institutional forums, which were more representative and ensured that a member of the university's executive sits on the committee.

The period in which I was heavily involved in SASCO coincided with a period in which the country was adopting new policies and, to some extent, reforming older ones. One such scenario was the critical debates of the mid to late 1990s about the introduction of GEAR. As students on the ground we had been dealing with a high demand for entrance into universities by black African students from poor families. These students were a mixture of those who met (and even exceeded) minimum requirements to study at our universities and those who had poor matriculation results but wanted to study further. As the years went by, the most contentious issues for student leaders in engaging the management of universities and technikons were around access and redress.

Three years into South Africa's democracy it was unacceptable that the racial demographics of many of our universities still reflected the apartheid legacy. Across academic faculties, it was clear that white students were studying Engineering, Science and Technology, while black students were spread between Humanities and Management. We fought very hard for our institutions to have what were called 'bridging year programmes' for black students to enter those technical fields.

On many campuses SASCO dominated student politics but at the PE Technikon there were heavy contests between AZASCO and SASCO for leadership of the SRC. For at least three years the SRC had an almost 50–50 split of representatives from AZASCO and SASCO resulting in political manoeuvring and continuous philosophical debates among the student leaders.

The issues of student admission and their general welfare became issues of serious political/philosophical debate about what would be the most suitable approach to addressing these questions in conditions of a political transition characterised by a negotiated settlement. For instance, the issue of incremental student fees was the major issue all student leaders had to confront. In SASCO we always settled for an approach that was not too obsessed with the percentages themselves; we rather considered the overall impact on students and their families. We also placed on top of our agenda the call for registration fees to remain at R750, regardless of any study fee increase, so that students were not disadvantaged by these increases and prevented from even registering at the technikon.

The terrain of higher education has changed rapidly since I left the student movement in 2000. I got employment in the private sector in East London and, for two years, was formally outside of an institution of higher education, although I kept contact with former comrades informally and kept abreast of political developments through the various networks I had developed.

The greatest reforms in the higher education sector were to come in the period between 2000 and 2007 when then Minister of Education, the late Professor Kader Asmal, introduced a policy framework of 'size and shape', which was meant to introduce bureaucratic mergers of the universities and reconfiguring the higher education landscape in South Africa. Some universities were to be merged due to financial and governance problems, while others were to be reoriented due to poor academic output. While this restructuring was being planned there was an underlying question of how to ensure that the old divisions between historically black and historically white universities should not be entrenched by the mergers.

Our history of uneven distribution of resources between black and white universities during apartheid meant that whether the new government should be strengthening historically black universities or sustaining historically white universities became a crucial issue of public dialogue. The mergers that have since ensued have been largely about merging the old technikons with the traditional universities, resulting in what are now called comprehensive universities.

My personal journey through this system continued in 2003 when, after two or so years in the private sector, I decided to pursue further studies at a university. The questions now for me were:

would a university accept me into its system? Would I need to do further courses to be accepted? What type of courses would I need to take and would I cope? So, as national policy dialogue continued on reforms in the higher education arena, my challenges were more about how I would manage moving from a technikon to a university.

Fortunately, I gained admission to the University of the Western Cape's (UWC's) Institute for Social Development at honours level. The director of the centre at the time, Professor Pieter le Roux, interviewed me and opted to give me a chance. This was not officially the policy but the director was allowed to use his discretion to accept a student who either had no prior university training or no formal education at all. There were a few fellow students with whom I attended the honours course who had entered the university through the policy of Recognition of Prior Learning (RPL).

I have since been in various programmes, including completing a Master's in Sociology at Colorado State University, sponsored by the African American Institute of South Africa (AISA), an opportunity I got as a result of the democratic changes in South Africa. After returning to South Africa in 2007, I took up a lecturing position in the Department of Sociology at UWC for a brief period before joining the BANKSETA as a research manager. This position exposed me to another component of the higher education and training landscape – the skills system.

Entering the world of SETAs

I got to work in the BANKSETA for three and a half years at a time where SETAs (Sector Education and Training Authority) were trying to embrace a more research-oriented approach rather than one focused on accreditation and provision. Since the promulgation of the Skills Development Act of 1998 and the subsequent creation of the SETA system, which is responsible for the implementation of the National Skills Development Strategy (NSDS), there has been a perception among the public of failure, corruption and mismanagement of funds by these institutions.

Four key issues have dominated the discourse of the SETA system and why it has failed. Firstly, the various programmes, such as learnerships and internships, have been seen as either ineffective or poorly conceptualised to address South Africa's high unemployment challenge. Despite the huge numbers of learners (reported to be over

50 000) who have gone through various SETA programmes since 2001, when the first NSDS was introduced, there still seems to be a dominant general perception that the system is failing.

Secondly, the lower numbers of qualified artisans in South Africa is also attributed to the SETA system's failures, which privileged private provision of short courses and skills programmes that did not lead to qualifications that directed learners to apprenticeship-based fields like artisanal type training.

Thirdly, the lack of a proper implementation of RPL to create developmental opportunities and upward career mobility for mainly black, semi-skilled workers is also a serious issue of concern for this system. RPL has a political dimension as it is often argued that should RPL be a success, the notion of a 'skills crisis' can be contested, given the tacit knowledge residing with many workers and citizens who were denied opportunities to gain qualifications in the past.

Lastly, there is a 'value for money' argument about the SETA system, which is known to be worth over R5 billion per annum, with an additional estimated R4 billion in the National Skills Fund (NSF), which is meant to support non-governmental organisations' (NGO) initiatives of skills development or entrepreneurial development in civil society. It can also be argued that the absence of a clear industrial strategy in the earlier phase of South Africa's transition has contributed to uncertainty over the aligned skills agenda to accelerate economic development through rebuilding of the manufacturing base. The question 'training for what?' remains unanswerable in a context in which the ultimate goal of skills development is the narrow advancement of profit maximisation.

The introduction of the third phase of the NSDS in 2009 has seen some radical changes with regard to governance and financial administration of the skills-development system. The NSDS III also seeks to move SETAs from quantitative targets to substantive qualitative targets that include an improved management system that considers wider societal relevance. The strong focus on intermediary level skills, such as artisans, has galvanised all role players around this vision, although there still remains a caveat of employment creation despite the gradual increase in the number of artisans qualifying through the trade tests.

These changes are influenced by a nuanced shift from a notion of skills as active labour market policy to a conception of skills within a discourse of post-school education and training (PSET) which is an overarching vision of the Department of Higher Education and Training (DHET) under the leadership of Minister Nzimande. The post-schooling approach has sought to transcend what was previously perceived as a wide separation between higher education, vocational education and the SETA system, which had resulted in fragmentation rather than coherence in the post-schooling arena.

Essentially researchers in the field and commentators have been drawn into protracted debates about institutional configuration and provision within the system; debates that have often resulted in a reductionist way of approaching the skills question. This reductionism has not always occurred consciously – it is, to some extent, a function of the political moment that we are currently in as a country, wherein there is increasingly a declining emphasis on deeper ideological questions. This has resulted in a dominant practitioner mould of analysis that also prevails in public discourse on skills and education. As a result, the popular discourse on skills and education largely favours supply-side restructuring or 'state efficiency' and individual responsibility above the necessity of fundamental economic restructuring of the capitalist economic system.

To paraphrase Tony Brown,* skills have emerged as a temporal 'spatial fix' to the current global economic crisis. Brown expands the point and says:

> This focus on skills as a fix is not simply a revival of an older attempt to improve competition; it addresses the situation from the wrong starting point. Skills are just one factor among many in economic and industry development. Capital investment, research, product strategy, innovation, technology and organisational development are equally important.

In South Africa it has become the daily dose of radio and television current affairs talk shows to perpetuate the view that our economic problems can be explained by arguing that citizens don't have the 'right skills' and that the existing institutions are unable to 'align' their training programmes tightly enough to the demands of the

---

* See Brown, T. 2011. 'Spatial and Financial Fixes and the Global Financial Crisis.' Paper presented at the International Conference on Researching Work and Learning (RWL7), Shanghai, 4–6 December 2011.

market. Furthermore, this received view is repeated by politicians across the spectrum of ideological orientation, who see the essential problems of development in South Africa to be the so-called mismatch of education and the economy.

Working for the government

Analysing what government should do and being employed within the government to be part of the 'doing' are two different challenges. I had an opportunity to be employed in the democratic government for about 14 months between 2011 and 2012. Working as Director: Public Liaison Services in the Director-General's office in the Department of Agriculture, Forestry and Fisheries gave me an insight into one of the most critical sectors of the South African economy, which has the potential to alleviate poverty and provide food security to millions of people. The accepted figure for the number of people who are food insecure in South Africa is about 11 million. That means about 11 million fellow South Africans may go to bed on an empty stomach in South Africa each day.

For a country endowed with natural resources and numerous institutions, this alone should be a signal for wide-scale revolt. Since 1994 the government has attempted different kinds of agricultural policies that are aimed at stimulating the sector while addressing the historical legacy of the racialised exclusion of the majority from productive growth in the sector. The internal policy dimension of the state and the contending ideological assumptions are key challenges in evolving policy that makes a difference in people's lives. I found that in sectors like agriculture, things take longer to be implemented and even when implementation is possible, there are layers of bureaucracy that one has to overcome before changes on the ground can even be possible.

One example of a policy that could make direct changes in a shorter period to many people requiring less technology is the Zero Hunger programme. This programme was implemented in Brazil during President Lula da Silva's era and has been considered in various guises by the South African government. The policy is basically about procuring large-scale food requirements of the state (for example, for school nutrition, hospitals and correctional services) from small-scale farmers rather than from private-service providers. Properly implemented, the programme could create at least 250 000 jobs and stimulate the small-scale agricultural sector while also contributing to the cultivation of land lying fallow in the old Bantustan areas. This would be a model that would not require direct confrontation with Capital nor require special regulations for businesses.

Rather, it would merely be the state redirecting its resources in a coordinated way to uplift a large section of the population. The spinoff of such a programme would be the creation of local food networks that can contribute to poverty alleviation in localities in which there are few job opportunities and a virtually non-existent manufacturing base. The process of adopting radical policies takes a painstakingly long time in South Africa because there are intergovernmental cluster committees, internal departmental structures, scientific committees and a number of other structures that regulate how government works and these all need to give their approval. While, on the one hand, working for the government is often perceived as part of narrow material accumulation and a status symbol in parts of our society, there is also, on the other hand, a pervasive negative perception of government employees as corrupt and lazy. I had to contend with these perceptions frequently as a government employee.

Conclusion

My diary is meant to tell a long story in a brief way about how I experienced being both a student and a professional within the South African higher education system over the period since 1994. The opportunities have widened my outlook about national policy developments within the transitional context of our country. The higher education and training system provides a window of hope for millions of people, particularly those from poor families. In order to appreciate where we are today, we must acknowledge the journey we have travelled. For me the terrain of higher education and training can be the basis for meaningful change to ameliorate our socio-economic challenges. The system does not need to be dominated by employers or big business but it should be a vehicle to address the large social challenges still confronting our society 20 years into the democratic era.

The year 2014 signifies an important milestone for South Africa. Four successive national elections have proved to be mainly peaceful and reflective of the 'will of the people'. Moving forward, the country requires a socio-economic order that is more inclusive than we have experienced to date. We have large numbers of young people who are unemployed and there is rising inequality between the rich and the poor.

The capitalist class has reaped the best rewards from the democratic era, as have professional elites, who either have gainful employment or, have been part of commercial transactions that have produced handsome profits. The ANC government has adopted a National Development Plan (NDP) for South Africa, which is underpinned by a vision of improved changes to the period 2030, but even before implementation this NDP has been criticised for having a neoliberal bias and possibly prescribing a framework not too different from that of the much maligned GEAR.

Re-engineering our communities: What 20 years of freedom means to me

Thamsanqa Ngwenya

Public servant and specialist on West Africa

MaDLAMINI WHO LIVED AND DIED under apartheid, hailed from the hilly village of eMkhakhweni in rural KwaZulu-Natal. She managed to raise 11 children by herself, largely in the absence of her husband, who initially had to work for white-owned companies and later as a priest. Although she did not have any formal education, she understood the liberatory power it had for her children, most of whom were girls. She and her husband refused to sell their children's labour and make them toil someone else's land. Instead, she went about getting her community to understand the importance of sending girl children to school, something that was not a predominant view at the time.

Her vision of a free and equitable South Africa was anchored on self-worth, social enterprise, community cohesion and taking care of others to attain social progress and achieve community preservation. This meant rising above the odds imposed on her people by a racist, oppressive and segregationist regime of the National Party. She believed that in a society shaped by oppression, it is the responsibility of the strong to protect the weak.

Even though she had no education or leadership position, she understood her responsibility to her family and community. Her spirit of social enterprise and innovation based on values of selflessness inspired me as a voting officer in a KwaMashu hostel as I cast my own vote on 27 April 1994. It was a vote for independence from a repressive, racist, authoritarian and corrupt regime. It was a vote for self-rule and determination. It was a vote to shape our own destiny as Africans so we could decide the nature, form and character of our state that fully promotes and protects fundamental human liberties and set us on a path to socio-ecomomic freedom.

This was to be self-rule based on our own prescripts of governance,

305

mirroring the aspirations of our forebears who fought in resistance wars against colonialism, our liberation activists, some of whom paid the ultimate price, and the ordinary folks like MaDlamini.

As I stood in that long line waiting to exercise my right to choose those that would represent me in Parliament, I thought of those who had paid the ultimate price in pursuit of freedom. Above all, I thought of people like MaDlamini, who had lived and died under apartheid, deprived of their dignity as human beings. Her story is not unique, but exceptional. It is mirrored in many corners of our country, where organic social enterprise built on the spirit of human resistance, community cohesion and instilled hope against state-engineered adversity.

My own understanding of liberation is contextualised on my upbringing in apartheid South Africa. As a six-year-old growing up in the small town of oPhongolo, I witnessed African men treated as sub-human and made to labour with their picks and shovels in severe heat, supervised by a young white man sitting under the shade of his umbrella enjoying whatever drink from his flask. This was my moment of exposure to the reality of oppression in our country. I have experienced going into the post office with two distinct entrances, one for 'Blacks only' and the other for 'Whites only'. The use of derogatory word 'kaffir' was normal. This applied to shops, pharmacies, public toilets, etc.

So it was no wonder that during my years at Mlokothwa High, a boarding school that was a melting pot of political education and activism, I came to reflect deeply on the experiences of my fellow Africans working on the sugarcane farms in oPhongolo. It was during this time that I wrote a poem that I have come to use as a reflection of the journey we have taken as a country to gain full enjoyment of civil liberties. In 1988 I wrote:

Rise kaffir boy!
Kicked at the back
Shoved and bulldozed
Misled and misinformed
Mis-educated and led astray.

Sadness and confusion
Happiness and sorrow

Love and hatred
Trusting and suspicious
All in one soul
Kaffir boy!

Waking up all smelly on a sunny Monday
Suffering from *ibhabhalazi*
Preparing for the journey to work
A journey to exploitation
Why *kaffir* boy?

Look up!
Look up to where your life is,
Look up in search of freedom
Freedom to live a free life
Free from *kaffired* life
Of the unjust world of exploitation and powerlessness
Rise *kaffir* boy. Rise!
Rise to political freedom
Rise *kaffir* boy, rise
In pursuit of economic independence!

Voting on 27 April 1994 represented a new chapter from the one described in my 1988 poem. As I stood in that long line I recalled the experiences of men in my village who had left their families to work in the coal and gold mines of Witbank and Johannesburg, and the dehumanisation of African labourers by their white employers. And I also thought about the internalised acceptance of such inequality by my schoolmates during my primary school years at the two-classroomed Jabulisani Combined Primary (built for farm workers' children), where my father was the principal.

Clearly, 27 April 1994 represented the dawn of the promise of freedom, not only from the bondage of oppressive racist system, but critically of hope for a different economic freedom and condition. With my vote, I was making a declaration that no one should rule me – and my fellow Africans – without my consent. No one should deny me and my fellow Africans equal opportunities in life, thus guaranteeing my dignity.

My vote was also an expression of my gratitude to fellow Africans, both in Africa and the Diaspora, who had campaigned against that repressive regime. South Africa's new Constitution, which is celebrated internationally for its protection of civil liberties, could not have come into life had it not been for this solidarity with the oppressed of my country of birth. As a result of their solidarity and their support of the national liberation movement, leaders of the Frontline States, such as Kenneth Kaunda, Samora Machel and Mwalimu Nyerere, caused great suffering to their own people and economies. Their support was appreciated and has been acknowledged by the African majority, who have named certain locations within the townships and informal settlements after these revolutionaries. I am eternally grateful for their solidarity, which inspires me not to relent in the fight for full restoration of our dignity.

The international character of our struggle for freedom was also entrenched in our institutions of higher learning. It was at the University of Durban-Westville (UDW) that my personal intellectual growth was nurtured. I was privileged to rub shoulders with students and comrades who had conviction of steel. Most of them have gone on to be the finest government technocrats in this country. The debates we had in the bus from Ntuzuma and KwaMashu townships to and from campus were deeply enriching, as were those we had on campus about the direction our government should take to advance freedom and the development of the black majority. At UDW, we jealously guarded the autonomy of our institution and the principle of academic freedom. It was impossible to have attended such an institution and been indifferent to any form of injustice.

When the debate on the African Renaissance and Africanisation of South African universities gained traction, UDW was once again at the forefront. Predictably, there was an unprecedented onslaught against those African intellectuals who championed this course. Today, the story of a 'rising Africa' is a dominant narrative accepting that Africa's time has dawned. This programme was characterised as being a narrow nationalist project aimed at affirming and empowering Africans at the expense of others. Critics never understood this as a national project that attempts to create an African scholarship, which places Africa at the centre of existential reality. The same applies to other aspects of our nation, such as renaming places and institutions after those we salute for their contribution to the struggle for freedom, artistic and athletic excellence. Of course, this is not understood and appreciated in a similar way across our nation.

I vividly remember how eThekwini Council pushed through a resolution to rename Durban streets after people such as Kaunda and Nyerere, and the opposition to this gesture of transformation. One notable objection was expressed in a letter to the editor of *The Mercury* of 3 October 2007, titled 'Names Belong in History's Dustbin' written by Duncan Du Bois, a DA councillor for Ward 66. I was as infuriated then as I am today when such sentiments are expressed, either brazenly or in subtly condescending ways. The final destruction of the brutal apartheid regime would have been impossible without the support of fellow Africans and leaders, such as Kaunda and Nyerere.

Therefore the issue of renaming the country's symbols and architecture should be located within the broader framework of resistance to dehumanisation and as an exercise in self-definition. The liberation of this country not only ensured that the ideals of freedom that Kaunda and Nyerere stood for are achieved, but also ensured that the ideal of Pan Africanism is realised.

While I feel discomfort with government's focus on renaming old buildings and roads rather than building new institutions that we can name after those we wish to honour, I nonetheless accept that as a society we must appreciate that our history is shaped by deep pain caused by the dehumanisation of the African majority. In this regard, restoration of our dignity, apart from social and economic justice, will have to include renaming those symbols that inflict collective pain to our national psyche. Without doubt, we need to move beyond renaming exercises, and affirm the liberation of African people through unapologetic programmes of socio-economic empowerment.

The question as we mark the 20th anniversary of a democratic South Africa is, what does this milestone mean to me?

On a personal level, it has been a great honour to serve in the reconstruction and development of my country and mother Africa. I have been privileged to meet amazing human beings in the course of my education and work and been able to drink from different cups of knowledge and wisdom, shared with me by all kinds of people. Unlike those who lived and died under apartheid, having been denied all possible opportunities to realise their God-given talents and potential, I have had an opportunity to realise mine, albeit not all of them.

In my short life, I have met heads of state and government, ministers, kings and queens. I have walked the corridors of the United Nations and the African Commission of Human and Peoples' Rights to address important issues of humanity. I have received fellowships and awards in recognition of my contribution to human freedom and progress. I have represented the interests of my country on various platforms, including negotiating agreements with other nations to advance such interests. In a nation of over 50 million people, I have had the rare privilege to serve my country at the highest level possible.

In equal vein, I have witnessed the hardships and lack of freedom of fellow human beings in other parts of the world. I have witnessed extreme underdevelopment and indescribable poverty, hopelessness, fear and entrenched states of despair. I have also experienced the highest level of development and quality of life in the Western world. I know what oppression and freedom mean. I know what apartheid denied the likes of MaDlamini. I equally know what the madness of the apartheid system denied the world in terms of our possible contribution to the betterment of humankind. I know we could have given more to the world in arts, sports, entrepreneurship, science and technology.

When we talk of 20 years of freedom, I think of the extreme contradictions of what this means to different sections of our society. We have people like me for whom 1994 represented a dawn of new possibilities. But this has not necessarily been the case for everyone. Our country is at a crossroads. While some have it easy, others struggle to sustain life, and the possibility of realising their hopes and dreams of a better tomorrow is not certain. They struggle to survive to the next day in the hope that it will be better than the one before.

Among the issues that face us, is, how we can give meaning to the socio-economic rights that are contained in Chapter 2 of our celebrated Constitution of 1996. We also contend with issues of social cohesion, poverty, widening inequality, competing interests across race groups, indifference to critical social policy issues, the slow pace of economic transformation, land reform and the lack of inspirational leadership across all sectors of society. These issues deserve decisive and resolute engagement if we are to successfully tackle them to build a solid future for future generations.

However, those who should provide leadership and produce

meaningful knowledge to solve our common challenges are loud in their silence. There are growing controversial issues and policy decisions that call for honest and courageous engagement instead of a preoccupation with political correctness. If not dealt with, these shortcomings could potentially compound our sense of despair.

The public discourse is dominated by a few voices, aided by privileged access and control to political power, money and the manipulation of media platforms, which are used to push certain partisan value systems. Disturbing acts of opting out of democratic processes are perpetuating the crises facing our country. As we drift further away from the dreams and promises of 1994, we collectively bear the responsibility of betraying those who fought and paid the ultimate price for our freedom. As we reach the 20-year mark of our country's negotiated political settlement, there is a resurgence of the radical rhetoric of African nationalism that suggests that 1994 may not necessarily have represented true freedom and social justice.

The issues of land reform and equitable access to our natural resources have once again taken centre stage. Central to this is how we resolve the legacy of land dispossession, economic exclusion and under-developement that has bred deep poverty and inequality. Freedom to me means the rebuilding of our country through inclusive commercial pursuit, founded on values of self-love and compassion towards others. These are values that are imbued and woven in our own concept of ubuntu and knitted across humanity through Afrocentricity.

Freedom means rebuilding self-confidence, self-reliance, active and responsible citizenry, which appreciates that 20 years in the life of a nation is nothing. It means paying tribute to those who lived and died under apartheid and those who fought and engaged in selfless struggles to make sure that my generation could inherit a dream worth pursuing. It means re-engineering our communities to believe in their inherent abilities to build their own meaningful communities that gurantee a complete sense of security, economic activity and social enterprise. It means understanding that government cannot do everything, but it can enable us, through correct, bold and empowering policy interventions, to embark on a sound path to a different future than the one designed for us by apartheid.

It means those in leadership across all sectors of society must lead not only for their own advancement and that of their families and clans, but for the whole nation and future generations. Freedom to me means that my daughters and my nephews and nieces can grow in a country where their safety and security is a given and non-negotiable. It means every child must have a place under the sun, where their potential can be harnessed. It means providing an environment where people can pursue individual dreams, not limited and constrained by poverty and barriers to entry due to prevailing social conditions that favour the dominant in society.

To build a winning nation, we have to embark on a radical psychological shift rooted in Pan Africanism. Our freedom as South Africans cannot be about some sense of exceptionalism that locates our thinking and practice outside of Africa rather than within. We must never be indifferent in our thinking towards any form of injustice. MaDlamini and others like her would most certainly look at the 20 years of freedom with a certain level of appreciation as core civil liberties are woven into our system. They would deplore that in some quarters of our society, even though the 'Whites Only' signs have been removed, the treatment of some remains that of a *'kaffir* boy'. It means that those who benefitted and built their lives of comfort on the sweat and blood of the oppressed must first and foremost acknowledge this reality and get off the horse of denialism.

I am equally certain that they would deplore acts of self-inflicted underdevelopment as perpetuated through burning down and vandalising community property, like healthcare centres, libraries and multi-purpose centres, in the name of the struggle for services. They would probably understand that the promise to a better life for all is taking a long time. However, I doubt they will ever understand how destroying what we could use as building blocks for thriving communities is justifiable in the elimination of poverty and inequality.

Because of MaDlamini, my parents could give me a better shot at life and compassion for others. Thus, freedom to me means learning from the selfless determination of the likes of MaDlamini and engaging in a continuous struggle for total emancipation. This should be my generation's contribution to the advancement of humanity.

Traditional initiation in democratic South Africa

Nkululeko Nxesi
Community development activist

Background

TRADITIONAL INITIATION IS ONE of the oldest practices of many African tribes and ethnic groups on this continent. Long before colonialism and apartheid, African boys were subjected to this practice as part of their rite of passage to manhood.

Different ethnic groups practiced this custom in different ways. However, the common feature in all these groups was that initiates would go to the mountain for a period of time, where they would be circumcised and be taught the traditional norms and values of their particular ethnic group and African society at large. These teachings included, for example, respect, self-reliance and communalism; but, most importantly, these teachings included how a man should act and behave, and their role in their families, the communities and society at large.

When initiates came back from the initiation school, there would be *imigidi* by the families and the whole village. The chief would welcome the initiates and the principal of the initiation school would prepare a big feast for the members of the community.

After the initiation period, these young men, who would have been welcomed into a new societal stratum, would be expected to conduct themselves in a very respectful manner, and to get married and start a family. During the era of wars these young men were then integrated into the nation's fighting brigade.

The apartheid era did not stop this tradition as many tribes continued to practice it. The most noticeable feature of traditional initiation under apartheid was the establishment of traditional initiation schools in urban areas. Although this was unusual and foreign, and traditional leaders and practitioners and custodians of culture were not happy about it, they were not able to stop this. This was linked to the rural–urban migration that had taken many parts of South Africa by storm. As the years went by, some black African families who had moved to settle in urban areas lost touch with their rural origins and were forced to conduct this practice in urban areas.

One of the visible impacts of colonialism and apartheid to traditional initiation practice was the 1913 Land Act. Due to forced removals and land-grabbing by the white apartheid regime, black Africans could not utilise the secluded land they preferred for traditional initiation purposes. In Port Elizabeth, it was reported that apartheid officials used this cultural practice to police and monitor liberation fighters. They were kept in traditional initiation schools under strict controls.

Initiation during apartheid was used as a training ground for cheap labour (for the white capital). It was instilled in the minds of those who practiced this tradition that for one to be accepted in the mines and other related jobs, one had to have undergone traditional initiation to become a man. There was a generally accepted view that to be a mineworker or be involved in any other hard labour, one needed to be physically fit and healthy. At the same time, to go for traditional initiation one needed to be older than 20 years, fit, strong and healthy. Traditional initiation was then used as a clear test that you were ready to go and sell your labour to white capital.

Ironically, traditional initiation had more value and was respected more during the apartheid era than in the post-apartheid era by the African people. In the post-apartheid era, this practice is controlled largely by young people who do not have the much needed experience and knowledge.

Situational analysis
In present-day South Africa, traditional initiation is practiced differently by different ethnic groups in different provinces. The Xhosa nation, largely based in the Eastern and Western Cape, is well-known for practising this tradition. Boys are usually sent to the traditional schools during the December holidays. Unlike other ethnic groups, Xhosas are not keen on taking their boys to initiation schools in winter. The significance of this is the fact that the summer holidays are longer than the winter holidays and this allows for enough time for traditional teachings. Summer circumcision is also linked to a human right issue – the right to education. A boy's right to

education is less violated if he is initiated in summer than in winter, where boys are sometimes abducted while still writing their June examinations.

Most Xhosa families still believe in the original traditional processes and procedures. This is despite the emerging evidence of an increasing number of deaths as a result of botched circumcisions that point to a need to rethink certain aspects of the culture in order to save the lives of our young children. Generally, Xhosas (in both the Western and Eastern Cape) record about 20 000 traditional initiates in a season. This clearly indicates that a large number of boys go through this practice, and even subject themselves to this process.

One prominent politician was forced to go to the initiation school recently. Those who abducted him believed that he could not be well-respected as a political leader in his ethnic group and family if he did not go through his cultural practice. Even the popular and controversial gospel singer, Lundi Tyamara, a self-confessed drama queen, had to subject himself to this culture at his older age.

People in North West also practice this culture. The prominent African ethnic groups in this province that take their boys through this rite are the Batswana and amaHlubi. Batswana are in the majority here and they practice initiation in both winter and summer.

Bapedi, based largely in Limpopo, usually conduct this practice in the winter season. This is one of the few African ethnic groups that still adheres to the original African way of conducting this traditional practice. Bapedi initiates usually stay for about three months in the initiation school, which partly explains their low death rate as they have sufficient time to heal. It is rare to hear about deaths among the Bapedi as a result of traditional initiation. In fact, it would be a shame and taboo, unlike in the Xhosa and Pondo nations, where it is fast becoming a norm to hear about '*ukufa kwabakhwetha*'. A distinct feature of Bapedi culture is that their boys are taken to the school at the young age of 12 or 13 years. While that is the case, the initiates are treated with care and respect; hence they all come out alive without any complications.

Vhavenda and Tsonga people also practice this rite. Usually they conduct it in the rural areas of Limpopo. Vhavenda are very secretive about their processes and procedures.

AmaNdebele and Tsonga in Mpumalanga also practice this tradition, and this province has been recently affected by initiation-related deaths. The amaNdebele people strongly believe in this tradition and they do the initiation under the strict control of traditional leaders. The king is the person who issues *ingoma* once in four years. This signifies the importance of this practice to the amaNdebele. They have low death incidences. In 2012, 32 initiates died in Mpumalanga and this sparked countrywide shock as amaNdebeles are known for their clean, strictly controlled and healthy process. After the death of these initiates, the two kings and their chiefs met with the relevant stakeholders, including the Department of Health in the province, to ensure that there would be no more deaths going forward.

In the Free State, there are amaXhosa and Basotho who follow this culture. The general perception is that there are no initiation-related injuries and deaths in this province. However, anecdotal information indicates that there has been a gradual increase in the number of deaths and assaults of initiates. Like the Bapedi, Vhavenda amaHlubi and amaNdebele, Basotho are very secretive about their initiation procedures. As a result, injuries and deaths of the initiates are rarely reported.

Gauteng has many traditional initiation-related challenges. Traditional initiation is being practiced here by Sothos, Vhavenda, amaXhosa, amaNdebele and Tsonga. It is practiced mainly by Basotho in the Sedibeng area and by amaNdebele in the Ekurhuleni and Tshwane municipalities. The recent inclusion of Metsweding into Gauteng has meant that most Ndebele rural areas are part of that province. This has increased traditional initiation activities in Gauteng. Here it has been associated with crimes that have included the abduction of boys at gunpoint and the rape of young girls by young men from the initiation schools as part of cleansing and testing their 'machines'.

There are provinces where traditional initiation is not practiced much. These included the Northern Cape and KwaZulu-Natal. This does not mean that there are no cases of it in these provinces. For instance, in places such as Kokstad, Umzimkhulu and Harding, boys travel to the Eastern Cape to places like Mount Ayliff, Mount Frere and Mbizana for initiation. KwaZulu-Natal introduced medical circumcision after King Zwelithini made an announcement that his nation has adopted a policy of male medical circumcision (MMC) as part of their HIV-prevention strategy.

In the democratic era post-1994, traditional initiation has encountered many challenges. The culture has lost the respect and dignity it had prior to this period. Given the protection of the cultural rights in our country's Constitution, and given the fact that this country is led by black Africans, one would have thought that cultural traditions would have been more respected and gained more recognition. However, traditional initiation is marred by the following challenges.

Deaths in the mountain

Each and every season over the past five years, children have died in the traditional initiation schools. These deaths have been increasing consistently, especially in the Eastern Cape. In June/July 2013 traditional initiation season, 39 initiates were reported dead. Also, it is important to note that there were about five more deaths in hospitals after the season. In September 2013, one boy died in Mthatha. Most of these deaths occurred in the initiation schools. One vivid picture in my mind is of two boys from a village called KwaMadiba in Mbizana. We went there at about 11:00 pm to pick up the corpses of two traditional initiates. This place is next to the Mthamvuna River and we could not get the car there because of the rough, mountainous terrain. So we had to travel about five kilometres on foot to pick up the corpses. It is sad that in our post-democratic period some people die like dogs as if they have no human rights.

Many deaths take place in illegal initiation schools and are usually conducted by illegal and inexperienced bogus traditional surgeons.

Abductions and kidnapping

A growing phenomenon in the traditional initiation practice is the abduction of young boys who are forced into circumcision schools. Children as young as 12 and 13 years are kidnapped, coerced or subjected to peer pressure to go through traditional initiation against their will or without their parents' consents. Clearly this is a violation of their fundamental human rights, which include the right to choose and the right to health and safety.

One instance is where a mother came to report the abduction of her son to the traditional initiation forum and the forum took this to the police. Her 13-year-old son had been taken by a certain traditional surgeon who was feared in the community. We went with the police to rescue the boy. Along the way the mother refused to cooperate with the police because she feared repercussions and attack by this illegal traditional surgeon and his gang. The boy was left at the initiation school going through traumatic and painful experiences. Even today I still wonder what happened to that young, innocent and vulnerable boy.

Another case worth mentioning is that of a boy who was vulnerable and orphaned. This boy was taken by a mob of drunken 'men' from his adopted home. They grabbed him, put black tape over his mouth and circumcised him in front of the gate. And then left him there. This is not traditional initiation! Clearly this is criminal behaviour done in the guise of initiation. This points to the vulnerability of children and young people in our country, despite our Constitution, which compels the state to ensure the safety of its citizens, especially vulnerable groups, including orphans.

The injuries

Some traditional initiates survive the illegal and unsafe traditional initiation. However, some of them come back injured. In the 2013 winter initiation season, about 300 initiates were injured and taken to public hospitals. In the OR Tambo district in the Eastern Cape, some hospitals could not cope with the influx of the initiates. This influx put burden on the already ailing rural public healthcare system. Some initiates needed to have their penises amputated because of the severity of the injuries. It is estimated that Eastern Cape currently has about 400 men with botched circumcision-related amputations.

Those who suffer such injuries have deep emotional and psychological scars. They are subjected to ongoing social ridicule from family members and their peers. It has been reported that some inhumane remarks have even been passed by the very same traditional surgeons and nurses who were responsible for these atrocities. The big question here is why these people are not being arrested. They are known in the community and some by the law enforcement agencies, including the police. Is the justice system of the democratic state not concerned about this? Some police and magistrates have been heard saying that they do not have a role in the traditional initiation and that the custodians of the practice should be left to handle it. However, deaths are deaths regardless of their causes.

Marginalisation of women

For centuries traditional initiation has been the domain of men. Women have played only a limited role, usually associated with the preparation of grass for the initiation house and food for initiates (in some places). However, with the advent of democracy women need to redefine and embrace their roles and participation in this important but strained traditional practice. With the increase in the number of deaths and injuries, women are becoming more involved and could provide the much needed solutions.

Violence against single parents

Most victims of illegal traditional initiation and botched circumcision are boys who come from single-parent families. Illegal and inexperience traditional surgeons and nurses target single mothers and force them to sign consent for boys to go for traditional initiation even if these boys do not qualify for a number of reasons. Some women have been blamed for conspiring with these illegal and inexperienced surgeons and nurses to sign fraudulent consent forms and deliberately forge identity documents. A case in point is where an initiate who had used his brother's identity document died in the initiation school. The gender dynamics of this problem force the policy-makers and programme designers to look deeply into how women can be educated not to sign-off the death of their boy children.

School attrition

One of the worrying realities about the traditional initiation is the increasing school dropout rates of the newly initiated boys. There is a growing trend in rural areas that when boys come back from the initiation schools they stop attending their conventional schools. This feeds into the growing pool of criminal elements in this country. This practice is linked to the increased abuse of alcohol and drugs. Unlike in the past, traditional initiation schools have been turned into drug and alcohol zones. Some boys go to initiation never having taken drugs or alcohol and come back using them.

Due to the above-mentioned challenges there are strong indications that this longstanding traditional practice is under attack from a number of sources. First, modernisation is putting pressure for the practice to adapt or be resigned to the past. Secondly, commercialisation has been blamed for the mushrooming of illegal initiation schools that are negligent, which leads to injuries and deaths of initiates.

There has been a view that this practice has lost its relevance and usefulness as it no longer serves its original purpose: moulding young boys into responsible men. As a result, some people are advocating for alternatives.

In the summer 2013 traditional initiation season, 42 initiates died across the Eastern Cape. Add this to the 39 who died in the winter season and we have a total of 81 in 2013 in Eastern Cape alone. More than 500 initiates were hospitalised during this period. The Community Development Foundation of South Africa (CODEFSA) established a rescue centre in Palmerton Methodist Church in Lusikisiki in order to protect the boys and provide medical care. While interventions have been put in place by government working with the House of Traditional Leaders, CODEFSA and other stakeholders, the end to these fatalities seems not to be in sight. In light of this, there are a lot of discussions on whether traditional initiation is still relevant. If it is still relevant, how can it be made safe so there are no deaths or amputations?

Based on the above numbers, one needs to ask whether government is doing enough to root out initiation-related injuries and deaths. My view is that government's response has not been equal to the task at hand. There have been mixed reactions by various government departments and leaders. Many feel that traditional initiation is a cultural issue that falls into the ambit of traditional leaders. Other government officials feel that traditional initiation must be totally banished as it is killing children and is no longer relevant. Others are quietly and secretly pushing for the integration of MMC. While these debates go on, people are dying.

What is also saddening is the fact that the dialogue about this is not robust or coordinated at all. The only government departments that have taken an active interest are the National and Eastern Cape Departments of Health and the Eastern Cape Department of Local Government and Traditional Affairs. Both the MEC for Health, Sicelo Qqobana, and MEC for local government, Mlibo Qhoboshiyane, provided the much needed voice and support for the campaign to promote safer traditional initiation. The House of Traditional

Leaders in the Eastern Cape under its leader Inkosi Ngangomhlaba Matanzima is also deeply involved in campaigns for safer traditional initiation. The Department of Education in the Eastern Cape has been involved in school road-shows and deploys some of its officials to monitor the traditional initiation schools. Police have been providing very few responses. It is clear that government at national, provincial and municipal levels can do much more than they are doing at the moment. Five-year national and provincial strategic plans are needed to address this problem. This plan, led by the House of Traditional Leaders, has to be comprehensive and commit various stakeholders, including government, civil society and the private sector, to act against these senseless initiation-related injuries and deaths.

Government needs to take this matter as seriously as it does other initiatives, such as the HIV and AIDS and the Arrive Alive campaigns. Part of the response to this challenge is to search for evidence-based alternatives. These could include the integration of traditional initiation schools; chief led and controlled initiation schools, the development of ethnic-based initiation models such as the Pondo, Xesibe, and Mpondomise, to mention but a few.

MMC is being presented by some, including some healthcare practitioners, as an alternative to traditional circumcision, largely because of safety concerns. So far, close to a million MMCs have been conducted throughout the country with a few complications and deaths reported here and there.

While MMC has been presented as an HIV-prevention strategy it is also a safer option against possible botched circumcisions and deaths. If these traditional initiation-related deaths and injuries are not stopped immediately, MMC will completely replace them in this country. And this would be unfortunate as MMC has no cultural values.

However, while MMC is said to be medically safe, it faces challenges of acceptance. First, it suffers from social stigma and is seen as a foreign practice that is designed to eradicate traditional initiation practices. Secondly, like other HIV-prevention strategies, MMC is biomedical and does not cover 99% of the components of traditional initiation, which includes education on values and culture. The third challenge of MMC is how to increase its uptake in areas that are strongholds for traditional initiation, including the rural areas. In the Eastern Cape, for example, young boys choose traditional circumcision over MMC because of the social stigma attached to MMC. This is despite their knowledge that they might not come back alive from traditional initiation school. This is the risk they are willing to take rather than be stigmatised and isolated by other 'men'.

Some have called for the integration of MMC within the traditional setting. The argument is that the coexistence of the two will ensure safer circumcision while addressing the social stigma associated with MMC. It will be important to see how this can be achieved. At the moment those seen competing with MMC, which has an advantage of being well-funded with millions and millions while a traditional initiation programme is not subsidised by government at all.

As culture is not static, there is a need to explore measures that will help traditional culture adapt to the current social, economic and health environment while ensuring that a tradition does not lose its essence, and original meaning and content.

Conclusion

In conclusion, challenges associated with traditional initiation go beyond botched circumcision, deaths and amputations. There are issues of child trafficking, abductions, women abuse, rape, child abuse, and alcohol and drug abuse. All these point to the breakdown of families and social disintegration.

Moving forward, in a quest to solve the challenges facing traditional initiation, the following questions need to be asked:

- What is the role of traditional initiation in the consolidation of a democratic South Africa and building a better and just society?
- Is traditional initiation still relevant and who owns this culture?
- Is traditional leadership best placed and able to respond to the challenges experienced by and during traditional initiation?
- Is traditional leadership through the House of Traditional Leaders given enough resources to deal with the current challenges facing the practice?
- Are human rights considered in traditional initiation practices?

Is it fair that young boys must die in the name of traditional culture?

It is clear that in order for these challenges to be overcome, there is a need to build competent communities, well capacitated to address this. A new movement built by those who support a safe and values-based traditional initiation needs to rise.

How communities respond to challenges facing traditional initiation will determine the relevancy of this traditional practice in this democratic dispensation.

Social dialogue: New light on an old story

Raymond Parsons
Academic and business leader

Sowing the seeds of social dialogue in South Africa

APRIL 2014 MARKS THE 20TH anniversary of South Africa's liberation from apartheid. What does one say when one looks back over two decades that hardly seemed to have begun and yet are now over? 'History', CV Wedgwood said, 'is lived forward but is written in retrospect. We know the end before the beginning and we can never wholly recapture what it was to know the beginning only.' When we examine the role of social dialogue in South Africa over the years, we find that it took root in soil that had been fertilised by social and economic trends and by political developments as well. It was Nelson Mandela, who had a vision of what he wanted South Africa to become, who mobilised the forces needed to develop social dialogue as a major factor in the country's crucial formative years, and to whom credit must be given for the confidence it generated at the time.

Nelson Mandela successfully launched South Africa into its post-apartheid era in 1994 and his death at the end of 2013 unleashed a widespread reassessment of what the country had achieved on the eve of its 20th anniversary of democracy. It is difficult to find new words to describe the historic contribution that Nelson Mandela made to stability and progress in the early years of democracy. While it is easy to look back through rose-tinted glasses at the advent of democracy in this country, the fact remains that it was a period fraught with risks and challenges, which only the statesmanship and leadership of the highest order, provided by Nelson Mandela, could have successfully managed. As *Financial Times* writer Alec Russell has pointed out, the policy of reconciliation was not a miracle in a biblical sense, but a carefully thought out, deliberate strategy.

It is perhaps understandable that many of the tributes to

Madiba have tended to focus on the 'reconciliation' philosophy and strategy that he represented, while downplaying the fact that it was inextricably linked in his mind to nation-building. As we celebrate our 20 years of democracy, we must recall that Nelson Mandela believed in creating strong institutions to underpin and sustain democratic processes on a long-term basis. Hence his belief right at the outset that social dialogue, as embodied in the National Economic Development Labour Council (NEDLAC), was necessary to provide the socio-economic dimensions to the reconciliation and nation-building to which he was so deeply committed. In this spirit of inclusiveness, he reached out to key stakeholders like the business community, collectively and individually, right from the outset to help undo the legacy of apartheid. But we run ahead of ourselves.

Events and actions prior to 1994 had begun to sow the seeds. Already in the early 1990s, it had been decided to set up the National Economic Forum (NEF), comprising elements of the outgoing government, business and labour, to focus on short-term issues affecting day-to-day economic governance prior to the inevitable political change that was coming. It was referred to at the time as the 'golden triangle' of government, labour and business, and it enjoyed Madiba's blessing in its transitional role. The NEF provided the various constituencies with some understanding of the perspectives and concerns of the other participants, and helped to develop some capacities among them. Valuable inter-constituency networks were built up during this period and many of the participants in the NEF are still in public life in South Africa. The NEF was a good apprenticeship for the more formalised NEDLAC that still lay ahead.

It proved to be a distinctly important institutional bridge between the 'old' and 'new' regimes. It is worth recalling that there was a valuable spinoff from the NEF having some of the key stakeholders under one roof in also dealing with the endemic political violence that characterised the early 1990s and which threatened to derail the political negotiation process. These developments led to a crucial National Peace Accord (NPA) at the time. The negotiated NPA was an important mechanism for keeping contemporary political violence to manageable proportions and involved more or less the same 'actors' as were participating in the NEF. We were all linked to a greater or lesser extent to the tough and tumultuous political process then underway, apart from the NEF's normal agenda.

Nelson Mandela and NEDLAC

Social dialogue was, therefore, the route that Nelson Mandela wanted to go. Informal processes had formal outcomes. Negotiations in the second half of 1994 centred on how social dialogue could best be institutionalised based on research both here and abroad. NEDLAC was then established as a statutory body with its structure, operational powers and characteristics being prescribed in the NEDLAC Act 35 of 1994. The NEDLAC Act was one of the first pieces of legislation passed by the new Parliament. NEDLAC was to be a major instrument of post-conflict rehabilitation and to inaugurate a new era of inclusive consensus seeking and, ultimately, decision-making in the economic and social arenas. The enabling legislation formally spelt out NEDLAC's task to pursue the goals of growth, equity and participation.

NEDLAC came into being on 18 February 1995. It was officially inaugurated by Nelson Mandela, whose speech and demeanour on that occasion reflected his great pride at having brought this key institution to fruition. High expectations and enthusiasm in many quarters, perhaps in retrospect excessive, surrounded the launch of NEDLAC. It was, and remains, institutionally distinctive in several ways. It is the most representative policy body in South Africa, since it includes government, labour, business and 'the community'. It is an agreement-making body of broadly equal partners and not merely an advisory body. Of the 60 or so countries, mainly emerging economies, who have NEDLAC-type structures, NEDLAC is among the very few that is a negotiating body and not only an advisory one. It also requires mandated representatives, which means that constituencies are held accountable for the consequences within their sphere of influence.

During its first few years, NEDLAC's main focus was on negotiating the introduction of the government's new labour market policy and legislation, although its agenda gradually broadened over time to include a formidable range of socio-economic issues. But labour market issues dominated the early period. Labour market changes, after all, lay at the crucial intersection of economic, social and political policies so were bound to be heavily contested. It proved to be a stern test of the fledgling organisation. In the absence of an overall social accord, the labour reform process, although necessary, dissolved into piecemeal negotiations out of which several serious unintended social and economic consequences emerged in subsequent years. As we have seen above, there had already been a positive history of social dialogue up until then, but the anticipated social compact had not yet materialised.

There was a lapse in the commitment to NEDLAC in the handling of the Growth, Employment and Redistribution (GEAR) strategy, which was launched in June 1996. A decision was taken at the highest political level that the implementation of GEAR as a 'stability pact' was urgent and that consultation at various levels would be kept to the minimum. GEAR was regarded as non-negotiable and withheld from NEDLAC. 'I confess that even the ANC learnt of GEAR far too late – when it was almost complete', Nelson Mandela later admitted (quoted in *Thabo Mbeki and the Battle for the Soul of the ANC*, William Gumede, 2005). Whatever the strategy and tactics behind the handling and implementation of GEAR, it eventually cast a long shadow over Cosatu's participation in NEDLAC. It also frustrated the work of the NEDLAC Public Finance and Monetary Policy Chamber for several years, which became a lightning conductor for Cosatu's opposition to GEAR.

Perspectives on the role of NEDLAC after 20 years

During its two decades of existence at the apex of the pyramid of social dialogue in South Africa, NEDLAC has found itself driven into an ever-widening socio-economic agenda, which has itself presented increasing challenges. It has had both successes and failures and has undoubtedly also been a source of deep frustration for NEDLAC participants, even those recognising that social dialogue inevitably requires time and patience. It is inescapably a time-consuming process. In practice it has become not only an institution in which to reach formal agreements, but has also evolved into an instrument of consultation and coordination on many policies and events. Important events like the Jobs Summit (1998), the Growth and Development Summit (2003), a collective response to the global financial crisis (2009) and aspects of the New Growth Path (2010) have fallen under NEDLAC's umbrella. The range of activities covered by NEDLAC is well reflected in its successive annual reports.

Yet the criticism has persisted, including from participants. To give the most strident of those their day in court, the most sweeping of all questions must be posed: would South Africa have been better off without NEDLAC? While much more empirical analysis needs to be done to evaluate NEDLAC's interventions in specific policy matters, the overall judgement must be 'no'. Without the conflict-management potential of a structure like NEDLAC, which Nelson Mandela foresaw, the transition to a successful democracy stood to be jeopardised. 'Consensual stability' in the early years was something to which NEDLAC could positively contribute. The recurring spectacle of a new government, business and labour sitting down together, to discuss policy under the auspices of NEDLAC, even amid robust debate, was reassuring to investors and boosted confidence.

That said, there has, against the background of the Marikana tragedy in August 2012 and recent developments on the labour front, been renewed focus on the structures of social dialogue like NEDLAC. With a shift in policy-making processes post-Polokwane, the impact of the global crisis and the rising tide of social unrest around workplace and service delivery issues in recent years, the role of NEDLAC has been challenged. On all sides, deep disappointment has been expressed that the institutions ostensibly designed to promote social dialogue, such as NEDLAC, appear to have failed us in these circumstances. Although social dialogue may have widened, the extent to which it has deepened is clearly still an open question. The networks of trust originally created by NEDLAC have been eroded. While there are issues on which economic ideology and race will continue to divide South Africans, they should be able to address common challenges in ways that do not force them to pay an even higher price for their divisions than they already have done. What is the perspective here?

There are two key perspectives to bear in mind. Firstly, promotion of the convincing reasons for the creation of NEDLAC also made for excessive expectations as to what social dialogue could achieve in the short term. Given the bitter legacy of apartheid, it was too optimistic to expect significant levels of trust to be established overnight. The intense enthusiasm that greeted the advent of democracy could not last as and when the real problems of governance crowded in, and with Nelson Mandela in office for only one term. Social dialogue, as important as it is as a mechanism to manage change, can in 20 years only do so much to repair decades and even centuries of mistrust and suspicion. To that extent, criticism that NEDLAC is failing to meet its goals is not based on a realistic analysis of what institutionalised social dialogue can legitimately achieve in a country like South Africa.

Secondly, no institution, no matter how rich its history, can shirk the challenge of taking stock of its role in a rapidly changing socio-political environment, both globally and locally. Government and the social partners have recognised that, after two decades, the relevance and functioning of NEDLAC need to be critically interrogated to assess its performance. Some serious institutional, capacity, and operational challenges have been identified, which need to be addressed. For if function declines, so also do status and influence. Do the benefits of NEDLAC still outweigh the costs? Therefore, in 2013 NEDLAC commissioned a wide-ranging independent evaluation of the institution and its future strategy. NEDLAC's constituencies are now considering the findings and, hopefully, decisions will be taken during 2014 to revamp and reposition the organisation. In particular, ways must be sought to ensure that NEDLAC becomes an active driver of effective social dialogue, rather than just its passive custodian. It is possible to give NEDLAC 'a new face'.

Trust and the creation of shared prosperity

Nevertheless, trust goes further than being embodied in formal institutions, as important as these are for the country. Trust needs to be more visible in our way of life in intangible ways, but with tangible outcomes. Nor can trust be created by a magic wand or because rhetoric claims it is a 'good thing'. Trust evolves and is renewed by people and groups working together to resolve problems and issues when it is in their common interest to do so. They do so by exhibiting a genuine desire for compromise and to find solutions without seeking to impose heavy ideological 'baggage' of whatever kind on others.

The National Development Plan (NDP) has suggested the possibility of a 'social compact' marked by equity and inclusion, for which it says a number of conditions must be in place. A successful social compact will require a much greater degree of convergence around aims and means than has hitherto been apparent. It is the absence of many of these requirements in South Africa that has hampered the maturing of social dialogue in general and the proper functioning of NEDLAC in particular. The NDP rightly concludes that this says a great deal about the history of the country and the lack of trust. If the implementation of the NDP is to succeed, then the emphasis given by its authors to the importance of developing solidarity and consensus-seeking is not misplaced. It develops from building confidence in joint ways of solving problems in a tolerant and 'give-and-take' mode.

In my recent book, *Zumanomics Revisited: The Road from Mangaung to 2030* (2013), one message is that a major lesson of the mixed economy in South Africa, and an economy that we want to see bigger, stronger and better in the years ahead, is that capital and labour need to coexist. This means that they must both get beyond caricatures and narrow self-interest, and seek to fundamentally understand each other better. They remain too important and too interdependent to do anything else. Power, shared accountability and responsibility require cooperative behaviour from participants. There is, indeed, time for robust and sharp debate, but there is an even greater potential for constructive cooperation and effective leadership on issues of common interest.

This approach was well captured in the Dinokeng scenarios, released in 2010 by a team of experts, in which they referred to three possibilities for South Africa, which are still relevant:

- walk alone
- walk behind
- walk together.

How we 'walk together' should now become the central theme as we salute the 20th anniversary of our democracy and hold our fifth general election in 2014 as an important reflection of it. Effective social dialogue and the leadership that must drive it are essential bridges between the present and the future in South Africa. Social dialogue should also not just be what various participants 'demand' of one another but also how they can add value to the longer-run solutions of otherwise seemingly intractable situations. While the structure of social dialogue may change, it still provides us with values and principles that transcend the circumstances in which it was originally forged. The fundamental challenge for South Africa remains how to reconcile a growing economy and the liberating effects of individual freedom with the goals of an inclusive society, even at the cost of some disturbance to a few cherished ideological shibboleths.

Looking for pragmatism and unity

Both Marxism and free-market fundamentalism basically represent a reluctance to accept theoretical models simply as analytical tools to understanding economic phenomena and as merely suggesting possible means to achieving certain ends, without being the ultimate word or an insuperable obstacle to compromise. Both extremes usually constitute a refusal to accept the discipline of empirical and evidence-led observation, trial and error and piecemeal, rather than utopian, change, as reflecting the real complexities and trade-offs facing decision-makers. In addition, to quote Nobel Prize holder, economist Professor Paul Krugman, we should be contemptuous of those 'who take a position and refuse to alter that position no matter how strongly the evidence refutes it, who continue to insist that they have The Truth despite being wrong again and again'. The strength of the NDP is that it creates a pragmatic framework within which it is possible to manage trial and error in policy as South Africa moves forward to 2030, while nonetheless giving a broad sense of direction.

In this sense, 2014 is not so much a crossroads but a T-junction for South Africa, as we will need to make key choices about the future direction of our economy and our society. We need to find within ourselves the magic with which to transform our economy towards 5%, 6% and even higher average growth performances, as some other leading emerging economies have done. We still face the triple challenges of unemployment, poverty and inequality. The NDP offers us a vision for 2030 that needs to be translated into reality through collaborative effort. We must, nonetheless, ensure that social dialogue does not become a smokescreen for procrastination or inaction but rather a spur to better outcomes. Participation and effectiveness need to be balanced. We need to encourage institutions and mechanisms that, however much talk is put into one end, will grind out the decisions and implement them within reasonable timelines at the other end.

It is effective social dialogue that is the essential tool to reduce the 'trust deficit' in South Africa. We need more trust among major stakeholders in the economy, including an 'active citizenry', to help provide the ideas, commitment and leadership needed that will lift

South Africa beyond current dogmas, tensions and disputes. In this way we can build on our strengths and address our weaknesses as a country. This is not something that is merely 'nice' to do but, as the NDP emphasises, is imperative in building a climate of solidarity to get superior outcomes and better delivery. Building trust is globally closely associated with stronger economic performance and social stability. In turn, there remain the irreducible elements of a shared responsibility in South Africa, because a united and cohesive society is an essential prerequisite for peace and prosperity.

What might frequently be seen as evidence of 'solidarity' or 'unity' in South Africa seems to be event-driven rather than organically based. Focal points like the advent of democracy in 1994, the rugby successes in 1995, the global economic crisis in 2008, the Soccer World Cup in 2010, the death of Madiba in 2013 – these events appear to bring the nation together for a brief moment and give us a glimpse of what might be possible. Yet we appear unable to sustain it for long or capitalise on it. It soon relapses back into underlying tension, conflict and polarisation, with solidarity hanging by a thin rope waiting for the next big event to give it another temporary boost. 'Unity' in South Africa is rather like jungle-man Tarzan swinging precariously from tree to tree, with big spaces in-between. We need to root our sense of solidarity more deeply by organically strengthening the structures through which we are meant to collaborate and collectively work on an ongoing basis, thus being less dependent just on 'events' to display intermittent 'unity'.

'Reinvesting' in social capital in South Africa
This must be the mantra for the future. The breakdown of trust into unpredictable and negative behaviour turns too many processes into a game in which all lose, and in which the values that Madiba espoused are forgotten or sacrificed. Cooperation through effective social dialogue is necessary to help consolidate our young democracy and to take it to the next level. We need to 'reinvest' in the fundamentals on which value-adding social dialogue is based and South Africa must strengthen what is often called the 'social capital' of a country. The revitalisation of NEDLAC remains an important component of this 'reinvestment'. The costs of failing to collaborate at strategic moments in South Africa have become high and are, to conclude, well-illustrated in the following story.

A scorpion came to the edge of a river and asked a frog whether he would carry him to the other side, for which he would reward him. The frog hesitated and said he feared the scorpion would fatally sting him on the way over. The scorpion reassured the frog that it was in their mutual interest to cooperate, and so the journey commenced. Halfway across, the scorpion did sting the frog.

In his dying throes the frog gasped: 'Why did you do that? Now we will both drown.'

'I couldn't help it,' replied the scorpion, 'I just can't change my nature.'

We in South Africa will simply need to change certain fundamental attitudes to collective effort if we want to get better outcomes than that of the frog and the scorpion post-2014.

A reflective essay on transformation in South African universities

Edith Phaswana
Academic

Introduction

I ENTERED THE SOUTH AFRICAN ACADEMY in 1994, a very opportune and historic moment in South Africa. A new country had just been born. For me, this was also a space imbued with feelings of ambivalence. On the one hand, I was extremely excited that the long-awaited South African 'miracle' had been achieved: apartheid and its evil laws had been abolished. The idea of living as a second-class citizen in my own country diminished instantly the ANC victory was announced. On the other hand, I was sceptical on two levels: (1) Would the new government be able to usher in a 'better life for all,' as suggested in those posters on electricity poles in my community? My distrust was, in part, influenced by my observations of liberation victories all over Africa and, in particular, our neighbour, Zimbabwe. (2) Would all citizens be open to the possibility of a total change in the way they lived their lives? Would the supporters and beneficiaries of apartheid be willing to transform and embrace the overwhelming change that confronted them, particularly the willingness to share the privileged spaces and positions they have previously occupied? How feasible would it be for those who suffered under apartheid to reconcile with their former oppressors? In my view, these were the two difficult challenges the new dispensation was presenting to South African citizens.

No wonder we witnessed a mass exodus to Europe, Australia and North America immediately after independence, notwithstanding the fact that there were those who emigrated for better opportunities elsewhere. Simultaneously, I was extremely proud to be in South Africa at this opportune time. I wanted to be part of this history-making, to witness first hand the changing structures and relations, the transformation and resistance, the lows and highpoints of this transition.

334

The impetus to contribute an essay to this collection was partly motivated by the need to embrace one of my acquired personal freedoms since 1994, 'freedom of expression', while also taking the responsibility not to deliberately hurt others. On this 20th anniversary of our democracy, we have nothing to celebrate more than our progressive Constitution. I therefore responded positively to the editor and exclaimed that if this essay made others uncomfortable, I would have reached my objective in writing it. This discomfort is necessary to encourage dialogue and debate in national discourse.

Another motivation stems from the need to encourage others to overcome their fears, in whatever form they manifest themselves. The ideal to achieve freedom, in my view, was based on the desire to confront and challenge systems of domination that impinge on the rights of others. Here my persuasions dictate that the idea of freedom would be in vain if I still lived in fear. On this note, I celebrate the fearless struggle for political freedom of the mid-1980s when I was growing up. The struggle removed a huge veil of fear for me and the many young people who participated in it. These included the lack of fear for authority at all levels. If one has been able to confront the gruesome and evil apartheid state apparatus, what more is there out there to fear in our democratic dispensation? If one was able to survive under institutionally designed deprivation for the most part of one's life, what again is there to fear? Over the past 20 years I have observed that fear has been the main barrier to people's enjoyment of their personal and collective freedoms in the new South Africa. As Steve Biko said: 'the most potent weapon in the hands of the oppressor is the mind of the oppressed.'[*]

This is one of the worst legacies of apartheid and it is difficult to eradicate in the psyche of many people. It is in thinking about the number of people who are still trapped and bound by fear that the need to encourage and liberate others arise and I do this by tracking my own trajectory within the various educational spaces I have occupied since 1994. Finally, I embraced this volume because it is not an academic tome in which gatekeepers in the field of knowledge production might attempt to silence my subaltern voice.

My aim in this essay is to share my subjective views, experiences and observations over the past 20 years of being in the higher

---

[*] Wilson, L. 2011. *Steve Biko: A Jacana Pocket Biography*. Johannesburg: Jacana.

education sector, both as a student and a lecturer. This is a reflection of my own expectations, aspirations, trials and tribulations within a field where age, gender and race remain unequally represented, despite government's efforts to fast-track transformation.[*] Like many influential sectors, the higher education sector remains predominantly white and male. While racism is highly significant in South Africa, in most cases issues of sexism, xenophobia, classism and homophobia are often ignored. Hence, I intend to interrogate some of these issues in an attempt to expose the transformation myth pervasive in our higher education system. As space precludes thorough treatment here, I will focus on particular issues that have caught my attention during my student and lecturing years.

My student years

My first entry point as a student was at the University of Pretoria[†] in 1994. At the time there were few blacks at this type of institution. Official statistics suggest that between 1993 and 1999 university enrolment increased from 43% to 52% for female students and from 29% to 59% for Africans.[‡] The Council for Higher Education's Annual Report (1999) further indicates that enrolment patterns suggest that historically Afrikaans-medium universities and technikons were the first choice for students. I therefore form part of the exodus to these universities and it would be worthwhile to reflect on my own experience at the time. In this sense, I celebrate 1994 for widening access through equal opportunity policies and initiatives in higher education institutions.

As a black student, I found myself in an environment in which there were no role-models. This did not surprise me as it did not simply 'happen' but was reflective of the legacy of apartheid. In 1993, only 7% of academic staff at universities were black and 87% were white.[§] I was never taught by a black lecturer in any of my classes throughout my three years at this university. This is confirmed in the Council on Higher Education's report, which concluded that 'academic staff at the historically white universities remain

---

[*] Here I deliberately exclude my experiences at a former black university and a UK university.
[†] A historically white Afrikaans-medium university.
[‡] Annual Report 1999, Council for Higher Education.
[§] Ibid.

overwhelmingly white especially at the historically white Afrikaans universities where black (African, Coloured and Indian) academics together constituted under 3% of the total in 1998 and where very little change in this regard has been evident in the past five years [since 1994]'.* What this meant for me as a black student was that I had no sense of belonging and identification at this institution. I felt alienated and this was exacerbated by situations in which some lecturers would converse in Afrikaans with white students in what was supposed to be an English class. It was not feasible to envisage myself as a lecturer at this university.

I can cite a number of horror stories we experienced and witnessed at this institution, including humiliation and rejection. I discuss some of these exclusionary practices in another volume.† They include being forced to translate study material from Afrikaans to English, and being ridiculed because of class size – as if it were our problem as students. Yet, they were aware of the structural challenges that led to this situation. This should not invalidate the efforts of some of the progressive lecturers who supported us. I happen to meet some of these lecturers in various academic circles and I acknowledge those who deserve my gratitude.

Incidentally, I recently shared a table with one of my former lecturers at a staff workshop. Although I personally never experienced her prejudicial side, when I approached her she remembered which class group I was in. She tried hard to explain how underprepared they were as lecturers to deal with change during our time, without me questioning her. She appeared extremely uncomfortable because I did not respond to her lamentations and she left the workshop within half an hour.

In some universities we are beginning to see slight improvements, such as increasing numbers of black students and lecturers, slight improvements in race relations, acknowledgement of the unequal educational backgrounds of students and many initiatives and programmes to support underprepared first years. However, an open letter directed at Professor Botman of the University of Stellenbosch opened some of the healing wounds of 20 years ago.‡ In this letter,

---

* Annual Report 1999, Council of Higher Education.
† See *Stepping Up: Stories of a New Generation of South Africa's Leaders*. 2012. Botsotso.
‡ See bonfire.com/stellenbosch/2012/08/06/open-letter-to-professor-botman-vice-chancellor-and-rector-of-stellenbosch-university.

Pieter Odendaal raises some pertinent issues indicative of historically white universities' persistence in promoting racial domination and their reluctance to transform and create meaningful experiences for black students.

What is encouraging and affirming of our democracy is the opportunity created for Odendaal to demonstrate courage by drafting this letter. In our days, this would not have been possible as we felt unwelcome and there were no proper channels through which we could engage with such issues. Many cases reported were either dismissed or not attended to. Our institutions of learning need to produce critical thinkers and observers such as Odendaal, who will challenge systems of domination and dismantle power structures that seek to perpetuate the persistent racism and sexism prevailing in our institutions of higher learning. In future, I would like to see an increase in the number of student voices, and their inputs and suggestions taken seriously and acted upon.

Female students and sexual harassment at universities

Although sexual harassment is a global phenomenon, recently there have been media reports about escalating levels of sexual harassment at our universities. The Wits University sexual harassment saga, involving four lecturers, is one of the many cases reported lately.[*] This is astonishing in an environment designed to nurture rational and critical thinkers, and agents of change. Unwarranted social influences should not be allowed to flourish in the academic world.

When I was at university, it inspired independent and critical thinking, and knowledge creation and its application in real life. In essence, our research should not only advance knowledge but be able to effect change in our society. However, despite the voluminous body of literature universities produce on sexual and gender-based violence, female students find themselves having to deal with certain male lecturers who perceive them as easy prey. Over the past 20 years, as a student and a lecturer, I have witnessed a number of situations where cases of sexual harassment between lecturers and students were swept under the carpet, even though they were public knowledge in the entire university.

---

[*] See www.news24.com/SouthAfrica/News/4th-Wits-lecturer-quits-over-sexual-harass-ment-20131101.

The limitation of our democratic dispensation is evident in issues of sexual and gender-based violence. A lack of commitment from high-level decision-making structures is evident in how cases of harassment are handled, both in the public domain and at universities. Here I want to emphasise my earlier point about who sits on high-level decision-making structures in South Africa. Globally, it is mainly men in positions of power and they tend to protect each other in such matters, hence, the patriarchal lack of sensitivity around these issues. It is, therefore, not surprising that cases of sexual harassment are often neglected.

As institutions of higher learning, we have not as yet done enough to empower our female students to expose sexual and gender-based violence. A year ago, a female tutor approached me about incidences of sexual harassment involving two male tutors and two first-year students. The victims had been courageous enough to report the incident to this tutor. This was taken up with the relevant university structures. However, the case was dropped because the victims felt uncomfortable and decided to drop the charges. This was exacerbated by the long waiting period and the number of hearings the students had to undergo. Unfortunately, during all this time the perpetrators were suspended on full pay and were later reinstated. In reflecting on the whole process, there was inadequate support for the victims at the higher level, illustrating the insensitivity to cases of sexual harassment.

This shows that some universities are inadequately prepared to support victims or to discipline perpetrators of sexual harassment. The internal processes and the dynamics of handling sexual harassment cases can be complex. What is encouraging about the Wits University case is that it was highly publicised and dealt with at the level of the vice chancellor's office. This resulted in the victims successfully laying charges and the perpetrators being dealt with. Ultimately, this may encourage other female students to come forward.

Experiences of inequalities at universities

Seven year later, I pursued my postgraduate studies at the Rand Afrikaans Universiteit and the experience was slightly different. Here, I got in touch with lecturers who were willing to embrace us in an alien culture and environment. Perhaps this was because it was seven years later and also a postgraduate class.

However, the inequalities in our country hit me hard in one of these classes. As part of our summative assessment, we were required to present real innovative projects we had earlier designed and implemented in our communities over the entire study period. I remember how the white students were proficient in using technology and created PowerPoint presentation, flyers, posters and business cards. My context dictated that I could only type and staple black and white pages. Despite my intellectual ability – confirmed on various assessment levels – I felt intimidated when the first two speakers presented, but there was nothing I could do about it even if I had wanted to. My turn came and I presented from my black and white pages. At the end, I was selected as a top achiever, independently, by my peers and by the external moderators. Despite the structural challenges, I managed to use my own agency to survive in this environment.

In sharing this story, I would like to encourage those students who find themselves materially deprived because this has not improved for many black students over the past 20 years. Seemingly, there are no indications that it will improve in the near future unless a miracle happens. However, I would like to emphasise that lecturers who do understand the inequalities pervasive in our society try to counter these problems.

I can still remember the comments from our external moderator when he motivated for why I should win the prize despite lacking the sophisticated graphics. He stated that the university worked differently as it sought to develop individuals with advanced analytical and critical thinking skills, individuals who could master theory and be able to apply it in real life situations. He further argued that although he appreciated the good efforts in creating PowerPoint slides and posters, any skilled personal assistant or graphic designer could produce these. He further highlighted that if a university graduate possessed such technical skills it was an added advantage but it was certainly not a must at this level. I dwelt on these important aspects of his speech, I excelled in my studies, and ended up being awarded a Ford Foundation Fellowship to pursue my PhD in the United Kingdom.

In this Master's class, our lecturers played a very important role in getting us to understand the inequalities created during apartheid so that we would be able to responsibly forge the new country that we all aspire to live in. This had a huge impact on me and has certainly influenced how I live with people from various backgrounds.

To demonstrate the extent of the support I received, I was a single mother to a six-year-old daughter at the time and when my lecturers realised that I would sometimes miss classes due to childcare, they allowed me to bring my child to the class and organised a playroom for her, which is not the norm at institutions of learning. This was done by individuals who were willing to take risks. As a lecturer I occasionally come across like-minded colleagues who are willing to listen to students' social problems and advise accordingly.

My greatest weapon over the years has been my positive attitude towards change without comprising myself in any way. I still have the courage to confront issues and dissatisfactions when they present themselves. True freedom involves being able to dismantle systems of domination, to resist the imposition of particular forms of social influences and supreme ideologies and to refuse to compromise oneself. My appreciation for this democratic dispensation was further intensified as I realised that educational boundaries are gradually being eradicated for blacks and women. This might be incomprehensible for those who profited from the past situation and therefore I am not alarmed by their antagonism towards widening access for black students and employment equity policies.

However, I would like to suggest that equity should not be promoted at the expense of quality. In recent years, concepts of 'equity' and 'quality' are highly politicised due to the structural and historic educational challenges created during apartheid. Due to pressures exerted on universities to transform, some universities find themselves hiring just anyone to fulfil the quota. Sometimes these universities attempt to counter this by constantly shifting promotion criteria to prevent new entrants from advancing into higher ranks. Regardless of the equity versus quality debate, this should not compromise the education of students.

My lecturing years
Since 1994 gender and racial equity have been government's priorities on the transformation agenda of the higher education sector. In his foreword to the *White Paper on Higher Education 1997*, Minister Sibusiso Bhengu declared:

341

The transformation of the higher education system to reflect the changes that are taking place in our society and to strengthen the values and practices of our new democracy is, as I have stated on many previous occasions, not negotiable, the higher education system must be transformed to redress past inequalities, to serve a new social order, to meet pressing national needs and to respond to new realities and opportunities.*

This White Paper further notes: 'the composition of staff in higher education fails to reflect demographic realities. Black people and women are severely underrepresented, especially in senior academic and management positions'.†

Surprisingly, 20 years into democracy the participation of black and women academic staff has not increased much, particularly at senior management level. This is despite innovative recruitment and retention strategies. A recent study found that gender parity increased by 5% between 2001 and 2010.‡ These authors also found that gender parity occurred at lecturer and junior lecturer level with a sharp decline of female academics as the seniority of the ranks increase. In 2010, approximately 23% of the professors at universities were female. These figures are unacceptable for a country that is committed to transformation. Although minimal, this slight increase in female participation is encouraging relative to where we were 20 years ago and can only be attributed to the equity policies adopted during this democratic dispensation.

In reflecting on these statistics, what does this discrepancy mean for the female voice in university structures and for sexual equality? As I indicated earlier, there is a lack of political will, commitment and support from university management structures as these are mostly male. Management also tends to turn a blind eye to these exclusionary practices. This inadequate representation of women at high levels of decision-making disadvantages women's voices. In most cases, the argument against the recruitment and promotion of black and women academic staff to senior level is based on two errors that

---

* Foreword by Minister Bhengu. *The White Paper on Higher Education 1997.*
† *The White Paper on Higher Education 1997.*
‡ See Boschoff, N. & Bosch, A. 2012. 'Women in South African academia: A statistical profile, The South African Board for People Practices Report 2012, (Chapter 3, pp. 13–19).

indicate a lack of commitment: (1) substandard staff quality, and (2) insufficient or low research capacity.* To what extent this is true for all female and black academics remain a big question. For instance, how does one explain the 50% research output for female academics in education, public/community health, language and linguistics between 2002 and 2004?† Is the yardstick for research output the type of research field and discipline?

If not, one wishes to see a situation where talented women are periodically recognised and promoted accordingly to high-level management positions. The post-apartheid government's insistence on equity is sometimes met with strong opposition from some male academics who think they are naturally entitled to be in high-level management positions. Selection committees for recruitment are still dominated by whites and males with reluctance to diversify them or sometimes without representation from unions. Incidentally, my own selection interview was conducted by four white men and it felt so 1960s. Even though I was finally appointed I found it severely narrow-minded and antediluvian in this day and age.

Women in senior academic positions

Sometimes the struggle for gender equity can be thwarted by tensions between race and class, which become obstacles for other women's upward mobility. Over the years I have observed that women in senior positions also perpetuate patriarchy by downplaying sisterhood when they enter these spaces. A black female colleague from another university experienced a challenge when she applied for promotion to associate professor level. She was denied the opportunity even though she met the requirements. Apparently, the white female head of department, who had fewer publications than her, could not support her application citing more criteria (H-index, number of articles) than were suggested in the promotion policy.

Suppose this colleague had been supported and promoted. In a few years' time she could become a professor and increase the representation of women in higher ranks. I can cite similar cases in

---

* See Prozesky, H. 2006. Gender Differences in the Journal Publication Productivity of South African Academic Authors. *South African Review of Sociology*, 37(2), 87–112.

† Table 1.7, p. 64 in Mouton, J. & Gevers, W. 2010. Introduction in *The State of Science in South Africa*. Pretoria: Academy of Science of South Africa (ASSA), (Chapter 1, pp. 39–67).

my own university, where there is currently a high staff resignation rate of black academics citing similar experiences. If I happen to know or hear of a black lecturer leaving our faculty, I have made it my mission to find out their reasons for leaving, as I have no confidence in exit interviews.

It is easy for women to criticise men for creating barriers for upward mobility of women. However, when women occupy senior leadership positions they, unconsciously or consciously, often perpetuate the system of domination. On this note, I would argue that real transformation will not emanate from equalising men and women, nor black and white but through clearing the entire system of individuals who remain intransigent and closed to critically engage with an academic sphere that is evolving.

Incompetence

The democratic system is gradually changing the racial composition of our institutions. As a result, there is an increased presence of black lecturers in historically white universities, albeit concentrated at more junior levels. Despite the fact that the general culture in academia is predominantly white and further crippled by a racialised and gendered perception of being, I have witnessed cases of incompetence and lack of commitment towards students. I have also observed that the higher the rank these individuals occupy, the more arrogant they become towards junior staff and students. Some of these individuals are so fixated on personal achievement that they tend to forget that parents spent a fortune sending their children to universities.

If we are to fight the injustices prevailing in our country, we will have to improve certain standards and work ethics learnt during apartheid, without compromise. How do we defend a situation where a colleague shows incompetence by missing classes, not marking students' work or, worse, demeaning students? A black postgraduate student once shared an experience where she had queried her mark and was told by the white male lecturer: 'I know you deserve more but I have decided to give you this mark.' This demonstrates incompetence. In most cases students are not equipped to deal with difficult lecturers. Issues such as these could lead to some students not being able to meet the course requirements. Such individuals impinge on the freedom of others. There's a need to empower students to be able to challenge and report poor conduct by lecturers.

Equally problematic among these historically white universities are some of the managers who perpetuate systems of domination and control that are reminiscent of what prevailed during the dark years of apartheid. If left unchecked, these individuals could derail the progress already made at our institutions. Their level of incompetence is quite astonishing: a culture of entitlement, nepotism and corruption continues to take place, with impunity, at these institutions. As much as there is corruption at the national government level, I find that some senior managers can be equally corrupt. The lack of respect and mistreatment of junior staff, and the unequal distribution of resources based on racial and gender lines are some of the observations.

Within the higher education landscape in South Africa, the most vulnerable groups in the staff hierarchy are temporary/contract lecturers and administrators. In most cases these are women from all racial backgrounds. In comparison to those at senior levels, they are the ones keeping the system running yet they remain unappreciated. The university benefits a lot, while they get little in return. In addition to these groups, immigrants working at our universities are expected to be forever grateful for whatever South Africa has to offer, despite the high level of skills some of them bring into this country. I have observed a high level of exploitation of migrant workers from African countries in our institutions. Due to their relative vulnerability, these groups tend to carry the heaviest workload and are often underpaid. Despite their exceptional performance levels that surpass some of their local and permanent counterparts, they continue to be taken advantage of. As a result, this has also created animosity.

Some senior academics seem to expect to be worshipped. It is really pathetic to realise how most academics are unconscious of their prejudices, be it towards migrants, gay people, black people, women or young people. This pathology of expecting to be treated with respect while mistreating others is what I detest in dealing with seniority. In observing some of their contradictory practices and listening to their chauvinistic comments, my respect for some of these senior colleagues has gradually diminished.

Concluding remarks

Overall, in sharing some of these experiences, I would like to show that to some extent the democratic dispensation did usher in attributes of a miracle. However, it has not sufficiently dealt with systemic and structural prejudices in our institutions or shaped cultures. Furthermore, the essay has demonstrated that over the past 20 years our institutions have failed to train those who operate under a prism of prejudice to unlearn their ways. If systems have been in place, they have not been effective as they have not broken barriers but have merely restructured the patterns of suppression.

As I have already indicated, institutions of higher learning should invest in educating young men to support their female counterparts to become agents of change against gender violence. This would have far-reaching outcomes in future as these young men take up positions in various workplaces or assume other social roles.

Memory, race and denial: The unfinished journey towards restorative justice

Mzukisi Qobo
Academic

Introduction

MEMORY IS A DOUBLE-EDGED SWORD. It holds the promise for restoration. Yet it can also be destructive. In societies that have been torn apart by civil strife, war or racial discrimination, as was the case in South Africa, leaders have a powerful role to play in harnessing memory as a force for good. Commitment by citizens to a shared social purpose can also help to mobilise positive energy that could take us beyond the fractures bequeathed by the past.

Many South Africans from all walks of life have different memories about what happened in the past, hold different world views on what it means to coexist in the present, and view the strategies for building a better South Africa through different lenses. In this essay I draw on my own personal experience as a starting point for offering an analytical and critical perspective on the new South Africa. I also reflect on the achievements of the African National Congress (ANC) government since the end of apartheid, as well as on the intractable challenges that still confront us today.

Memory and the violence of apartheid

The memory of the struggle for liberation evokes conflicting feelings. There is the satisfaction of triumph in our having overcome what had seemed insurmountable during the monstrosity of apartheid; a sense of deep respect for those who sacrificed their lives to make the dream of a free society real; a sense of pride at how we managed to work through our differences in the initial phase of democracy to stabilise society and install a new democratic government; a sense of resentment at the fact that deep-seated inequalities along racial and class lines are still very much with us; and a sense of anger at the complacency of the ruling party and the growing vice of corruption

347

that breeds cynicism and undermines the cause of freedom.

During the liberation struggle the powerful drive for justice was not so much in the songs or the revolutionary literature from older comrades, but in the searing images of injustices that you witnessed daily in a country that was fractured racially. The expectation that South Africa would one day be different, the dignity of the black person restored, fuelled the commitment of liberation fighters and kept many going in the face of a system that was meant to crush their spirit. My own conscious encounter with what was fundamentally wrong with the social structure of South Africa was at the tender age of ten, during the 'pass' raids of the early 1980s.

As I grew up, I witnessed women with screaming children on their backs being chased by white policemen. Some would be kicked to the ground before they got pushed forcibly into the white vans fitted with sirens. You would know when this was about to take place when a shrill cry of '*Kubomvu!*' echoed across our section of the township. Loosely translated, this meant 'it is red' or 'danger is about to descend'. This was normal in townships across South Africa.

Before then, I never questioned why townships were populated by black people only, or what gave rise to this particular type of settlement. Neither did I question the white men's assumed position of superiority and the servile existence to which blacks were subjected. For me, this was the life I knew.

Soon enough, my political consciousness set in. I would ask my parents many questions of a political nature. Most of my peers' parents worked as labourers at the railways, industrial areas of Epping or were domestic workers in the northern suburbs, such as Durbanville and Bellville or the southern suburbs of Rondebosch, Newlands and Constantia. These areas were inhabited exclusively by whites and the few blacks there were either 'garden boys' or 'maids'.

Once in a while during school holidays, I would go to these exclusive suburbs to visit my mother who was a domestic worker there. Life in the suburbs was a sharp contrast to the dusty streets of Langa. Unlike in the township where my family shared a room of about 25 square metres with two other families and shared ablution facilities with six other families, in the suburb one family of four would own a multi-room home on spacious grounds and have a swimming pool.

Whenever I visited the suburbs, the rustling sound of trees and the mellifluous chirping of the birds were a novelty for me. I would feel 'privileged' to visit my mom's place of employment. It was on one such visit, when I was ten years old, that I encountered the menacing impact of the racism of white South Africa when the police confronted me. I had just alighted from a train at Newlands Station when I was suddenly stopped.

Two police officers got out of their van and demanded to know what was in the plastic bag I was carrying. They muttered abuses and quizzed me on what was I doing there. I remembered just enough Afrikaans words to tell them that my mother was a domestic worker. I was clearly an unwelcome sight. They emptied the contents my bag unceremoniously onto the ground and left. The full force of the abuse weighed heavily on my heart as I picked the clothes that I would require for my short stay in the staff quarters at the back of a mansion inhabited by my mum's white employers in Newlands. I asked myself what it is that I did to deserve such callous treatment. I could not imagine a white child my age being subjected to a similar violation. This and many subsequent incidents of far worse police brutality against people with black skin instilled in me a fear of the police but, importantly, also a sense of anger and a desire for justice.

Anyone who grew up in the townships during the apartheid era did not need to be schooled in Marxist literature to develop a sense of righteous indignation about South Africa's racialised and oppressive social structure. Many black youth in different parts of the country witnessed violence. Some lost relatives and friends at the hands of the brutal security forces, and others were separated from their parents and siblings for years because they were either detained on Robben Island or in exile.

Apartheid violence was also painted in other softer but dangerous forms: it was etched in the uneven provision of education and the poor quality of schools for blacks; in the differential allocation of public resources; in the varying types of human settlement for blacks compared to that enjoyed by whites; and in the allotment of one's chances to succeed in life based on skin pigmentation. As one economic historian put it: 'Imposed discrimination restricts access to the law and education, to health and entertainment, to dignity and progress.'* That was the narrative of apartheid.

---

* Kiewiet, CW. 1956. *The Anatomy of South African Misery*. London: Oxford University Press, p. 7.

The outlines of the apartheid system

Those who viewed the apartheid system as simply about granting self-determination to various racial groups ignore the basic historical fact that the construction of South Africa was facilitated through large-scale conquest, dispossession, coercion and exclusion of the African majority from economic ownership.[*]

South Africa's evolution, as Charles Feinstein observes, began with the brutal assertion of British power in a mission to extend British imperial authority over independent black states, a process in South Africa that was accelerated on the back of the development of the mining industry.[†] The apartheid system was a continuation of this racial order in more vicious forms. Not only did this system build different pathways to economic life in South Africa, with the white race at the top of the political, social and economic hierarchy, but it made these privileges and exclusions a fact of nature.

As Merle Lipton points out, apartheid consisted of two apparent elements: the hierarchical ordering of the economic, political and social structures on the basis of race and the legalisation and institutionalisation of this hierarchical, discriminatory and segregated system, enshrined in law.[‡] For example, the idea of whites-only settlements was appealing to many white communities. It worked for them. They had little interest in knowing how their servants' lives were unfolding on the other side of the divide in the townships. Of course, this does not mean every white citizen swore by apartheid.

Some whites protested against the system, opposed conscription into the military, joined liberal interest groups, raised their voices in Parliament as members of the Progressive Federal Party or joined the liberation struggle. But those who protested openly could hardly be regarded as a representative voice of the white population. Many whites went about their lives as if it were normal to sit on a 'Whites Only' bench and enjoy the sight of their children playing at an exclusively white public park.

---

[*] For a detailed discussion of South Africa's economic history, see Feinstein, HC. 2005. *An Economic History of South Africa: Conquest, Discrimination and Development*. Cambridge: Cambridge University Press.

[†] Ibid: p. 35.

[‡] Lipton, M. 1986. *Capitalism and Apartheid: South Africa, 1910–1986*. Cape Town: David Philip, pp. 14–15.

Like black youth who grew up in the townships knowing that their positions in society were as part of the underclass, and their start and destiny in life were at the bottom of the ladder, white children conversely grew up exposed to privilege. It was normal for them to learn by observation that those who were servants in the household were black and that positions of authority – their teachers, doctor or police – were all white.

White children growing up under apartheid also had their own title of privilege as *'Klein Baas'* (or 'Little Master'). Their profound disadvantage was growing up with a false paradigm of social relations and a disturbing sense of entitlement that they were a superior race. This explains why even today there are cases of white youth, who were born at apartheid's end or post apartheid, unleashing violence on black youth in universities such as in the Free State. Even today, very few white parents encourage their children to socialise across race lines or to even learn another South African language other than Afrikaans or English – for the latter are regarded as the languages of knowledge and authority.

Apartheid was not devised by a deranged few, but was the brainchild of well-educated and conscious intellectuals. Intellectual networks and cultural organisations such as the Broederbond infused it with pseudoscience and passion. It was supported by white communities because it conferred privileges upon them. It was pervasive in churches, the workplace, music, the arts, and on sports grounds. The state, as Michel Foucault reminds us, is given authority in its repressive functions by the already existing power relations in society; and on its own the state cannot occupy the whole field of actual power relations.[*] In South Africa's case, the apartheid state stood on the perverse legitimacy of the votes cast by the white community.

Although since democracy there has been a shift in race relations and some integration in the suburbs, however shallow, as a result of the growth in the black middle class, it is doubtful that there has been a radical shift in racial attitudes beyond the imperative of tolerance and genteel politeness. These are small victories nonetheless. Things may have generally improved under the ANC government, but at the core the socio-economic structure, in particular race-based inequalities, leaves much to be desired.

---

[*] Foucault, M. 1994. *Power*. New York: The New Press, pp. 122–3.

The rationale of the struggle and counter-movement

The struggle of black people has been about creating conditions of justice and equality – rooted in the idea that we are all created in God's image and are, therefore, equal before his eyes. Restoring the dignity of the black person has been an overriding objective. What the apartheid system did was to disfigure the sanctity of human life as rooted in a common divine source. It allocated opportunities on the basis of a sole, shallow criterion – skin colour. It set in motion a wheel of race-based inequalities that would operate even after the laws that created them had disappeared.

There are those who protest that their success has nothing to do with apartheid but everything to do with the sweat of their brow. For them, they got ahead of everyone on the account of their 'merit' without any baton of privilege gained pre 1994. They do not consider that many who grew up in Umlazi, Langa, Alexandra or Giyani were deliberately crippled and deprived opportunities through legislation in order to channel the lion's share of state resources to the advantage of the white minority.

It is this absence of a self-reflexive awareness of the white identity as an artificial mark of 'excellence' that was constructed historically and given a particular position of privilege in the social hierarchy that makes it harder for them to understand the necessity of reverse discrimination in the distribution of opportunities today in order to level the playing field.

Expectations of freedom and a dream of a better future

When I was growing up, my conception of freedom was no different from that of many of my peers in the township. We saw the future as bright and through the prism of unmediated possibilities. We expected liberation to mean more than voting every five years. We came to understand that discrimination on the basis of race is not natural, and would one day crumble and be replaced by a government established on the basis of the will of the people. We hoped that such a government would do everything in its power to create social and economic advantages for the black majority so as to level the playing field. It would not just be about service delivery within the social framework that was built by the apartheid system, but that, fundamentally, it would change the social structure, level the economic playing field, and reformat the spatial arrangements altogether.

When I was growing up in Langa, then Khayelitsha, we dreamt of a life where we would one day experience what it means to have dignity as black people and as equal members of the human race. We thought we would take charge of the economy. I was enchanted by the rhetoric and romanticism of the struggle. In the 1980s and early 1990s I had faint knowledge of the African National Congress since it was banished in exile.

I did not know what Mandela looked like except through those youthful pictures that were hoisted by activists of the Release Mandela Campaign in the mid-1980s. These images also became iconic features in the many rallies organised by the United Democratic Front (UDF) that I attended religiously in Athlone, Mitchells Plain and Gugulethu. The UDF had come into existence in 1983 as a coalition of student activists, inchoate grassroots civic formations, former Robben Island prisoners, women's organisations and trade unions, to protest against the sham reforms that were proposed by President PW Botha, beginning with the tricameral Parliament that had separate representations for whites, Indians and coloureds.

In my early youth in the late 1980s, messages of leaders such as Christmas Tinto, Dullah Omar, Cheryl Carolus, Terror Lekota, Jay Naidoo and Trevor Manuel resonated deeply with how I felt and gave me hope for a better future. The UDF suffered a momentary setback after the Botha government proclaimed a State of Emergency in 1985, followed by another in 1986.

It was in the late 1980s that my family relocated from Langa to Khayelitsha, after unsuccessfully resisting forced relocation to this new area that looked like a dump. It was located far from places of employment, functional hospitals and other decent public services. It was only over time that it was just modestly developed and attracted even more migrants from the rural Transkei. A bustling social life took shape. By then, apartheid's influx control system had been dismantled.

During my high school years (1989–93) in Khayelitsha, I was naturally drawn to student organisations such as the Township Student Congress (the proxy of the then banned Congress of South African Students) and South African Youth Congress (the proxy of the then banned ANC Youth League). In the early 1990s, President FW de Klerk had already signalled that he was taking an irreversible path to enacting serious political reforms largely for pragmatic reasons.

De Klerk was always known as part of the *'verkrampte'* group, or the conservatives within the Nationalist Party, until he saw an opening worthy of exploiting in the context of a world that was going through seismic shifts: the Soviet bloc was collapsing and could no longer be used as a justification for the continuation of apartheid. The apartheid government could no longer quell sporadic internal revolts successfully and guarantee lasting peace to its white constituency. Moreover, the economy was wobbly.

De Klerk had calculated that the only viable way to secure the continuation of the Nationalist Party within a reformed power-sharing arrangement in future was to speed up reforms. Eventually, a path was opened up to the first free elections in 1994. I voted for the first time then.

The hopes and dreams of a materially better life warmed my heart. Many people showed an extraordinary amount of optimism that their lives would soon be better. 'Let's give our leaders a chance,' was a popular refrain. During the first phase of democracy, post-1994, it was very rare to encounter vocal criticism of the ANC from the black community. The promise of the Reconstruction and Development Programme to create peace and security for all, ensure nation-building, bring about land reform and improve housing standards, further lifted the hopes of many.

This was also an auspicious moment to cultivate reconciliation and foster bridge-building across the racial divide. However, there was no white leader who played a role akin to that of Mandela to galvanise the white community to pull collectively in support of political and economic change. Instead, many were concerned about their whittling privileges and threats to their social power. Their sense of entitlement blinded them to the fact that long-term stability could be guaranteed only through sharing of the economic resources of the country.

Conclusion: An imperfect future?

South Africa's democracy is 20 years old. Much progress has been made to improve the living conditions of the majority of South Africans. The diversity of political expressions as constitutionally guaranteed, and broadened access to basic services, such as water, sanitation and electricity, are important improvements.

There are still, however, fundamental gaps in critical areas of public service delivery, educational standards and outcomes, economic participation and race relations. The expectations of many on substantive issues of economic redistribution and putting in place a fundamentally different value system in governance have not been sufficiently met.

There is yet to be a shared values framework on levelling the playing field and empowering the historically excluded groups. Alongside resistance to substantive political and economic change from those who benefitted under apartheid, the ANC governing deficiencies have also slowed down the pace of change.

There is a general sense that the euphoria that greeted South Africa's transition to democracy in 1994 is waning in the face of the continued economic pressures felt by young black South Africans. The crisis of legitimacy arising from governance weaknesses that confronts the ruling party today makes it harder for it to persuade broad sectors of society to support a socio-economic change agenda.

Large-scale economic changes in the form of, for example, the format of the land reform programme or a more extended role of the state in the economy for purposes of achieving results that go beyond market mechanisms require advancing better arguments, engaging persuasively with a diversity of social actors and demonstrating clear benefits. Just as the cost of social instability can affect all sectors and classes of society, albeit with varying degrees of intensity, the benefits of inclusive social and economic policies are likely to make everyone better off in the long run. It is thus in the best interest of those who are better off – predominantly white – to explore a more effective framework for social and economic transformation.

The ruling party's priority should be to ruthlessly deal with corruption within its ranks and in government while it makes a bold and persuasive case for economic change, and shows that it has the leadership equal to the task.

Mediations of the geopolitics of South Africa's freedom

Chengiah Ragaven

Academic and social activist

Where it all began

THE MEDICAL SCHOOL AUDITORIUM was packed to its capacity and the main contenders had not yet come. The day was hot, as Natal days are, and as usual the air conditioners were out of order. Outside in the sweltering weather, angry students in groups were discussing the various contentious items on the agenda. The meeting was scheduled for 2:00 pm and it was nearly 3:30 pm. Finally the meeting was called to order with Thami Mhlambiso in the chair and Sumara as the secretary. First item on the agenda was whether the University of Natal-Non European Section (UNNE) should disaffiliate from the National Union of South African Students (NUSAS).

This had been a contentious matter over the past years, with UNNE affiliating one year and disaffiliating in the next. As soon as the item was mentioned a number of hands shot up, not without an uproar. The first one to speak was Kadar Essack – a serious-looking scholar who, I was told, headed the Non-European Unity Movement. He berated NUSAS as a liberal, albeit racist, movement masquerading as representing the interest of the oppressed students in the country. He said that they were the elite of the South African white English and Jewish society, whose parents and grandparents were the 'owners of the means of production'. Their liberal protests had not changed the slave conditions of the people of colour. Much of what he said passed me by and for the first time I realised that I was extremely unschooled in the politics of the country.

During my high school days I had accompanied my older neighbour to Durban, where Chief Luthuli and others spoke of the freedom struggle, which I could understand aside from certain political terms. But this was different in that it was 'academic', I was told.

He sat down amid loud clapping.

Next, Asha Ntanga spoke. Studying law, he commanded tremendous respect within the student body, which was evident when he stood and bowed to students. He thanked the chair and the last speaker and said that while he agreed with some of the previous remarks, there were issues that needed to be addressed. Having gone to previous NUSAS congresses, he had studied the 'rationalising' process of the so-called whites. He argued that to understand the 'enemy', 'we' needed to interact at some level if 'we' were going to be the 'intelligentsia' and we needed to get to 'know' them. We needed to 'know' how the 'other' thinks and functions. Thus far we have worked, he argued, on assumptions. He argued that NUSAS would give us that unique opportunity to 'understand' in order to 'counterargue' their assumptions. Only then could there be 'transformation' in the whole country and make this a truly African society.

He was superb in his arguments and humble enough, although 'aristocratic' in his style of presentation. The contentious and house matters lasted until 6:00 pm that momentous day. I say 'momentous' only because my life's direction changed dramatically from trying to become a school teacher to becoming an agent for political and revolutionary change.

Joining the Student Representative Council (SRC), I felt, was one way of 'educating' my political realities. Soon after that the Sharpeville massacre occurred. Students were mobilised and demonstrations took place throughout Durban and its environs – joining the rest of South Africa and the world at being outraged.

People had been haemorrhaging for a long time under the racist English and Afrikaner, colonial and apartheid systems respectively, and suffered murders and other atrocities for over 500 years. But, somehow, Sharpeville seemed to conjure up, within South Africans and civilised people throughout the world, an unprecedented outrage at the audacity, criminality and barbarity of the South African government, military forces and police, especially its Special Branch. Some argued that no single event so far had raised so much hostility within the country and 'conscientised' the people, not only in South Africa but in the world at large. It seemed as if something was changing in the country, but one thing for was sure: South Africa was not the same after this.

People were becoming much more critical of government policies and, in turn, the state was becoming much more vicious.

The liberation's civic and social movements were becoming much more active and militant. The process exposed me to 'knowing' the various 'liberation' actions of the past: the massive peoples' protests of the 1950s – especially in the cities and the role of the trade unions, strikes, political ideologies of change and the sufferings of the poor people across the continent. Names of movements and individuals were becoming clearer and also some incoherent notations of international organisations and movements.

On the campus things were rapidly changing. More and more students who were expelled from the University of Fort Hare were coming over to the UNNE campus with their history of political leadership – Robert Sobukwe, Nelson Mandela and Gatsha Buthelezi, among others. Johnny Makhathini soon 'disappeared' from the campus and was reported to be with the ANC in exile. Ernest Gallo was reported to have been murdered in Swaziland or Botswana by the South African authorities.

Political orientation

My entry into this enfolding history: I was born on the sugar plantations on the Natal South Coast in a village called Reunion in the 1930s. My grandparents were indentured sugar-cane labourers brought to South Africa to work the lucrative sugar-cane industry of the British between 1860 and 1900. Politics to the community was totally foreign, especially since the labouring Indian community knew little English and even less politics. My generation was one of the earlier to enter the higher education sector.

As a result, our understanding of the social, political and economic dynamics was rather superficial, and my own political experiences were a 'miracle' at best. By now I was 'fired' from 'platoon school' – a community inaugurated and funded school – and the odd *locum tenens* positions, through the agencies of the South African Bureau of State Security.

The more the intimidation from the authorities, the greater my engagement in the protest movements in Durban and within politics at the university. By now I had joined the SRC and its affiliates. Steve Biko and Ben Ngubane from the medical school joined me in mobilising forces in many activities on the campus. In the meantime, I was working in factories, the post office, a laundry, in whatever jobs I could get.

I became a regular victim – detained frequently, interrogated, threatened and bullied. In the meantime, there was a realisation that students across the country were becoming conscientised and the UNNE delegation visited students and various conferences – NUSAS, church conferences and schools – to influence students to participate actively in the political directions of freedom and justice.

Police brutality was becoming commonplace in townships which, in turn, was conscientising parents and elders. This was increasing membership of dissenting political movements. It was in this atmosphere that I was elected vice president of World University Service and the National Union of South African Students. No one present at these conferences would argue that student leaders such as Asha Ntanga, Thami Mhlambiso, who later became the ANC representative at the United Nations, and Thumba Pillay, a former high-court judge, did not 'educate' the assembly of 'realpolitik' of South Africa and the real world.

I was elected president of the SRC in 1966–1967, with Ben Ngubane as the vice president and Steve Biko as a council member. The issues were becoming much more complicated and the political divisions became sharper as the state and its international surrogates played a desperate game of divide-and-rule. We were also discovering 'informers' on the campus.

My term concluded, and a few months later I became one of the first 100 persons to be strapped with a stringent five-year banning order and further house arrest. By this time, over a period of about ten years I had accumulated ten credits towards my BA degree – 'not bad for a sugar-cane labourer's family member', I was teased by my colleagues. While under restrictions, I received a letter from the International University Exchange Fund in Geneva stating that they were offering me a scholarship to study at Goldsmiths College, University of London for a degree in Education but this would mean 'exileship'. It will always be difficult to describe the thoughts and emotions, which have since become a part of my being. Bittersweet at best!

I departed Durban on a bright Sunday morning, saying farewell to the beloved country and a large family. Arriving in London I was picked up by the London Students Union of University College and driven to Goldsmiths in Lewesham, a suburb of London. It was their winter break and it was bitterly cold. I was accommodated in an old building on the campus and an occasional student walked past the window. I had never experienced loneliness in South Africa but I now began to understand that 'disease'. These were terrible times – the university was closed for its winter vacation, which lasted over a month.

Term began with excitement and soon I began my studies in earnest. Debates here were mild and polite with the occasional disagreement. I was asked to give a few talks and these were received with great interest and students were not unfamiliar with apartheid in South Africa.

I visited the London office of the ANC, met a few officials, stuck a few stamps on envelopes and got a cursory preview of its functioning. I participated in an open meeting where the main topic of discussion was the financial statement of the annual dance! The treasurer had not presented the financial statements for months and he argued that since the ANC was a liberation movement and, as such, its activities were confidential and secret, he was not obliged to produce statements. The house was in uproar. I was being educated in the exile politics of the ANC.

While concentrating on my studies in Sociology and Education with some of the best minds from the London School of Economics, I began to attend the big London protests on various conflicts, including the anti-apartheid struggle around the world. Robin Margo, a South African Rhodes Scholar at Balliol, visited me at Goldsmiths and encouraged me to apply to Oxford. I did and was accepted at New College to read Politics, Economics and Philosophy.

I soon became the president of the Graduate Common Room and initiated various contentious issues to be debated, learning 'global politics' on the way. Margret Ling from Sommerville and Richard Wainright from Balliol became close friends and we set up an African discussion group. This was followed with campaigns on Broadway. Seretse Choabi, a rather serious scholar from Magdalen, joined us and briefed us on the goings on in Lusaka where he made frequent trips as he was on the governance structures. Once Glen Scott from Magdalen and I asked Seretse if he could speak to Oliver Tambo about our joining MK and got the reply that we should continue our studies as this would be useful to the future South Africa.

From Oxford I moved to Sussex to read for an MA in African Politics and the Sociology of Development. Here I met 'liberals turned Marxists' from South Africa, mostly at the Institute of Development Studies.

My questioning the ideology and philosophy of the 'development thesis' was rather painful for the ideologues of 'white supremacy', whose 'superiority with our wealth' was the 'signifier' for our development. The debates continued all over campus, not only on South Africa, but on Latin America, women's studies, communism, Pan Africanism and a whole range of international issues. Closely examining these issues, I realised that Latin American politics was so engineered by American involvement, and that international politics was far more nuanced that meets the eye, that I decided to undertake research on Latin American politics with special reference to political torture by the state with the connivance of the United States.

I registered to do a DPhil at Cambridge, with a year in Libya teaching in the Oasis of Sabha, which was the birthplace of Colonel Gaddafi. The tragedy of that African state has a long unwritten saga – a lesson for South Africa.

Still unable to return to South Africa, I married my American girlfriend who was on her way to Montreal, Canada, to study medicine at McGill so I became an adjunct professor at Concordia and was there for almost 13 years.

Here I translated my intellectual experience to Third World politics in general and South Africa in particular. Gathering a few students and one or two South Africans, I set up the ANC branch in Montreal. Little did I realise that this unit would be so influential in Canadian politics – so much so that when Mandela made his first visit overseas he visited Montreal, where a huge gathering of over 20 000 people came to see him at the city hall.

In the meantime, I had given hundreds of lectures, attended meetings and conferences. I had, in fact, in my Oxford days hitchhiked all over Europe and talked wherever there were audiences organised by my friends, especially in Demark, Sweden and Norway. With a few exceptions, people seemed ready to offer support wherever we went. I mention this as it will be important in my summary.

After Mandela's visit, we made arrangements to return home. We received a warm welcome by the ANC branch at Isipingo and I toured the universities talking about the impending change to be implemented and the promises we had made to the international community once we returned. But this was a dream that some of us carried, while the gatekeepers had other ideas.

Geopolitics

The leadership realised after CODESA that the United States, Britain and Europe had masterminded the agenda. While the Constitution was a fine document, I learnt in a law class that 'prostitution' was a regular feature in 'controlled societies' as I had seen in Latin America. Little did South Africa realise after its 20 years of democracy – that its agenda had been crafted by the World Bank, Wall Street, the IMF, Washington and Brussels, all of whose shadows hovered before, during and after CODESA. The 1% made sure that South Africa was not going to 'cross the shadow line' of its hegemony. The economic policy was fashioned by Washington, with the Pentagon as a close partner after the collapse of the Soviet Union. It laid bare as it were, to no challenges beyond. They had hatched the plans for Gaddafi earlier and were not going to fail ... having created the eminent persons group; one or two unwittingly uttered a few sentences I picked up at the Oxford cocktails circuit.

South Africa needs a 20-year review to ask, what went wrong? Our education is in a shambles after having introduced America's material education. The Department of Home Affairs gives passports to the world's most notorious criminals, such as the 'White Widow'. We allow the CIA and Mossad free rein in the country. We allow foreign multinationals to dump food and the likes of Monsanto to introduce genetically modified seeds, which will destroy rural farmers. We have created a petty bourgeoisie elite to mimic 'white chicks' and 'dandy boys' and the media promotes crass values and conspicuous consumption.

Might it not be argued that the 'transformed' Home Affairs allowed some of the major criminals of the world to enter the country? State housing is in a shambles, as are the other agencies of the government, from the central decision-makers to those on the margins.

What were our leaders in Lusaka, London, Germany, France, USA and Canada doing in their offices when the rank and file were engaged in raising consciousness and funds for the central office? Might it be that for the 50 years or so as 'we' sat in our offices, there were others wearing the hats of 'diplomats'? And living the easy life while they masterminded our future for failure, relying on the likes of the CIA, Mossad and MI5. Are they the funders of most of the parliamentary groups – with their multinationals, banks and business houses – masterminding our 'so-called' leaders and their opposition? How is it that the 20 000 or so who gave evidence at the 'important' Truth and Reconciliation Commission where real tears were mixed with crocodile tears were not heard in the 'transformation dialogue'. Where have all those brave people gone? The answer is blowing in the wind!

Conclusion

As a moral philosopher and a serious analyst, let me argue that the 'revolution' was aborted thanks to the geopolitics and the 'realpolitik' of Henry Kissinger, who remains the guru of American politics. Long before Nixon, at the time of John Kennedy, the mafia, the money lenders, the feds, the military–industrial complex, NATO, the CIA, the world's banks and the neo-cons set the agenda and 'executed' people that entered the orbit of 'objection'.

I wrote a paper a year or two ago, yet to be published, noting the mineral, oil, land and labour wealth, among other things, of Africa, arguing that its potential is immense and that the appetite of the European is endless. And their plan, in fact, is that Africa must be 'controlled' and South Africa in 'exile' let this happen with the help of the local leaders. The West was fully aware that we had not prepared for an African liberation, economy, culture, education and, finally, for an African pride – whatever that might be – but rather were a shadow of the nation we had been.

But the control of Africa had one great obstacle – Gaddafi – whose African nationalism outshone many present-day leaders. Where are today's Julius Nyerere, Léopold Senghor, Kwame Nkrumah and Patrice Lumumba?

International scholars have written about how the CIA, Mossad and Britain took the Sannusi, trained them with the Jihadists in Virginia and London and then sent them to cause the 'revolution' with NATO waiting to initiate the 'No fly zone'. Muammar Gaddafi's crime: no cheap oil and planning to set up an African bank – which would destroy the dollar and later the euro. What African, I ask you, would take such a risk? And the unkindest cut of all is that 'an African was seen to support that murder'.

Otherwise the country will 'bow' until AFRICOM takes control of it (that is, if there is anarchy as a result discontent and thus Western powers send the so-called stabilisation forces), if it has not already; South Africa will be turned into a police state with the excuse of 'fighting crime', which it has orchestrated in the meantime; there will be a build up of the military to challenge the Jihadists – a pretext to ravage Africa, which make imperialism and colonialism seem like a Sunday afternoon tea party.

I knew Alan Paton and met up with him in, of all places, the Durban Magistrates' Court, where both of us were charged with 'crimes' we didn't commit. Strangely we were fated to meet in court and we said sad farewell to one another, never to see one another again. This reminds me of *Cry the Beloved Country* all over again.

Indeed, as President Jacob Zuma stated in Parliament recently, South Africa has progressed in so many ways, yet more change is required.

Revisiting Mandela's Rainbow Nation 20 years on

Mugabe Ratshikuni
Diepsloot activist and aspirant scholar

Introduction

TODAY ALL OF US DO, BY OUR presence here, and by our celebrations in other parts of our country and the world, confer glory and hope to newborn liberty. Out of the experience of an extraordinary human disaster that lasted too long, must be born a society of which all humanity will be proud. Our daily deeds as ordinary South Africans must produce an actual South African reality that will reinforce humanity's belief in justice, strengthen its confidence in the nobility of the human soul and sustain all our hopes for a glorious life for all.

These were heady days, when former President Nelson Mandela spoke these words at his inauguration on 10 May 1994. The eyes of the world were on South Africa, a country that had seemingly achieved the impossible: a negotiated transition after years of racial disharmony, discrimination, injustice and much bitterness. What we were witnessing was a triumph of the human spirit over injustice, discrimination, violence, bitterness and hatred. It was the stuff of dreams. But 20 years after this iconic moment, a period that will fascinate historians forever, it behoves us to ask a few questions: Have we truly created the society 'of which all humanity will be proud' that Mandela spoke about on that memorable day? Have we managed to 'sustain all our hopes for a glorious life for all' or has that hope completely vanished? What of the nation-building agenda? Are we any better 20 years later? Have our expectations, hopes and aspirations on that day been fully met or is that an unfair question to ask?

The miracle of 1994

The year 1994 was significant for me as it was my first year of high school as a boarder at a private school in Pretoria called St Alban's College. I had grown up in the former homeland of Venda in what is now Limpopo, where I had attended a private primary school called Tshikevha Christian School, which was founded by the Association for Christian Education in Venda (ACEV) in partnership with some funders from the Netherlands. This school had a passion for what it termed Christian Education. So, coming to Pretoria and enrolling at St Alban's College was a new and exciting experience for me. I was the fourth brother in my family to attend this elite school and, as a bright-eyed 14-year-old, I felt I could take on the world and overcome any obstacles that life threw at me in order to achieve my big dreams. This was very much in line with the mood of the times in the triumphal and optimistic post-election South Africa.

Prior to the elections, I remember the prevailing mood among my fellow learners at St Alban's College. Now, St Alban's has been a mixed-race school from the 1980s, so it had a good mix of black and white learners and, as is typical of South Africa even today, most of the black kids were very aware of the political dynamics in the country, while most of the white kids were, at best, indifferent or were ignorant of what was happening around them. There were some young white friends of mine who would comment on the political situation at the time, but their sentiments (which you could see were inherited from their parents), were those of fear, apprehension, pessimism and 'doomsday prophecies'. As the tension increased before elections and we had daily reports of violence and death in the hostels around Gauteng because of fighting between Inkatha Freedom Party (IFP) supporters and those of the African National Congress (ANC), my white friends at St Alban's would talk of the civil war that they foresaw after elections. They spoke of the country completely collapsing and how they and their parents had prepared for this eventuality and were ready to leave, fly out into the sunset and leave us 'darkies' to fight among ourselves, as had so often happened in the 'postcolonial African state'.

These were, in Dickensian terms, 'the best of times and the worst of times': for someone like me who had grown up politically conscious, in a family that was steeped in politics, it was exciting, but for my fellow white learners it was all terror, doom and gloom.

Of course, history records that the elections went smoothly, the violence subsided, a Government of National Unity was formed and South Africa became the envy of the world, as the moment captured in Mandela's inaugural speech, part of which is quoted above, clearly encapsulates. So, none of the doomsday prophecies of my fellow white learners at St Alban's College in 1994 came true and South Africa proceeded to 'normalise' as we got about the business of building the 'desired nation' that Mandela spoke about. The post-election euphoria in 1994 was electrifying. The miracle of the negotiated settlement, the relatively peaceful elections and the uneventful transfer of power from the National Party to a Government of National Unity, led by the ANC, had stunned many people, not just abroad, but even within South Africa, who had expected a more negative, disastrous outcome.

I was 14 years old at that time, but almost 20 years later, I remember it as vividly as if it were yesterday. I remember the magic of the time, the belief within the nation that we could, indeed, be great, that nothing that we envisaged, hoped for, aspired to, dreamt of, was beyond our grasp. It was a time when, to quote from an old book of wisdom, 'all things were indeed possible'. We had crossed the Jordan River and were now on our way to Canaan, the Promised Land. The black majority was full of expectations: houses, jobs, quality education and improved lifestyles, while white South Africans were grateful that the black majority hadn't sought to avenge the years of subjugation and humiliation. Grateful that the 'new era' that was ushered in during Mandela's speech on the 10 May 1994, hadn't taken away their comfy, cushioned lifestyles, as they had presumptuously predicted. The 'miracle of Mandela' of the 'Rainbow Nation' had captivated everyone and there was a genuine belief on all sides that we were on our way to building a non-racial, just and equitable society that would be the envy of all of the people of the world.

In looking back at 20 years of democracy and analysing whether this democracy has, indeed, lived up to our aspirations, hopes and expectations, we have to remind ourselves of the magic of those early days, days when South Africa did stand tall among the nations of the world. We have to remind ourselves of how close this dream came to being stillborn. How sensible, visionary, astute leadership and cool, calm heads took the nation by the hand and led it through a time that could have been very tricky, that could have degenerated into chaos, bloodshed and yet another 'sad African story'. In that sense, we have been very successful as a nation. We managed to navigate our way through the toughest of times, where there was lots of uncertainty, anxiety, mistrust, doubt and hostility and came out 'on the other side' with our hopes, our dreams, our aspirations still intact. If anything, we came out on the other side, not necessarily unscathed as a nation, but our dreams and aspirations had been refuelled, re-energised and re-invigorated.

Given everything that we've been through over the past 20 years, it is easy to forget all this and just get caught up in the pessimism of our everyday struggles and day-to-day living, but it is incumbent upon us to remember those early days and get a true sense of what this nation can truly be, what it can achieve, that we can, indeed, scale the heights of the world and soar with the eagles, taking our place among the great nations of the world.

Rugby World Cup 1995: Mandela's Rainbow Nation
Speaking at the same occasion of his inauguration in 1994, President Mandela had this to say:

> We enter into a covenant that we shall build the society in which all South Africans, both black and white, will be able to walk tall, without any fear in their hearts, assured of their inalienable right to human dignity – a rainbow nation at peace with itself and the world.

The Rugby World Cup in South Africa in 1995 was one of those seminal moments in the life of this young nation, which those who experienced it will treasure forever. In racialised South Africa, almost everything is seen through the eyes of race. Even our sporting preferences are divided along racial lines. Football, a global sport loved by people of all colours and shades the world over, is seen predominantly as a 'black sport' as a result of our divided past. Rugby, alongside cricket, is seen as a 'white sport'. These are the types of crazy, typically South African anomalies that our racially divided past has bequeathed to us.

Although seen as white sports, I grew up playing cricket and rugby in our massive backyard back in Venda in the 1980s with my brother, who is a year younger than me. While other kids were kicking around a soccer ball in the streets, we played rugby and cricket, coming up with all kinds of innovative ways of playing each other in order to express our passion for these two sports that we both love. It was very unusual in a 'black area' like ours to find two youngsters kicking around a rugby ball or batting and bowling against each other in an intense, competitive cricket match, but, because our older brothers were attending a private school already in the 1980s and playing these sports at their school, we got to understand, love and appreciate these two sports at a young age. The other kids in the neighbourhood kicked a soccer ball around, completely fascinated by the sports we were playing, but they were unable to understand and participate because these were 'white sports'.

So the 1995 Rugby World Cup was a big moment for me and served up so many special moments that will live long in my memory. I remember that priceless moment in the very first match between South Africa and Australia at Newlands, when Springbok winger Pieter Hendriks rounded Wallaby legend David Campese and scored a try in the corner: South Africa went on to win the game. I remember that quarter-finals match against Samoa when Chester Williams scored four tries, a very powerful nation-building symbol at the time. In a country that was still trying to find its way to racial harmony and unity, the image of a coloured player scoring four tries for his country in a World Cup quarter-finals game was a powerful symbol of the 'desired South Africa', where people of all races, colours and creeds could become whatever they set their hearts on, with the right application, commitment and focus.

I remember the epic semi-final match between France and South Africa at a rain-soaked Kings Park Rugby Stadium – the tension of that final scrum with France right on our try-line and the sense of relief and euphoria when the referee blew his whistle and South Africa were confirmed as Rugby World Cup finalists at their first attempt on home soil. What joy, what hysteria. It was like we were all in a dream that we just didn't want to wake up from. There were so many iconic images, in an iconic game graced by *the* icon, the Rugby World Cup 1995 final at Ellis Park: those planes flying over the stadium before the game started; Joost van der Westhuizen's wonderful tackle on the man mountain that is Jonah Lomu who had run through (and over) all opponents with impunity; Joel Stranky's dropkick that won the match and the tournament for South Africa in extra time; and a packed Ellis Park, in unison, singing 'Shosholoza' like they'd been doing it all their lives. And, last but not least, two magic moments: President Nelson Mandela appearing to shake the players' hands before the game, wearing Springbok captain Francois Pienaar's number 6 jersey, and Francois Pienaar holding aloft the William Webb Ellis trophy, proclaiming, 'We did not have 63 000 fans behind us today; we had 43 million South Africans'.

What powerful, nation-building, unifying images these were. Rugby, the sport that symbolised and typified 'Afrikanerhood' and was one of the pillars of the 'Afrikaner Nationalism' that had taken the country down the evil path of apartheid, was now being used, in a new South Africa, to showcase to the world the 'Rainbow Nation' that Mandela and Desmond Tutu had spoken about. What a turnaround for the books! What a special, priceless moment in the life of this very young nation, this 'democratic project' built on the ideals of non-racialism and equality. Who will ever forget this?

For, once again, in that moment of triumph, we showed the world what a unified South Africa with no discrimination and one common goal could achieve. We stood again as giants, having temporarily overcome our demons, our divisions, our fears and our insecurities, to reveal to the world, the beauty of this 'Rainbow'. It was a poignant moment, a definitive event, one of the first shared triumphs of this newly unified South Africa, competing on a global stage.

The dream deferred

Despite these moments of great triumph, our unity, our bond as a nation, has been tested and found wanting on many an occasion over this 20-year period. One only has to read the comments of most of our newspaper articles online to realise how racially polarised and sensitised we still are as a nation. A few major scandals that have occurred over the years have tended to bring this racial tension almost to boiling point. A video of Afrikaner policemen unleashing a savage police dog on a terrified black man while laughing about it, which was seen throughout the nation, brought back images of apartheid to the black majority and threatened to unleash the dormant anger that they have seemingly suppressed for so long, but once again cool heads prevailed and the nation moved on. Farm workers are still being ill-treated by their white bosses and white farm bosses being murdered by their black workers. Afrikaner students at a university in the Free State made older black women, who do menial jobs at the university, drink their urine and laughed about it.

All of these and many other temporary crises have tended to raise the racial tempo within the country and expose the deep racial prejudices that still exist within too many of us as South Africans. But has the dream of a non-racial Rainbow Nation failed? Has the dream died at all, amid pressures to 'transform' South African society and redress the imbalances of the past?

The answer lies in that beautiful poem entitled *Harlem* by Langston Hughes.

Here's the point: the non-racial dream, like all other parts of the 'South African dream' (a better life for all, decent jobs for everyone, decent housing and living conditions) has been deferred/delayed, but not necessarily denied. Deferred dreams do not necessarily equate to denied dreams, so no, the dream hasn't died at all. It just requires greater effort, more sacrifice and costlier commitment from all of us. It requires more patience, and greater involvement in the nation-building project from everyone. Our dream is alive – it hasn't yet been exterminated. As we celebrate 20 years of freedom, it is incumbent upon us all to realise that what we do *with* this dream, what we do *for* this dream, will determine whether it dies a painful death or inspires us to greater heights as a nation. The dream of a Rainbow Nation is Tutu's dream, Mandela's dream, our dream as a people.

The poem *Hold Fast your Dreams,* by Louise Driscoll, is most poignant in this regard. So, please fellow South Africans, in celebrating 20 years of democracy, remind yourselves of the high moments, soberly reflect on the low points but in doing all this, hold fast your dream – the dream of a rainbow nation: the dream to build a society, 'in which all South Africans, both black and white, will be able to walk tall, without any fear in their hearts, assured of their inalienable right to human dignity – a Rainbow Nation at peace with itself and the world'. Remember how tall we walked in 1994? Remember what giants we were in 1995? Hold fast the memory; hold fast the dream. This is what it means to live in a democratic South Africa. This is what democracy means to us: to keep the dream alive and do everything within our powers to bring it to pass. It is on such a people, with such a resolve, that the 'sun shall truly never set', to steal from Mandela's final few words on that memorable day in May all of 20 years ago.

Still seeking the 'Promised Land': A Jewish perspective on free South Africa

David Saks

South African Jewish Board of Deputies

SOUTH AFRICA'S TRANSITION FROM white minority rule to multiracial democracy at the end of April 1994 actually began more than four years previously. On 2 February 1990, President FW de Klerk had launched the country on a dramatic new course with his announcement in Parliament that the 30-year-old ban on the African National Congress and other political organisations was being rescinded. This had been a true game changer, one that at a stroke ushered in a new era of negotiations that, for the first time, involved representatives of the entire population. Whatever the immediate future held, everyone at the time recognised that South Africa would never be the same again.

Reactions across the greater South African population naturally varied, from unrestrained jubilation on the one extreme through to baffled fury and fear, on the other. Within the Jewish community, the mood was generally one of cautious optimism – whatever direction events were destined to take, De Klerk's reforms were clearly a step in the right direction if any progress was to be made in resolving the country's mounting problems. However, from a Jewish perspective, the new era did not get off to the best of starts. Infuriated by the radical changes ushered in by De Klerk, white right-wingers countrywide launched a series of demonstrations, in the course of which there were anti-Semitic demonstrations, such as burning Israeli flags and blaming Jews in general for selling out the white race. The community then received a nasty jolt from the other side of the political spectrum, when the newly released Nelson Mandela was photographed warmly embracing Yasser Arafat, leader of the Palestine Liberation Organization (PLO).

At the time, the PLO was officially still very much committed to the destruction of the State of Israel and Arafat was popularly seen as being among the worst enemies of the Jewish people. Thus, the present seemed to threaten mounting anti-Semitism from right-wing extremists, while the prospect of black majority rule in the future suggested that the Jewish community's longstanding Zionist loyalties would, at the very least, come under significant pressure from the new regime.

Ultimately, the subsequent unfolding of events served to largely allay these concerns, albeit not completely. After that initial flare-up, right-wing anti-Semitism tended to manifest at a low level – in any case, blacks and communists were the bogeymen primarily on the radar of this disaffected sector of white society. The latter, as a political force at least, went into terminal decline after the 1994 elections, and the spectre of anti-Semitism from this quarter likewise ceased to be of serious concern to the Jewish community. Overall, the withering away of the right-wing threat (bar sporadic and easily contained incidents) has been one of the major positives of the post-1994 era. At the time, however, no one knew how far this shadowy constituency might go in its determination to reverse the course of history and cling on to its privileges.

So far as the Arafat incident went, Jews had to adapt to the new reality that the incoming new regime would be a great deal less friendly to the State of Israel than they would like, as well as the existence of deep-rooted support for the Palestinian cause within those circles. What served to reassure them was the ANC's firm recognition of the legitimacy of the State of Israel and of its right to exist within secure borders, this to be achieved through the creation of an independent Palestinian state coexisting alongside it. It further helped that South Africa's transition largely coincided with the launch of the Israeli–Palestinian peace process, through the signing of the 1993 Oslo Accords.

This held out the hope – sadly illusory, as things proved – that just as blacks and whites in South Africa were coming together to finally resolve the issues between them, so were Israelis and Palestinians doing likewise. Once the peace process collapsed into violence at the beginning of the new century, attitudes towards Israel correspondingly hardened within the ruling party, which, in turn, has led to a number of verbal spats between government and the Jewish leadership. Despite this, the Jewish community's traditionally strong Zionist loyalties have shown little sign of weakening, beyond the emergence from its ranks of a small number of dissidents who have involved themselves in anti-Israel activities.

Notwithstanding these early hiccups, the leadership of the major Jewish community organisations, in particular the South African Jewish Board of Deputies (SAJBD) and Chief Rabbi Cyril Harris, from the outset took a decision to actively identify itself with the transition process and to lead the Jewish community in doing likewise. In doing so, it was making a welcome break with its previous stance of political neutrality, for which its predecessors had been much criticised by more progressive members of the community. Whatever the failures of the past, it was recognised that the time had come to seize the moment and join with other South Africans in forging a new and, hopefully better, society for all. For this, attaining universal democratic rights was just the first step.

In large part, the decision of the Jewish leadership to become part of the transition process was driven by the need to allay the inevitable feelings of anxiety about the future that were rife among its constituents. Rather than remaining passive bystanders, with all the feeling of helplessness and irrelevance that this would engender, Jews were urged to become positive agents in their own destiny. The mere fact of becoming positively involved would act as a morale booster. Certainly, it would be an effective antidote to the mood of fatalism and helplessness that had exercised so baleful an influence during the apartheid era.

The previous decade had been a disastrous one for South Africa, with political violence, the continual erosion of civil rights and the rule of law under successive States of Emergency and a near-catastrophic economic downturn having seen an unprecedented rate of emigration by Jews and other sectors of the white population. During the early 1990s, while the last vestiges of apartheid were being swept away, violence and economic decline continued apace, leading to further emigration. Some indeed welcomed the dawn of a new era and sought to play a constructive role in bringing it about, but many others feared that the country's destiny was to become yet another authoritarian, dysfunctional failed state of the type so common in postcolonial Africa.

In the end, the triumphant success of South Africa's first-ever democratic, non-racial elections on 27 April 1994 confounded the doomsday predictions of the Afro-pessimists. Perhaps the

most miraculous aspect of the transition was not merely the fact
that the elections themselves went ahead so peacefully, but that
practically overnight the ruinous political violence that had wracked
the country prior to this, permanently ceased. This was followed
by what might be termed the 'Mandela honeymoon', a period of
general thankfulness and relief among whites and blacks alike that
their country's seemingly insurmountable problems had at last been
resolved and that all now were equal partners in building a better
society. The inspiring leadership of Nelson Mandela, who went
to extraordinary lengths to reassure the anxious white minority
that they need not fear a future under black majority rule, was a
significant factor in all of this.

Uplifting as the first elections and subsequent presidential
inauguration were, in practical terms the hard work really
commenced afterwards. The legacy of apartheid included enormous
gaps between black and white, both economic and educational. The
challenge now was to begin closing these gaps as quickly as possible.
During this time, individual Jewish business leaders became involved
to a striking extent with supporting outreach and upliftment
initiatives promoted by Mandela. Another Jewish businessman
and philanthropist, Bertie Lubner, was, with Chief Rabbi Harris,
responsible for the establishment of Tikkun (today Afrika Tikkun).
This was conceived as being a specifically Jewish-headed initiative
aimed at assisting South Africans previously disadvantaged under
apartheid and was very much inspired by Mandela's appeal to the
Jewish community to assist in this regard.

These initiatives initially met with some opposition in Jewish
circles; given the mounting financial pressures that Jewish welfare
institutions and other communal bodies were coming under, some
community members argued, in effect, that charity should begin
at home. Over time, however, it has come to be broadly accepted
that concrete actions, not just by government but by civil society
as a whole, are needed to put right the enduring harm wreaked
by apartheid. Today, a wide range of Jewish communal bodies,
including synagogues, Zionist organisations, youth movements and
schools, include social outreach on behalf of all South Africans as a
permanent component of their day-to-day activities.

At the SAJBD's national conference in 2011, Deputy President
Kgalema Motlanthe appealed to the Jewish community to bring to

bear its skills and resources to assist in the areas of job creation, education and skills development. The SAJBD responded by launching its Jubuntu project, which documented what Jewish organisations and individuals were doing in these areas and provided practical guidelines as to how the lessons learnt through these projects could be replicated and expanded upon by others working in the field.

Central to the nation-building process was the drafting of a new national Constitution, with a Bill of Rights that would safeguard the hard-won freedoms of the liberation struggle. Civil-society organisations were invited to give their input to this process, and the SAJBD, through its Constitution and Legislation Subcommittee, became much involved. In particular, the SAJBD emphasised the necessity of the right to freedom of expression being qualified as to exclude 'propaganda for war, the incitement of imminent violence or the advocacy of hatred based on race, ethnicity, gender or religion, and that constitutes incitement to cause harm'. This limitation was ultimately incorporated into the relevant clause in the Bill of Rights and is a crucial component of the legislation prohibiting what is regarded as 'hate speech' in South Africa. The SAJBD subsequently also gave important input into the Promotion of Equality and Prevention of Unfair Discrimination Act of 2000, likewise in the area of prohibiting certain forms of hate speech. It has had occasion to invoke these clauses on numerous occasions in the course of confronting anti-Semitic discourse in the public domain, including in the media and the political arena.

In various other areas of public policy, the Jewish community has, at the representative level, likewise sought to play a meaningful part in the formulation of public policy, the fostering of a robust human rights culture and identification with national symbols. Its representatives have been involved in a range of civil society initiatives, among these the Hate Crimes Working Group, the Right2Know Campaign and interfaith initiatives such as the annual Reconciliation Day Interfaith Walk in Cape Town. The countrywide attacks on foreign migrants that took place in the early part of 2008 elicited a swift response from the Jewish community, whose multifaceted relief efforts on behalf of the victims were coordinated by the SAJBD in Johannesburg, Cape Town and Durban.

The Jewish leadership has also tried to instil a greater identification with South African symbols and holidays. For example, in 2005 the SAJBD held a commemorative evening to celebrate the 50th anniversary of the Freedom Charter and the following year led a Jewish delegation to participate in the 30th anniversary of the 1976 Soweto Uprising. For the 2010 FIFA World Cup, it coordinated an ambitious 'Jewish 2010' project aimed at making Jewish visitors to the country feel welcome. Much more work needs to be done, however, before it can be said that the greater Jewish community genuinely identifies with the post-liberation national culture. In this respect, Jewish attitudes have, unfortunately, tended to mirror those of the larger white population of which they are a part.

Since 1990, a process of re-examining the mainstream community's political behaviour under apartheid and, specifically, its attitudes towards the anti-Jews who had been involved in the liberation struggle has been underway. This has taken the form of museum exhibits, academic symposia, panel discussions at national and regional conferences and numerous books and articles. The most recent event was a round-table discussion involving SAJBD president Zev Krengel and anti-apartheid veterans, Denis Goldberg, Albie Sachs and Anne-Marie Wolpe, held at the historic Liliesleaf heritage site in Rivonia. By no means have all community members been comfortable with all of this.

Veteran communal leader Solly Kessler had been one of the more progressive voices during the apartheid era but, on one occasion, felt compelled to warn against too much 'breast-beating and self-flagellation' over past events. Others asked why Jews should be continually excoriating themselves over their collective behaviour during the apartheid years when no other sector of the white population was doing likewise. It was further argued that Jews, as a traditionally persecuted minority who, in addition, had been targeted by anti-Semitic measures by the pre-1948 National Party, at least had something of an excuse to remain politically passive.

On the other side of the spectrum, former Jewish activists (few of whom, it must be noted, had ever been much involved in Jewish communal life) objected to what they saw as mainstream Jewry's claiming credit for what they had done to oppose apartheid now that it was fashionable to do so after having signally failed to support them at the time. Such individuals also tended to be far more critical of Israel and of the Zionist ideology in general, which has generated a fair amount of tension within the community.

South African Jews are passionate (to the point, perhaps, of obsessiveness) about recording their own history. Since 1994, a stream of popular and scholarly books has appeared, not only on Jewish involvement in the anti-apartheid struggle, but on such subjects as the legacy of Jewish life in the country districts and the development of Zionism and Judaism in South Africa. The same period saw the establishment of the South African Jewish Museum in Cape Town and the South African Holocaust Foundation, whose centres in Cape Town, Durban and Johannesburg now provide an important educational service in teaching schoolchildren and the public at large about the dangers of prejudice and the values of tolerance.

The mainstream religious leadership has also sought to become more involved in building a cohesive society in South Africa. Chief Rabbi Harris, whose dynamic leadership during the transition years saw him receive, among other things, the OBE shortly before his untimely death in 2005, continued to play a leading role in this regard. His successor, Chief Rabbi Dr Warren Goldstein, has been involved in high-level interfaith structures. Among other writings, he has authored a 'Bill of Responsibilities', which has been widely adopted within the various faith communities. Within the more strictly Orthodox sectors of the community, however, there has been a general turning inwards and focusing on specifically Jewish communal issues to the detriment of involvement in the wider society.

As the organisation mandated to protect the civil rights of South African Jewry, the SAJBD strenuously combats all instances of anti-Semitism. In this regard, such quasi-government institutions as the South African Human Rights Commission and Broadcasting Complaints Commission of South Africa have proven to be effective vehicles through which to address these issues. A very positive aspect of South Africa has also been the dramatically low rate of anti-Semitic incidents recorded annually, when compared with figures in other countries, among them Canada, Britain and Australia.

This is surely testimony to the strong anti-racist ethos that South Africans have succeeded in fostering post-1994 (although even prior to this it is fair to record that for many years, anti-Semitic sentiment had rarely translated into actual acts of hostility against Jews). It is likewise important that South Africa has adopted a 'unity in diversity' approach to nationhood rather than following a melting-pot model in which all ethnic, religious, linguistic and cultural differences are subsumed. One of the vehicles aimed at protecting and promoting different forms of group identity is the Cultural, Religious and Linguistic Commission, set up in terms of the new Constitution in 2002. Former SAJBD President Marlene Bethlehem was appointed by President Mbeki to serve as one of the first deputy chairpersons of this body, and she has continued to be active as an ordinary commissioner since the conclusion of her term of office. Overall, it can certainly be said that the prevailing culture of respecting diversity has played a role in discouraging prejudice against Jews and other minority groups.

The fact that anti-Semitism levels have been comparatively low in South Africa does not mean that serious cases of anti-Jewish behaviour have been entirely absent. Over the past two decades, there have indeed been a number of such incidents, all triggered by events taking place internationally. During the late 1990s, Jewish institutions were among those targeted in the spate of terrorist bombings carried out in Cape Town by suspected Islamist militants. In mid-1997, a Jewish bookshop was firebombed because a Jewish woman in Israel had displayed an offensive image of the prophet Mohammed and, the following year, the Wynberg synagogue was bombed immediately after a US bombing raid on Iraq. Since the beginning of the century, fortunately, attacks on Jewish installations, when they do occur, have taken more innocuous forms, such as the daubing of offensive graffiti. Jewish cemeteries, particularly in the country areas, are frequently vandalised, although in most cases casual vagrancy or juvenile delinquency rather than anti-Semitic motives have been the probable cause.

Following the collapse of the Israeli–Palestinian peace process in September 2000, anti-Israel rhetoric has frequently crossed over into offensive and sometimes inflammatory rhetoric about Jews in general and South African Jews in particular. This has occurred primarily during times of conflict between Israel and its neighbours, such as during the 2006 war against Hezbollah in Lebanon and the three-week war against Hamas and other Islamist groupings in Gaza at the end of 2008. The latter period saw anti-Semitism in the country reach levels not seen since the 1940s.

In January 2009, Deputy Minister of International Relations Fatima Hajaig caused an international storm when she said (to enthusiastic cheers) at a Lenasia protest rally that the Western powers were being controlled by Jewish money power, hence their failure to come to the rescue of the Palestinians. Hajaig was subsequently censured by the Cabinet and compelled to apologise by Acting President Kgalema Motlanthe. That same year, the South African Human Rights Commission upheld a complaint by the SAJBD of anti-Semitic hate speech against Cosatu's international relations spokesperson, Bongani Masuku.

If it has been necessary to sometimes adopt a confrontational stance when Jewish civil rights are threatened, the Jewish leadership has nevertheless remained committed to participating in the nation-building process, whether in the constitutional, socio-economic, political or civil society arenas. Indeed, it is recognised that such participation helps to build bridges of friendship and understanding that make the upholding of Jewish civil liberties that much easier.

Running counter to this, however, has been a persistent strain of negativity within Jewish circles, which, in turn, is reflective of common attitudes within the white population in general. The extent to which the upsurge in violent crime has undermined the community's faith in the future can never be over-stated. Alongside this must go the enduring concerns, common to the population at large, over declining public services, high level and now ubiquitous corruption and, for minority groups at least, dissatisfaction over affirmative action-related policies and a general sense of being marginalised by the majority black population. Notably, whereas there were at least nine MPs of Jewish descent in the 1994 House of Assembly (one of whom, Tony Leon, served as Leader of the Opposition in the years 1999–2007), today only one remains, indicating how traditionally high levels of Jewish involvement in the political life of South Africa have become a thing of the past.

With the strong perception that public services are in decline, one of the main pre-1994 fears and one that has regrettably been largely borne out, the Jewish community has gone about developing its own parallel institutions, including security, schooling, social services and medical assistance. While this has somewhat absolved responsibility from the state, it has placed great financial strain on the community.

The sustainability of Jewish communal institutions remains a continued source of concern, and the problem will become all the more pressing should there be a renewed upsurge in emigration. Fortunately, rationalisation strategies, enabling organisations to share resources to avoid a costly duplication of services, have been successfully implemented in all the main Jewish population centres. For example, welfare in Johannesburg now falls under the umbrella of the Johannesburg Jewish Helping Hand and Burial Society (Chevra Kadisha).

The fact that the great majority of Jewish school-going children attend Jewish day schools does have its downside. Apart from the inevitable financial strain it entails, it also serves to keep young Jews apart from their peers until university. To address this problem, Jewish educators have sought to partner with non-Jewish schools, both at the social and social outreach levels. A particularly successful initiative has been the annual Cycalive, whereby learners from Torah Academy join with those from other Gauteng schools in cycling from Johannesburg to Durban as a fundraising and friendship-building exercise.

On the threshold of the 1994 elections, it was estimated that the Jewish population in South Africa had declined by nearly one-third over the previous two decades, and it continued to decline, even after 1994. In 1998, a survey of Jewish attitudes towards various aspects relating to South Africa was commissioned. Its results provided a sobering picture of a community whose members, and particularly its younger members, increasingly no longer saw a future for themselves in the country and either intended emigrating or were strongly considering doing so. In his address to the SAJBD on the occasion of its centenary conference in 2003, President Thabo Mbeki felt sufficiently concerned to draw attention to this and urged the community to rediscover its faith in South Africa.

In general, reports on the state of South African Jewry in international Jewish publications, backed by the undeniably depressing statistics of the time, adopted a lugubrious view of a community in crisis and on the verge of dissolution. That Jews were perceived to be giving up on the country and moving elsewhere also generated concern locally. A revealing (if somewhat 'politically incorrect') joke of around that time was that when the Jews started leaving, you knew that trouble was coming, when the Greeks did so, the trouble had already arrived, and when the Portuguese began leaving, it was too late already. Jews were thus represented as being, as it were, a weather-vane people whose collective antennae, sensitised by centuries of wandering and persecution, were at some level more in tune with the hidden historical forces shaping the destiny of their society.

In fact, by the time Mbeki made his speech, things were already beginning to change for the better for South African Jewry. There had been a noteworthy drop-off in emigration, which has continued to the present day to operate at more or less normal levels (with some immigration and returning émigrés offsetting those losses). An estimated 70 000 Jews remain in South Africa, of whom around two-thirds live in Johannesburg and most of the remainder in Cape Town, Durban and Pretoria. Added to this were the unexpected but very heartening results of a follow-up survey, conducted in 2005. This time around, a substantial majority of respondents said that they were either 'very likely' or 'likely' to remain in South Africa in the foreseeable future.

Added to this were the impressively high levels of involvement in Jewish communal, religious and cultural life, for which South African Jewry had always been renowned throughout the Diaspora and which, if anything, have only intensified. When this is seen alongside the gratifying extent to which Jews remain involved in the general affairs of the country, it can be said that for the Jewish community, the first 20 years of multiracial democracy in South Africa have been essentially good. Had those who were present during the democratic transition been able to look two decades ahead, one can say that, on the whole, few would have been disappointed by what the future showed them. It certainly helps that South Africans have faced up to and overcome far more daunting challenges than those that currently confront it.

At the beginning of 2014, South Africa remains a work in progress. No gains, democratic or otherwise, are permanent; they must be continually safeguarded and strengthened, and that, among other things, means responding effectively and forthrightly whenever the fragile system is abused. In a democracy, there is no room for sentimentality when it comes to dealing with misuses of power by those entrusted with authority. South African Jews, along with their fellow citizens, nevertheless, can take heart from the historical experience, which demonstrated both to themselves and the world at large, what people of such widely different backgrounds can achieve when they put their differences aside and work together for a common cause.

My miniskirt, my freedom

Matshepo Seedat
Observer of culture and social trends

NELSON MANDELA ONCE SAID, 'FOR to be free is not merely to cast off one's chain, but to live in a way that respects and enhances the freedom of others.' Through these words, Madiba taught us that while we strive for our own freedom, we need to remember that the freedom of others is also in our hands. I mean, how can I profess to be free when I am oppressing another?

Apartheid has demonstrated that oppressors are themselves oppressed, although not in the same way that the ones they oppress are. The oppressor turns out to be the more oppressed as their oppression is on their conscience.

It has been 20 years since the end of apartheid and the dawn of a democratic South Africa! So much has happened; there is so much to reflect on. I was way below the voting age when black South Africans were allowed to vote for the first time in 1994. I do remember, though, accompanying my mother to the voting station and seeing the longest queue I had ever seen in my young life. What captured me was a middle-aged man who collected tips from the voters as they stood in the queue. The voters were tipping him for his impersonation of Nelson Mandela.

He must have gone home a very wealthy man on that day. Everybody wanted to hear Mandela, that was who their vote was about. He had brought them hope and a voice through which they were waiting to express their wishes. Nelson Mandela – he was their door to freedom.

We looked to Madiba to bring us all that we were unable to have before our democratic dispensation. I didn't know what bondage and freedom was. All I knew was that, standing in that queue, not a single individual was complaining. All had waited all their lives to cast their vote and choose the government that would lead them.

I cast my very first vote five years later in the second democratic elections in 1999, my final year of school. I did so with the understanding that I would not have been in the Model C school I went to throughout high school had it not been for the ANC government – the government of Nelson Mandela. I would not have been able to speak English with a twang because I would have been forced to complete my curriculum in Afrikaans had it not been for the class of 1976 who stood up against Afrikaans as a medium of instruction in schools.

By now, I can say that my political consciousness has improved and that most of my adult life has been lived in political consciousness. That is how I know that I enjoy a range of freedoms. I have freedom to practice my religion. Under apartheid, religious activities were disrupted by apartheid forces and people were not free to practice their various faiths. I am free to marry outside of my racial group and not be in contravention of the Prohibition of Mixed Marriages Act. I am free to pen my thoughts on freedom because I have freedom of speech. I have neighbours from different racial groups, the pleasure of whose company I could not have enjoyed during apartheid and its Group Areas Act. All these freedoms are not to be taken for granted and I, for one, do not.

I have come to cherish freedom. However, freedom is quite complex. Freedom in the South African context, or any context, cannot be confined to what apartheid denied us. Freedom is a complex notion as it comes with responsibility. Freedom and responsibility go together and must always be juxtaposed against each other.

It is true that there are many different types of freedoms: freedom of expression, freedom of choice, freedom of association, and freedom of movement, to mention a few. For me, a freedom that I did not know I had been lacking is the freedom to express myself through what I wear. I was not aware that I had been denied this freedom until I experienced it in a different context, culture and geographical location.

Over the December holidays of 2012 my husband, two small children and I took a holiday to southeast Asia to Singapore. Packed in my suitcase were four pairs of denim jeans, knee-length cargo pants and a summer dress that reached well below my knees. With my South African mindset, I chose my clothing mindful of the fact that the entire trip would be travelled in different modes of public transport, such as trains, busses and subways.

While in Singapore I observed that shorts as well as short skirts and dresses were common. While travelling on the subway, I observed women going to work wearing shorts formally, while those at leisure dressed down their shorts. While shopping at the malls in Singapore, I observed how articles of clothing, be they dresses or skirts, were shorter than what I would normally find here in South Africa. This inspired me, as I was getting hot while seeing the many tourist attractions that Singapore has to offer either on foot or by public transport, to set about shopping for some appropriate tropical-weather clothing. I found a bright orange dress that measured six fingers above my knees. In South Africa, I would have considered this to be too short for a wife and mother of two to wear, considering I was travelling on public transport.

So, I put on my dress and off we went sightseeing to Sentosa Island. I walked half a kilometre, half expecting the treatment I would have got had I dressed like this on the streets of South Africa: disgusted stares, wolf-whistles, snide comments and scorn. To my absolute amazement, not a single person, male or female, gave me or my exposed legs a second look. Not even the gentlemen who lurked around the red light district. No one groped me or assaulted me for showing too much skin. I got on the subway and sat down while my dress went inches higher and the old Malay lady sitting next to me, wearing a long garment and head scarf didn't even look at me or my receding hem line. Not even when I returned to my hotel after the night safari at the Singapore Zoo around midnight along the streets packed with women of the night (and I fitted in perfectly with my petite, bright orange dress), did I get an unusual look. Getting back to the hotel I had my aha moment. I had just had the most liberating experience. I had walked the streets of Singapore and travelled on a bus and the subway in a miniskirt and the Earth had not shaken. I had worn my miniskirt because I was responding to the climate in Singapore, which is tropical, but not much hotter than South Africa.

This was strange, indeed, because I know what happens when I dare show a little skin in South Africa. I once ran a marathon wearing running shorts and then decided to go grocery shopping. I will never forget how two gentlemen dressed in overalls sniggered at me at the supermarket, saying, '*yini ngathi, ucabanga ukuthi ungumlungu?*' before telling me I would get raped if I walked around dressed like that. Infuriated, I turned and walked away towards my husband, needing to feel safe. This and other incidents, unsavoury looks, scoff and snide comments, to mention but a few responses, are the reasons I am comfortable in below-the-knee skirts. Whether for professional or leisure dress, it is the safest choice.

Having described my definition of freedom, I realise that freedom is not isolated from responsibility. I relate my experience with the full knowledge that in as much as I should be afforded the freedom to dress in a way that pleases me, I also have a responsibility to adhere to particular situations or places. Places of worship and workplaces, for example, have a prescribed dress code, which requires compliance. Therefore, when one has chosen to dress in a particular manner, it needs to be done with responsibility, firstly to oneself and then to the social environment in which one exists, but never with fear of intimidation or violence.

A freedom I believe I am denied in my beloved South Africa, I experienced in another country. With little personal experience of how life was before freedom, I had not been able to make a comparison of pre- and post-1994, but I could do so on one tropical summer day in a land far away from home. I must admit, nothing jolts you into reality like having a liberating experience when you least expect it.

That one can base their idea of freedom on a garment will sound strange to many, especially men, but the ability to walk the streets at whatever time, dressed in any manner one chooses, is a liberating experience. Freedom means different things to different people. For me, it means that nobody should misconstrue one's intentions and should understand that a miniskirt is a response to climate conditions, and that it is as much a fashion statement as a trench coat is, not a sexual statement!

However, in South Africa a miniskirt is not just a miniskirt, but an excuse for sexual violence against women. In South Africa, women are blamed for wearing miniskirts and claims are made that they are asking to be raped. I would argue that I am justified in believing that I should be able to enjoy the freedom to wear a miniskirt and take public transport.

Of all the freedoms that have come with democracy, many of which I personally enjoy, it is this one freedom that I yearn for. This is the freedom to express myself through my dress without any fear of abuse, sexual or otherwise.

I still grimace at the thought of the young Nwabisa Ngcukana being stripped and sexually molested at Noord taxi rank in 2008 for wearing a miniskirt. The young woman was not asking to be sexually assaulted, nobody ever does, even in the way they dress. This and similar examples reveal that South Africans are trapped in perceptions about dress that are outdated. Those who perpetuate such acts are not mindful of the rights and responsibilities of every individual. They easily forget that the South African Constitution guarantees the 'freedom and security of a person and the right to be free from all forms of violence from either public or private sources'. Every citizen has the right to make choices without fear of intimidation and violence.

The protest march led by talk show host Redi Tlhabi on 4 March 2008 against the violence that was suffered by Nwabisa Ngcukana reminded me of the brave women who marched to the Union Buildings in 1956 against the pass system. What would Sophie de Bruyn, Rahima Moosa, Helen Joseph, Lillian Ngoyi and many others say about this incident? Their cause may have been a different one but their pursuit was the same – they marched in pursuit of freedom. They took a bold step and today we can proudly say we have attained that freedom. I am certain that they would be proud that they have set a profound example and demonstrated to the following generations how to take a stand and make their voices heard. However, they would be pained by the thought that although South Africa is a free society, women are under threat from violence and rape and are not free to wear what they want.

Rape statistics prove that not only is rape prevalent but that the outrage and outcry of a nation have not been heeded by the rapists and would-be rapists. We as a nation carry the responsibility because we know the rapists – they are our fathers, brothers, uncles and sons. While South Africa battles violence against women, it is clear that we need to change the way in which South African men perceive women, and educate them about what constitutes violence towards women.

In the course of writing this I spoke to some men and asked for their opinion on miniskirts and their interpretation of this troublesome garment. The responses were varied. Some thought that religion is to be blamed for South African men's opinion of women wearing miniskirts, some blamed culture and others blamed a lack of education. I found one man's response interesting. He said that the length or shortness of a skirt depended on whether the woman was in Sandton City or at Noord taxi rank. My next question was: What is the difference between the people who are in Sandton and those who are at Noord? The immediate response was 'education'. Those who were not educated about women's rights were stuck in the past and did not accept this modern dress sense.

In the traditional sense, as women mature and become mothers they are required to cover up. This is the kind of practice that has made society unaccepting that a miniskirt is a kind of dress. More enlightened and more educated men were more accepting of miniskirts, if worn appropriately at the appropriate time and place.

According to the World Health Organization 2013 *Fact Sheet on Violence Against Women* in countries such as Tanzania, Bangladesh and Peru, the first sexual experience of many women in rural villages is forced. This report supports the notion that rural men are more prone to sexual violence than men in urban areas. This further bolsters the fact that cultural beliefs and a lack of education in men creates a lack of understanding of what sexual violence is. The report further explicates that one of the risk factors of being a victim of sexual violence is low education. Now that we know the root cause of sexual violence, we ought to be developing educational programmes on women's rights.

Singapore ranked 58 out of 128 countries on the 2013 Global Gender Gap Report. South Africa ranked higher, at 17 (www.weforum.org). Yet my experience in Singapore is in contrast to my experiences in South Africa. Singapore has gender disparities but their gender-based violence statistics are incomparable with South Africa's the most common violence reported against women is domestic violence.

In his article, posted on kunjalo.co.za, entitled 'Miniskirts are Fashion, Not Sexual Statements', Busani Ngcaweni asks, 'How do we build an understanding that miniskirts are fashion, and not sexual statements?' It is a question I ask today. How do we transform the mindset of the would-be rapist who insists, 'She is wearing a miniskirt so she is asking for it'? How do we bring an acceptance that women are not asking for anything by wearing a miniskirt but seek your respect.

Education is one of those aspects which define freedom for many.

Under apartheid, education was inferior for black people. While some might argue it has improved, it has still to reach its potential. If education is the missing ingredient in reducing violence against women, we have more work to do as a society. We need to educate and the education needs to start at a tender age. Parents have an enormous responsibility to teach their boy children that women deserve to be respected and protected so that they grow up with that knowledge. If we do not do that, we would have failed.

Showing flesh is a no-no at a taxi rank or in a rural village because people there still hold on to their deep cultural beliefs, which seek to portray women as sexual objects rather than equals in a society. Surely the Constitution is the supreme law of the country and any cultural beliefs and practices that are contrary to the Constitution should be abolished. This education should also include information about what the Constitution proclaims about the rights of women in a free and democratic society. School-based programmes to teach young people about sexual violence is a step to be explored.

To quote from the Australian ballroom dancing film *Strictly Ballroom,* 'A life lived in fear is a life half lived'. To live in fear means that we are denied a part of ourselves that makes us able to live wholly and to our full potential. It means that somebody has stolen a part of the freedom we are meant to enjoy. It means that our decisions are made based on what others believe to be correct, when, in fact, those beliefs are an infringement on somebody else's rights.

I can harp on about how much my freedom is taken away by those who I fear would assault me if I wore my miniskirt and expressed myself freely. But, as Nelson Mandela said, the people who are not free are also the abusers and the rapists. They have also not experienced freedom in its entirety because they are not living in a way that enhances the freedom of others.

As a result of the mentality of some men in our society, it is not only the women who are not free – both men and women have not come to the totality of their freedom. For men, it is most likely because they have not freed their minds and have not lived in a way that respects the cultural freedom of women. For women it is because they are not permitted to fully express themselves.

Twenty years down the line let us not have merely cast off the chains of apartheid, but let us live in a way that respects and enhances the freedom of women to wear their miniskirts.

The unrelenting spectre of ethnicity in South Africa

Jeffrey Mathethe Sehume

Trans-disciplinarily researcher

Introduction

Twenty years into democracy South Africa finds itself awkwardly navigating a path that seems unconducive to building national unity – as is the case in most of postcolonial Africa. Part of the reason for these countries' failure to realise the dream of progress and unity is the spectre of ethnicity, used in the past for convenient political ends, constricted economic gain and sectarian social identification. While this phenomenon is not unique to Africa, its pliability to exploitation for narrow interests, coupled with the failure of political leadership, has rendered the continent unable to overcome these hurdles; instead, it seems to be trapped by and defined in them.

What is the background to this circumstance?

Given that most multi-ethnic societies have developed mechanisms to surmount the challenges that accompany diversity, the nagging question remains: why does the continent look like it is defined by these challenges, which resulted in the Democratic Republic of Congo imbroglio and South Sudan impasse? Among the untold negative effects of this inability to manage ethnic diversity sustainably, one scarcely needs to mention the human lives lost and environmental destruction.

And given its privilege in witnessing the cumulative damage associated with ethnic politics and leadership lacuna on the continent, why does South Africa look set to replicate the undesirable routes that led to ethnic tension and conflict, instead of consciously mobilising projects aimed at forging national unity? One wonders if it has not fully embraced the vision and practice of building networks for ethnic cooperation that are ultimately necessary to spur shared growth and progress. Still, one would like to believe that the long-

391

fought for struggle for liberation from discriminatory ideas and acts was motivated by goals of eventually establishing a society that is appreciative of the benefits accruing from promoting non-racialism and non-ethnicism.

After all, such cognitive and material benefits were seen in South Africa during the early years of democratic rule, when a spirit of working together in trust was evident in newly deracialised workspaces and places of interaction. The crowning achievement of this zeitgeist came with the sporting triumphs symbolised by the national team lifting the Webb Ellis rugby trophy in 1995 and the local football team being crowned in the 1996 Africa Cup of Nations. During this period in our history, we seemed to tower above all expectations. There was none of the doom and destruction that was predicted when racial and ethnic groups were compelled to live and work together. It is to be recalled that in the same year of the country's first free elections in 1994, a mass genocide came to light in Rwanda. Such ethnic cleansing – where nearly a million people were slaughtered – magnified, on a much larger scale, other known inter-ethnic conflicts that have occurred in many countries, in the name of religion or politics.

What price is freedom?

Around this same period, the example of South Africa in negotiating its inherited past and navigating the difficult demands of its black and white social groups, served as a model to countries like Northern Ireland in how to craft reconciliation programmes. As a collective, we avoided the implosion and ethnic massacre predicted by naysayers on both the local and international scenes.

Yet, the South African national reconciliation project, espoused by the democracy's founding fathers – Madiba and Tutu – in the medium term, has proven not to be sustainable to weather the storms inflicted on its hull, especially since these storms carry the hopes of many for a better life for all. It can be reasonably said that the reconciliation project would have found supportive ground to flourish and been accepted by many if it had delivered beyond mere promises, a life that is not circumscribed mainly by poverty, unemployment and inequality. What then is responsible for this turn of events and is it inherent in the very make-up of every society with multiple social groups defined either by racial or ethnic affiliations?

How could we, by advantage of reflection, have avoided the storms confronting our Rainbow Nation ship and steered it in the direction of the nation's interests? Are there identifiable models gleaned from elsewhere that we could embrace in our aims to construct frameworks of cooperation across, within and beyond Babel towers of exclusivist ethnicity?

What is clear is that for South Africa to thrive and realise its ambitions, given that it was the last African country to gain independence even from internal colonial rule, it should and must have heeded lessons gathered from experience of the last 60 years of postcolonial self-rule. This is even more urgent because the country possesses both human and natural resources that can be harvested for shared gain by all inhabitants without regard for ethnic belonging, in relative contrast to some countries, where there is an ethnic mindset and leaders use politics for the economic advancement of certain ethnic groups. As it is known, such a mindset has the effect of reducing politics to a zero-sum game instead of encouraging a win-win situation. Moreover, such a mindset is short term in orientation, peddling to sins of incumbency that do not benefit the country and all citizens for the better in the long term. This is one of the major differences between, say, Western democracies – where the road to politics is monopolised by the wealthy – and the proverbial postcolonial country, where politics is a route to selective economic enrichment, without, in the process, considering the collective wellbeing.

Ethnicity and politics

Still, perhaps it was naïve not to anticipate the manner in which 'ethnicity', as a social category, would be used and exploited by certain interests, even if it was for narrow political and economic reasons. It reveals inexperience and unfamiliarity with the basic laws of politics not to anticipate that a rich conceptual and material resource like 'ethnicity' would be applied for shared national interests when there is much to mine for thin personal benefit.

Ethnicity and politics are familiar bedfellows, marshalled on many occasions before to leverage popular support, outwit enemies, secure a stake in the collective cake and commit bigoted acts of intolerance like Afro-xenophobia. Three decades into democracy, are South Africans guilty of perpetrating the misdeeds mentioned above?

If the answer is in the affirmative, why have they allowed themselves to fall into the trap, used to vivid perfection, first during the entire colonial enterprise, which culminated in slavery, and, second, in the primitive racial ideology that brought about apartheid?

If no, how do we account for the re-emergence of slim ethno-nationalist sentiments, whereby some people are wearing apparel emblazoned '100% Tsonga', and violence against so-called African foreigners is excused in the name of protecting what rightly belongs to the indigenous populations. The irony of African groups giving themselves the geographic descriptor 'indigenous populations' of southern Africa, is not lost on Africa's first world people, the Khoisan, whose initial inhabitation of these lands, long before any other social group, is abundantly documented in archaeological and physical evidence. At the same time, stating this historical fact is open to further misuse by sectarian sects who proclaim that this region was 'an empty land' – *terra nullius* – when the first European naval merchants landed on these shores.

It may be that ethnicity is a convenient descriptive category, employed to explain complex human traits not neatly bounded by conceptual boundaries that also neglect nuances that cannot be called, for example, culture, ideology or economics. In its fullest sense, ethnicity therefore has to reckon with potentialities inherent in every human being to be more than the sum of the total parts contained in the term. These other parts existing independently would allow a child born in post-1994 South Africa to easily identify with children born in different circumstances in different regions, classes and religions. A common denominator enabling these trans-boundary linkages could be technology, media access, and other empowering globalisation mechanisms that create virtual friends in social network platforms – friends known to each other by monikers and pseudo-identities that transcend race and ethnicity.

Then again, there is merit in the argument bandied about by cynics that ethnicity is the new race. A significance of such a possibility means ethnicity is now a concept and practice used to access positions of power, and with monopoly of the levers of power comes the political, economic and social dynamics of inclusion and exclusion.

One person's self-characterisation is value-laden towards specific results, just as much as such characterisation can lead to the othering of others deemed dissimilar, exotic, strange, or different in complexion or mental attributes. Popular stereotypes accorded to some ethnic groups in the country are an outcome of the fine play between according conceptual features and manners in the same breath as the practice of validation or prejudice would follow from these stereotypes. Examples of these stereotypes include, for instance, that Afrikaners are loyal to their *volk*; amaXhosa are educated tricksters; the English are insincere with their smiles; amaZulu are stubbornly proud, and Bapedi are entrepreneurial.

Another argument by those of a progressive bent would value the possibilities offered by the re-emergence of ethnicity in reclaiming identities maligned during colonial times and apartheid. To them, the country should be commended for avoiding the path that befell most countries whose only national representation revolves around ethnic skirmishes. In their case, the supposed tension among the 11 or so ethnicities reflects healthy evolution of multi-ethnic countries finding out what they are all about. The thinking goes that it is something to be expected in nations living in an interregnum or periods of interval between a niggling past, urgent present and deferred future.

International benchmarks

This may provide an explanation of how hugely populous countries like India, China and Indonesia have seemingly somehow managed to mobilise their assorted ethnic groups in a singular direction of shared common interests premised on shared values. China, for one, is notable for achieving the rare feat of launching the material upliftment of the lives of hundreds of millions of people, while simultaneously marshalling national unity – amid countless acts of social dissent – within its 56 ethnic groups, admittedly a speck minority within the dominant Han majority. Also, it would appear that an important variable available and relied upon in the Middle Kingdom, enabling the expression of national unity, is the achievement of the collective improvement of material conditions for many. An inability to realise this enables people to hijack projects geared towards national unity for sectarian ends or fosters an environment inimical to joint social cohesion.

There are three proposed factors behind this argument.

Consequences of unchecked ethnicity

First: The unrelenting spectre of ethnicity can be bothersome for South Africa since it threatens to derail the ambitious projects espoused in its key blueprints, namely the 1996 Constitution, part of whose Preamble says that 'South Africa belongs to all who live in it, united in our diversity', plus the 2012 National Development Plan (NDP), which echoes that 'South Africa belongs to all its peoples. We, the people, belong to one another. We live the rainbow.' To this extent, it remains a source of reassurance to notice the overwhelming support across ideological lines for these two living documents of our post-1994 society. Their spirit and praxis is embedded in instituting an attainable future that almost all can share in.

To be sure, there is much to celebrate in overcoming the legacy of centuries-old colonialism by improving, in a short period, the lives of many. Still, it is not inconceivable for these notable gains to be undercut by perceptions that the country has not radically transformed from the poverty, unemployment and inequality much evident in the pre-1994 era. In response to the bonhomie greeting the announcement of the 2013 matriculation results, the education commentator, Jonathan Jansen, ruffled many feathers in his 5 January 2014 *Sunday Times* article when he stated, 'if you removed the top 20% of schools – mainly former white, privileged schools – from the national averages, then a very dark picture emerges of a mainly black and poor school system performing far below what the combined results show (of a 78% national pass rate)'. Since this racial dichotomy is similarly replicated in other sectors, such as the economy, healthcare, access to basic technology and learning infrastructure, it is rather understandable when comparisons are established between the pre- and post-1994 periods.

In cases where racial or ethnic dimensions are expressed in material conditions, some have said these marginal conditions benefit the status quo of those in political and economic power. On the rest of the continent, the maintenance of the dependent condition of the poor has served the elites well. Precedent is highlighted by the very motif used during apartheid to establish the Bantustan system of social engineering, with different privileges given to black and white people and selected strata of the black communities to the exclusion of others. This divide-and-rule method worked well until it was no longer viable in terms of politics or economics. Consequences of the homeland structure are plain in 2014 in the unresolved land question, uneven infrastructure maintenance culminating in service delivery protests, and in the fibre of ethnicised discourse crudely symbolised in the belief that the current ruling clique articulates a transition from Xhosa to Zulu, which will culminate in the Venda ascendance.

Second: The insistent spectre of ethnicity should be a worry since it speaks to a self-destructive prophesy made famous in the May 2000 issue of *The Economist*, about the continent and its people being 'hopeless' to rise above their inherited colonial circumstances to triumph as, for example, Far Asian countries managed to do after World War II.

Learning from others

What guarantees can be offered that South Africa can circumvent the structural challenges associated with its multi-ethnic make-up that are hobbling the development prospects of South Sudan, post-Gaddafi Libya and northern Mali, and creating religious-cum-ethnic conflicts in Nigeria and free-for-all looting in the Democratic Republic of Congo? The calculus of ethnic balancing is important in separating those countries advancing to higher trajectories, in spite of their ethnic challenges, from those that are mired in ethnic battles. Good management of ethnic or tribal belonging creates the conditions necessary for building national unity, which is indispensable to permitting people to think, dream and realise success, not in terms of ethnic or tribal identity but as travellers sharing the same boat.

This delicate ethnic calculus was raised in the 1940s by the brilliant scholar, Geoffrey Cronjé, in his overlooked paper, *Afrika sonder die Asiaat* ('Africa without the Asian'). This paper is especially interesting given the debate currently raging in KwaZulu-Natal around the obvious economic contributions to the province of the Indian communities and the rights of the African black majority to profit from transformation projects initiated by both government and industry. Of course, such a debate is implicated in tussles experienced wherever people from different social groups compete for shrinking material resources, compounded by expanding and urbanising populations and external global financial pressures on local economies. However, what is unfortunate is the crude tribalist turn this debate has taken in the wilful neglect of South Africa's history of ethnic-based dispossession, political opportunism and ethnic economic exploitation. The noted commentator, David Welsh, writing in the *The Rise and Fall of Apartheid* (2010), warns against ignoring this history of 'the politics of ethnic outbidding'.

Why should our country heed the lessons from postcolonial Africa's ethnic scuffles and be mindful of our heritage of identity politics? As a geographic entity, our country has come a long way from the days when it was conceived as largely a multinational ethnic society and its laws were oriented towards supporting this. In later years, during the height of resistance against apartheid and with the introduction of the tricameral Parliament in the early 1980s, much progress was made within the assorted liberation movements to conceive the country as more than 'four nations'.

While it is undeniable that in key sectors, such as educational and economic opportunities, South Africa remains a country of two unequal nations, as the recent matric results and various General Household surveys reveal, some progress has been made towards constructing an edifice of one nation, unified in its diversity, as the NDP elaborates. Failure to address the material conditions for the many who, for example, are still battling to access clean, drinkable water, would spell doom for the political, economic and social foundations for the collective acceptance of the NDP as a living document that should be responsive to changing circumstances while, nevertheless, retaining its essence.

What should be a basis for making the NDP tangible for people, given the many challenges remaining in South Africa in the 21st century? Firstly, there has to be acknowledgement of the facticity of our past, present and future history. To borrow liberally from theorist Ambalavaner Sivanandan, one cannot get rid of the spectre of ethnicity by avoiding recognising the very concept of ethnicity. There is no doubt that ethnicity is a comforting instrument for people's definitions as individuals and a collective, particularly in a globalised world where the dominant identifications revolve around commodities such as Facebook, iPads, Coca-Cola and McDonald's, in contrast to the marginal status found in identification with homegrown heroes and heroines, such as the great sculptor Jackson Hlungwani and the poet Sol Tshekiso Plaatje.

Third: The baggage and fortune of our inherited racial, class and ethnic identities will cease to matter much when basic welfare services and conditions for economic growth are put in place by responsible stakeholders. This is an abiding lesson from China, which has more than 50 ethnic groups, where the lives of more than 600 million people were lifted from poverty. In other words, where water, education, employment and security are provided equitably, and opportunities for individuals and groups are available without discrimination, the resort to chauvinistic identities no longer matters in public discourse, even though it will inevitably remain in private realms of the family. As Sivanandan says[*], 'practice defines the terminology, not terminology the practice'. One does not have to be a Marxist to welcome this perspective. As Pope Francis asked in his papal exhortation, 'How can it be that it is not a news item when an elderly homeless person dies of exposure, but it is news when the stock market loses two points? This is a case of exclusion.'

Conclusion

There can be no doubt that the NDP's vision of forging non-discriminatory practices is within grasp if all organs of society, such as the media and schools – as the most powerful organs for transmission of values and positive meanings – have to reconnect with the idea of nation-building made famous by the late editor of the *Sowetan*, Aggrey Klaaste. The media are central here in that they 'provide the materials out of which many people construct their sense of class, of ethnicity and race, of nationality, of sexuality, of us and them'.[†] Surely, the news media's propensity for exposing corruption and maladministration is not the only reason for its existence.

Most nations that aspire towards and achieve their goals are motivated at heart by the promotion of good stories that serve as an inspiration to others, such as the recent exposure of two young wunderkinds – inventor Siyabulela Xusa from Harvard and the youngest medical graduate from the University of KwaZulu-Natal, Sandile Khubeka, who completed his MBChB degree at just 20. Harping on about negative stories betrays something of a self-hate mentality that produces nothing but cynicism, apathy and a collective inferiority complex, highlighted for the entire world to witness at Madiba's memorial last year.

---

[*] *Frank Talk* 1(5). 1984.
[†] Hall, Stuart et al. 1980. *Culture, Media Language*. London: Hutchinson.

Practical national unity has simple elements. In *An Ordinary Country: Issues in the Transition from Apartheid to Democracy in South Africa* (2002), Neville Alexander counsels that such unity begins with every South African endeavouring to know more than two local languages. It is also important to accept the local and global identities that one has to negotiate on a daily basis, and accept difference as a human reality without explicit discrimination.

Democracy: The double-edged sword

Nono Simelela
Clinician and global expert on reproductive health

Introduction

As I pondered this essay before I even typed one word, it became clear to me that I had taken on something much bigger than I had originally thought – that it was going to be impossible to write about democracy as a concept; that this was going to be the story of my life. I did not want to step back from the challenge and embraced this opportunity to take stock, introspect and look back at my life and the forces that have shaped and continue to shape me. I feel humbled by the fact that I have been given such an elegant way of finally moving the dialogues from my head to an essay that will hopefully liberate me and tempt many more to shun fear and embrace life – not life in general but their own lives, warts and all.

This realisation is a product of democracy: I can write without fear that someone will detain me and lock me up for expressing my ideas. Before democracy people got shot for speaking out!

Sadly, the status quo has not changed and we are still polarised, no longer according to our colour but according to our political affiliations. Anyone who dares speak out against those in power pays a price – a price determined by what you have said and how your statements impact on the popularity of those in power. How sad that one moment we celebrate democracy and the next some are silenced, isolated and demonised for speaking out. What does our democracy mean in the here and now?

Democracy has given me back my birthright – the power to choose who to become.

It is quite likely that common threads will run through this collection, yet I know not what these common threads will be. Will the stories convey sadness, loss and regret? I am willing to bet that the readers will be inspired.

As I reflected on this, my anxiety was slowly replaced by anticipation. I look forward to reading what others have contributed and, perhaps, through this effort, strangers could become friends and perhaps a common vision might emerge, one that will hopefully ignite a flame of love for ourselves as a people and for our common humanity.

What I do know for sure is that as a woman, my story will resonate with many others and I dare to propose that pain will emerge as a common thread but that, in the final analysis, hope will triumph. I say this because life has taught me that I can define myself however I want, and live up to that definition. I love that about being mature: Ha ha! Although I have not even started my story, as I've said, I know that all the stories by women will have a common thread running through them irrespective of their backgrounds or experiences. The common thread is the fact that the story of women's lives is one of pain. Each of us has experienced some kind of pain. There is no hierarchy in pain, hence I assert that all women have suffered in one way or another. Democracy remains an unfinished story.

I was born at Bridgeman Memorial City, which has now become Garden City Clinic. My parents lived in Sophiatown in a one-roomed house they rented from an Indian landlord in 1958. My mum worked as a nurse at the Munities TB Hospital just off the Jukskei River. My mother's family was originally from Greylingstad and the tradition back then was that family supported one another so those who could make a better living closer to the city often provided support for other family members; the circles of support could extend well beyond the nuclear family.

Being the first of three children means I was a source of great joy for my parents. Back then, marriage was a solid institution with many positive aspects. My mum tells of how her return from hospital with a new baby girl elicited a unique and special reaction from my dad: 'Her name is Princess – she is my princess!' This statement marked the beginning of a relationship that I can barely describe: fiercely protective, profound and filled with a sustained love – the best a dad can give and be for his daughter. My dad also expected a lot from his Princess and, upon reflection, the force emanating from this name shaped me as my life unfolded. He set a tone for my life back then, as he sometimes does now, except that now I write my own script, choose my own cast and act when I want to. I am quite happy to have no royal blood in my veins. I can make things up as I go.

My arrival prompted a short relocation to Natalspruit, where I lived with my maternal grandma. The tiny room in Sophiatown had damp and my parents were worried that these unhealthy living conditions would affect my health adversely. My dad prioritised my wellbeing above everything, even if it meant staying with his in-laws, something that could be considered to be unmanly. This firm principle was sustained years later when I had my own son, Thabi. My husband lived in Tembisa, where the bucket latrine system was used. My father argued that this was not the best place to bring up his first and only grandchild and he refused to allow my husband to take us home to Tembisa, as was traditionally expected. He firmly stood his ground and insisted we stay with them, 'Until you improve the living conditions in Tembisa'.

My parents sent me to a convent school for girls in the previous Bantustan of Bophuthatswana. I was not yet five years old, skinny and mischievous. As the youngest learner in the first grade, I received a lot of attention from my teachers, who were all matronly nuns whose life purpose it was to make sure we all got an education but, more importantly, that we became staunch Christians. The school, its ethos and everything Catholic about it had a profound influence on my view of the world back then and I have spent a huge part of my life expunging some of the dogma that was drummed into me. I think I have succeeded through the help of many patient souls: friends and therapists. I have unlearnt a lot, maybe too much, but what I know for sure is that it cannot be normal to separate boys and girls at such a formative age. Young people must be taught how to interact and live together in harmony from a tender age. Single-sex schools must be banned! I am sure there will be many whose views differ. But I earned the right to have this opinion and I state it without prejudice. I own the narrative!

Preparing for life

The education I received from the school was something else though – it was to become my passport to a life that was full of opportunities. Let me not get ahead of myself. What I remember and embrace is the discipline that was instilled in us, the commitment to do our best and to strive against all odds to do as well as possible in all our subjects. In this school, the teachers identified one's strengths and helped one become better; they instilled a sense of responsibility that enabled me to survive the worst times in my life. When you are down it helps to remember that there was a point in your life when you were the best. The fact that they were all nuns and that I never got to see their hair at all in the seven years I spent in their company is something I reflected on only much later.

It was only in my last two years of high school that I met and was taught by a male teacher – a charming young soldier from the South African Army who taught us mathematics. This was a scarce skill and the nuns from Ireland could not find one of their own to teach it to us. The soldier did a great job despite the fact that his uniform distracted us. He also played the guitar on weekends and most of us never realised he was white.

Boarding school meant going home twice a year. I missed being home in Rockville and later Meadowlands. In Rockville my family lived in the Zulu section and I had to walk long distances to visit my Sotho friends on the other side of the township. Separation was a ploy to divide-and-rule but this was lost to us. As kids we found the walks exciting – something to look forward to. We dressed up and made our way across the township. Can you imagine? A group of pretty young girls, singing and laughing and feeling free in the township? Who can do that these days? Our children have freedom and yet they remain caged behind high fences and so do we. We hardly know our neighbours. Worse still, if they happen to be from another African country, we don't even greet them. This is how free we are.

That my school was in a Bantustan did not matter to me at the time. I was too busy striving to get good grades to qualify for a scholarship and did not pay attention to the politics outside the safe boundaries of my school. Of course, the fact that outside the school I was unable to exercise my right to walk freely or shop in the same shops as white people, and that Africans had to stand in different queues, irritated and subconsciously bothered me. I once asked my father if the pocket money he gave me was different from what white children got. When he asked why, I said I wondered why I had to stand in a different queue to pay for the same things. I started to believe that perhaps blacks emitted an odour that only whites could smell and that this must be so unbearable to them that we just had to be separated. I made my mind up then to study biology and medicine to figure out what was different.

I have many great memories of my childhood. I stayed with my grandfather in the village next to the school during holidays, so I learnt how to herd cows, sheep and goats. I could run barefoot with my nephews, chasing anything on four legs. I slept under the skies, listening to the jackals and hyenas. I learnt how to sweep a kraal, use cow dung to make the floor smooth and climbed the mulberry tree to hide from my grandmother. My grandfather was a pastor of the Methodist Church and prayer was central in my upbringing. At home, my father also made sure we said a prayer as a family every evening before bed.

My father studied in Kilnerton and later at the University of Fort Hare, where he earned his degree. He was and remains a towering figure in my life – a man of immense knowledge who loved to teach. He was quick with his hands as well and a slap across the face was not confined to children; teachers who were in his employ also tasted some of his slaps. I don't think his attitude would have led students to toyi-toyi or teachers to abandon teaching and protest his 'unique' approach to discipline because they 'understood' that his focus was on producing good results, first-class students and people who were disciplined. I also often laboured under his intense discipline.

I was comforted by the warm words shared by many when he finally passed on. People from near and far, many of them products of his teaching skills and many more who had become leaders in their own right paid tribute to him at his funeral. His nickname was Caesar – his love for literature was too great to quantify. My dad made sure I achieved – between him and the nuns, there was no room for mediocrity. My siblings and I often reminisce about having to recite Shakespeare, sometimes having to repeat the same passage dozens of times until Tata was satisfied. Good times, hard times!

What has all this to do with democracy, you may ask. I suppose, what underlies this story is the fabric that underlies the lives of many young people who grew up in the apartheid era. Those of us who found solace in family did not experience the high levels of violence and social disintegration that has become so common in South Africa today. So what has democracy bought us? Or should I ask, what price have we paid for this democracy, this freedom we talk so proudly about? Well, I am not sure if we are free at all, free from want, free to walk anywhere we want without fear of being attacked, raped or killed. While I was denied the freedom to walk where I pleased by the apartheid regime, I am still not free to do this now, even though I claim to live in a democratic country.

As a young woman, I was shaped by many forces – religion, family, beliefs, culture, friends and the politics of our time. I developed a keen awareness of the political dispensation and its full impact, like many other women. The desire to pursue a career in medicine was further cemented by a horrible experience I had close to the end of my boarding school days. One day I got food poisoning. I dare not attribute this to the food that we were given at my new boarding school in Taung, another nun-controlled place with its good, bad and ugly stories. I was lying weak and dehydrated on a stretcher in the local hospital, which was also under the management of Catholics. Despite my condition, I noticed that there were a lot of people sitting under the trees near the casualty area, waiting to be seen.

A white, male doctor was attending to these poor people, many of them elderly. The doctor asked each of them to 'breathe in and out' as if he were listening to their lungs, but his stethoscope was not in his ears – it hung on his shoulders as he moved from one patient to the next. He kept making notes in the files. What was he writing? He was not examining these people. How could he, with his stethoscope hanging around his neck? Oh my God, he did not give a damn about these poor people! He was just prescribing without actually doing anything. I felt sicker than I already was. My resolve to become a doctor was cemented on that day. I felt helpless then but I don't feel so today, thank goodness. I have often thanked that uncaring man – he does not deserve to be called a doctor – who pushed me to achieve. I hope he died a happy person!

Sadly, there are too many horror stories about our current health system, if I am indeed objective and passionate. How different are the experiences of those who have lost loved ones as a result of a failing health system from those of the elderly people I saw many years ago being denied proper healthcare? Where is our democracy? What has it brought for our people when they are ill? It is a tough issue to confront and yet it is a reality, 20 years after we earned our democracy.

Fast track my life to varsity, where a different kind of force took shape and a new chapter and struggle began. By the time I hit university in 1976, the country was on fire. I was enrolled at Fort

Hare for my first year of study towards a medical degree and before year-end, we were sent home as we had protested the brutal murder of Steve Biko. Life was fast and too full, and coping was a challenge. Coming from a protected, regimented life, where everything was a sin unless the nuns said it was not, I was faced with too many issues. I was on fast-forward, free fall, with no limits. I had to stop and check myself and, whoa, life was just too demanding.

The predominant narrative was survival and maintaining my focus on my studies. Not being connected too closely with those driving protests, I was indirectly fighting my own struggle. I had been denied entry to the only medical school and I was determined to get there against all odds. I took extra classes and even though I was not from a 'poor' family, I worked during the holidays and made sure I got ahead of the lectures as we had lost so much time when we were suspended by the authorities during the numerous strikes that had dominated my first year.

The death of Biko propelled our struggle to another level. In my own tiny world, I fought domination by men, by the system, by others who found me different. The school and the nuns had not prepared me for the real world. 'Being clever' was not enough – I had to be streetwise. Family life was also in a state of 'change' – in many ways we were disintegrating from without and from within. My dad was struggling with the aftermath of the 1976 uprisings. Schools were no longer the same; discipline was not easy to enforce and students had turned into activists. Learning now meant something else. People like my dad had to find ways of maintaining their vision of producing educated activists, but this was too complex. Other more powerful forces were at play.

I watched my dad lose his passion for teaching, mainly because he was much older and his health was starting to fail, and going to work meant facing empty classes as students continued to focus on fighting the regime. Events moved fast and my dad resigned and rapidly lost his zest for life. A part of me slowly died with him but my determination to pursue my dream was fierce. Now I had another reason to fight and win: I had to trounce and beat the system, to validate my father, to honour his efforts and his life's commitment. I was not only determined to make it but I was going to make sure he was alive to attend my graduation as a medical doctor – and he was!

At this stage of my life, even as I was slowly but surely making headway in my career, I had to grow up very quickly and unlearn dogma. Engaging on a day-to-day basis with men for the first time at varsity was very difficult. There was a complex interplay of power, lies, cheating and all the things that constituted 'sin' during your formative years. Relationships and sex were taboo subjects in our household, so my mentors became my university friends, who were a risk-taking bunch from all walks of life. I learnt very quickly that reading Mills & Boon was not exactly the most appropriate life-skills programme. Life was full of young men who were all out to experiment with anything that wore a skirt and had boobs!

Not all was doom and gloom though because some of the guys had attended boys-only institutions and were also a bit naïve when it came to the opposite sex. So, there were many first times on both sides. This would have been easier to handle if much of the fumbling had not brought with it unacceptable levels of abuse, cheating, lying and all manner of unpalatable behaviour, which seems to have escalated to very high levels in this country earning us the title of the world's most violent society. We can spend time arguing about how experts arrive at this conclusion but the fact is, women in this country are abused on a huge scale. Did we set enabling conditions by not fighting back? Did we just accept our fate and collude in the silence that became entrenched and institutionalised in our communities?

I have since educated myself through reading about the lives of women who led the struggle for our democracy and, sadly, I have recognised that they often paid the ultimate prize as women in the struggle – they paid for favours with their bodies. A question we have to confront is, how has such a destructive force been allowed to grow unchecked? The same stories that were told back then are still part of our narrative: girls abused and raped for wearing miniskirts; toddlers raped and condoms shoved into their tiny vaginas; babies raped until their bowels spill out to rid some man of HIV – a myth no one can find in any history books! What a price to pay for *democracy*! Can we celebrate democracy when our narrative is punctuated by such gross and horrendous violations – especially the murder of innocent babies? How different are we from the Syrias of this world? Do we need to line up the bodies of all the children who have been murdered since the dawn of democracy on a slab, count and compare and declare ourselves better than countries like Syria? Where is democracy? Can it save us from ourselves?

In the context of the above, my own life seems tame and safe. My own struggles were, however, real to me and the forces referred to earlier continued to pull, shape, break, make and toss me about. For reasons I cannot fathom now, I had a picture of my ideal partner in my head. Of course, I learnt the hard way that such a creature has yet to be born. In my misguided idealism, I am sure that I lost many opportunities or maybe saved myself more angst – one has to live with one's decisions. I learnt very early on that regret is a total waste of emotional space and time. Whenever something goes horribly wrong I just pick myself up, often with the help of family and friends, and embrace life.

This part of my life is the most difficult to reflect on because it is personal and brings the lives of others into some scrutiny. The most challenging part of being a grown-up, educated and so-called accomplished woman at a tender age can be a recipe for success and/ or a spiral down to the darkest abyss of life. As a young woman, I made some of my most important decisions from a position of fighting 'dominion'. I rebelled in my own way against what my father, in particular, had defined as an ideal partner for me: he had to be educated, come from a 'good family' (I'm still not sure what that means) and be from the same class as me.

Tales of adulthood

Being rebellious and wanting to settle a score with my dad for my strict upbringing, I exercised my democratic right to choose whomever I wanted. I went for someone who did not meet any of those criteria and, in the words of Khalil Gibran, love burnt and shaped me, wounding me deeply and softening me at the same time, alas. Not that all was bad from the outset, but when you build a life on a foundation without common values, aspirations and ideals, there is nothing to hold the centre together. Anyway, the forces that influence and drive our lives took centrestage. Suddenly I was faced with the feelings of 'differentness' alluded to earlier. I am Xhosa and my late partner was from a Tsonga/Pedi background. I did what I could as a 'child bride' (I was 23 when I got married), but I failed spectacularly. Firstly, being an educated woman was a sore point: in spite of working long hours at the hospital, I was still expected to do what a *makoti* does – the washing and all that. This meant that some days I started work without having had any sleep at all.

This was a sophisticated kind of bondage and I bore the cross while crumbling inside. I still fought to survive and decided I would not learn the language of my in-laws, nor cook the traditional pap. I still don't know how. This remained a sore point for which I was cursed, condemned and isolated.

All this led to the demise of my first and only marriage. I felt bitter because I felt I had given up many of the things I held dear to make this union a success. Although a staunch Catholic, I had agreed to be married by an Anglican priest, and for many years I laboured under the false dogma that the breakdown of my marriage was a result of this 'sin' I had committed. Now I know better. As I continue to pursue my spiritual journey, I have let go of all the hurt and bitterness and now have good relations with my in-laws – they are part of who I am and I respect the lessons I learnt from them.

The last but most profound experiences of democracy for me unfolded when I took over the reins as director of an HIV programme at the most difficult time in South Africa's response to the pandemic.

This is a story that requires a separate book – one I am working on. I walked into the medical post as one of the most naïve activists you could find in this country. I think that naïvety was the one thing that contributed to my ability to survive that very tumultuous time in the history of the response. I say this because by remaining naïve I remained optimistic that sanity would prevail in the end because nothing else would make sense. I believed strongly that our democracy would not permit the senseless loss of life when we knew what needed to be done. Now that democracy was a reality, none of our leaders would allow more people to die when such death could be prevented and our people spared the pain of loss and humiliation from the stigma and all that goes with HIV and AIDS.

I reckoned we were in a good place in that we had the right leadership, we had excellent scientists, we were part of the global community grappling with this pandemic and, hence, what we had to do was to put an evidence-based analysis of the facts and propose a programme to tackle the epidemic. I was not prepared for what unfolded as we battled not only the international community but also our own leaders, who we held in high esteem and regard. I was grateful that I could scrutinise information (thanks to the sustained fight for democracy), grateful that I could use this to the benefit of the people, but perplexed by the fact that those who had paid a great price for this democracy would be willing to deny the full expression of our great Constitution, which includes the right to healthcare.

The story of how the war was fought and won is known to many of us. For those in the background, there remains a tiny remnant of fear that in South Africa politics can always trounce science – and 'denialists' could revisit our backyards.

An example of politics trouncing science is the entire issue of male circumcision and the deaths of initiates. How can we all watch as young men lose their lives, and suffer untold misery with penile amputations and many other complications in this day and age? Where are democracy and the voices of the people? Has culture remained static? Should we say to those who insist on maiming these young people, how can we accept double standards? Instruments have evolved from spears, to knives, then blades and now to surgical implements. Communications has moved from letter writing to mobile phones. I hear no protest that we should revert to sending people on horseback to deliver messages from one village to another.

For me, democracy is a double-edged sword. Although I am contributing to shaping policies and plans and questioning where we are going as a country, I still feel oppressed by unspoken pressures from a wide range of places: the workplace, society, family, and sometimes, the things in my head.

Our democracy has brought more good than bad but we have to raise the level of the content and discussions on the meaning of this democracy as we move into a new administration. The predominant question should be: how best can this hard-won democracy benefit the poorest of the poor, not only the privileged few? We need not look further than the headlines of our daily newspapers to see heart-wrenching stories of South Africans who have yet to feel the impact of democracy.

For many it remains an elusive destination; the journey is still confusing and many struggle to feed their families. Should we be seeing people scavenging in dustbins in a free South Africa?

Coming back to my story, what has democracy done for me as a South African woman? Obviously, I am where I am because of our history and struggles – kudos for that. My weapon for success continues to be education. My psychological strength comes from spiritual mentors who teach me not to live in fear, and I see more breakthroughs in my life when I apply that principle. Democracy has taught me that those in power are also human and need support and guidance, so I have learnt not to fear speaking my mind, albeit in a respectful manner; I don't want to taint my father's legacy.

Conclusion

Democracy means honest hard work and commitment by those tasked with the role of shaping policy and more hard work for those tasked with bringing those policies to life. Democracy is respecting each other and not using others, especially women, as punching bags. Democracy means accepting all children as our collective responsibility, doing things differently to address their needs and nurturing them. Violating them must bear severe consequences. Democracy for me is the understanding that one day I will pass the baton to someone else and I would like them to feel proud and ready to continue building this, our great nation.

I am trying hard to balance my reflections. On the one hand I see a South Africa that has truly emancipated its people, women especially. I celebrate the fact that we have more career options for young people, that young people are taking charge of their lives, but I also know that in many ways we have failed to arm these unpolished gems of our nation as we should have. We need to ask ourselves why it took Oprah to build our children an academy. Where are the successful black women of our country? Education is the one and only sure way to lift people from poverty and despair to their full potential, and yet we miss so many opportunities, not just as successful black people, but also as a democratic government.

The gap between the haves and those who live in abject poverty is something we seem to have accepted as a given. It is someone else's problem, but we never stop to ask whose. I certainly don't intend to paint everyone with the same brush here but have our souls and our ability to care for one another died with no hope of resurrection? If the answer to that is yes, then apartheid and its demise have given birth to a monster without a name.

My story will not be complete if I don't acknowledge all the forces, good and bad, strong or weak that coalesced to shape me and eventually contributed to who I have become, though a work in progress. I acknowledge the apartheid regime for igniting my passion for medicine while simultaneously putting all kinds of blockages and obstacles in my path to achieve this dream – yours was a doomed force! I also thank my family, and everyone who knew us and crossed our path, for everything that was given to me, things that were given up for me, for the love and profound support. I especially and sincerely thank my mother – an angel lent to me by the Almighty.

My children deserve a special mention for the lessons they continue to teach me. Motherhood is bittersweet. In the words of Khalil Gibran: 'Your children are not your children. They are the sons and daughters of Life's longing for itself. They come through you but not from you, and though they are with you yet they belong not to you.' I guess this is what we all must remember – we have to leave this country in a better shape than it is in now – for the children.

Operating the apartheid machinery from within: What freedom means to me

Ntsiki Sisulu-Singapi
Woman's development practitioner

FREEDOM MEANS BEING ABLE TO exercise one's free will to reach one's full potential, uninhibited by laws, culture or religion, while respecting the freedom of others to do the same.

To arrive at what 20 years of democracy have meant to me, it seems necessary to reflect on my roots and where I am today.

I remember my home address as being 2693 Rockville, Zulu section, Moroko. When the address was actually written down it didn't contain 'Zulu section', yet we all referred to it as such. I didn't realise until much later that what we called 'Zulu section' was actually a part of Soweto set aside for Zulu-speaking people. My aunts lived in the Sotho section, while my coloured-looking grandmother lived in a section of Rockville where people were given plots on which to build their own houses.

I finally began to realise that this separation by ethnic groups, which was probably initiated by the apartheid system, was self-perpetuating. These divisions were so engrained in our consciousness that we didn't question them but actually 'normalised' the situation.

Black South Africans who still live in these areas continue to refer to them as the Zulu and Sotho sections. Other ethnic groups lived in Mabopane East, which later became Soshanguve, an abbreviation for *So*tho, *Sha*ngaan, *Ngu*ni, *Ve*nda, these being the languages spoken in this township.

Getting into a taxi every day that takes you to Rockville, Zulu section or Sotho section, is very damaging to our consciousness of who we are and where we live. This separation became so ingrained that it became the 'norm' – an unquestioned and unchanged norm. The only thing that has changed has been the renaming of the streets. As significant as this is, it only scratches the surface of undoing the damage of the past. However, the street names should, in time, give

414

rise to a new enquiry for those who care enough to want to know the significance of the street names. But because the names of the sections have remained the same, there will be an ongoing subliminal conditioning of at least three generations after those born in the 1940s of who our oppressors were as they still feature prominently in our daily drives to and from work and school.

This is because the intention of the apartheid government was not only to separate the white minority from the black majority, but also to separate blacks from one another along tribal lines in order to make it difficult for blacks to organise and gain political power. We must purposefully gain control of our minds and our unity to build a nation that values humanity. We must strive towards self-actualisation, which can come about if we make a concerted effort to recognise the full extent of what it means to be free.

Democracy in and of itself does not automatically translate into a sense of freedom and, so, over the past 20 years our young democracy has been preoccupied with governing towards a better life. This preoccupation can be seen as an entrapment of sorts, given the power that comes with governing within a yet-to-be-transformed system.

There have, nevertheless, been some visible changes, made possible by freedom. People no longer have to contend with appalling gravel roads; a neighbourhood dump (*isganga*); teargas or police dogs; the 2:00am house raids; petrol bombs; sleeping in cold cars at night; travelling as cargo in the belly of a ship to Robben Island to visit *utata'mkhulu*; 4:00am alarms for school; 4:30am school pick-ups, then three hours in the Kombi to a school only a short distance away; shooting at Kombis taking children to multiracial schools and hitchhiking to Swaziland in a soft-drink truck. Now my children can go to and from school unhindered, one can visit Robben Island as a guest and take a leisurely drive or flight to Swaziland as and when one chooses.

The dusty gravel roads of Rockville, Soweto, raised us. We learnt to ride our bikes on those roads. Rollerskating was more difficult on the dusty roads but we tried. If we found a concrete driveway in someone's yard, it felt like an arena.

August was not then referred to as the windy month but rather the dusty month, so clothes were turned inside out before they were hung up early on the outside washing line so that by the time the dust came they would be dry and off the line.

People did, however, have a sense of pride in ensuring that their front yards were neat. So, each morning, almost like clockwork, each household would water their yard before sweeping it. Over time, the residents used the rocks of Rockville to decorate and demarcate their yards. Sometimes they painted these white and planted flowers or grass. Some streets seemed to excel at this and their yards were a pretty sight.

Today it's rather disappointing to see some of the weed-filled and unkempt front yards. One wonders what happened to that sense of pride we had in the little front yards of those homes our parents didn't even own as they were on a 99-year lease.

Has freedom of movement come at the expense of self-respect and pride in our communities and the little that we had but did not own? Granted, a large number of families and returning exiles moved to the suburbs, where municipalities attend to the cleanliness of the streets, but the question remains, what values had been instilled in those who were left behind? What values did those who left take with them?

If, with freedom, we lost our sense of self and community, we are not free at all but are simply living in a democracy in which the full human potential is of no consequence. We seem to have adopted a predominately Western, individualistic way of life and we barely know our neighbours. Instead of making the suburbs more community-oriented, we have been transformed by them and we have conformed to the norms we found in them. When we grew up we knew all our neighbours, even those who lived opposite gogo's house.

A visit to gogo, both maternal and paternal, was the highlight of many of my weekends. I wore clothes made by my 'coloured-looking' maternal grandmother, Elizabeth Mashile, who, because she was classified coloured was taught to make a whole garment and later became a supervisor in a garment factory. However, gogo Mable Nkonyeni, affectionately called gogo Mantso, her dark-skinned younger sister, was taught only how to make a sleeve or a collar of a garment and no more.

Under apartheid, it was instilled in one generation after the next that you are defined by the colour of your skin – that being black meant that you were worth less than whites and, therefore, deserved to know less. In turn we taught this to our children so that, as a people, we came to believe and demonstrate that we were, indeed, worth less, given the evidence that we knew less and, over time, we became less in comparison to whites.

Gogo Albertina Sisulu, my paternal grandmother, was orphaned at the age of 15, became a missionary-schooled midwife, married Walter Sisulu and became involved in the struggle against the apartheid system that defined black people not by their humanness but by the colour of their skin. The price for being an enlightened black person who would not accept the white definition of blackness was detention, house arrest and continuous harassment by the police. She spent 26 years without her husband due to his imprisonment and had to raise five, and later seven, children on her own. For a while, three generations of Sisulus were imprisoned at the same time.

In 1994, I was sitting alone at 5:30am in the Gilmore House dormitory TV room, watching CNN updates on developments in South Africa. I was waiting until 6:00am to vacuum classrooms at Hope College in Holland, Michigan – one of my three jobs.

Once I figured out the system, I always scheduled my classes for 9:00am so I could vacuum classrooms from 6:00 to 8:00am for US$6 per hour. Twice a week between classes, I would spend an hour or two in the maintenance office, taking calls from students about their maintenance problems, for US$4.25 per hour. By night and over weekends, I was also a residential life staffmember and attended to students' concerns in the dormitory and their overall wellbeing – including diversity management and building a general sense of community – for US$400 every fortnight.

Three-month-long summers were spent on campus because travelling home to South Africa was simply not affordable for either my parents or me. During summers, when I didn't have classes, I worked when I could in factories. In my third year at university, I remember working in a sweet factory from 6:00am to 2:30pm, without lunch. When my mother visited me she said I smelt like mint. Because some students remained at school during the summer holidays, there was an opportunity to earn additional money as a house manager.

There were also opportunities for a social life in one form or another within the local community, which was increasingly Hispanic, and also in other states where there was a large South African community. Although my social life meant less pay.

417

Be that as it may, my ability to move and engage and earn at the manual labour level was a choice. I got the opportunity to study because of a scholarship I received based on results obtained during summer classes before being admitted, but I was afforded access because of the struggle by South Africans for freedom. So it was the lack of freedom that resulted in this opportunity but it also made it very difficult for me to get a travel permit that would allow me to travel beyond Lesotho and Swaziland. Going beyond there sent you into exile with very little possibility of return. Of course, some people were not even afforded a travel document to go to Lesotho or Swaziland in search of better education and liberation strategies.

After our education we believed that service to our people through governing was what would allow us to transform this machinery that had destroyed the very essence of blackness. It was not enough to return to South Africa with an education from the United States, only to be in the private sector or in private practice as a clinical psychologist. There was a sense and belief that freedom is not free and that governing wasn't easy – but then who should do it if not I? I remember my father and mother grappling with their own difficult question; at that time it was, 'If we don't send our own children into exile, whose children should be sent?'

A commitment to serve meant going into the public service. But what we are running, using our political freedom, is essentially machinery set up and handed over by apartheid South Africa. We have expanded it, we've allocated more money to it, we've anchored it on a great Constitution, but could it be that we struggle to deliver on great policy and legislative framework is because we are trying to do so within the apartheid machinery?

We need an appropriately transformed and systematically operated state machinery – with adequate checks and balances – to implement policies that are meant to give the majority of the people of South Africa a better life, regardless of where they are in the socio-economic sphere.

We should, where necessary, remove individuals who are not pulling their weight from public service, and do so swiftly. We can't wait to react until we have another service delivery protest. But more importantly, we need to recruit a cohort of state employees who will serve for the greater good rather than self-interest. Everyone, from our garbage collectors and street sweepers to our police force and administrators must take pride in serving our people to the best of their abilities. We all need to take pride in ourselves across the socio-economic spectrum. If we feel that we need to build our cohort of civil servants, we must allow ourselves the necessary time to do so, but we must be as focused as we were in pursuit of freedom.

I find no reason why people in informal settlements should live in squalor except for a lack of pride in themselves and their community and country. The high levels of gender-based violence know no colour, socio-economic status or creed, and reflect on our lack of mechanisms within communities, the private sector and the state to care for and protect the vulnerable. We will be truly free only when we liberate our minds and stop depending on others to do everything for us. Every one of us needs to recognise our own ability to exercise our free will to reach our full potential.

There is no doubt that the responsibility on the part of the state remains paramount but individuals need to take greater responsibility and seek to uplift themselves.

We need good leadership at all levels to help prevent the cycle wherein each time an incident erupts our response is looting, shouting, killing and blaming someone else for it – then returning to where we were before without taking responsibility for fixing the situation. We shall be free only when, within our communities, government and the private sector, we can influence each other for the better.

Affirming my potential, believing in change

Onkgopotse JJ Tabane
Communicator

Introduction

In 1994, when Nelson Mandela was made president, I was a student leader at the University of the Western Cape. I was the president of the Anglican Student Federation and had just been elected as international convenor of the International Anglican Youth Network (IAYN). My responsibilities included overseeing offices of the IAYN based in the United Kingdom and United States from my room at Dos Santos residence on campus. I was going around the globe addressing various student and youth groups about the future of South Africa.

The most recent had been an address to students in various colleges affiliated to Durham University in the United Kingdom. In this secluded part of Britain the only information that people had about South Africa was from the BBC World News – the narrative was simple: there was an impending bloodbath. I was at pains to paint a different picture. It did not help matters that my trip to the UK coincided with one of those 'black-on-black' violence episodes in Natal, where several people were killed in what had become commonplace violence between members of the African National Congress (ANC) and the Inkatha Freedom Party (IFP), resulting in an impasse and Chief Buthelezi's refusal to participate in the elections. When this is beamed on prime time news just before your talk about South Africa's elections being peaceful, you have loads of salt being taken with your talk.

A few months after I had made this optimistic speech, the ANC was voted peacefully into power during the first democratic elections, making Nelson Mandela the first democratically elected president of the Republic of South Africa. These elections happened largely without incident. Twenty years later, there are still people who hang on to the pessimism that saw a pre-election panic and the stockpiling of food in anticipation of the bloodbath predicted by some in the international media who did not know any better. And as I write this some are asking, 'Now that Mandela is gone, what will happen to our country in the next 20 years?'

I am a prisoner of the spirit of optimism that saw Mandela walk out of jail a better person, able to embrace those who had incarcerated him. The 20 years of democracy are a personal testament for me to what can be achieved if we affirm the basic potential in all human beings and if we believe in the inevitability of change by embracing it. I can write until the cows come home about what this democracy should mean to all of us but maybe the story of my personal opportunity to be part of the new South Africa is a better story to tell. Such a story adds to my tools of analysis and reflection about what this freedom means and how it should be established going forward.

Mindset shift: Thinking like freedom
One of the most frustrating things about the new South Africa was being expected to lay down the instruments of war when there was still a war to fight. It was clear that oppression, and economic bondage, in particular, did not disappear on the day Mandela walked out of prison or even on the day that he occupied his office at the Union Buildings. When Mandela called on the armed struggle to be suspended, it was an act of untold bravery and leadership – because, in fact, the war was not over. A friend and mentor of mine, Father Michael Lapsley, was sent a letter bomb that was meant to kill him way after Mandela was released and the call to lay down arms had been made. This is a hurtful situation, when you are expected to lay down arms with no guarantee of a similar cessation of hostilities by the opposing side. So many people died after that call that it militated against arguments to build for peace – look at the assassination of Chris Hani, look at the Boipatong massacre, and so on. All of these things sought to militate against a mind-shift change ahead of the 1994 elections, some were designed to disrupt the march to freedom.

So the call to change tack found me as a student leader who had been in student struggles since 1989. Back then, the army was present on campus to quell any protests. A few years later we became part of the establishment – the Student Representative Council (SRC) was now a part of the university council. The SRC was outnumbered by other stakeholders on the university council, and it was bound by decisions made there. So, if the university decided to increase fees, you had no leg to stand on because you were a party to the decision, having been at the meeting. It took courage to ensure that student governance was no longer about demand and protest, but that it became a constructive engagement with all stakeholders on campus – the mind-shift was one of the most difficult challenges for student leaders during this period of transition.

In 1996 this found expression in the way that we dealt with the annual protestation over financial exclusions at UWC. The SRC that I led took the extraordinary step of writing to students and saying, 'No need to come early to campus this year – an agreement has already been reached with management about how the financial exclusions are to be handled.' In summary, students were to be assisted on a sliding scale to ensure that arrangements were made for those who owed fees from the previous year. Now, this kind of agreement was usually finalised after much protesting and marching during the registration process.

A new dawn had arrived – we had access to the finance books of the university and were able to have an intelligent conversation with the university about how we could be accommodated. Consequently, a letter was sent to students jointly signed by the university rector and me on behalf of the students. This move annoyed the political opposition, whose only hope of political mileage was when the 'ruling student political party' was seen to be failing to persuade management not to exclude some of the worst-performing students at the beginning of each year.

Why the long story? Various parts of our society had to adjust to the way in which they approached challenges in the context of a new South Africa, where 'our' government was now in charge – whether in wage negotiations in the workplace or fighting for better conditions. To rise to this challenge one has to accept that freedom comes with responsibility and so in 1993, once the student body was part of determining budget, my demands in the boardroom for a moratorium on fee increases had to be tempered with the reality of the financial situation of the university. Today, some of the service delivery protests that are plaguing the country are a cry for information and involvement. Initiatives such as the Open Government Partnerships are aimed at educating people on how public participation can be made meaningful enough to enable them to be part of the planning for their own development. Integrated Development Plans (IDPs) are an innovation of the legislative framework in local government to ensure that communities own the developmental agenda, but there is still much to be done before people realise the power they have by shaping these IDPs.

Affirming the potential within

One of the most acrimonious debates of the new South Africa is about affirmative action. Recently there was a big fight about whether people without 'experience' should be given jobs or promoted over their white counterparts. The recent spat among the DA party faithful about this subject served to underline the fact that even after 20 years we still are not sure how to handle the fact that affirmative action has an element of positive discrimination – it also involves taking a level of risk that is based on the unscientific conclusion that someone who may not have 20 years' experience may rise to the occasion and be a success.

And so, the story of my career confirms to me the correctness of having adopted affirmative action. There is no shame in admitting that my own career would not have taken off as it did if our freedom had not been ushered in 1994.

In 1997 I wrote my final examination and added another degree to my qualifications. I got married while still a student and was a father at 25 – a youngster with a wife, a new baby and no full-time job. I had a part-time job as a facilitator of student leadership workshops and relied on my friends and family to pay the rent for the house I had rented in Mowbray in anticipation of the birth of my first-born son, Resego. So I was a man in search of any job.

A comrade from my student days, Andile Nkuhlu, and his twin brother, Ayanda Nkuhlu, who were partly responsible for my entry into politics at UWC, received a call from Mohammed Valli Moosa, the Minister of Constitutional Development and Local Government at the time. He had just interviewed about 12 people looking for an interim spokesperson. His spokesperson, Mpho Mosimane, had gone overseas to study so he needed a stand-in for 18 months. I submitted my CV and waited to be invited to an interview. Valli Moosa was one of the most dynamic ministers in Nelson Mandela's Cabinet. He was bright and had a high media profile, having been at the forefront of the UDF in the build-up to freedom. So I knew, as I was preparing for the interview, that I would be meeting someone who, as they say, does not suffer fools gladly. The interview was as informal as it was serious.

My friends were in his office when he paged through my CV and conducted a 10-minute interview in which he complimented me on my English and Philosophy marks and even better marks in my second degree in law. So I thought I had passed the first hurdle. And then came the killer question: 'But ... you have never worked. How do we know you can do a full day's work?' My friends looked visibly uncomfortable – they had brought in someone for the position of spokesperson who 'had never worked'! The job of a spokesperson in those days was known for high pressure and a lot of responsibility.

'If you read my CV carefully, you will realise that I have done leadership roles... everything up to the International Anglican Youth Network where I supervised people across the world... and this is, well... more than a full day's work.'

It was an answer that I had not rehearsed but it did dawn on me that student governance, community service and activism had prepared me for this moment just as surely as my academic studies had. It counted, suddenly, that I had been on the governing board of the university and part of international conventions and that I had spoken at conferences across the world. It counted, suddenly, that I had been involved in various youth and student publications and so I could answer that while I had never received a payslip, I had potential – even though I had never been a spokesperson and didn't even fully understood what it would take to do a job of that nature.

Affirmative action can be complicated in its implementation – identifying talent and believing that making such a maverick move, giving a rookie a chance, will not backfire and embarrass you. So, I was sent to President Mandela's spokesperson for a follow-up interview. The late Parks Mankahlana was a pleasant fellow. He welcomed me into his Cape Town office and made me feel at home. 'Chief,' he started off, 'this is not an interview – it's a meeting.' I was puzzled. Two hours later, after sharing stories of how we used to deal with the media during our student days, I left not knowing whether I had the job or not.

He had said, 'I have a position here for a researcher. If they don't want you there, please consider joining us here to support the president.' Here I was in the highest office in the land and suddenly I had a job offer. The very idea of even being here, speaking to this spin-doctor-in-chief was an honour. Before 1994 I would have been arrested for protesting outside this office – today I was meeting with the right-hand man of Nelson Mandela.

'Take him or I am taking him,' said Parks Mankahlana to Valli Moosa. And so I received a call while I was conducting a student workshop at the ML Sultan Technikon in Durban saying, 'You start Monday!' I was appointed to my very first job as a spokesperson for a minister. At 25, I must have been the youngest spokesperson; my counterparts were fellows who knew how to have journalists eating out of their hands.

Fast-forward to 2002. I was appointed as the government communicator of the year, sharing the inaugural award with friend and fellow comrade, Sipho Ngwema – an affirmation of the value of in-service training and belief in potential. I can proudly hold up my story as a practical expression of the intention of our new constitutional order – to give those who would otherwise not have stood a chance an opportunity to excel.

The negative narrative of transformation is that people who are promoted to meet the requirements of employment equity are naturally mediocre and are a recipe for a drop in standards. In implementing such policies care needs to be exercised to provide the support that is necessary for those people to succeed.

The question of redress in the implementation of transformation imperatives in our country is paramount but has to be matched with the relevant mentoring and support. I had not studied PR101, neither was I given a crash-course on how to be an effective government communicator. The absence of an orientation course for government communicators continues to be the Achilles' heel of the civil service. The opportunity for me to start a communications career was a direct result of having been given an opportunity. I was able to take that skill and apply it in the private sector, where I later went to ply my trade.

Back to the future: The past is very much with us

One of the stark realities of our democracy is something that former President Mbeki termed the two nations theory. Many people at the time criticised him for being divisive and negative. These two nations exist even after 20 years and live side by side in the new South Africa. When I went to work for the private sector, these two nations came to life for me.

First stop: the Chamber of Mines; next stop, Adcorp Holdings; and then onto the Altron Group of companies. I went from dealing with budgets to dealing with business targets. These were two different worlds. My first meeting was like a movie from the past. It was a meeting of all chief executives of the mining industry and the new irritant in their coffee – the Minister of Finance, Trevor Manuel – who was planning to introduce what is called 'mining royalties', a natural follow-up to the mooted 'Transformation Charter' of the mining industry. I could not believe it. The venom in the room was almost palpable. I was new; this was my first meeting. You know what they say about biting your tongue in your first board meeting? It was clear to me that we have a long way to go in building bridges.

Fast-forward to two months later: the Chamber of Mines was sitting with the officials of the treasury and Minister Manual, sipping coffee and being very polite to one another and back at the office the temperatures are calmer. I cannot recall whether the royalties bill was ever passed. I remember vividly, though, that it was the one issue that exposed the chasm between business and government. Mbeki, with all his theories about the two nations, was the first to shy away from the TRC-proposed wealth tax. This was the beginning of a slippery slope, where business was expected to volunteer change. Had a firmer stance been taken, maybe there would have been no need for BEE legislation.

It became increasingly clear to me that the new South Africa, where freedom was meant to be embraced, was still a site of struggle, where not all communities embraced change. This chapter of my life was to be dedicated to dealing with this. It struck me when I entered the private sector that a many black people in corporations had lost their sense of activism. There was a real sense that once they made it into the echelons of power, their sense of justice got blunted by the privileges that came with their positions in corporations. I found myself questioning whether, as a movement, we had a strategy about how we could deploy some of our own in this corporations to effect change.

When I joined the Altron Group, as Group Corporate Affairs Executive, I was the only black executive in the group executive committee of a R21 billion company. Every meeting was a fight about the pace of change. I didn't mind being an irritant. In theory, there was no resistance to change as the company went along with my suggestions to develop a five-year transformation strategy, among others. In practice, a lot of transformation initiatives were either 'unfunded mandates' or were simply ignored. This is, after all, what they had hired me to do.

My experiences at this company sharpened my sense of activism again. To be any sort of activist in corporate South Africa is a lonely undertaking indeed. This is why I admire people like Jimmy Manyi, who was not afraid to tell home truths in public about the laxity of transformation in corporate South Africa. During my time in corporate South Africa as an employee, the Black Management Forum was very vocal about the need for change. Under Manyi's leadership, a lot was said about what needed to be done to change the face of business in South Africa. This was when Broad-Based Black Economic Empowerment (BBBEE) was introduced in response to the 'rent-a-black' habit that was taking root, as business was scrambling to curry favour with government by giving activists and politically-connected people meaningless shareholdings in companies, while they continued to run the companies as if nothing had changed. It became clear to me that the question was less about the noise that one can make in public against the lack of transformation, than it was about doing the necessary work of activism that would bear results, company by company. Sadly, this is lacking and continues to be the bane of black activism in the new South Africa. This is no reflection on Manyi, whose transformation activism I admire. It is simply the kind of physiological inertia on activism that is gripping us post 1994 – a sign of the times.

While at Altron, I invited Comrade Manyi to address a transformation conference that I had called for all directors of the company. His articulation of the problem statement of BEE in the country was impressive. With the advantage of having chaired the employment equity committee, it was good to have someone from outside affirming all the things I had been saying internally about the need to increase the pace of change. This speaks to the support that we should be giving each other as black executives who have a responsibility to effect change in corporations.

Exercising freedom: A treacherous assumption
Our Freedom was tested as a country in 2008, when the former president was recalled from office. This bloodless coup d'état was

followed by Mbeki's ousting from the ANC leadership in Polokwane. With all its negative connotations, and the ill-advised removal of the president six months before a general election, this development was maybe attesting to the maturity of our politics. There was no rebellion of any kind, not even from Mbeki, who had every right to take the ANC to task. But this development was to result in a split in the ANC, or so it seemed at the time. A few leaders who had been in the ANC for years considered this development unjust and left the organisation – another exercising of freedom.

This development found me at a political crossroads and I decided to leave the ANC to join the Congress of the People (COPE). It is hazy to me now what it was that broke the camel's back for me, but among other things, it was when the entire leadership of the ANC in its NEC undertook to 'find a political solution' for the charges facing Jacob Zuma at a time. I thought we had completely lost it as a movement. I attended what was called the November conventions and from there I was sucked into a movement that was to result in the formation of COPE – the full story is yet to be written about that. What is important is that, here I was in the new South Africa, having the ability to choose a different political home. What was to follow by way of hostility from the ruling party made me ask the question: Are we ready, as a society, for divergent views and political tolerance? Mutterings that 'it is cold outside the ANC' and a campaign to 'come back home', indicated that we were not ready to explore the real meaning of exerting our freedoms. It almost feels like treason to even think of being in an alternative political party.

The venom directed at black people who join the Democratic Alliance (DA), for example, is an example of the political immaturity of our country.

The formation of the Economic Freedom Fighters (EFF) is another development that has brought to the surface the exercising of freedom in the new South Africa. After being expelled from the ANC, Julius Malema reinvented himself, presumably propelled by a sense of justice that he believed was not served in his disciplinary case. But, ironically, this was the same Julius Malema who had declared that he would die for Zuma and would carry him into the Union Buildings with 'orange overalls' (referring to prison garb should Zuma be found guilty of corruption).

Epilogue: I am free

Twenty years on, I can look back and say, thank you, ANC. The ANC has laid a good basis for us to build as a country. Sadly, there is not yet a mature alternative that can take over from the ANC at this stage. Not that the ANC will 'rule until Jesus comes back', as Jacob Zuma attested. Our freedom must mean people can choose other political parties but it must also mean that people can continue choosing the ANC if that works for them. Coming back to the ANC was a decision I made, because I want to fix our century-old movement to rise to the occasion of dealing with the issues of poverty and inequality facing our people. Opposition politics over the last 20 years has proved futile beyond the mere correctness of the existence of an opposition. Their contribution to rolling back poverty has been suspect. COPE was the worst – it seemed to have taken the bad parts of the ANC and perfected them: leaders plotting against each other; the greed over leadership; the accentuation of the politics of the stomach. I said to myself, 'This is not what freedom should mean'.

While many people may argue over theory, my own story is a story of what the ANC should have and has tackled to various degrees over the last 20 years. The ANC sought to give opportunity to people who otherwise would not have had a chance. Despite initial dithering about taking on economic freedom, the ANC has put a solid policy in place in the BBBEE Act, strengthening it recently with the amendments of the codes of good practice. The Constitution, which people today take for granted, was a key achievement of the last 20 years. It is the Constitution that guarantees the freedom of expression for individuals and companies and, for that matter, the freedom to choose to what extent they want to be a part of the new South Africa.

The narrative of the new South Africa, therefore, can never just be about corruption – as if corruption was born in 1994. Neither can it be just about poverty as if poverty that manifested for generations can be eradicated in a short 20 years. As we celebrate 20 years of freedom, let us acknowledge the huge strides that have been made. As for me, I have plenty to celebrate – the new South Africa has meaning for me. I can truly say, 'I am free.'

In education,
money still matters

Mpho Tshivhase
Young academic

> The educated differ from the uneducated as
> much as the living from the dead.
> (Aristotle)

Introduction

I WAS RAISED IN A COMMUNITY where education is an absolutely necessary step for any person who wants to improve his or her family's financial status. In my community, in the Makwarela Township in Venda (Limpopo), education is seen as a vehicle one can use to move away from poverty. The notion of a 'gap year' was completely foreign to me because where I come from it is the norm to proceed to tertiary education immediately after matric. A gap year would be viewed as a waste of time in much the same way as failing a grade is – in the words of my mother and her friends, 'Failing a year is equivalent to losing one year's salary'.

When I thought of the difference one year's salary would make to my family's financial state, even if just to relieve my mother from paying for my living expenses, I was motivated to continue studying and make a success of it. When it came to education, the operating principle was: every child *will* gain basic and tertiary education and eventually get a job. This was a path set forth by every parent in the hope that their children would live better lives. In most impoverished communities, education is regarded as the surest way to overcome poverty and secure a better quality of life, and this has proven true in enough cases to render such a belief valid.

Our country's Constitution tells us that education is a *fundamental* *right* for all its citizens,* and on paper this is true. However, in practice, education in our country seems, to me, to have become a tool for exclusion and discrimination; it discriminates against the poor, and elevates the rich. Sadly, education has been reduced to a status-affirming commodity rather than a developmental tool grounded in equality and excellence. I think the commodification of education has hindered and continues to hinder the development of underprivileged people.

I celebrate our country's achievements over the past two decades – I particularly appreciate the substantially decreased racial hatred in our country. However, I am disappointed at the state of our education system. I am afraid that our education system has become a platform for a new form of oppression whose devastation is suffered most by poor people. I will share my views on the implications of the commodification of education for the poor and suggest possible ways to minimise discrimination, in relation to education, against poor people. I believe that for South Africa to develop it must academically advance the lives of its underdeveloped citizens.

Implications of commodifying education

What I have in mind when I speak of 'commodified education' is a system that is governed and validated in monetary terms. Currently, access to education depends on the amount of money one can pay, so that entry into a tertiary institution is but a dream for people who come from households with a monthly income of R1 800, as is the case with most housekeepers in our country. Educational quality and institutional reputations are weighted according to the amount of money parents pay to have their children enrolled. It is believed that the higher the tuition fees, the better the education. The students' capabilities and skills are also perceived to be dependent upon the institution's reputation so that students from 'rich' (private) schools are taken more seriously than students from 'poor' (public) schools. Money determines the probability of gaining access to education, especially at tertiary level.

I point to tertiary-level education because of the financial cost of the successful completion of a degree in South Africa. Also, tertiary

---

* Bill of Rights of the Constitution of the Republic of South Africa Act 108 of 1996. *Government Gazette*, No. 17678. Pretoria: Government Printer.

institutions, unlike some primary and secondary schools, do not operate on a 'no-tuition fee' policy. Everything at tertiary institutions costs money: tuition, books, accommodation, transport, food, etc. Consequently, people with little or no money are excluded from gaining access to tertiary institutions because they simply cannot afford it.

A related implication of commercialised education is the misrecognition of students. Because money governs institutions, students are no longer primarily seen as learners. Students are misrecognised as clients paying institutions for service. The institutions make a lot of money from students' tuition fees and so students have come to represent monetary gains: the more students enrolled, the more money for the institutions. What used to be known as 'student services' departments are now 'client services' departments. Such language indicates that institutions value students as clients – patrons. This misrecognition inadvertently clouds the characterisation of education as a *right*. The commodification of education is incompatible with the fundamental principles of an education system that aims to edify its citizens and equip them with the skills necessary for personal and societal development. Students should be seen primarily as learners who are guaranteed an education, not clients who can be exploited for money.

Apart from excluding poor people from tertiary institutions, the commodification of education has also turned our focus way from a culture of meritorious excellence to a culture of producing and maintaining high throughput rates. A positive trajectory of matriculant pass rates has become the yardstick of a good school. Seemingly, the education department's primary objective is to maintain high matric throughput rates, thereby making the production of quality students secondary. Throughput rates are commendable only when they are achieved meritoriously. This misplaced focus neglects the development of pupils into strong candidates for tertiary institutions as some may be pushed through to maintain high throughput rates. Losing focus on excellence plagues tertiary lecturers with students who are inept for tertiary level education, which stunts their academic development.

Another issue that stunts academic development is exposure to technology. The infrastructure in most impoverished public schools does not include the facilities for basic computer literacy. A student who has no idea how to use a computer is much worse off than one who does. Some of us were lucky enough to have Computer Studies at school. Even then we were confronted by classmates who had computers at home so we were a bit behind, but we caught up. There is time to catch up at high school but the tertiary schedule is not as forgiving, and a lot of work is done electronically. In this techno age, computer illiteracy, on top of having to adjust to a big institution in a city, can disorientate students.

Even a six-floor library can unnerve a student from a school that does not have one. What is more, there are students from the rural areas whose command of English is so poor that they struggle to comprehend the course material. It is cruel to admit such students to a university and expect them to compete equally and flourish when they are not equipped to do so. It is highly prejudiced to expect students who do not have the necessary foundational training to successfully apply themselves, become educated and gain skills that will make them employable. Tertiary education is a race to success with the odds in favour of privileged students.

Getting a diploma or a degree is an expensive exercise. Students are expected to register before lectures begin, and, sadly, if you cannot afford the registration fees, the next name on the waiting list will take your spot. The message is, 'If you cannot pay for your tuition, we will not educate you'. It is much like a hotel policy – if you cannot pay our rates, you cannot sleep in our rooms. I understand that universities have operating costs that are partially paid for by the tuition fees. However, I believe that universities could cut down on many things aimed at advancing hierarchical benefits that separate lecturers from executive management.

If I had to choose between a kitted-out kitchen with a personal chef or subsidising a poor student's tuition and/or boarding, I would choose the latter. As a woman, I don't want chocolates when I enter an institution in the first week of Women's Month* because I believe this money would be better spent feeding students who cannot afford to feed themselves. When it comes to educating our citizens, I believe that every rand counts. Some institutional managers are neglecting to prioritise. Tertiary institutions are places for educating

---

* Some tertiary institutions have a tradition of giving their female staff members chocolates in the first week of Women's Month.

impressionable and often eager minds, not an arena for showcasing luxurious offices. Money should be reallocated to funding students' academic advancement because education takes priority over inessential comforts.

Two years ago it was reported that approximately 4.7 million adults in South Africa were completely illiterate.* An additional 4.9 million were functional illiterates who had dropped out of school before Grade 7 (ibid). In a country with a population of about 51 million, this means that almost a quarter of the citizens are not well educated. Given the number of illiterate people in this country who are having children and struggling to send those children to school, because, let's face it, the child grant upon which they so heavily depend is peanuts, there is a high probability of those children also being illiterate so that generations on the cycle of illiteracy continues. This cycle points to a failure by our country to make education accessible to *everyone*.

It is clear that education is not truly a *fundamental right* – it is an *affordable right*. Only those who have the money to pay for education enjoy it as a right; those who cannot afford it experience it as a privilege that they can't access. In celebrating 20 years of liberation, it is really difficult to celebrate education, especially in relation to the poor.

Financial aid

I recognise that the government is making some effort to give people access to education in light of it being a fundamental right. I, in particular, know of the National Student Financial Aid Scheme (NSFAS). I admire the scheme's aim to help alleviate poverty. However, it still excludes people who do not have the money to register as the language of the NSFAS Act[†] suggests that a student must be registered with a tertiary institution before applying for the study loan.

As much as I understand the logic behind considering only registered students for funding, I would like the government to make

---

* SABC. 2011. *4.7 Million Adults Illiterate in South Africa*. NGO Pulse. Available at: www. ngopulse.org/newsflash/47-million-adults-illiterate-south-africa (accessed 28 October 2013).

† National Student Financial Aid Scheme Act 56 of 1999, Chapter 1. *Government Gazette*. 413(20652), 19 November. Government notice no. 1400. Pretoria: Government Printer. Available at: www.info.gov.za/view/DownloadFileAction?id=70624 (accessed 28 October 2013).

provision for students who qualify for the loan but do not have the money for registration. Personally, I am stunned that our government is willing to pay unemployed people a grant for making babies, but has no grant for people who want to study but cannot afford to register. The message seems to be that it pays to make a baby. This is a very dangerous message to send to uneducated people – who are most likely also financially illiterate – because they see having children as a means to receive an income.

I often hear this in taxis and supermarkets queues: young women planning to buy clothes or pay for a hairdo with their child grant; unemployed men contesting the women for the money so they can grab a beer. Yeah, that's right – the child grant is not always being used for its purpose and unemployed people seem to be making more babies to get paid. Herein priorities are skewed. If it were up to me, I would make education an uncontested priority and give money to those who want to enrol at a tertiary institution before I even thought about giving money to someone who neglected to consult a family-planning clinic.

Bursaries and other grants are a possible solution. A related problem is making the information available to those who need it. Often, information about bursaries is made available on university websites. For a student in the rural area with no access to a computer, let alone the Internet, the websites are useless. We might suppose that the universities' Open Days are another possible way of advertising the bursaries, but often the students cannot afford to travel to the institutions. By the time the student gets to register, deadlines for bursary applications are closed.

Bursaries are awarded on merit. This seems like a great yardstick but it has its drawbacks. For instance, a student who went to a school that is disadvantaged cannot really compete successfully against one who went to a school that not only developed them academically but socially as well, giving them the skills necessary to understand the workings of society at large and ways to develop conscientiously within that society. Applying for a bursary is essentially a self-marketing exercise. Applicants have to convince the reviewers that they are worthy of investment.

Marketing oneself is not something one learns in an English class. One learns this in Career Guidance, which most impoverished schools do not offer because they are still finding the task of teaching challenging in itself and so they are unable to produce self-sufficient and independent pupils. Viewed from this angle, bursaries are another area of exclusion because they are not always allocated where they are needed most. It may be worth exploring efficient ways of informing impoverished students of bursary opportunities in their senior high school years so that they are mindful of maintaining high grades in order to have a shot at securing a bursary. Introducing Career Guidance classes may be a good start.

The NSFAS is quite popular among students and it is often helpful. However, the NSFAS is a loan, which means that students start their career with a debt. It is outrageous that a student has to get into debt to pay for education – something our country regards as a *fundamental right*. Since when does a *fundamental right* come with such an exorbitant price tag? Viewed in this way, education is not available to every person but only to a select few who can afford it.

Chronic cycle of poverty

The chronic cycle of poverty is entrenched in the very schools that are meant to educate our people. The state of our education also highlights the disparity between the private and public schools – the rich and the poor. The gap seeps through from primary school all the way to tertiary education and sometimes into the workplace. Once again, this makes the playing field uneven. Where education is meant to be the one place where we can claim equality, in our country it is another sphere that highlights inequality and subsequently deepens the entrenchment of poverty.

Twenty years into democracy and we are sitting with a migration towards private schools and the private institutions are thriving because of this. The private and public school divide is indicative of the financial exclusion that is prevalent in our country's education system, and 20 years of freedom has not alleviated this problem. In fact, more and more parents are losing faith in the public school system but only a few have the resources to do something about it. Please note that I am not referring to public schools in the metropolitan areas in our country. I am referring to schools located in impoverished areas – schools with no playgrounds or electricity, classrooms without windowpanes and doors that do not lock. These are the kinds of schools that should not exist 20 years into democracy. This feeds the perpetual cycle of first generation scholars that is a long way from reaching its end. Our country has a lot of first generation scholars and this implies that the serious education problems plaguing our country are not properly addressed.

Commodifying education prevents the poor from developing successfully into first-rate citizens who can afford to live dignified lives by having access to the basic amenities, such as proper housing, sanitation and electricity which give a person dignity. A child from a low-income household may pass matric but get stuck at home unskilled and unemployable. Say this child produces offspring – and this is not an unusual occurrence, especially in rural and township areas – and gets a child grant – what you have here is two generations, possibly three, of unskilled and unemployable people who are stuck in a chronic cycle of poverty. One has to understand that this is not what any parent wants for his or her children, but in a country driven by money, a low-income-earning parent cannot secure tertiary education for his or her children. It is truly heartbreaking to pass matric with an exemption and be unable to study further.

Not having enough money to pay a registration fee is one of the most disappointing things one can experience. One feels as though one's bright future is slipping away. I remember the excitement of passing matric and telling everyone that my dream of becoming a psychologist was going to come true. This excitement was quickly followed by heavy disappointment when my mother could not afford to pay the registration fee. She was forced to make very quick plans because I *had* to go to university. My mother had to do her best to gather the registration fee all because of a clause in the education policy she had taken out for me years before that prevented the release of the funds because I had matriculated a year earlier than expected. We struggled, but a week into the first semester we managed to get me registered. But this was just one of many hurdles.

Apart from the fact that I had to catch up on a week's work, there was the matter of books, accommodation, transport fees, and other living costs. Due to limited funds, I had to stay with my aunt in Soweto. I would catch the 6:00am bus to arrive on campus at 7:30am. This meant waking up at 4:00am to boil water because we had no geyser, then getting ready by 5:45am to walk to the bus stop. On leaving, I caught the 16:30pm bus to arrive home at 18:00pm and then had to help prepare dinner, serve it and wash the dishes. By 20:00pm there was hardly an ounce of energy left in me to prepare for a test or an assignment, but my lecturers did not care; they assigned deadlines and meted out penalties when I missed them. These are some of the challenges one might face outside the classroom.

Waking up early and not having enough time to do academic tasks may be challenging but these do not completely hinder one from getting educated. But students heading families face even greater challenges than most people. The issue of child-headed families is a highly disturbing situation that our country is struggling to find a functional solution to.

In addition to financial challenges, one also faces social challenges. Such challenges should be considered when providing financial solutions to a social problem as the two inform each other in a person's efforts to gain education.

Conclusion

At bottom, our education system has (at least) three problems: inequality (evident in financial exclusion), inadequacy and underperformance (evident in lack of merit). And all of these are exacerbated by the commodification of education. Nevertheless, this trend can be stopped in its tracks by solutions that meticulously target the problems at their very foundation. Grants should be made available at different levels, starting with funding for application fees. Also, when students cannot make it to tertiary institutions for Open Day events, institutions should send representatives to the schools. Alternatively, teachers can be trained to be the representatives for their respective schools and liaise with institutions regarding applications and courses offered. These are small and doable solutions that can help large numbers of students.

Additionally, in order to create an education system that aims for meritorious achievements, we need teachers who are experts and passionate about their work. A strong foundation for education depends largely on the quality of our teachers. We also need a system that involves parents, and works with parents to help them understand what their children are studying so they are in an informed position when they support their children's academic careers.

Finally, the government needs to provide financial assistance in a way that ensures the funded students will succeed in getting their degrees. Helping students pay for tuition is often not enough because of other social challenges that can hinder their progress. We need a holistic system of financial aid that is tailored to the academic and basic social needs of poor students. Moreover, in order to improve our education system, we cannot wait for the government – it ought to be a societal project that all sectors buy into.

Changing narratives of race in the new South Africa

Cheryl Uys-Allie
Filmmaker

APRIL 1994 SIGNALLED THE DAWN of democratic rule in South Africa. For the majority of South Africans, it was a time of liberation and an end to prejudice and hopelessness. However, many white South Africans did not share the enthusiasm for a new South Africa. Those who could afford to do so, and could not imagine living under black rule, had been preparing their exodus for as long as those in exile had been preparing their return.

Spurred on by reports of white expulsion under Mugabe's rule in post-independence Zimbabwe, while I was growing up my family travelled to London then Portugal almost every year with our allowed allocation and eventually accumulated enough savings overseas to purchase property. We did not grow up living for today but rather saving for tomorrow. My family was determined not to face a similar fate under black rule to those who still call themselves 'Rhodesians'.

And so, as privileged white South Africans, my parents fled, selling up all they had worked for, shipping what they could across the Atlantic, to start over again as immigrants. They left in April 1994.

Emancipation and liberation

Slowly but surely the activism bug grew inside me as I witnessed the folly of running from my destiny. Something told me I belonged in Africa. Subsequently, my own trajectory as a journalist and documentary filmmaker took me through Africa and the Middle East.

At that time South Africans did not consider themselves 'Africans'. Only on crossing the Limpopo River would you be in 'Africa'. I began my cross-Limpopo work in 1991, fuelled by the optimism generated by Ghana's independence in 1957.

This is the background that inspired and confirmed my roots as a white African. It is this period that shaped the trajectory of my life, my future, and that of my children today. But the saddest part of enlightened change and my transformation is not being able to take those you love along with you. Once you have left your so-called 'tribe' it is impossible to go back and more difficult to expect to be accepted back into the fold.

My marriage in the late 1990s to a black South African was a culmination of my beliefs and a divine celebration, but one deeply mourned by my parents. The first year of my marriage I cried myself to sleep, haunted by my guilt at being happy, knowing that what was right for me had broken their hearts. We grow up programmed to please our parents. This I did until the day I introduced my husband-to-be – and this is when things fell apart.

The return of my parents to South Africa after unsuccessful emigration, quickly cemented their racial outrage: their love for me, I learnt, was conditional upon my marrying into their white tribe. My journalism and film work as a documentary cinematogrpher is an ongoing answer and a work in progress to the problems caused by hatred and love in the world.

On a planet ever more populous and imperilled by resource scarcity, hatred and the lack of respect for diversity intensifies many of our dangers. My life and work is aimed at reducing our fear of the unknown by uncovering and discovering, through film, the necessity to love and respect one another. And, in particular, to restore to historic consciousness the need to recognise the planet's greatest asset: women.

I am African, South African, female, middle class, white and free.

Liberation! There are few words as promising, uncompromising and potent in the human story. Perhaps 'mother' or 'prayer' to some, even 'God' to others, but, whatever to liberate means to unchain, to set free and deliver the most precious attribute: freedom. Freedom fulfils potential and sustains dignity and makes one free from being uneducated and unemployed and free from starving in the midst of plenty.

I was in Mozambique in my mid-20s, with a pocket full of dreams working as a filmmaker when Nelson Mandela walked free. I was bursting with an activist's dreams about her African future and trying to make sense of lives trapped in racial confusions.

After a year in Portugal on a scholarship at Lisbon University, my racial innocence had still been intact. In spite of reading about political liberation, from the removal of Salazar in Portugal to Cabral and Samora Machel, I was caught by surprise in Nampula, Mozambique. There I shared an apartment with a spirited East German woman who had married a Mozambican. They had fallen in love in what was then the German Democratic Republic, a former communist state until 3 October 1990, and she had followed him home to Africa.

Every part of my being was challenged by how normal it seemed. From that moment, the trajectory of my liberation began. My film work for the United Nations on the run-up to Mozambique's first post-war elections was wrought with a colour-blind mind, and the light it threw over everything was dazzling. Wherever I looked there was fusion. A merging of friendships that was not perplexing but soulful. Could this be what they call spiritual freedom?

On the road to living and working in Rwanda I crossed the Rubicon: being a journalist, covering the aftermath of the continent's most gruesome genocide, removed any lingering traces of being 'white'. I became African. The horrifying scale of what extreme hatred can do scoured the final stains out of my Uys ancestry. My skin remains white, and while I can't alter biology, I do claim that I'm cosmopolitan-African: perhaps 'Afropolitan' would be a useful term.

Early years in green and gold

Our genealogy is interesting and my journey from my preteen years on a farm in Heidelberg in the 1970s to university was fairly characteristic of a privileged white South African. My ancestor, Dirk Cornelius Uys, died on his farm in Stellenbosch in 1758. Bone and marrow, as the saying goes, that makes me as South African as soil and climate can achieve. But we were English-speaking – the only ones in the valley. Thus my sense of being 'different' was born.

I had been brainwashed into the standard racial hierarchy of the times and place. I caught the bus to school and never saw a black child riding with us. After school, one of our black farmworkers, Kayvas, would wait at the bus stop with my horse, Mickey. I would hand him my schoolbag and ride home.

At primary school I was also the only '*Engelsman*' and at first knew not a word of Afrikaans. This soon changed, as I discovered

442

I take to languages with ease. I am now useful in five. Happily, the Grade 1 teacher took a liking to me and I rapidly acclimatised to one of the world's youngest languages.

A row of majestic blue gum trees lined the short road up to my teacher's home, where I swiftly acquired the nuances of Afrikaans. I saw my first rugby jersey in gold and green: stickers of players adorned the older boy's bedroom wall. Blue gums still stir a deep nostalgia in me.

As a child, 'our' farmworkers, their wives and children were my only contact with black Africans. At one time we farmed up to 5 000 chickens, had a dozen cattle, a couple of horses and fields of maize and sorghum (commonly referred to as 'mielies' and *'kaffir koring'* in the valley). In retrospect, my father was the exception among local farmers, having built concrete houses with potable water for his workforce. Other farms retained clustered villages of mud huts and had no intention of improving living conditions for 'their' workers.

In the 1970s my mother had a permit to enter the local township, Ratanda, where she delivered trays of eggs to a Mr Tshabalala once a week. I'd be upfront by her side on the rare occasion and have a strong recollection of passing the military checkpoint and entering a very different world, a contrast that still simmers in my memory. I believe we caused some consternation among other white farmers in the valley. Something I never quite understood.

This perplexity grew as I tuned in to the disjuncture between what I believed were my father's views at home on politics and my then Afrikaans-medium school's nationalist rhetoric with the daily flag-raising ceremony to national anthem chorus. BJ Vorster, of Biko infamy, was prime minister at the time and I vividly recall my father's scoffing at his statements on the news, especially after returning from a call-up to border duty in what was then South West Africa, and Angola.

The tension between school behaviours and our opinion at home grew steadily and by the age of ten it just seemed too much. It spilled out one night when my father sensed my distress. He was a chartered accountant by profession and a military historian by design, well aware of South Africa's layered history in warfare. I explained how embattled I felt at the gap between what was being said at school on the playground and in our home. I felt out of place. In a word of today: alienated.

When he heard this, he visited the school and I was immediately transferred to an English-medium school, where I was naturally top in Afrikaans. I then went on to a private girls' high school in a leafy Johannesburg suburb. Supposedly integrated, it had but 12 black girls in the boarding house. They kept very much to themselves (or was it the other way around?), plaiting each other's hair and wrapped up in warm fluffy blankets in the winter term. They spoke to one another in a vernacular, which only enhanced the separation between 'them' and 'us'. I noticed, however, that the white girls from Malawi, Zambia and Botswana floated in friendship with the black girls with an ease that fascinated me. At 14, a friend from Gaborone invited me home with her for the holidays. The result was a deep shift in perception and a growing understanding of what was so wrong with my own country.

I was head boarder in my final year and eager to take on the world, so I applied for Rotary Exchange. As my father was a Rotarian he arranged for me to interview at a club other than his own. The club he approached was the Rotary Club of Lenasia and Eldorado Park, so-called Indian and coloured townships near Soweto. To my amazement, the members took on the prospect of a 'white' girl representing a 'black' club. The year was 1985. Their conditions were about to change my life.

They suggested I live with both Hindu and Muslim families on weekends and spent school holidays in Lenasia, Fordsburg and Mayfair during my matric year. Doing so I would grasp what it meant to live under apartheid. Until then, the word 'apartheid' was little more than a blunt term I had heard bandied about in the media and I'd never heard of Nelson Mandela growing up. But in those households I learnt about and felt the daily weariness of humiliation. Of grown men and women, as mothers and fathers, business and community leaders, who had to swallow insults in silence to keep the peace.

Naturally, some families were sceptical. How could a kid from middle-class white South Africa possibly know and feel what, in truth, was happening to the South African psyche? Well, they had a point. One could succumb to compassion fatigue. Shrug it off as history and do one's best in sympathy. But Gaborone was on my mind. A small steeliness was becoming a growing component in thinking and listening. The exchange year I spent in Germany among upper-class families sped by with little effect, somehow reinforcing and ennobling the experience of Lenasia and Eldorado Park.

At university I was elected to the SRC. Among those who appeared quite radical on campus were some who were uncovered as police informers. It was the era of the '*rooi gevaar*', with communists supposedly lurking on every campus committee. Students were looking over their shoulders. Suspicion was as omnipresent as the Cape's blustery south-easter.

To be honest, I was scared of police intimidation and uncomfortable with toyi-toying and remained pretty much a voyeur on the sidelines. But my political compass was set on course. I knew I needed the political education I would acquire in student leadership. So I set my sights on the least troublesome SRC ticket: rugby. In short, I became the first woman to chair the Intervarsity Rugby Committee at UCT.

In any event, I attended underground meetings, listened to much passionate anti-apartheid speechmaking and saw a great deal of attitudinising about the downtrodden by people who went home to comfortable suburbs. I became aware of an ever-growing discontent with my place in South African society, where the more things changed the more they stayed the same. I was determined to do something and, casting around for the means, chose filmmaking as my agency-of-change.

My first degree in languages gave me French, Portuguese and German, the three historic languages of African colonisation. This allowed for work across the continent at a time when few white South Africans ventured beyond the Limpopo. The year was 1991. A second passport was arranged in Lesotho and off I went. With my white South African eyes the mix of colourless relationships was, as I recall, a blinding revelation of what could be.

But by the time I was living in Rwanda in the aftermath of Africa's most shocking systematic genocide, I was a lot more attuned to and accepting of cross-racial relationships. Then, in 1995, an innocent question posed by my mother while I was visiting home took me by surprise. She asked what Christmas in Kigali had been like. I'd told her of a function I had attended at the Milles Collines, a hotel frequented by expats and aid workers, and she asked whether there had been any 'whites' there. I was stunned for a moment, then realised I actually didn't know, and better still, I didn't care. The question of race had become the least of the issues I was grappling with at the time. Much like the burqa and hijab in Saudi Arabia being the least of the many empowerment issues Saudi women are concerned with, yet an issue of great concern to Westerners.

Non-comrades in a new South Africa

Having never overtly traded as an anti-apartheid activist, I somehow feel caught in a generational vacuum and feel somewhat detached from South Africa's anti-apartheid history, yet I do still very much feel part of its future. I believe there is a generation of us non-comrades, who are educated and active in the economic engine rooms of our country, a generation who needs South Africa to succeed.

To me there appears to be a dearth of political leaders in our generation but I believe these will emerge as the older cadres step back. I don't believe that many educated and economically active South Africans of my generation (between 35 and 55) would choose to go into politics today but many of us do feel an obligation to public service. To be allowed the opportunity to clean up the kleptocracy our land of plenty promise has become.

Change had come to the southern tip of Africa, and the tide had turned for the better, but only for some. However, the realities that played out around the time of negotiations become more and more fascinating as they are unpacked and reflected upon so many years later. With time, I have come to understand how well-orchestrated the 1994 elections were, securing the wealth of those whites in power by sharing with a small elite made up of 'buffer' blacks, suddenly wealthy beyond belief and now with their own interests to protect, and, indirectly, those of their white predecessors, now comrades. Clever, but also somewhat subversive, under the pretext of what has become known as Broad-Based Black Economic Empowerment (BBBEE).

In 1994, taken up by the euphoria of a new nation, I applied to the Ministry of Foreign Affairs with great enthusiasm. A chance to represent a country I could be proud of would indeed be a privilege. I few months later I received a letter thanking me for my application, which had been among 12 000 others. Disappointing, yes, but the first time I felt what so many had felt for so long – that the colour of my skin was no longer an automatic access card but was, in fact, a liability.

I did become a diplomat incognito in many ways, representing and sharing what I had witnessed as a journalist and, later, a filmmaker. I travelled extensively across Africa and the Middle East and, by the time I turned 30, had covered stories in over 15 African countries, interviewed business and government leaders, and shared a lot of the suffering and disillusionment of the many displaced and disenfranchised Africans at the hands of civil wars, corruption and dictatorships. There were always pockets of hope and light cast by people who prioritise the interest of others, mostly women, with a multiplier effect, often far beyond their own communities.

The 21st century is about women, and especially women in Africa. Prominent female leaders have emerged across the continent, from Malawi's President Joyce Hilda Banda and Nobel laureates, Leymah Gbowee and Liberian President Ellen Johnson Sirleaf, to SA's own Dr Nkosazana Dlamini-Zuma, current chair of the African Union. The emphasis on the struggle towards economic freedom is paramount to the African agenda. As President Johnson Sirleaf remarked at the 50th anniversary of the African Union in 2013, African women have always been entrepreneurs and it is now time for us to free ourselves of imposed borders across the continent.

My work across Africa opened doors I never knew existed. Certain questions began to hammer and call for clarification. Uppermost was the nature of democracy in Africa and, for me, the status of women. By 2000 my life had taken a swerve towards love, marriage and children.

I married a magnificent man, and if the concept of *Imago Dei* means anything, well, there you have it: a South African born of Somalian decent, of godlike stature and a practising Muslim. The son of an Imam and school principal. His work took us to the Middle East for five years, first to Saudi Arabia and on to Beirut, Lebanon. While he excelled in the corporate world, I learnt what I could of Islam and Arabic and made several films while mothering a son, Tareq, and daughter, Aliyaah, my beautiful children. Middle East political turbulence and their irreconcilable conflicts were a perfect apprenticeship for unravelling the complexities of African societies.

Our Arab Spring

My return to Africa underscored how our struggle to find a form of democracy was similar to that of the Middle East. Both were in search of a political accommodation that would fit their unique features of culture and history. Winning the right to vote did not automatically confer the right to healthy employment, high school education or safe housing. Wherever I travelled the same pattern emerged: searing poverty and a ruling elite, who, in real terms, were indifferent, or put the blame for failure anywhere but on their own decisions or treasury. Was I missing something?

Then the so-called Arab Spring ignited in Tunisia. To all intents and purposes, it looked like a political revolution. But on closer examination, the trigger was nowhere near political. Mohamed Bouazizi was an illiterate street-peddler, who burnt himself to death on a public square in protest. The outrage that followed drove Tunisia's president into exile in Egypt.

Bouazizi was not protesting anything more than for a licence to trade his way out of poverty, a right denied to him several times by corrupt police, and against the random confiscation of his goods by local officials, whose bribes he could no longer afford. Bouazizi's death by fire was a demand for freedom, not political democracy. In South Africa, Andries Tatane suffered an almost similar fate. Human rights being indivisible, Tatane's martyrdom spoke to his claim to own a house of brick and mortar with basic services – a bitterly contested right in South Africa.

Bouazizi's example set the Arab world aflame. From Libya to Syria and Egypt, protests have erupted into violence and death on a large scale. It seems to me that the example of Bouazizi and many others in the Arab world – unrecorded in Western media – illustrates that wide-spread unrest is a call for freedom. A call to liberate human potential from the shackles of deadening poverty by freeing them to pursue economic activity. In South Africa, our Arab Spring is yet to come.

In short: liberation is economic, and freedom is its means. Anyone embarking on 'the long walk to freedom' must pass beneath the portals of economic freedom.

My MBA degree at UCT made it clear that a country being democratic is not enough, and that a majority cannot turn what is wrong into right. Even if the Arab Spring prevails – doubtful as things stand – and various forms of democracy are established, real freedom depends on the strength of institutions, those of law and order; the sanctity of contract; the right to legal protection; a free press or the struggle for one; police that are friendly to the people they are paid to protect; and politicians accountable to their constituents. A tall order, as I observed through my work in several African states and certainly in the Middle East. Just how tall and uncertain I learnt when invited to create a film documentary on the 50-year anniversary of the Africa Union in Addis Ababa in 2013. When all of Africa's states gathered to celebrate the kick-start of another 50 years of African advancement, there were several authentic political claims made on the podium.

With the death of Meles Zenawi and loss of office of Thabo Mbeki, Africa lost two intellectual politicians (ignoring of course Mbeki's damaging opinions on HIV and AIDS). One a so-called dictator and saviour of Ethiopia, and the other, an architect of post-apartheid South Africa. Far apart, yet agreeing that unless and until Africa creates a productive middle class like South Korea or Singapore, its states will be parasitic, surviving mainly on taxation and rent. This is a recipe for stagnation.

Anyone can step into an Internet café and call on unlimited information. The cyber rules allow this magic facility. But step into the street in almost any African city and the absence of rules bites you. Of course, in theory everyone is protected by some law but, in practice, arbitrary decisions and corruption prevail, stifling creativity and innovation.

Economic liberation is women's emancipation

The power of women acting collectively and mobilising actively should be Africa's agent of change. Africa's digital experiment with the future is an amazing spectacle in the hands of women. It might leap-frog Afro-pessimism and create, for the entire world to see, a truly convivial, 'democratic developmentalism' that may have been the dream of Zenawi and Mbeki, in turn.

To fully develop, Africa must listen to the voices of its mothers and allow for the voices of the next generation to be heard. Powerful female voices are emerging across the continent, from Dambisa Moyo (Zambia), the author of *Dead Aid*, to activists like Waris Dirie (Somalia), who fought against the 'tradition' of female genital mutilation. More and more young women in South Africa and across the continent are stepping up, like Tendai Wanyika (Zimbabwe), who passionately implores the older generation to guide and impart their wisdom but at the same time allow the next generation to own the agenda for the next 50 years and to be allowed to lead the struggle for Africa's economic liberation – and female emancipation.

Politically, we remain a country of contradictions. Since liberation in 1994, there has been significant accommodation made for women in leadership positions, both in business and in government. Women would argue that, at higher levels, a glass ceiling is still very much in place. On the one hand, South Africa celebrates her women, while on the other we remain humiliated by having the oft-quoted highest statistics, worldwide, of rape, domestic violence and abuse against women. We are an opinionated generation with high expectations of ourselves and those around us. We are quick to judge our leaders and criticise decisions without necessarily being able to supply the solutions. Those of us with strong views do have an obligation, or responsibility, to engage where we can and to make what is wrong, right.

May each film I make be an opportunity to educate, to liberate. Mandela, the most iconic symbol of liberation in our time, will always serve as a testament to the sacrifices made by many for the freedoms celebrated over the past two decades. He was a man who sacrificed his family, for me to have mine.

Breaking the post-apartheid socio-economic impasse in Africa

Herbert Vilakazi
Scholar and rural development activist

THE DEEP, WIDESPREAD CRISIS OF poverty, unemployment and inequality has caused a serious disturbance in the minds and souls of everyone in South Africa. Severe poverty, unemployment and inequality are the roots of the dehumanisation and brutalities that show themselves at all levels of society.

Our leadership and intellectual elite, inside and outside government and political parties, have presented in the media their opinions on the causes of the crisis, as well as proposals on how the crisis can be ended. The National Planning Commission has presented a major document to Parliament, detailing what should be done. The proposals put on the table, so far, from inside and outside government, still leave a lot to be desired. The commission urges that the entire citizenry of the country should participate in the vast project to solve the crisis before us, but then warns against populist pressures in the process. The poor, unemployed and ordinary workers in urban and rural areas, who are the vast majority, have every right to have their imprint on public policy and to demand the allegiance of government and political leaders.

We must, however, guard against a false notion of democracy: when the masses want major changes, particularly changes in the life of the poor, working and unemployed in urban and rural areas, science and specialised knowledge come into prominent play. We cannot rely on mass meetings of political parties, or hundreds of people in consultation in public halls, to propose how the problem of poverty, unemployment and inequality should be solved, just as we cannot call a mass meeting to get a plan on how we can send a rocket to the moon. That is useless populism that will not get us anywhere. From the 'people's assemblies' we shall get only *demands* for jobs, for the end of poverty, for equality, for health, and education. *How* all of this is to be done will not come from the assemblies but from individuals who have specialised knowledge; at the end, the *how* must be taken back to the assemblies for serious study, questioning, amendments and approval. The understanding of modern social and national problems requires comprehensive knowledge based on a thorough understanding of economics and economic history.

Capitalism produced not only the advanced industrial societies of the West and Japan, but also colonialism and underdeveloped countries. South Africa is a by-product of this twin process. To know how poverty, unemployment and inequality can be eliminated in South Africa requires a correct understanding of how the problem arose, but also a correct knowledge of economics and of the economic history of the modern world.

The historical roots of our problem go way beyond apartheid. Apartheid is simply an Afrikaner term for a policy and process that existed before 1948, which Afrikaners wanted to pursue in their own way. Our problem are rooted in a process that goes back to Smuts, to the 1920s and 1930s, to 1913, 1910, 1906, and to the conquest of African people in the 19th century.

The roots of our problem lie in colonial conquest. Colonialism gave rise not only to a colonial state, but also to a colonial economy and a colonial ideology. Here is a peculiar phenomenon: the death of a colonial state is survived for decades, even centuries, by the colonial economy and the colonial ideology. The colonial state died in South Africa but was survived by the colonial economy. Our economy still bears the very serious scars and shape of a colonial economy. The representatives of the Mother country, England, settled here, together with a population from other parts of Europe: hence the designation 'settler-colonial society'. The European population in this colony became the largest in Africa, giving rise to very strong emotional bonds between this settler community and the West, and imbuing Western rulers with the feeling that the bond between this settler community and the West was untouchable. (This is the emotional bond which exploded in anger against President Mugabe.)

This gave rise to two grossly unequal parts of South African society: the African part and the white part. Africans make up the vast majority of society, and a large proportion live in pre-industrial rural areas. Africans became the primary labourers. This vast sector is poor and has the worst facilities and infrastructure. The other part is the white community – a very small minority that is, by and large, wealthy compared to Africans. The white population has the best facilities and industrial infrastructure and is intimately linked with the industrial Western capitalist economy.

Colonialism and the African slave trade created the racial problem. Sobukwe was correct: there is only one race – the human race, distinguishing human beings from animals. The lines of division between human beings based on skin colour, hair texture or culture, making one community superior and another inferior, are creations of social and historical events, particularly of the ruling classes. The colonial rulers, who brought people from India to the colony to meet their labour needs, created a special status position for these workers: thus the South African 'Indian' emerged.

Another status position was created for the children of the sexual union between Europeans and Africans: thus South African 'coloureds' emerged. The identity and status of Indians and coloureds flowed from the struggle and tension between Europeans and Africans. Over and above the economic and political roles of these groups, rulers created separate statuses for them. The intention was to make these communities closer to whites than to Africans, for the security of whites. A recent creation has been the 'black middle class' and a 'black capitalist class', as protection for the capitalist social order: this is a very tiny slice of society, which is merging with the middle and upper classes of whites, Indians, and coloureds, making up the so-called 'non-racial' South Africa. The 'black' middle class and 'black' individual capitalists have become detached from the colonial economy in which the overwhelming majority of Africans are trapped.

The problem of inequality, poverty and unemployment remains. The World Bank, not for the first time, has warned about the growing problem of inequality in South Africa: 'The policy challenge is to find a way to break this vicious, self-perpetuating cycle of inequality...' The crucial question is: how can we eliminate this inequality, poverty and unemployment, and the racial problem in South Africa?

Thinkers who have proposed solutions to this crisis have failed to accept the fact that the current South African economy still bears the scars and shape of a colonial economy. The majority of Africans are trapped within deep underdevelopment in pre-industrial rural areas. Through the migrant labour system, some millions were forcibly brought to work in mines and urban areas. A large proportion of the African rural population has migrated, together with their poverty and misery, to urban areas, forming shantytowns attached to the original townships.

These millions of Africans constitute the colony inside South African society: Africans constitute the colonial economic component inside the South African economy. Figures indicate that most working-age urban Africans are not workers in modern industry and commerce but are in what is called the 'informal economy' – in our terms, the 'colonial economy'. This is the fundamental problem of South Africa.

The underdevelopment of African rural communities – and their off-springs in urban areas – is now the heavy drag that is pulling down the entire South African economy. The national economy cannot develop any further as long as it contains this colony. In accounting terms, when conducting an audit of the national economy, the colony, comprising the vast majority of society, is simply entered in the loss column. The cost of the colony to the national economy is many times greater than the gross national product (GNP) of the country. The colony is now sapping and negating the vitality and growth potential of the national economy and society in the same way that US militarism and wars are sapping and negating the vitality and growth potential of the US economy and society.

The cost of Iraq and Afghanistan already runs to trillions of US dollars. South African economists and statisticians often calculate and bewail the cost of a holiday to the national economy. The cost of the colony to the South African economy, the cost of unused capacity of tens of millions of African people, should also run into trillions of rand: that is how big the South African economy can be if the colony were eliminated. That is the 'potential economic surplus', in Paul Baran's terms (as elaborated in his 1960 *Political Economy of Growth*).

We cannot eliminate the colonial economy in our midst guided by the principles of modern economics. Modern economics is a reflection of the workings of advanced capitalist economies. In the history of capitalism, the colony was simply an object and site of economic vandalism and plunder. This was during the stage of plunder wages and complete denial of democratic and human rights to the colonised. Except for the relation of vandalism and plunder, the colony was separated from the metropole. African rural areas were as separated from the industrialisation and modernisation process taking place in the white community as the Belgian Congo was separated from Belgium, as Northern Rhodesia was separated from Britain. The metropole accordingly waxed fat with extraordinary wealth drawn from this relationship.

The ending of the plunder wage structure, and the relative triumph of democracy and human rights, changes the dynamics of the capitalist economy. The profit rate goes down. The urgent need now is for true unity and integration of the national economy – for the elimination of the colony. The future development of the country must now depend on the skills and educated intelligence and health of these millions of people currently cut-off from modern industry, commerce and agriculture.

The World Bank stated some decades ago that the Achilles' heel of the South African economy is the smallness of its domestic market. The buying power of the overwhelming majority of the population, trapped in the colonial economy, is very small. That is the killer to the national economy. We must put in place a policy that effectively eliminates the existence of this colony within the national economy.

Modern economics misguides us. The main reference points in modern economics shall always be industrial capitalist economies. For example, World Bank economists begin their account of stagnation and decline in the South African economy by referring to problems in the world economy: 'A weakened global economy and dampening of consumer and business confidence are triggering a slowdown in South Africa's growth momentum … South Africa is highly integrated with the global economy, and is therefore susceptible to the ongoing slowdown in the Eurozone countries and China…' Economists in the South African Reserve Bank think likewise.

In formulating the strategy for eliminating poverty, unemployment and inequality in South Africa, we cannot be guided by the list of needs provided by thousands of people in public meetings around the country. Those formulating the strategy cannot take the 'supermarket route', that is, they cannot take a trolley and fill it with dozens of needed goods and services mentioned by the masses of people during consultations.

Serious economics and economic history advise us differently. There has always been one sphere of economic action that has jump-started the engine of economic growth and development, which then spreads the growth dynamic to the rest of the economy. The 17th-century European Agricultural Revolution was the prelude to the Industrial Revolution of the 18th century; the African slave trade and African slavery in the 18th and 19th centuries jump-started the engine of the European-centred world economy; cotton and the textile industry were the economic basis of the Industrial Revolution; the construction of railroads jump-started the engine of US economic growth in mid-19th century; oil, Californian gold and the automobile industry jump-started gigantic US economic growth in the second-half of the 19th century and early decades of the 20th century; and mining jump-started the engine of industrialisation and gigantic economic growth in late 19th and early 20th centuries South Africa. For some decades now, the construction, sale and purchase of housing has been a crucially important basis of the growth of the US economy, and the massive collapse of housing has been a fore-runner to the collapse of the economy.

Economics and economic history teach us that the strategy for eliminating massive, national underdevelopment should take a mono-causal path, not a multifaceted, 'supermarket trolley' path, in which up to 15 or more different actions are to be done at the same time. The latter path boggles the mind, and none of the 15 or more different actions on the shopping list can be satisfactorily realised. A serious strategy for eliminating massive nationwide underdevelopment focuses initially on one or two economic areas, and triggers growth there, which then starts the engine of growth and development in the entire economy.

The measures that must kick-start the economic process leading to the elimination of the colony within the South African economy must occur within the colony itself, not outside the colony. The initial, main measures must be in the home-base of the colony, African rural areas, and from there move to the off-springs of rural areas, the shantytowns and townships, leading to the growth and rejuvenation of the national economy.

The present massive underdevelopment of the majority of society, Africans, is rooted in the fact that the Agricultural Revolution, which was the basis of the Industrial Revolution, did not occur within the African community – the Agricultural Revolution did not occur within the colony. It occurred only in the white community.

It is a major error among economists guiding our government to assume that the Agricultural Revolution that occurred in the white rural community renders the Agricultural Revolution in the African community unnecessary.

This error follows from the wrong assumption that the white-dominated industrial economy of the nation is the major actor, the Big Brother, of the other twin, the colonial economy; that the white economy shapes the national economy. That was the case in the colonial era; in the postcolonial era of our time, it is the colonial economy, the colonial population, which, in the deficit sense, shapes the national economy.

The National Development Plan tells us that 60% of the people are now in urban areas. That has led some industry-centred economists to think that African rural areas are of minor significance in the national economy, which they identify with the modern white economic sector. It is one thing for the majority of rural people to disappear because they have been absorbed by national industrialisation, as happened in England; it is something else for the majority of rural people in the colony to disappear because underdevelopment and misery in the colony's rural areas have forced them to flood the cities, when there is no prospect of their being absorbed by developing industry in the white economy.

The millions of Africans who have been forced by underdevelopment and misery to migrate to urban areas, who actually constitute the larger bulk of the unemployment problem, have moved to urban areas because of the big default in the nation's economic history: the fact that South Africa's Agricultural Revolution took place only in white rural areas. African rural areas, the site of the overwhelming majority of society, remained pre-industrial.

The first act needed to eliminate poverty, unemployment and inequality in South Africa is to initiate an Agricultural Revolution in African rural areas. This is to cut the roots of massive poverty, unemployment, diseases and abnormally high death rates in South Africa. The aim of this policy should be to increase and improve the capacity of every rural household in the colony to produce needed food for sustenance. Rural Africans should also be encouraged to grow once again, the traditional African crops that kept Africans free from modern diseases for thousands of years.

The error in the agricultural development policies of most

provincial governments, and of the national government, is that the aim is to produce successful individual commercial farmers, as part of the strategy to create a black capitalist class. The focus is not on developing the capacity of an entire rural community to produce sufficient food to meet household needs, first and foremost, and then, following that, to develop marketing channels and agro-industry.

Rural development strategies, so far, are heavily weighted in favour of assisting small 'black' farmers intent on becoming successful commercial farmers. The considerable amount of money and attention being given to African farmers do not reach the millions of people in communal lands: these millions of people are so poor that they do not qualify to be considered as small commercial farmers! They live a hand-to-mouth existence, that is, they are in self-subsistence agriculture.

Here is an example from KwaZulu-Natal: more than half of all arable land in the province, 5.4 million hectares, is in communal land areas, under the sovereignty of traditional leaders. This is the source of the heavy statistics on poverty, diseases and the high death rates in KwaZulu-Natal. What is amazing is that the Siyavuna Strategic Plan (2004–09) for African rural areas in the province does not apply in communal lands! The problem, here, is that in a community of, say, 100 households, government can sponsor one or five individuals to become successful, small commercial farmers and still leave the majority of households in that community ravaged by poverty and unnecessary deaths.

The World Bank, until a few years ago, advised Third World governments to take action against communal property in rural areas, and put in place policies that would instate private property in land – a desired framework for capitalist society. This thinking also influenced our government policy with regard to communal land. Rather than deal with communal land and traditional authority structures, it was thought better to devise a new policy of granting 'title deeds' to individual households or to deal with 'cooperatives'.

Even the policy to encourage the formation of cooperatives in rural areas is still driven, and hampered, by the aim of creating successful capitalist farmers and to encourage the passion for individual wealth, which has brought about degradation to our social life. This logic leads to the emergence of a tiny minority in the community that is successful financially, while the majority is left in poverty.

The aim of policy in communal lands should be to develop the entire community, assisted by the existing communal heritage and sentiments: the current favoured policy of helping to develop individual black farmers should be part of the development of the food-producing capacity of the entire commune, or should exist side by side with the development of all households within the community.

In our economic history, the necessary step of initiating the Agricultural Revolution in African rural areas was skipped. The Agricultural Revolution took place only in the white community, involving only a very tiny section of the nation. This does not mean that we can just move forward from where we are: we need to go back to repair the massive damage that was inflicted on the African countryside and African people; this, in turn, will begin to repair the enormous damage inflicted by this default to our towns and cities and to the national economy as a whole.

The entire process is a single chain with interconnected links of food production, health, mortality rates, community life, morality, rural industry, a mutually-supportive interchange between rural and urban, employment, buying power, the size of the domestic market, the scale of social pathology, investment opportunities, and more power to industry, commerce and to the national economy. We must focus on the first link of the chain and with full strength and determination as a nation, initiate the Agricultural Revolution in African rural areas in the colony. This is a revolutionary change that will reverberate throughout the length and breadth of our society. The chain-reaction from this will lead to reverse migration – to masses of people in towns and cities moving back to the revitalised and modernised rural areas where substantial job creation will be occurring.

I repeat: the first link in the chain has to be massive changes in the African countryside to make a modern society. The first act in the rise of capitalism was a massive transformation of the English countryside; the French Revolution began in the countryside; what made cotton 'king' in US economic history, making it the foundation of the rise of the mighty US economy during the first two or three decades of the 19th century, was the rise of African slavery in the rural South; the greatest drama of the 1917 Russian Revolution occurred in the countryside; Stalin's path towards the industrialisation of the Soviet Union began in 1929 with massive violence in changing the Russian countryside. The Chinese and Cuban revolutions were massive movements of peasants led by urban intellectuals.

Our slogan towards the creation of a new South Africa should be: To the countryside!

The rise of the modern Chinese economy is another striking confirmation of the fact that the countryside is the springboard for the creation of modern society. We really have to begin with the maligned Cultural Revolution, led by Mao Tse-Tung, from 1966, which saw hundreds of thousands of urban Chinese compelled to go to the countryside, 'to learn from peasants', to bring about a synthesis between urban knowledge and science, on one hand, and peasant knowledge and science, on the other hand.

Modern analysts, however, date the birth of modern China to 1978, when the Deng reforms began. What is striking is that this new stage in the building of modern China began in the countryside. In an official publication of Chinese scholars, we read: 'Reform was first implemented in the rural areas, and then gradually carried out in cities; even when the focus of reform had shifted to cities, it was first tried in the special economic zones, then in coastal areas, and then in the interior'. The important point for us is that this is a single chain with interconnected links, and that the first link that was grasped with determination of the Chinese government was transformation in the countryside. In the early 1990s, economists calculated that almost half of the acceleration in China's economic growth rate during the first phase of reform (1978–83) came from improved agriculture and rural development. The steps that were first taken in rural China were the first link in the single chain that led to China becoming in our time the second biggest economy in the world.

A crucially significant lesson for us is that Chinese peasants, given assistance and freed from the dictatorship of government and urban activists, not only produced sufficient food for over 1 billion people, but also, on their own initiatives, developed non-agricultural economic activities called township enterprises. These small, peasant-controlled companies produce light industrial products needed by local people, and these have become the roots of the emergence of rural industrialisation and small-scale urbanisation in the countryside.

Even more important for us is that these companies have played the most crucial role in absorbing millions of unemployed in rural China. 'The industrial output value of township enterprises accounted for 9.1 percent of the gross national industrial output value in 1978, 16.3 percent in 1984, 23.8 percent in 1989, 30.8 percent in 1991 and 36.8 percent in 1992.' 'A total of 10 million surplus rural labourers were absorbed by these enterprises per year, and by 1988 employed 95.45 million people, almost equal to the figure for workers in state-owned enterprises.' It was the productive activities of rural Chinese people, using a mixture of traditional Chinese science and technology and modern Western science and technology, which played a very significant role in launching China into being the leading economic power in today's world.

We must do in African and coloured rural areas of South Africa what the Chinese leaders decided to do with regard to the Chinese countryside. Indeed, in the late 19th century and early 20th centuries, African rural producers were becoming the leading participants in the new national market, actually surpassing white rural producers. The leaders of the white community, imbued with the gospel of the 'White Man's Burden', were disturbed; hence the white legislation which forbad Africans from entering the new market as equals of whites.

Our greatest challenge as government and nation is the elimination of the colonial economy within the national economy. The colonial economy in our midst is the seedbed of our crushing poverty, unemployment and inequality. Our first act should be in the countryside of the colony, through initiating the Agricultural Revolution in African communities. It is through this strategy that we can effectively work to become one mighty nation, instead of the present weak 'two nations'.

References

Gao Shangquan, Liu Guoguang & Ma Junru. 1999. *The Market Economy and China*. Beijing: Foreign Languages Press.

Dwyer, D, ed. 1994. *China: The Next Decade*. Harlow, Essex: Longman.

Gao Shangquan. 1997. *The Reform and Development of China's Rural Economy*. Beijing: Foreign Languages Press, pp. 169, 173.

The art of governing: Knowledge and experience for change and development in a new democracy

Nomonde Xundu

South African Health Attaché, Washington DC

Student years

I WAS NEARLY FIVE YEARS OLD when I held the hem of my mother's dress as we walked through the gate that separated the Makinana Lower Primary School Cottage, a newly opened school at Eziphunzana in Duncan Village, East London. This is the first time that I became aware of my surroundings, during January 1964. Half a century later, it gives me pleasure to share these personal reflections as we celebrate 20 years of our democracy. We as a society have gained some good experience, which should inform our strategic direction towards the realisation of a better life for all.

As the youngest of eight children, seven of whom were girls, brought up in a female-headed household, I became committed to the virtue of fairness in society. I became acutely aware of the importance of education for the wellbeing of society and I went through school determined to gain knowledge and education. It was in matric when the Black Consciousness Movement (BCM) became a force in the Eastern Cape.

When the 1976 uprisings spread across the country, it was clear in my mind that I would use education and knowledge as a powerful tool against apartheid – a ticket to lift my family and community out of poverty and demonstrate to the apartheid regime that black Africans are equally capable – one of the key teachings of the BCM. I chose to study Social Work. Practising as a social worker in the early 1980s sharpened my understanding of the socio-economic determinants of wellbeing. I arrogantly refer to myself as the self-appointed champion of the underdog. In order to broaden my area of influence, I registered to study Medicine at the University of the

Witwatersrand (Wits) in 1986 when my son was four years old. The residence I stayed in, where the majority of African students stayed was the Glynn Thomas House Residence, where most of the campus student political activities were engineered from.

During the 'clinical years' of medical training, African students were not allowed to rotate through previously 'white-only' hospitals, like the Johannesburg Academic and the JG Strijdom. On the other hand, white students had the freedom of exposure to the whole spectrum of illnesses, including dealing with trauma and other complex medical and surgical conditions, at all of the hospitals in the circuit. This caused racial tensions among medical students at Wits. After much negotiation and pressure from student activists, Wits opened white hospital rotations to African students, except for Obstetrics and Gynaecology training. Professor Joe Veriava and others who were members of the National Medical and Dental Association (NAMDA) pushed for the opening of all disciplines at all hospitals and to all medical students at the Wits Medical School. This policy was changed in 1991. This was around the time that the apartheid regime and the ANC were talking.

When I graduated with an MBBCh from Wits in 1992, South Africa was firmly on course towards a regime change, towards a democracy. About 15% of the students who graduated in 1992 were black Africans. My classmates either had plans to specialise or go into private general practice. I was confused!

Early years of the AIDS epidemic

Public Health had a lot of appeal to me. I was always looking for a strategic interface between social work and medicine, to be relevant and responding – a niche for best impact. While the health sector was engaged in organisational transformation, there was an alarming increase in the spread of HIV among blacks. HIV and AIDS found in South Africa a vulnerable society in transition. Dr Jonathan Mann, the pioneering coordinator of the Global AIDS Programmes at the World Health Organization (WHO), aptly made the observation that, 'those people who, before HIV and AIDS arrived, were marginalized, stigmatized, and discriminated against, become those at highest risk for HIV infection' (healthrigh.org). The pressing challenge was not so much in analysing where it came from but where it was going and how best to halt the spread. The association with homosexuality, sex work, promiscuity and high AIDS-related mortality rates instilled fear, anger and stigma towards those infected with HIV and AIDS in the society.

Within a short space of time, and because of the social/sexual networks in many communities, HIV found its way through the general population – propagating like wildfire in informal settlements and rural areas. New infections of tuberculosis of the lungs increased in an unprecedented way. Miners were expatriated in large numbers because of AIDS-related illnesses. Babies were not thriving and their mothers were diagnosed with HIV. All while South Africa was going through fundamental regime change.

The National AIDS Convention of South Africa (NACOSA) worked closely with the government of President Mandela and produced the first National AIDS Plan (NAP), which was shaped by healthworker activist groups from within and outside of the country. The NAP was adopted within months of the first democratic election in 1994 and there was optimism that the epidemic could be avoided. The NAP took a broad approach, recognising that 'the spread and prevention of HIV could be dealt with only within the context of addressing the underlying socio-economic factors'. The NAP was about 'social medicine'; it recognised the firm links between poverty and ill health. National antenatal HIV prevalence surveys suggest an exponential rise from 1992 to 2002. AIDS-related mortality was also high, with no hope for either a cure or a vaccine.

In January 1996, I got on a registrar rotation with the Department of Internal Medicine at Public Hospitals, Johannesburg. Young people were presenting to hospital with unusual cases of strokes, wasting disease, shingles, tuberculosis and meningitis caused by fungal infections. There were talks in my professional circles about the perceived paralysis of the ANC government in the face of the HIV and AIDS calamity.

I questioned whether a specialist qualification in Internal Medicine is critically necessary for me to make a relevant contribution to the most pressing public health challenges facing our new democracy and the majority of South Africans. As a young woman who understood poverty, a single mother, a qualified and experienced social worker, a medical doctor who had spent some time in public health hospitals, who had the scientific knowledge and background necessary to inform PHC programmes and public health, I concluded that I was not on the track that would lead me to my perceived niche. So I put myself on the market for work in the public health policy environment. Some of my colleagues questioned my sanity. I was introduced to Dr Liz Floyd of the Gauteng Department of Health (GDH).

I went to work as a GDH Medical Adviser for HIV and AIDS and STIs on the last day of March in 2000. Professors Alan Kaerstedt and Haroon Saloojee, whom I found committed to the public health system, provided the much needed academic and technical support. There was global activism on HIV and South Africa was in the spotlight.

The biennial International AIDS Conference was held in Durban in June 2000. Judge Edwin Cameron and the young Nkosi Johnson were some of the prominent speakers from South Africa. Even with the heated discussions, demonstrations and insults that were thrown at our government policies, I had no reason to believe that my government had intentions to deny the majority of its people the best affordable healthcare available. It seemed to me that people were talking past each other and the interests were many and varied. The National Strategic Plan 2000–05 (NSP) was now in place, it was funded fully through a conditional grant and plans were afoot for the establishment of the South African National AIDS Council (SANAC). The significance of the conference was largely the push for access to antiretroviral therapy (ART).

I obtained the Wits Diploma in Tropical Medicine and Hygiene (DTM&H) and completed all the course work towards an MSc in Medical Epidemiology and Biostatistics at the School of Public Health which considerably improved my understanding of infectious diseases and epidemiology. I could engage better with experts in these fields. I developed policy guidelines and treatment protocols for the management of sexually transmitted infections (STIs) and the management of HIV and AIDS in the province. I would draft the policy documents and send them to experts and district managers for comment. The long working hours as a medical registrar turned out to be a walk-in-the-park compared to navigating the policy space on AIDS at the GDH. I soon realised that policy-making and policy development is politics.

It became imperative that I understand the culture and policy-making processes of the African National Congress (ANC). So I joined the Ward 100 branch of the ANC after the local government elections in 2002. The ward had a councillor from the Democratic Alliance (DA) while the majority of the people in the ward were Africans living in the informal settlement of Zandspruit in Randburg.

I was astonished to see how little the DA councillor cared about the living conditions of the people of Zandspruit. We revived the branch and I was elected to the BEC as the secretary in 2003. During this period the provinces were required to develop plans for the implementation of the national policy on the Prevention of Mother-to-Child Transmission of HIV (PMTCT). Dr Nono Simelela, a specialist gynaecologist and obstetrician, was the National AIDS Programme Manager and she chaired the National Task Team for the development of PMTCT guidelines. I represented Gauteng in this task team. Experts like professors Haroon Saloojee, James McIntrye, Glenda Gray, Jerry Coovadia, Dr Anna Coutsodis, Dr Tammy Meyers, Dr Ashraf Grimwood, UNICEF, and provincial PMTCT representatives were in the PMTCT Task Team. Draft guidelines on the use of single-dose Nevirapine (sdNVP) in the primary healthcare setting emerged from the task team's discussions. Some of the critical questions that were raised by principal policy-makers related to short- and long-term safety, especially the risk of drug-resistance development. Things got serious to the extent that the government was instructed by the Constitutional Court to make sdNVP available at all hospitals in the country. It was policy-making by regulation in our new democracy! By the time the ruling came, the programme was already underway in Gauteng.

It was useful to have support from the Perinatal HIV Research Unit (PHRU) at Baragwanath Hospital (Bara). Ms Florence Ngobeni, who worked for the PHRU and who had lost a baby to HIV, became a powerful advocate for PMTCT in the province. It was around the same time, too, that post-exposure prophylaxis (PEP) policies for sexual assault cases were being developed and implemented. I practiced these during my overtime work at the Nthabiseng Rape Centre at Bara under the leadership of Dr Thami Bomvana.

My social work skills and experience came in handy in this environment. Ms Sally Mbulaheni, the nursing sister responsible for the centre, still associates me with the centre.

The AIDS debacle

Another programme that took off around the same time was the Diflucan Donation Partnership Programme (DDPP). Mr Zackie Achmat of the TAC led the fight against access to AIDS drugs, including drugs for common and debilitating opportunistic infections (OIs). It was common to see AIDS patients with severe headaches and confusion caused by fungal infection of the brain; or with dehydration and wasting because of pain with swallowing. The cost of medication to treat these fungal infections was prohibitive. It was simply inaccessible to the people who needed it most and this caused a lot of unnecessary suffering. Pfizer Pharmaceutical Company offered a donation of Diflucan to the Department of Health. Minister Manto Tshabalala-Msimang accepted it on condition that it was extended to other SADC countries. This is one of the most exciting initiatives, led by Advocate Patricia Lambert of the NDOH. I had the privilege to lead the DDPP for the GDH.

Here was what could be achieved through a partnership of strange bedfellows – the government, AIDS activists, the pharmaceutical industry and the patients. Everyone was a winner! The majority of the people who needed and accessed these services have always been Africans, mainly women and babies. Clearly this was the most vulnerable population in South Africa. The majority of the affected people were poor, uneducated and unemployed. The face of the HIV and AIDS epidemic didn't change.

The ANC was preparing to go its 51st National Conference in December 2002. Two of us were nominated by the branch to attend the conference in Stellenbosch and we ended up fielding three Ward 100 delegates because Comrade Greg was on the parliamentary list. It was my first ANC conference. It was an electrifying experience! Comrade Mbhazima Shilowa led the Gauteng delegation with a clear position and mandate. My MEC, Dr Gwen Ramokgopa was at the conference too. Comrade Mary Metcalfe was one of the few leaders who stayed with the general membership at the student residences.

I remember comrade Nelson Mandela walking in after the opening plenary session had started and the house burst out singing. President Mbeki had to stop reading his report to allow for Madiba's thunderous welcome to subside. When he got up to speak, Madiba started off by apologising for walking in late and explained why. To me his key message was that the ANC should not operate from a position of fear as it was gearing up for the 2004 national elections, because the people don't easily forget who it was that liberated them. He made the examples of Frelimo in Mozambique, SWAPO in Namibia and ZANU-PF in Zimbabwe. I left the 51st Conference of the ANC with a clear socio-economic policy direction and a strengthened resolve to do what I could to keep the ANC in power and to drive the implementation of its policies in the government.

After the ANC national elections campaign kicked off, the BEC was dissolved and I was given the task of BET coordinator. Comrade Sipho Majombozi was the Zonal Elections Coordinator for Zone 14. I took the work seriously. Our door-to-door campaign exposed me to the reality of the terrible living conditions of the majority of the people in our ward. The ANC had to win in the branch because I believed it was the only party that was serious about improving the lives of the people in the ward.

We were in Zone 14 with comrades who are in leadership positions in the ANC now, such as Bafana Sithole, Chris Vondo, Hlengiwe Mkhize, Khusela Sangoni and others. HIV and AIDS was definitely an election issue in 2003/04. The TAC was in a battle with the pharmaceutical industry and the government on intellectual property (IP) rights and access to ARVs. Advocate Boyce Moerane, at the brief of the Director-General for Health, Dr Ayanda Ntsaluba, represented the government in support of the TAC at this case. I didn't know the details but the TAC and the state won the case. Generic antiretroviral medicines could be imported and bought at more affordable prices. This case became a global precedent on matters relating to IP and public health. Today, South Africa still enjoys respect in the global community, at the World Trade Organization (WTO) and World Intellectual Property Organization (WIPO). Affordability was no longer a barrier to providing antiretroviral therapy in the public health system.

The TAC, aligned health professionals and HIV experts agitated for the introduction of ARTs at public clinics and hospitals. I was given the task of developing and driving the implementation of the provincial operational plan for the introduction of ART in Gauteng. Dr Laetitia Rispel, who was head of the Department of Health and MEC Ramokgopa provided all the supported I needed.

Cabinet adopted the National Comprehensive on ART in November 2003. Health systems strengthening was an essential of the plan. Opposition parties doubted that the government of the ruling party would ever be able to execute the plan.

It took me the first three months of 2004 to get all systems ready for the introduction of ART province-wide; at the same time, the ANC national elections campaign was reaching fever pitch. I was under pressure. Expectations were high. It was good pressure. Indirectly we carried the national burden because many people felt that if it didn't work in Gauteng it would be difficult to get the programme off the ground anywhere else. Failure was not an option. We were in the spotlight. There was a lot of support, too. The AIDS Consortium, a coalition of AIDS NGOs and PLHIV had a keen interest in what was unfolding. The media interest was also huge.

Convinced about the readiness of the province to deliver, Premier Shilowa made a public and media announcement of the commencement date of 1 April 2004. Dr Liz Floyd, Dr Abul Rahman (Chief of Operations), Dr Laetitia Rispel and MEC Ramakgopa engaged politically, with the provincial legislature, the PAC, the media and the public. Obstruction of any kind was not allowed to happen – I had a direct line to the HOD and to the MEC. People needed the treatment and the ANC had to deliver on its promise. We were governing, leading and addressing one of the most important challenges facing the people of the province.

The ANC elections campaign was becoming more demanding. So I decided that I should hand over the BET coordination responsibilities to another comrade and focus on the ART roll out. I called comrade Greg and advised him of my decision. Of course, my request was not approved by the BET; the comrades promised to beef up support around me and took on some of the functions. So I soldiered on. I was on the edge with everything. I must have been one of the most difficult people to deal with in my social circles (if there were any) at this time. From all angles the stakes were high.

We fielded ten full buses from Zandspruit to the ANC Siyanqoba national elections rally at the FNB Stadium. All clad in ANC-colour T-shirts and armed with vuvuzelas. The FNB Stadium was packed to capacity – opposition parties must have been shaken by the sight of this on television news.

I felt like a zombie at the rally. I was so tired! All was not in vain because the ANC took Ward 100 back from the DA with a landslide win of 93% at Zandspruit in 2004! This set a firm ground for the local government elections that followed. I was at pains to explain to comrades why I was not available to be candidate for councillor of the ward. Now Zandspruit has an ANC councillor in the Johannesburg City Council since. I was later co-opted to be an additional member of the Johannesburg REC in 2005. I graduated from the Gauteng Provincial ANC Political School in 2007.

Gauteng Province launched its ART roll-out programme on 1 April 2004 as announced. The Premier, MEC, and HOD were in the media at the health facilities that had seen the first clients and pictures were shown of them among boxes of ARVs that were ready for dispensing to children and adults. I was pleased we had managed to deliver to the people of the province. The opposition parties were proven wrong – the ruling party was delivering on a complex programme, firmly in the governing seat. This gave the Gauteng ANC national elections campaign a major boost!

The chief of operations reported that the ART roll out as the most successful programme in the department. We exceeded the target of putting 10 000 people on ART in the first year of implementation! I started taking print and electronic media interviews. Through due processes, I got a promotion to a managerial position of Director for HIV and AIDS, STIs and TB. Soon afterwards, Dr Nono Simelela resigned from her post of Cluster Manager HIV and AIDS, TB and STIs. I was devastated to hear of her resignation because I had always admired the skill with which she navigated the complex environment of HIV and AIDS in the country and abroad. I was deeply touched and surprised when she called to let me know that she had submitted my name as one of the people to be considered as her replacement. A few people also encouraged me to submit an application. I wished I had half the confidence they had in me. It was important to me to be recognised by her in this way but stepping into her shoes was unthinkable! I discussed the matter with my family and they also had mixed feelings about it. My mother gave me that look and smile that meant 'go for it' without saying it.

It was in July 2005 at the International AIDS Conference in Barcelona when I was told that Minister Manto was looking for me. Apparently the advertisement for Nono's replacement was in the Sunday papers at home. The minister wanted to make sure that I was aware of this. I looked at her with disbelief and was told that I, and others, had been targeted for the position. In my heart of hearts

I was thrilled at the idea! I actually wanted to do the work of policy formulation and programme design for the national fight against HIV and AIDS. My colleagues who thought the ANC government could not handle this had to see that not only could this be done, but it could be done in a nuanced manner that was informed not only by biomedical knowledge but also by an understanding of socio-economic and cultural vulnerability to HIV infection and to AIDS. My work would be cut out for me and I was getting closer to my niche space. I submitted my application.

I was appointed as Cluster Manager for HIV and AIDS, TB and STIs at the National Department of Health in December 2005. When most people were going away for the December holidays I was setting up office at the DOH in Pretoria. I was more convinced now that the government was committed to dealing HIV and AIDS. I understood my role to be using whatever reputation, strategic contacts, knowledge and experience I had to 'connect the dots' and get things going – to govern. My track record spoke to these issues and I was up to this challenge.

Tensions between the government and civil society at SANAC were not abating. Shy and soft-spoken, I was probably too 'grassroots' for some of the renowned AIDS specialists in the country but this didn't bother me. I was where I wanted to be, where I was needed most. At this stage of the fight against the epidemic, the country needed a rallying call that would be owned by a wide range of sectors in society. So, during the second half of 2006, SANAC mandated the DOH to lead the work of reviewing SANAC and the NSP 2000–05 towards renewal of both the NSP and SANAC. I took responsibility for both these processes.

When she became the deputy president (DP), Ms Phumzile Mlambo-Ngcuka's other responsibility was to chair SANAC. I could never have been more fortunate! Minister Jeff Radebe was appointed Acting Minister of Health for about six months or so. I was in the hot seat! The DP and minister seemed to be on the same wavelength and of equal resolve to confront all the national HIV-related tensions in order to focus on what was best for the country at the time. Again, my back was covered; I just had to go ahead with my work. Cabinet adopted the SANAC restructuring plan and Mr Mark Heywood, a nominee of civil society, became the Deputy Chair of SANAC.

Civil society felt that the writing of the NSP could not be left to an individual. I was to learn more about democratic principles during the development of this NSP. The DP tried to manage all the pressure points that civil society thought were divisive. Dr Mbulawa Mugabe of UNAIDS, Professor Helen Rees of the Reproductive Health Research Unit (RHRU) and Mark Heywood sat with me through the writing of the NSP.

I had hoped that the NSP 2007–11 would be launched on 1 December 2006. This was not to be. Instead, the DP read verbatim from the executive summary that I had developed as a framework for the NSP. Even though 'democracy' caused a delay of the launch, I was pleased beyond description. The media tried to play these developments down because there were some who were not happy with the cordiality that had developed between the government and civil society and the fact that the government never left the governing and leading seat during these processes. We rested during the December holidays – well somewhat.

The NSP writing process resumed early in 2007. The WHO released guidelines for the use of 'dual therapy' in PMTCT. This is about the addition of Zidovudine (AZT) to sdNVP. It was a huge challenge to navigate what I refer to as 'AZT politics' in the country, which related mainly to issues of the toxicity of the drug and the fact that it was going to be used on pregnant women. I read and consulted widely around the WHO guidelines. I found the counsel, support and guidance of Professor Prakash Jeena of UKZN, Dr Ameena Goga of the MRC and Professor Gary Maartens of UCT very useful on these matters. It was a back-and-forth discussion until a compromise position was reached. I prepared and presented draft policy recommendations to the minister and the National Health Council (NHC) aka MinMEC.

The members of NHC – provincial HODs and MEC, including SALGA and SAMHS – understood the environment within which policies on HIV and AIDS were processed. They were all warm and supportive and, to this day, show this disposition towards me. I attended several sessions with them, seeking approval for PMTCT dual therapy. Civil society, the media and HIV clinicians put pressure on the department to demand policy on dual therapy. Policy-making in a democracy is not easy. The DP had to intervene before the guidelines were approved by the NHC. This was a great relief and the outcomes of implementation even sweeter.

We concluded the work of the NSP 2007–11 in April 2007. It was endorsed by the consensus at SANAC. Cabinet then approved it, after which it was launched by SANAC. In the end, the delay bought us consensus and broad ownership. The country had a rallying call in the fight against HIV and AIDS. I noticed a striking resemblance between NSP 2007–2011 and the NAP of 1994. Things in HIV and AIDS work seem to act like a pendulum that swings back and forth in time!

During November/December 2007, I led my team on a country-wide road show in support of the implementation of the NSP. It took us six weeks to cover all nine provinces, spending two full days in each province. In the scientific environment, the key debates at the 4th International AIDS Society (IAS) Scientific Conference I attended in Sydney, Australia, during July 2007 were about: when to treat; long-term side effects; aberrations of the constantly activated immune system and how this causes inflammation and chronic diseases – the link between HIV and Non-communicable Diseases (NCDs); status of HIV and vaccines; prospects for a cure; infant feeding questions; and gene-based therapies; All of these remain the existential basic and clinical science research questions to date, more than 30 years after HIV was discovered and AIDS was defined. I presented a report on this conference and Cabinet discussed it at length.

In the global health space Minister Manto was serious about ensuring that regional and international communities understood Africa's perspective on issues and took them seriously. For various reasons, 'Africa' was not always speaking in the same voice on health matters. Negotiation became a skill I would acquire during trips to meetings in multilateral organisations. Knowledge, experience and political perspective came in handy during such engagements. In most instances, we got what we wanted in terms of the resolutions and outcomes of those meetings. I believe that this was so because of Minister Manto's leadership. For this, she was respected by many in the global health community.

The minister decided that I should be posted to Washington DC in 2008 as health attaché. I was to cover global health issues in the multilateral system in the United States and, to some degree, Canada. Under the leadership of Ambassador Baso Sangqu, I became South Africa's chief negotiator on the only two health-specific UNGA's Political Declarations, namely, on HIV and AIDS and on non-communicable diseases. I saw this as an opportunity to influence change and the adoption of the HIV and AIDS instead of HIV/ AIDS nomenclature. When negotiators finally understood that the term is not delinking but is defining, a consensus was reached for the preferred use of HIV and AIDS. I felt victorious when HIV and AIDS instead of HIV/AIDS was used in the UN Political Declaration that was adopted by consensus at the high level meeting of the UN in 2011. I am told that this was by no means a minor achievement! I dedicate this enormous achievement to the late Minister Tshabalala-Msimang who taught me to be proud as a South African woman in the world and never to be afraid to fight for what is right.

The UN Declaration on Non-communicable Diseases was the first on NCDs and much of the language was new. A lot of work was done in South Africa prior to the UNGA on NCDs. The sponsors of the work on NCDs, CARICOM are still grateful for South Africa's contribution during these negotiations. Minister Motsoaledi represented the country at the UNGA on matters relating to NCDs.

Conclusion

I feel honoured to be an active participant in the first 20 years of the ANC-led government. I hope that this essay conveys my key message about the power and responsibility of knowledge for governing in the post-apartheid South Africa.

There is convincing evidence to suggest that the lives of the majority of the people have improved. However, the scale, scope and extent of the devastating impacts of protracted apartheid on families and communities call for deeper and broader interventions. It is clear that political power is not enough for the kind of redress required. More work is needed to intensify targeted access to good quality education, and expansive and inclusive job-creating economic growth, while the country continues with delivery on social programmes.

Synergistic and strategic partnerships between capital, business and science, led by the government through priority setting, using the National Development Plan (NDP) as a guide, regulation and financing are key to economic growth and broad-based prosperity. There are many opportunities for win-win convergence approaches to accelerate the second transformation in South Africa. As the saying goes: 'to whom much is given, much is expected'. I owe it to my beloved country to give more back.

Acknowledgements

Often when books are released to the public, authors and editors heap a tonne of praise on those who made the publication possible. This is only right because these are the individuals and institutions that organised the intellectual and material resources without which the book would not have materialised. In this connection, I wish to acknowledge the following people who supported me throughout the process, from conception to the launch of this exciting book.

I thank all the contributors for entrusting me with their valuable work. We initially planned on 20 essays to reflect on 20 years of democracy. But the project elicited such an overwhelming response at some point, we had to increase the number.

The reading public will be the best judge of the quality of these tales of post-apartheid South Africa. But as editor, I am delighted that the contributors have told the unique South African story from their own perspectives – whether personal or political, they reflect on our 20 years of democracy and celebrate our successes and point to our shortcomings and the way forward. I would like to thank all the contributors to this volume for their effort and creativity – without them we would not have a book.

Second, I wish to acknowledge the generous material contributions of the following individuals and institutions:

- Nolitha Fakude, Mike Teke and Moss Moloi who dug into their wallets to fund this book.
- The Anglo American Corporation and the South African Roads Agency Limited, who saw value in sponsoring a book that tells the South African story.
- My publisher, Jacana Media, for your belief and investment in this product.
- My employer, the Presidency of the Republic of South Africa,

for allowing me space and time to work on this collection. This tradition started under President Nelson Mandela, and the Presidency continues to nurture and affirm scholar-bureaucrats to enable them to sustain the course of knowledge production, believing in the superiority of intellectual ideas to shape and move society.

• I am grateful to President Zuma, Deputy President Motlanthe, the ministers in the Presidency, Dr Cassius Lubusi and my colleagues in top management and advisory positions. They have all provided encouragement, learning opportunities and inspiration for my career as a writer.

• Finally, I wish to thank my family, especially my mother Nonhlanhla and my boys, Khulubuse, Mhlengi and Zamo. These wonderful people continue to be a source of strength and inspiration, adding important dimensions to my search for a purpose in life. All my friends, too, in their diversity and multitudes, who complement what family offers, I thank you.

Yet, as I mentioned earlier, there are men and women who deserve much more praise when such reflective and retrospective tomes are published. Here I am talking about the departed, known and unknown hero and heroines, who made the dream of a free South Africa possible. That we can convene such a diverse group of South Africans to tell their stories – many with powerful political messages – in this manner, with no fear of repercussion, is a fitting tribute to those who lost their lives fighting for us to be free to tell our stories today. To all the celebrated and unsung fighters, whose blood nourished the fruits of freedom, thank you! This book is a tribute to you.

Busani Ngcaweni

Contributors

Nazeema Ahmed is a mother to three phenomenal young women: Il-haam, Ibtisaam and Aaliyah, and a reader of Islam philosophy.

Nazir Alli is a chartered engineer currently serving as the CEO of the South African National Roads Agency.

Kim Catherine, raised in Eldorado Park and with roots in eMnambithi-Ladysmith, is a conscientious observer of transformation in South Africa and remains active in young women's struggles.

Dr Zosa de Sas Kropiwnicki-Gruber is a senior lecturer in Development Studies at the University of Johannesburg with research specialities in the field of child protection and child migration.

Amanda Dlamini is a PICA award-winning writer and was previously the editor of *The African Pioneer* newspaper. She holds qualifications from the universities of South Africa, Pretoria and Harvard Business School.

Wayne Duvenage, born a flower child of the '60s, was schooled in the kingdom of Shaka and in the wisdom gained from so many. He remains a passionately active citizen, knowing that while freedom has been bestowed to all, our prosperity has yet to be realised.

Jean Elphick is the national manager of Afrika Tikkun's empowerment programme for children with disabilities, working with parents and caregivers of disabled children in the townships of Johannesburg.

Kanya Kali was recently admitted as an advocate of the High Court. She holds junior and senior law degrees from the University of Johannesburg.

Wandile Goozen Kasibe is a Chevening Scholar with a B-Tech degree and three master's degrees in Fine Art, World Heritage and Museum Studies.

Bheki Khumalo has held various positions in the public and private sectors, including serving as spokesperson to President Thabo

Mbeki and several cabinet ministers. He has worked for Siemens, Sasol and Anglo American.

Sakhiwe Kokela is doing a master's degree in Public Policy at the University of Pretoria. She has been deputy chairperson of Seidet School Projects and marketing and projects coordinator for the Foundation for Ethical Youth Leadership. She serves as research intern in the office of the deputy president.

Nomfanelo Kota, passionate about diplomacy, believes that women's participation in decision-making can contribute to a better world as they hold 'half the sky'.

Khanyisile Kweyama is executive director of Anglo American Corporation in South Africa and vice president of the South African Chamber of Mines. She takes an interest in women empowerment and transformation issues broadly.

David Maimela is a political economy researcher at Mapungubwe Institute (MISTRA). He is former president of SASCO and remains active in the progressive youth movement.

Penelope Makgati is forging a path of her own in life as she takes lessons of wisdom from those who have gone ahead of her. She is a trainee speech writer for Deputy President Kgalema Motlanthe.

Professor Evan Mantzaris is a senior researcher at ACCERUS, School of Public Management, Stellenbosch University. He has written books and articles on corruption, working-class struggles and labour relations.

Professor Ntongela Masilela is a South African independent scholar, publisher and intellectual who presently resides in Bangkok, Thailand.

Dr Bandile Masuku is a specialist clinician with strong leadership credentials in the student movement, young doctors' association and now in the ANC Youth League.

Lawrence Matemba is a senior policy analyst in the Presidency. He holds a master's degree in Commerce from the Graduate School of Business, University of Cape Town.

Nozipho Mbanjwa is a financial journalist with CNBC Africa, managing director of Akwande Communications and an accomplished speaker.

Thaddeus Metz is Humanities Research Professor of Philosophy at the University of Johannesburg and is internationally known for his analytic approach to African ethics.

Bongani Mkongi is a former Member of Parliament and former Western Cape youth leader. He currently works as chief of staff in the Sport Ministry, and he is a volunteer for the Social Transformation Committee of the ANC.

Dr Setumo Mohapi is chief executive officer of Sentech and his wife Toivo is a young policy analyst who participated in the drafting of the National Development Plan.

Vusi Mona is General Manager: Communications at the South African National Roads Agency. He has led senior communications portfolios in government and previously worked as magazine and newspaper editor after attending a press fellowship programme at Cambridge University.

Zuki Mqolomba is an emerging economic researcher and writer affiliated to the Department of Public Enterprises. She holds master's degrees from the universities of Sussex and Cape Town.

Dan Tlhabane Motaung, a graduate of Wits University, is a reader of classics and history currently engaged as writer and communicator in the public service.

Moloto Mothapo is a University of Technology journalism graduate who currently heads the Department of Information and Publicity of the ANC in Parliament.

Vukani Mtintso is a former youth activist and development practitioner and now serves the African Union as special advisor to its chairperson, Dr Nkosazana Dlamini-Zuma.

Mhlengi Wandile Ngcaweni is an undergraduate Political Science and Development Studies student at the University of Johannesburg.

Dr Dumisani Ngcobo holds a doctorate in Social Policy and has studied at the Bard College in New York. He works as a social sector policy analyst and writes regular opinions pieces.

Siphelo Ngcwangu is a research associate at the University of the Witwatersrand's Centre for Researching Education and Labour (REAL). He is completing a PhD in Sociology at the University of Johannesburg focusing on the role of policy actors in the making of South Africa's skills system.

Thamsanqa Ngwenya works on international trade and economic development, specialising in Southern and East African economic integration. He holds senior degrees from the University of KwaZulu-Natal and Columbia University.

Josephilda Nhlapo-Hlophe trained at Swaziland University, Henley

Business School and at the Institute of Social Studies at The Hague where she studied Economics and Statistics. She has worked for the trade unions and participated in the drafting of the National Development Plan.

Nkululeko Nxesi is the executive director of the Community Development Foundation of South Africa whose tasks include promotion of safer and value-based traditional initiation.

Thulani Nzima is the chief executive officer of South Africa Tourism, a public entity that promotes tourism in South Africa.

Professor Raymond Parsons is currently in the Faculty of Economic and Business Management at North West University, and is a prominent economist who has been deeply involved in social dialogue processes in South Africa for many years within Business Unity South Africa.

Dr Edith Phaswana is a Ford Foundation alumni, scholar, social justice activist, decolonial thinker and youth development researcher in South Africa.

Dr Mzukisi Qobo is deputy director in the Centre for the Study of Governance Innovation at the University of Pretoria where he also works as a senior lecturer of International Political Economy.

Professor Chengiah 'Rogers' Ragaven, a graduate of universities like Oxford, Cambridge, Sussex and Durban-Westville, regards himself as an Intellectual Derelict in T.S. Elliot's *The Waste Land.* He was the vice rector at the Durban University of Technology.

Mugabe Ratshikuni is a dedicated scholar of life in all its complexities, young writer, poet and adventurer. He's also a passionate rugby fan who spends a disproportionate amount of time at his local pub drinking beer and trying to figure out the meaning of life in the new South Africa.

David Saks is the associate director of the South African Jewish Board of Deputies. He has authored, co-authored and edited a number of books on aspects of South African history, including its Jewish community. Prior to joining the SAJBD, he was Curator: History at Museum Africa. He holds a master's degree in History from Rhodes University.

Matshepo Seedat is a communicator and a traveller.

Mathethe Jeffrey Sehume is a researcher at the Mapungubwe Institute having previously worked in government and as a lecturer.

Dr Nono Simelela is a gynaecologist and women's rights activist.

She served as head of the country's AIDS programme when ARVs were first introduced in South Africa and currently serves as senior advisor on HIV and health-related matters to both the deputy president and the minister of health.

Ntsiki Sisulu-Singapi is a qualified clinical psychologist having trained at Roosevelt University in Chicago. She specialises in institutional support and capacity building for women empowerment programmes.

Onkgopotse JJ Tabane is a communications expert, business man and community activist. He is a doctoral candidate in Media Studies at the University of the Witwatersrand.

Mpho Tshivhase is professionally and academically affiliated with the universities of Pretoria and Johannesburg.

Cheryl Uys-Allie is a documentary filmmaker with extensive work experience across Africa and the Middle East. Cheryl has an MBA from the University of Cape Town (UCT) and is a fellow of the Public Values and Leadership programme at Duke University and UCT's Graduate School of Business.

Professor Herbert Vilakazi is an independent scholar on development issues, grounded in his knowledge of Anthropology, Economics, Sociology, Philosophy and History.

Dr Nomonde Xundu is health attaché at the Embassy of South Africa in Washington D.C., a position she took after serving as the head of Gauteng's Department for Health.

About the Editor

Busani Ngcaweni is a senior public servant working in the Presidency, South Africa. Avid reader of public policy and economic history, he writes regularly for weekly newspapers and journals and has contributed book chapters and reviews. His recent book, published by Africa Institute, is titled *The Future We Chose: Emerging Perspectives on the Centenary of the ANC"*. He holds degrees in Education and Urban and Regional Planning from the University of KwaZulu-Natal and has attended special courses in economic development offered by the London School of Economics and the Graduate School of the Chinese Academy of Social Sciences.